PEOPLE, PLACE

THE
ULTIMATE
BOOK
OF LISTS

PEOPLE, PLACES & THINGS

THE ULTIMATE BOOK OF LISTS

EDITED BY MICHAEL CADER

MACMILLAN

First published 1998 by Calder Books New York
as *The Name Book*

First Published in Great Britain 2001 by Macmillan
an imprint of Pan Macmillan Ltd
Pan Macmillan, 20 New Wharf Road, London N1 9RR
Basingstoke and Oxford
Associated companies throughout the world
www.panmacmillan.com

ISBN 0333 90624 1

5 7 9 8 6 4

A CIP catalogue record for this book is available from
the British Library.

Printed and bound in Great Britain by
Mackays of Chatham plc, Chatham, Kent

CONTENTS

PLACES

THE EARTH 76

THE SKY 110

REAL AND IMAGINARY PLACES . . . 116

THINGS

ANIMAL 130

INTRODUCTION

People, Places and Things: The Ultimate Book of Lists began with a very simple idea and extended itself into a broad and unusual reference work. Bookstores and libraries are full of what I call conventional naming books—usually, collections of first names to help inspire parents seeking monikers for their soon-to-be newborn. As this genre has grown, it has given rise to similar, if somewhat slighter, volumes: books to help name pets, for instance, and even books of things you would *never* want to name a child.

There are so many things in life that we like to—or need to—name: prized possessions for starters, like boats, cars, houses and property; but also all manner of companies, new products and inventions, web sites, characters, and more.

So on one level, this was created as a brainstorming source book. Divided simply into People, Places, and Things, it gathers together hundreds of lists with thousands of names, all intriguing models of the process in which we name the elements of our world, and inspiring examples for the continuing pursuits of naming.

Within the book there are a few different types of lists. Whenever reasonably possible, we tried to the make the lists as inclusive and comprehensive as they could be. For example, you will find every breed of cat, dog, and horse listed. In some instances, the pool of potential entries was so vast that we set a reasonable limit for ourselves, which is why you will find only 200 protagonists from literature. And while our exceptional sample of colours surely doesn't include every single variation, it does offer an impressive collection of hundreds of names. The intention was to bring together a fun and fantastic variety of lists as well as a compilation that was detailed enough to be used not just for inspiration but also for reference.

Which brings us to the second use of *People, Places and Things*. Quite often we've needed a list of names—such as the names of all the popes, or of the British monarchs—and have had no idea where to turn for such a list. This book uses this simple organizing principle to present an unique kind of reference, one that serves as the first and best place to turn whenever searching for the specific name of something in particular.

Whatever you need to find a name for, you're almost certain to find it here.

PEOPLE

AFRICAN RULERS THROUGHOUT HISTORY

Abdul Bubakar The ruler of the Futa Toro from 1879 to 1890 who attempted to revive the Tukolor confederation to oppose the French.

Abdussa Iami The first Fula emir of the state of Ilorin in Nigeria who died around the year 1830.

Abiodun The last great ruler of the Yoruba state of Oya in Nigeria who died around 1789.

Acheampong, Ignatious Kutu The military ruler of Ghana from 1972 to 1978.

Adama The founder and first ruler of the Fula emirate of Adamawa in Nigeria who ruled from 1806 to 1848.

Adandozan The ruler of the Aja kingdom of Dahomey in Benin who ruled from 1797 to 1818.

Ado The ruler of the Akan state of Akwamu in Ghana from 1689 to 1702.

Afonso The greatest ruler of the Kongo kingdom who brought Catholicism and technology to the Congo in the years of his reign, 1506 to 1545.

Agaja The ruler of the Aja state of Dahomey in Benin from 1708 to 1740.

Ahidjo, Ahmadou The first president of Cameroon from 1960 to 1982.

Ahmado Tijuni The Takolar ruler of Macina in Mali from 1864 to 1887.

Ahmadu Ibn Umar Tall The ruler of the Tukolar empire, which incorporated Guinea, Mali, Mauritania, and Senegal, from 1864 to 1893.

Aisa Kili Ngirmaramma The ruler of the Kanori empire of Bornu from 1563 to 1570.

Akonno The ruler of the Akan state of Akwamo in its zenith, from 1702 to 1725.

Ali Gagi The ruler of the Kanuri state of Bornu between 1470 and 1503. He is regarded as one of the three greatest rulers of a one-thousand-year dynasty.

Ali Yaga Ibn Tsamia The first Moslem ruler of the Hausa city-state of Kano between the years 1349 and 1385.

Alvere I The ruler of the Kongo kingdom from 1567 to 1586.

Amin, Idi The military ruler of Uganda from 1971 to 1979.

Amina The queen of the Hausa state of Zaria during a time of rapid expansion. This legendary figure, who extended Zaria's empire, lived in the 15th century.

Ansa Sasraku The ruler of the Akan state of Akwamu in the years 1681 to 1689, the period of the state's greatest military expansion.

Apithy The president and leader of the independence movement in Benin between the years 1963 and 1965.

Asipa A Yoruba warrior who was the founder of a royal dynasty at Lagos, circa 1700.

Azikiwe A leader in Nigeria's independence movement and its first president between the years 1963 and 1966.

Babari The ruler of Gobir when it was the most powerful state of Hausaland between the years 1741 and 1769.

Bagaza, Jean-Baptiste The president of Burundi from 1976 to 1987.

Bakaffa, Asma Giorgis An Ethiopian emperor from 1721 to 1730.

Bambatha A chief of the Zulu branch in South Africa who led a 1906 rebellion, circa 1865–1906.

Barends, Barend A Grigua chief and bandit leader between the years 1770 and 1839.

Barghash Ibn Said The third Busaidi ruler in Tanzania, from 1870 to 1888.

Bathoen, Bathweng Chief of Ngwaketse in Botswana between the years 1889 and 1910.

Behanzin The King of Dahomey during the French conquest, between the years 1889 and 1893.

Bhunu The ruler during the period of white takeover in Swaziland, between the years 1889 and 1899.

Bodian Moriba The ruler of the Bambara kingdom of Kaarta at its zenith, from 1815 to 1832.

Bongo, Albert Bernard The president of Gabon from 1967 to the present.

Botha P. W. The president of South Africa from 1984 to 1989.

Bukar d'gijiama The Kanuri ruler of the state of Mandara between the years 1773 and 1828. He also helped win independence from the Bornu empire.

Cabral, Luis de Almeida The first president of Guinea Bissau, from 1974 to 1980.

Cetshwayo The last independent king of Zulu in South Africa, from 1872 to 1884.

Changa The usurper of Munhumutapa kingship and the founder of the Changamire dynasty who died around the year 1494.

Chikuyo Chisamarengu The ruler of the Munhumutapa kingdom between the years 1494 and 1530.

Chilipadambo The ruler of the Msawe Kasungo Chewa kingdom at its zenith, between 1850 and 1880.

Da Cruz Family This powerful Portuguese-Afrikaans family were the rulers of the Massangano state from 1840 to 1888.

Daddah, Moktar Ould The president of Mauritania from 1960 to 1978.

Dawud The ruler of the Songhay empire between 1549 and 1582.

Dingane The second Zulu king, who ruled from 1828 to 1840, when he was assassinated.

Diogo I The ruler of the Kongo kingdom between the years 1545 and 1561 who tried to limit Portugal's encroachment.

Diouf Abdou The prime minister of Senegal from 1981 to the present.

Doe, Samuel K. The military leader of Liberia from 1980 to 1990.

Dogbargrigenu This semimythical founder of the Aja kingdom of Dahomey lived around the year 1650.

Dunama Dibbalemi The ruler of the Kanuri empire of Kanem during its apogee between 1221 and 1259.

Dunn, John The white chief of the Zulu kingdom between the years 1835 and 1895.

Egunoju The ruler of the Yoruba kingdom of Oyo in the 16th century. He founded its new capital.

Eyadema-Gnassinghe The president of Togo from 1967 to the present.

Ezana The king of Axum between 320 and 360. He introduced Christianity to Ethiopia.

Faku The paramount chief of the Mpondo between 1820 and 1867.

Fasiladas The emperor of Ethiopia between 1632 and 1667.

Galawdewos, Claudius The emperor of Ethiopia from 1440 to 1459 during the major conflict with the Muslims.

Gaseitsiwe A Ngwaketse chief and unifier in the years 1846 through 1889.

Gouled Aptidon, Hassan The first president of Djibouti, from 1977 to the present.

Gungunyane The last Gaza king. He succumbed to the Portuguese conquest, after reigning from 1884 to 1895.

Habyarimana, Juvenal The president of Rwanda from 1973 to 1994.

Haidalla, Mohammed The first president of Mauritania, from 1980 to 1984.

Haile Selassie The regent ruler, then emperor, of Ethiopia from 1916 to 1974.

Hamad II Ruler of Macina from 1853 through 1862.

Houphouet-Boigny, Felix The first president of the Ivory Coast from 1958; he favoured close cooperation with France.

Humai The first ruler of the Kanuri empire of Kanem to accept Islam in the late 11th century.

Ibrahim The titular king of the Kanuri state of Bornu from 1820 to 1846. He and his son were the last kings of the ancient Sefawa dynasty.

Ishaq I The ruler of Songhay from 1539 to 1549, he expanded its domain at the expense of the old Mali empire.

Iyasu I (Iyaso the Great) The emperor of Ethiopia from 1682 to 1706.

Jakpa Lanta The ruler of the Gonja kingdom from 1622 to 1623, then from 1666 to 1667.

Kabarega The last independent ruler of the Nyoro kingdom, from 1868 through 1899.

Kaboyo The founder of the Toro kingdom in the 1830s.

Kambarapasu Mukombwe The ruler of the Munhumutapa kingdom from 1663 to 1690.

Kasavubu, Joseph The first president of the independent Congo Republic, from 1960 through 1965.

Kaunda, Kenneth David The president of Zambia from 1964 to 1991.

Kayibanda, Gregoire The first president of Rwanda; he served from 1973 to 1977.

Keita, Mobido The president of Mali from 1960 through 1968.

Kenyatta, Joseph The first president of Kenya, from 1964 to 1978.

Kerekou, Mathieu The military ruler of Benin from 1972 to the present.

Kgama III The ruler of Ngwato from 1875 through 1923.

Kigeri IV Rwabugiri The king of Rwanda from 1860 through 1895.

Kimweri Ye Nyumbai The ruler of the Zilindi empire in the 19th century, one of the most powerful 19th-century leaders.

King, Charles P. B. The president of Liberia from 1920 to 1930.

Kofi Karikari The ruler of the Akan kingdom of Asante from 1867 to 1874, during the British invasion.

Kusi Obodum The ruler of the Akan kingdom of Asante from 1750 to 1764.

Lat Dyor Diop The ruler of the Wolof kingdom of Kayor from 1862 to 1864 and 1871 to 1882; responsible for the Islamization of West Senegal.

Lentswe The last independent ruler of Kgatla, from 1875 to 1924.

Lerotholi The king of Lesotho from 1891 to 1905.

Lewanika Lubosi The last Lozi king, from 1878 to 1884; he built the Lozi state into the greatest power of West Zambia.

Machel, Samora Moises The first president of Mozambique; he served from 1975 to 1986.

Macheng A Ngwato chief from 1858 through 1859 and 1866 through 1872.

Maga, Hubert Coutoucou The first president of Dahomey, from 1960 to 1963 and 1970 to 1972.

Maherero A Herero chief who freed the tribe from Khoikhoi domination; he ruled from 1861 to 1890.

Majid Ibn Said A Busaidi ruler from 1856 through 1862.

Makaba II The ruler of the Ngawaketse chiefdom at its zenith, from 1790 to 1824.

Malloum, Felix The president of Chad from 1975 to 1979.

Mawewe A usurper of the Gaza kingdom; he ruled from 1859 to 1862.

Mbandzeni The king of Swaziland who paved the way for European occupation by signing away Swazi resources to concession hunters; he ruled from 1874 to 1889.

Mboo Mwanasilundu Muyunda The first ruler of the Lozi kingdom in the 17th century.

Mirambo The most powerful 19th-century Nyamwezi chief; he ruled from 1840 through 1884.

Mnkabayi A Zulu princess and leading figure in Zulu politics from 1760 to 1840.

Mobutu Sese Seko Zaire's military president from 1965 to 1997.

Moshoeshoe I The founder and king of Lesotho;

he reigned from 1785 to 1870. His successor in name ruled 100 years later.

Moshoeshoe II Lesotho's constitutional monarch from 1960 to 1990, when he went into exile; he returned in 1995 and resumed rule until 1996.

Mumia The last independent ruler of the Wanga kingdom; he reigned from 1882 to 1926.

Musa The ruler of the ancient Mali empire at its zenith, from 1312 through 1337.

Mwambutsa IV A Burundi king during the colonial period, from 1915 to 1966.

Na Siri A late-15th-century Mossi ruler.

Neto, Agostinho Antonio The first president of Angola, from 1975 to 1979.

Ngouabi, Marien Congo president, 1968 to 1977.

Niani Mansa Mamadu The last ruler of the Mali empire, he died in 1610.

Nkrumah, Francis Nwia Kofie The first leader of independent Ghana, from 1957 through 1966.

Nzinga Mbande The queen of the Angolan kingdom of Ndongo from 1624 to 1626, and of Matamba from 1630 to 1663.

Oluewu The ruler of the Yoruba kingdom of Oyo from 1833 to 1835, during its final collapse.

Oranyan The 14th-century semimythical founder of the Yoruba state of Oyo.

Osei Bonsu The ruler of the Akan state of Asante at its zenith, from 1800 to 1823.

Ovonramwen The king of Benin at the time of British conquest; he ruled from 1888 to 1897.

Pereira, Aristides Maria The first president of Cape Verde; he served from 1974 to 1991.

Prempe II The ruler of the Akan Asante confederacy during its colonial and early independent period; he reigned from 1931 through 1970.

Roberts, Joseph Jenkins The first Liberian president. He led from 1848 to 1856, and from 1872 to 1876.

Roye, Edward James A Liberian president from 1870 to 1871.

Safori The founder of the Akuapem state in the late 17th century.

Sakura A Mali ruler from 1285 to 1300.

Sarsa Dengel Ethiopian emperor from 1563 through 1597.

Sebego A usurper of the Ngwaketse chiefdom in 1825; he ruled until 1844.

Sekeletu The king of Kololo from 1851 through 1863.

Senghor, Leopold Sedar The first president of Senegal, from 1960 to 1981.

Shaka The founder of the Zulu kingdom; he reigned from 1787 to 1828.

Siad Barre, Muhammed Somalia's first president, from 1969 to 1991.

Sobhuza I The king during Swaziland's formative period, from 1810 to 1839.

Soglo, Christophe The president of Benin from 1965 to 1967.

Soshangane The founder of the Gaza empire; he reigned from 1790 to 1859.

Stevens, Siaka Probyn The president of Sierra Leone from 1971 to 1985.

Sulayman The ruler of the Mali empire from 1341 to 1360.

Suluku Konte A Limba ruler of the Biriwa chiefdom; he died in 1906.

Sundjata Keita The founder of the Mali empire; he reigned from 1210 to 1260.

Sunni Ali The founder and ruler of the Songhay empire; he reigned from 1464 to 1492.

Tewodros II (Theodore) The reunifying emperor of Ethiopia from 1855 to 1868.

Tombalbaye, Françoise Ngarta The Chad head of government from 1859 to 1975.

Toure, Ahmed Sekou The president of Guinea from 1958 to 1984.

Umar Ibn Idris The ruler of the Kanuri empire of Kanem-Bornu from 1384 to 1388.

Vakaba Ture The founder of the Nyula state of Kabasarana; he died in 1849.

Verwoerd, Henrik Frensch The South African prime minister from 1858 to 1966.

Vorster, Balthazur Johannes The state president of South Africa from 1978 to 1979.

War-dyabi Ibn Rabis The ruler of Takur, the first West African kingdom to embrace Islam; he died in 1041.

Wegbaja The first ruler of the Aja kingdom of Dahomey; he died in 1680.

Wene The 14th-century founder of the Kongo kingdom.

Whitehead, Edgar Cuthbert The prime minister of Southern Rhodesia from 1958 to 1962.

Yambio The most powerful late 19th-century Zande ruler; he reigned from 1869 to 1905.

Yekuno Amlak The king of Ethiopia who restored the Solomonic dynasty; he ruled from 1270 to 1285.

Youlou, Abbe Fulbert The prime minister, then president, of the Congo from 1958 to 1963.

Zara Yagob, Jacob An Ethiopian emperor, considered the greatest of the medieval Ethiopian rulers; he reigned from 1434 to 1468.

Zauditu The empress of Ethiopia from 1916 to 1930.

Zubeiru The ruler of the Fula emirate of Adamawa from 1890 to 1893.

Zwangendaba The founder of the Ngoni kingdom; he ruled from 1785 to 1845.

AFRICAN TRIBES

Algeria Arab-Berber

Angola Ovimbundu, Mbundu, Kongo, Mulatto

Benin Fon, Yoruba, Adja

Botswana Tswana, Kalanga, Baswara, Kqalagadi

Burkina Faso Mossi, Fulani, Lobi, Malinke, Bobo, Senufo, Gurunsi

Burundi Hutt, Tutsi, Twa (Pygmy)

Cameroon Cameroon Highlander, Equatorial Bantu, Kirdi, Fulani

Cape Verde Creole, Afrika

Central African Republic Baya, Banda, Mandjia, Sara

Chad Sara

Comoros Antalote, Cafre, Makoa, Oimatsaha, Sakalava

Congo Kongo, Sangho, Bateke, Mbochi

Democratic Republic of the Congo (a.k.a. **Zaire**) Kongo, Luba, Mongo, Mangbetu-Azande

Côte D'Ivoire Baule, Bete, Senoufou, Malinke

Djibouti Somali, Afar

Equatorial Guinea Fang, Bubi

Eritrea Tigray, Tigre, Kunama

Ethiopia Oromo, Amhara, Tigrean, Sidamo, Shankella, Somali

Gabon Fang, Eshira, Bapounou, Bateke

The Gambia Malinke, Fulani, Wolof, Jola, Serahuli

Ghana Akan, Moshi-Dagomba, Eive, Ga

Guinea Fulani, Malinke, Susu

Guinea-Bissau Balanta, Fulani, Manjaca, Malinke, Papel

Kenya Kikuyu, Luhya, Luo, Kamba, Kalenjin, Kissi, Meru

Lesotho Sotho

Liberia Indigenous African

Libya Arab-Berber

Madagascar Merina, Betsimisaraka, Betsileo, Tsimihety, Antaisaka

Malawi Chewa, Nyanja, Tumbuko, Yao, Lomwe

Mali Mande, Fulani, Voltaic, Songhai

Mauritania Moor

Morocco Arab-Berber

Mozambique Makua, Lomwe, Thonga

Myanmar Bamar, Shan, Kayin, Rakhine

Namibia Ovambo, Kavango, Damara, Herero

Niger Hausa, Djerma, Fulani, Taureg, Beriberi

Nigeria Hausa, Fulani, Yoruba, Ibo

Rwanda Hutu, Tutsi, Twa (Pygmy)

Senegal Wolof, Fulani, Serer, Dialo, Malinke

Somalia Somali, Bantu

Sudan Arab, Beja

Swaziland Swazi

Tanzania African

Togo Eive, Mina, Kabye

Tunisia Arab

Uganda Ganda, Nkola, Gisu, Soga, Turkana, Chiga, Lango, Acholi

Western Sahara Berber, Arab

Zaire Congo, Luba, Mongo, Mangbetu-Azande

Zambia African

Zimbabwe Shona, Ndebele

CARTOON CHARACTERS

Alvin, Theodore, and Simon This trio began their high jinks on CBS in 1961.

Andy Pandy This cuddly panda created by Walter Lantz first appeared in the 1939 cartoon *Life Begins with Andy Panda.*

Asterix This feisty Gaul was created in 1959 by René Goscinny (writer) and Albert Uderzo.

Bam Bam Barney Rubble's son, who says only "Bam! Bam!" (*See* Fred Flintstone.)

Barney Rubble Sidekick to Fred Flintstone, resident of Bedrock. (*See* Fred Flintstone.)

Beaky Buzzard This extremely dumb buzzard first appeared in the 1942 *Bugs Bunny Gets the Boid.*

Beavis and Butt-head This insipidly stupid duo from the pen of Mike Judge premiered on MTV in 1993.

Betty Boop Created by Grim Natwick, this famous vamp batted her long eyelashes at depression-era crowds.

Betty Rubble Barney Rubble's loving wife and mother of Bam-Bam. (*See* Fred Flintstone.)

Bill and Ben Two animated flowerpot men, with their friend Weed, were created by Freda Lingstrom and first gained popularity in the 1950s BBC programme *Watch with Mother*. They were revamped and relaunched in the US and UK in 2000.

Bob the Builder A huge hit for HIT TV, Bob and his friends, the talking machines Scoop, Dizzy and Rollie spawned a hit song in the UK and big TV hit in America.

Boo Boo Yogi Bear's faithful sidekick.

Bugs Bunny Created over a period of time by many Warner Brothers studio employees, this rabbit became famous for his "What's up, Doc?" in numerous cartoons directed by Fred "Tex" Avery and Chuck Jones.

Bullwinkle Moose This dim-witted moose first

aired, along with Rocky the Flying Squirrel, on NBC in 1958 in *Rocky and Friends.*

C. Montgomery Burns This hard-hearted owner of the Springfield nuclear plant has a penchant for forgetting Homer Simpson's name.

Casper Introduced in 1945 in "The Friendly Ghost," produced by Famous Studios, this childlike ghost made friends with and helped humans.

Charlie Brown Known for being wishy-washy, Charles Schultz's Charlie Brown premiered in *A Charlie Brown Christmas,* on CBS on December 9, 1965, after a long run in the funny papers.

Chilly Willy Walter Lantz's Chaplinesque mute penguin debuted in 1953.

Chim Chim The pet monkey featured on *Speed Racer.*

Chip and Dale These two lovable, overly affable chipmunks debuted in Walt Disney's 1943 "Private Pluto."

Commander McBragg This raconteur first guest-starred on *The Hippity Hooper Show* in 1964 on ABC.

Daffy Duck First appeared in Tex Avery's 1937 cartoon "Porky's Duck Hunt."

Daisy Duck Daisy started her career as Donna Duck in Disney's "Don Duck" in 1939.

Daria Morgendorffer The smart but cynical 16-year-old girl debuted on Beavis and Butt-head on MTV, but moved to her own series starting March 3, 1997.

Deputy Dawg This slow-witted hound-dog lawman began sleuthing on his eponymously named show in 1971.

Dino Fred Flintstone's excitable pet dinosaur. (*See* Fred Flintstone.)

Donald Duck This cantankerous duck debuted in the Disney's 1934 "Silly Symphony: The Wise Little Hen," with a voice done by Clarence Nash.

Droopy Tex Avery introduced this sad-eyed bloodhound in "Dumb-Hounded" in 1943.

Dudley Do-Right Jay Ward introduced this bumbling mountie along with his adversary Snidely Whiplash.

Elmer Fudd This befuddled rabbit hunter began with Warner Brothers in 1937 in "Egghead Rides Again."

Eric Cartman The fat kid with a short temper who likes cheesy poofs on *South Park.*

Fat Albert Bill Cosby's character began his cartoon life in 1972 on CBS.

Felix the Cat The high-water mark of the silent cartoon age, the creation of this feline by Pat Sullivan falls somewhere between 1914 and 1925.

Foghorn Leghorn This Southern rooster began talking in "Walky Tawky Hawky" in 1946.

Fred Flintstone This variation of the Jackie Gleason *Honeymooners* character debuted on CBS in the fall of 1960.

Fritz the Cat First created by R. Crumb but sold to Ralph Bakshi and Steve Krantz, this cat starred in the infamous X-rated movie *Fritz the Cat.*

George Jetson Hanna-Barbera developed *The Jetsons* television show after the success of *The Flintstones.* Debuted on ABC in 1962.

George of the Jungle Jay Ward's satire on Tarzan began in 1967.

George Slate Fred Flintstone's immovable boss. (*See* Fred Flintstone.)

Gertie the Dinosaur This 1914 creation of Winsor McCoy of "Little Nemo in Slumberland" fame is credited with being history's first animated cartoon.

Goofy This slow-witted nice guy debuted in 1932 in Walt Disney's "Mickey's Revue."

Granpa Simpson The confused grandfather on *The Simpsons.*

Hank Hill Hank and his suburban Texas family were created by Mike Judge and were introduced on the Fox network in 1997.

Heckle and Jeckle These mischief-making magpies were introduced in 1946 in Paul Terry's "The Talking Magpies."

Huckleberry Hound This Andy Griffith-like dog starred in his own Hanna-Barbera show in 1958.

Huey, Dewey, and Louie This triumvirate of tot-sized terrors first appeared in Disney's "Donald's Nephews" in 1938.

Jiminy Cricket This streetwise little fellow burst onto the silver screen in Disney's *Pinocchio*.

Johnny Quest Hanna-Barbera created this world-hopping lad in 1964.

Jose Carioca This traditional Brazilian parrot first sang with Donald Duck in Disney's 1941 *Saludos Amigos*.

Josie and the Pussycats Hanna-Barbera debuted this all-girl group in 1970.

Kazoo The irascible little man from the future who only Fred Flintstone can see. (*See* Fred Flintstone.)

Kenny The little kid who dies in each episode of *South Park*.

Kimba the White Lion This peaceful character began in 1966 for Mushi Studio Productions.

Krazy Kat Introduced in 1910 by George Herriman, this cat starred in one-minute shorts at the end of Hearst newsreels.

Krusty the Clown The self-centred son of a rabbi has provided laughs for the children of Springfield since the first season of *The Simpsons*.

Kyle The leader of the pack on *South Park* who has a little brother he kicks like a football.

Lucy Van Pelt The domineering older sister of Linus and part of the *Peanuts* gang. (*See* Charlie Brown.)

Major "Diamond Joe" Quimby The less-than-honest mayor of Springfield on *The Simpsons*.

Marvin the Martian This faceless, pint-sized terror created by Chuck Jones first matched wits and weaponry with Daffy Duck in *Duck Dodgers in the 24½ Century*.

Mickey Mouse Introduced by Walt Disney on November 18, 1928, in "Steamboat Willie."

Mighty Mouse Created by Isidore Klein for Paul Terry's Terrytoons studio in the 1942 "The Mouse of Tomorrow," this parody of Superman was in love with Pearl Pureheart.

Minnie Mouse Also appeared for the first time in Disney's "Steamboat Willie."

Mr. Magoo This crotchety old coot was created by John Hubley and Robert Cannon in 1949.

Mr. Peabody This eyeglass-wearing dog/genius was introduced to Americans by Jay Ward, along with his sidekick and adopted son Sherman.

Ned Flanders The upstanding and religious neighbour of Homer Simpson.

Olive Oyl Popeye's wife.

Oswald the Rabbit Created by Walt Disney in 1927. The name of this floppy-eared rabbit was picked out of a hat.

Pepe le Pew Created by Michael Maltese, Pepe first wooed in "Scent-Imental Romeo."

Peppermint Patty is a tomboy who pines for Charlie Brown. (*See* Charlie Brown.)

Pink Panther Friz Freleng created this svelte cool cat in 1964 for Blake Edwards's movie of the same name.

Pluto Pup This dog was introduced in "The Chain Gang" in 1930 by Walt Disney.

Pokémon was launched as a Game Boy in Japan in 1995 by Nintendo, and the spin-off card games, movies and TV cartoons have been big hits.

Popeye the Sailor E. C. Segar created this spinach-loving sailor in a January 1929 comic strip.

Porky Pig Debuting in "I Haven't Got a Hat" in 1935 by Looney Tunes-Merrie Melodies, this pig usually played the straight man to his colleagues.

Reverend Lovejoy The preacher at the Simpsons' house of worship on *The Simpsons*.

Roadrunner In 1948, Warner Brothers introduced this bird in a cartoon directed by Chuck Jones.

Rocky the Flying Squirrel a.k.a. Rocket J. Squirrel, of Frostbite Falls. Rocky and his friend Bullwinkle do their part in the cold war against Boris Badenov and Natasha Fatale.

Rugrats First aired in August 1991 on Nick-elodeon, the Rugrats has become one of its most successful shows. Created by the duo Klasky and Gabor Csupo, ex of the Simpsons, the TV shows are syndicated worldwide and two movies have been spawned. Characters Tommy, Dill, Phil, Lil,

Angelica, Chuckie, Chas, Spike, Stu, Didi, Drew and Charlotte, Betty and Howard, Boris and Minka, Grandpa Lou (Lulu).

Seymour Skinner The Vietnam veteran and mama's boy who is the principal at Bart and Lisa's school on *The Simpsons*.

Scooby Doo This bashful dog and his teenage compadres began sleuthing in 1972 for Hanna-Barbera.

Scrooge McDuck This miserly curmudgeon first starred in Disney's "Scrooge McDuck and Money" in 1967.

Snoopy The lighthearted and adventurous beagle who sleeps on top of his doghouse is owned by Charlie Brown. (*See* Charlie Brown.)

Speed Racer The adventure-loving hero is the star of his own Japanese-made cartoon, which debuted in 1967.

Speedy Gonzales Speedy debuted in 1955 in a Warner Brothers cartoon directed by Friz Freleng. The flamboyant and quick-witted Mexican mouse was often pursued by Sylvester the Cat.

Spridal Speed Racer's kid brother who made his debut in 1967.

Stan Kyle's best friend on *South Park* who is in love with Wendy Testeburger but throws up whenever he sees her.

Sweet Pea Popeye and Olive Oyl's baby.

Sylvester the Cat A frequently frustrated scaredy-cat who debuted in 1942.

The Simpsons Matt Groening's Bart, Homer, and the family had their first telecast on the Fox network on December 17, 1989, although they were included as shorts on the *Tracey Ullman Show* beginning two years earlier.

Tom and Jerry a.k.a. Tom Cat and Jerry Mouse, was created by Bill Hanna and Joe Barbera in a 1939 cartoon called "Puss Gets the Boot."

Trixie Speed Racer's girlfriend who made her cartoon debut in 1967.

Tweety Bird "I taut I taw a puddy tat!" became the trademark of this canary preyed upon by Sylvester the Cat.

Wallace and Gromit The first really successful 'claymation' characters, Wallace the phlegmatic plasticine inventor, and his dog Gromit are the creations of Nick Park and Aardman Animation.

Waylon Smithers The bootlicking toady and right-hand man to Mr. Burns on *The Simpsons*.

Wile E. Coyote A devious coyote who is nevertheless constantly outwitted by the Roadrunner.

Willie The temperamental Scottish groundskeeper at Bart and Lisa's school on *The Simpsons*.

Wilma Flintstone Fred Flintstone's patient wife. (*See* Fred Flintstone)

Winnie-the-Pooh Originally created by A. A. Milne for *Punch* magazine in 1926, this bear's first animated cartoon was "Winnie-the-Pooh in the Honey Tree."

Woody Woodpecker This aggressive bird created by Walter Lantz first appeared in an Andy Panda cartoon.

Yogi Bear This good-natured bear created by Hanna-Barbera first appeared on *The Huckleberry Hound Show*.

Yosemite Sam This ornery gold-rusher is a member of the Warner Brothers cast of characters.

CASTE SYSTEM

The caste system, as it came to be called, arrived in India somewhere between 2000 and 1000 BCE. Brought by the invading Aryan tribes, who were anxious to preserve their racial identity, the caste system was imposed upon the native population as a method of social control. Initially the idea was to prevent miscegenation, but gradually it evolved into an enduring system of social stratification.

In its manifestation, the caste system gave social power and prestige to the Aryans, while subjecting the indigenous majority to an unquestioned level of servitude backed by heredity and the emerging religion of Hinduism, which sanctified the notion of reincarnation—the belief that the meritorious will attain higher status in their next life if they acquit themselves accordingly in this one. Thus, acceptance of, and obligation to, one's station in life was the norm, which itself added to the longevity of the caste system.

Originally the Aryan system of classes, or *varnas,* consisted of three levels: the **Brahmans**, the priests, who were associated with spiritual and bodily purity; the **Kshatriyas**, the royals and warriors; and the **Vaishyas**, the merchants, professionals, and agriculturists. In order to accommodate the conquered population another class was adopted, the **Shudras**, who were the workers and artisans.

The caste system, as one of distinct levels of social and spiritual purity, eventually came to be subdivided into many hundreds or thousands of castes, each one associated with a different standard of cleanliness. There emerged the concept of the **Harijans**, the untouchables, who were the lowest class. Their daily lives involved coming into contact with pollution and impurity. They were the labourers, the smiths, the cleaners, and finally the beggars and diseased. Each class was essentially a labour union with a monopoly on its specific trade, its status derived from the level of purity or monetary worth of its product.

The caste pyramid is as follows, from the top down:

> **Brahmans**
> **Kshatriyas**
> **Vaishyas**
> **Shudras**
> **Harijans (Untouchables)**

CATHOLIC CHURCH HIERARCHY

Pope Elected by the College of Cardinals, the pope is also known as the Supreme Pontiff, the Bishop of Rome, and the Vicar of Christ.

Cardinal Appointed by the pope, most of these "Roman Princes" reside in Rome and advise the pope.

Archbishop Archbishops preside over an archdiocese (one or more dioceses) and are the authoritative teachers of the faith within their region.

Bishop As supreme local authority, the office of the bishop succeeds to the role of the apostles in the early church.

Chancellor The chancellor acts as the record-keeper and secretary of the bishop.

Apostolic Chamber This part of the Roman Curia handles the administration of temporal affairs of the Holy See when vacant.

Prefecture of the Economic Affairs of the Holy See The Prefecture deals with the daily temporal affairs of the church, and is part of the Roman Curia.

Defender of the Bond This clerical or lay person with qualification in Canon Law works in the marriage tribunal with petitions for annulments.

Vicar General The vicar general is a cleric who acts in the name of the bishop throughout the latter's diocese.

Monsignor This ecclesiastical title of honour can be bestowed on priests and prelates by the pope.

Priest Priests may belong to either a specific religious order or a parish, and are responsible generally for three things: pastoral leadership, administration of the sacraments, and preaching and teaching.

Abbot Elected to his office, the abbot is the head of a specific religious community of men.

Nun These members of a religious community of women live under the vows of poverty, chastity, and obedience.

Deacon In a post revived by the Second Vatican Council, deacons may or may not be married members of the church who help celebrate the Eucharist, preside at baptisms, and preside for priests or bishops at certain liturgical celebrations.

CHARACTERS FROM CHILDREN'S LITERATURE AND FILM

Alice The inquisitive young girl from Lewis Carroll's *Alice's Adventures in Wonderland* and *Through the Looking-Glass*.

Amelia Bedelia This madcap maid, whose literal interpretation of everyday events results in ridiculous episodes, was introduced to the world by Peggy Parish in her 1963 *Amelia Bedelia*.

Anne of Green Gables The orphaned girl sent mistakenly to an elderly brother and sister who had requested a boy in L. M. Montgomery's 1908 book.

Arthur Babar's cousin who lives with him and Celeste in the old lady's home in Jean de Brunhoff's 1931 *The Story of Babar, the Little Elephant*.

Aslan The talking lion in C. S. Lewis's *The Chronicles of Narnia*.

Auntie Em Dorothy Gale's hardworking, unappreciated aunt in L. Frank Baum's *The Wonderful Wizard of Oz*.

Babar The well-dressed French elephant began his wanderings in Jean de Brunhoff's 1931 *The Story of Babar, the Little Elephant*.

Baloo The bear who befriends Mowgli in Rudyard Kipling's 1894 *The Jungle Book*.

Bambi The fawn who grows to be the wise old denizen of the forest in Felix Salten's 1928 *Bambi: A Life in the Woods*.

Barney The lovable singing purple dinosaur.

Benjamin Bunny Peter Rabbit's cousin first appeared in Beatrix Potter's 1904 *The Tale of Benjamin Bunny*.

Bilbo Baggins A merry, travelling hobbit in J. R. R. Tolkien's *The Hobbit, or There and Back Again*.

Black Beauty This graceful horse of Birtwick Park was introduced in Anna Sewell's *Black Beauty*.

Bobbsey Twins Bert and Nan, and Freddie and Flossie were introduced in Laura Lee's 1904 *Bobbsey Twins*.

Borrowers, The A minuscule race, entirely dependent upon human beings in Mary Norton's 1952 book.

Brer Rabbit This trickster rabbit first appeared in Joel Chandler Harris's *Uncle Remus: His Songs and Sayings*.

Captain Hook J. M. Barrie tells of this dreadful pirate leader with a steel hook in place of his right hand in the 1911 *Peter Pan*.

Cat in the Hat Dr. Seuss's beguiling cat whose high jinks give glee and dismay to two young children in the 1958 *The Cat in the Hat*.

Celeste Babar's cousin who becomes his queen in Jean de Brunhoff's 1931 *The Story of Babar, the Little Elephant*.

Charlie Bucket The chocolate-loving youngster was featured in Roald Dahl's 1964 *Charlie and the Chocolate Factory*.

Charlotte The friendly spider from E. B. White's 1952 *Charlotte's Web*.

Chee-Chee Doctor Dolittle's monkey in Hugh Lofting's 1920 *The Story of Doctor Doolittle*.

Chitty Chitty Bang Bang The remarkable flying motor car from Ian Fleming's 1908 story.

Christopher Robin The human child the animals of Hundred-Acre Wood go to for advice in A. A. Milne's 1926 *Winnie-the-Pooh*.

Cowardly Lion The lion seeking courage in L. Frank Baum's *The Wonderful Wizard of Oz*.

Curious George H. A. and Margaret Rey's inquisitive monkey began hanging around in *Curious George,* first published in 1951.

Dab-Dab Doctor Dolittle's duck who is also his housekeeper in Hugh Lofting's 1920 *The Story of Doctor Dolittle*.

Dinosaur Bob William Joyce's huge brontosaurus who befriends the family Lazardo in the 1989 *The Adventures of Dinosaur Bob and the Family Lazardo.*

Doctor Dolittle This animal-loving doctor was introduced in Hugh Lofting's *The Story of Doctor Dolittle.*

Nancy Drew The resourceful teenage detective in numerous novels by Carolyn Keene.

Dorothy Gale This little girl found Oz to be quite unlike her native Kansas in L. Frank Baum's *The Wonderful Wizard of Oz.*

Eeyore The gloomy donkey in the Hundred-Acre Wood in A. A. Milne's 1926 *Winnie-the-Pooh.*

Fern The farmer's daughter who saves Wilbur the pig from immediate slaughter in E. B. White's 1952 *Charlotte's Web.*

Flopsy Bunnies Beatrix Potter told the story of these lovable bunnies in her 1909 *Tale of the Flopsy Bunnies.*

Frances The witty and mischievous little badger from Russell Hoban's 1963 *Bedtime for Frances.*

Frog and Toad These friends were created by Arnold Lobel in *Frog and Toad Are Friends.*

George and Martha A pair of hippos who are very forgiving of each other's foibles and failings in James Marshall's 1972 book.

Glenda the Good Witch The witch who aids Dorothy in her search for home in L. Frank Baum's *The Wonderful Wizard of Oz.*

Grinch, The The dastardly grouch who despises Christmas in Dr. Seuss's 1957 *How the Grinch Stole Christmas.*

Gub-Gub Doctor Doolittle's ever-hungry pig in Hugh Lofting's 1920 *The Story of Doctor Doolittle.*

Hans Brinker This impoverished but virtuous son of a Dutch dike engineer is from Mary Dodge's 1865 *Hans Brinker and the Silver Skates.*

Hardy Boys The sleuthing Frank and Joe began in 1927 in Franklin W. Dixon's *The Tower Treasure.*

Harold The boy who creates his own world with his magical purple crayon in Crockett Johnson's 1955 *Harold and the Purple Crayon.*

Harry Potter The boy, created by J. K. Rowling, who began to take the world by storm in 1999.

Heidi This heartwarming orphan living with her grandfather in the Alps was introduced in Johanna Spyri's 1880 *Heidi.*

Horton The unflagging heroic elephant who alone hears a tiny voice in a dust speck from Dr. Seuss's 1954 *Horton Hears a Who.*

Jemima Puddle Duck The main character in Beatrix Potter's 1908 *Tale of Jemima Puddle Duck.*

Jim Hawkins The young narrator of Robert Louis Stevenson's *Treasure Island.*

Johnny Tremain The American Revolution-era - silversmith's apprentice in Ester Forbes's 1944 book.

Kanga The mother kangaroo in the Hundred-Acre Wood in A. A. Milne's *Winnie-the-Pooh.*

Kermit the Frog Jim Henson's lovable green muppet.

Lassie Eric Knight's 1940 story *Lassie Come-Home* tells the tale of the collie with astonishing intelligence, courage, and initiative.

Laura Ingalls The inquisitive and restless daughter of the pioneer Ingalls family in *Little House in the Big Woods.*

Little Lord Fauntleroy The little poor boy from New York who is discovered to be the heir to an earldom and English castle in Frances Hodgson Burnett's 1886 book.

Little Prince, The The inquisitive, planet-travelling prince from Antoine de Saint-Exupéry's 1943 book of the same name.

Little Toot The tugboat who consistently prevails despite being constantly faced with seemingly insurmountable odds in Hardie Gramatky's 1939 *Little Toot.*

Ma Ingalls Laura Ingalls Wilder depicts her steadfast and practical mother in the 1932 book *Little House in the Big Woods.*

Madeline The daring little girl who lives in Paris with Miss Clavel in Ludwig Bemelman's 1952 *Madeline*.

Mary Ingalls Laura Ingalls Wilder's older sister who is eventually blinded by scarlet fever in the Little House on the Prairie books.

Mike Mulligan Virginia Burton's character who must figure out how to save his steam shovel from being replaced by a more modern machine in *Mike Mulligan and His Steam Shovel*.

Miss Piggy Jim Henson's vain prima donna muppet, whose voice is supplied by Frank Oz.

Mrs. Tittlemouse Beatrix Potter's charming story of the matronly mouse in her 1910 *Tale of Mrs. Tittlemouse*.

Mowgli The human baby given shelter by a family of wolves in Rudyard Kipling's 1894 *The Jungle Book*.

Nellie Olson The shopkeeper's spoiled daughter in Laura Ingalls Wilder's Little House on the Prairie books.

Old Yeller The extraordinarily loyal and stubborn dog who aids his young master on a frontier ranch in Frederick Benjamin Gibson's 1956 book.

Oompa Loompas These mysterious short creatures are featured in Roald Dahl's 1964 *Charlie and the Chocolate Factory*.

Oz The great and wonderful magician who promises to return Dorothy to Kansas but turns out to be nothing but a fraud in L. Frank Baum's *The Wonderful Wizard of Oz*.

Pa Ingalls Laura Ingalls Wilder tells the tale of her hardworking and lovable father in her 1932 *Little House in the Big Woods*.

Paddington Michael Bond's accident-prone bear who is found after being left at the Paddington railway station in London in the 1958 *A Bear Called Paddington*.

Peter Pan The little boy who refuses to grow up in James Barrie's 1911 *Peter Pan and Wendy*.

Peter Rabbit The naughty young rabbit forever being chased out of gardens in Beatrix Potter's famous 1900 *The Tale of Peter Rabbit*.

Piglet The small, timid creature in A. A. Milne's 1926 *Winnie-the-Pooh*.

Pippi Longstocking The wild, adventuresome, freckled, braided red-haired girl from Astrid Lingren's 1950 *Pippi Longstocking*.

Prince Caspian The featured character in C. S. Lewis's 1951 *Prince Caspian: The Return to Narnia*.

Pushmi-Pullyu The remarkable two-headed animal from Africa described in Hugh Lofting's 1920 *The Story of Doctor Dolittle*.

Raggedy Ann The rag doll with a life of her own once the "real for sure" people in the house are asleep or away in Johnny Gruelle's 1918 *Raggedy Ann Stories*.

Ramona The plucky, adventuresome girl with spunk galore in Beverly Cleary's *Beezus and Ramona*.

Roo The baby kangaroo in the Hundred-Acre Wood in A. A. Milne's *Winnie-the-Pooh*.

Runaway Bunny The bunny who realizes that no matter what he does or where he goes, his mother will always love him, from Margaret Wise Brown's 1942 book.

Scarecrow The brainless companion of Dorothy Gale in her quest to return home in L. Frank Baum's *The Wonderful Wizard of Oz*.

Squirrel Nutkin One of the animal characters from Beatrix Potter's eponymous 1903 story.

Stuart Little This plucky and enterprising mouse with romantic inclinations comes from the pages of E. B. White's 1945 *Stuart Little*.

Tailor of Gloucester Beatrix Potter tells the story of this tailor whose clothes were made at night by fairies in the 1910 book *The Tailor of Gloucester*.

Thomas the Tank Engine Reverend W. Awdry's 1946 story of the fussy little engine whose perseverance earns him his own branch line.

Tigger The bouncy tiger who is always looking for something to eat in A. A. Milne's *Winnie-the-Pooh*.

Tin Man The heartless companion of Dorothy Gale in her quest to return home from Oz in L. Frank Baum's *The Wonderful Wizard of Oz*.

Tinkerbell The helpful fairy from James Barrie's 1911 *Peter Pan and Wendy*.

Tom Kitten This engaging little kitten was the subject of Beatrix Potter's 1907 *Tale of Tom Kitten*.

Toto The dog who accompanies Dorothy Gale to Oz in Frank L. Baum's *The Wonderful Wizard of Oz*.

Velveteen Rabbit, The The tattered, neglected rabbit who finds joy when it becomes the beloved toy of a poor child in Margery Bianco's 1922 book.

Wendy Peter Pan's friend who, by growing up, loses her power to fly in James Barrie's 1911 *Peter Pan and Wendy*.

Wicked Witch of the West Desperate to claim ownership of the silver slippers, she does everything in her powers to destroy Dorothy in L. Frank Baum's *The Wonderful Wizard of Oz*.

Wilbur The runt of the pig litter who is destined for slaughter until the interventions of Charlotte the spider from E. B. White's 1952 *Charlotte's Web*.

Wild Things The monstrous fantasy figures Max must tame when he's sent to his room after a temper tantrum in Maurice Sendak's 1963 *Where the Wild Things Are*.

Willy Wonka Roald Dahl tells the tale of the owner and inventor of the mysterious, magical chocolate factory in his 1964 *Charlie and the Chocolate Factory*.

Winnie-the-Pooh The slow-witted, vain, and extremely lovable bear who is forever in search of honey in A. A. Milne's 1926 *Winnie-the-Pooh*.

Zephir Babar's mischievous monkey friend in Jean de Brunhoff's 1931 *The Story of Babar, the Little Elephant*.

CHINESE DYNASTIES

BEFORE THE COMMON ERA (BCE)

2200	Xia dynasty (suspect due to lack of concrete evidence), 2205?–1766 BCE
	Shang dynasty, 1766?–1122? BCE
1100	Zhou dynasty, 1122?–256 BCE
	Western Zhou era, 1122?–771 BCE
	Eastern Zhou era, 770–256 BCE
700	Spring and Autumn period, 722–481 BCE
	Warring States period, 403–221 BCE
	Qin dynasty, 221–207 BCE
200	Western Han dynasty, 202–9 BCE

OF THE COMMON ERA (CE)

200	Xin dynasty, 9–23 CE
	Eastern Han dynasty, 25–220 CE
	Three Kingdoms era, 220–80 CE
	NORTH
	Wei, 220–66 CE
	WEST
	Shu Han, 221–63 CE
	SOUTH
	Wu, 222–80 CE
500	Western Jin dynasty, 266–316 CE
	Era of North-South division, 316–589 CE
	Sixteen Kingdoms, 301–439 CE
	BASED IN SHANSI AND SHENSI
	Han or Chao, 304–29 CE
	Later Chao, 319–52 CE
	(Former) Xin, 352–410 CE
	Later Xin, 384–417 CE
	Xia, 407–31 CE
	Western Xin, 385–431 CE

BASED IN SZECHUAN
Ch'eng Han or Shu, 301–47 CE

BASED IN HOPEI
(Former) Yen, 348–70 CE
Later Yen, 383–409 CE
Southern Yen, 398–410 CE
Northern Yen, 409–36 CE

BASED IN KANSU
(Former) Liang, 313–76 CE
Southern Liang, 397–414 CE
Later Liang, 386–403 CE
Western Liang, 400–421 CE
Northern Liang, 397–439 CE

NORTHERN AND SOUTHERN DYNASTIES,
  317–589 CE
Northern dynasties, 386–581 CE
(Northern) Wei, 386–534 CE
Eastern Wei, 534–50 CE
Western Wei, 534–57 CE
Northern Qi, 550–77 CE
Northern Zhou, 557–81 CE

Southern dynasties, 317–589 CE
Eastern Jin, 317–420 CE
Song, 420–79 CE
Southern Qi, 479–502 CE
Chen, 557–89 CE

900   Sui dynasty, 581–618 CE
      Tang dynasty, 618–907 CE

FIVE DYNASTIES ERA, 907–60 CE
NORTH: FIVE DYNASTIES, 907–60 CE
Later Liang, 907–23 CE
Later Tang, 923–34 CE
Later Jin, 936–47 CE
Later Han, 947–51 CE
Later Zhou, 951–60 CE
SOUTH: TEN KINGDOMS, 907–79 CE
(Former) Shu, 907–25 CE
Later Shu, 934–65 CE
Nanping or Chingnan, 907–63 CE
Chu, 927–56 CE
Wu, 902–37 CE
Southern Tang or Qi, 937–75 CE
Wu Yueh, 907–78 CE

Min, 907–46 CE
Southern Han or Yueh, 907–71 CE
Northern Han, 951–79 CE

1200   Song (or Northern Song) dynasty,
         960–1127 CE
       Northern Conquest dynasties,
         916–1234 CE
       Liao dynasty, 916–1125 CE

1300   Jin dynasty, 1115–1234 CE
       Southern Song dynasty, 1127–1279 CE
       Yuan dynasty, 1264–1368 CE

1900   Ming dynasty, 1368–1644 CE
       Qing dynasty, 1644–1912 CE

Republic of China, 1912–49
People's Republic of China, 1949–present

CLASSICAL COMPOSERS

Albinoni, Tomaso (Baroque) 6/08/1671– 1/17/1750; Adagio in G Minor, Concertos for Oboe op. 7 and 9.

Bach, Carl Phillip Emanuel (Classical) 3/08/1714–12/14/1788; Sonatas for Keyboards.

Bach, Johann Christian (Classical) 9/05/1735– 1/01/1782; Quintets for Flute, Oboe, and Strings op. 11, Symphonies op. 3.

Bach, Johann Sebastian (Baroque) 3/21/1685– 7/28/1780; *Art of the Fugue*, Brandenburg Concertos, *St. Matthew Passion*.

Barber, Samuel (Modern) 3/09/1910–1/23/1981; Adagio for Strings.

Bartók, Bela (Modern) 3/25/1881–9/25/1945; Concertos for Piano.

Beethoven, Ludwig van (Classical) 12/15/1770– 3/26/1827; Concertos for Piano, Symphonies, Sonatas for Piano.

Berlioz, Hector (Romantic) 12/11/1803– 3/08/1869; *Symphonie fantastique* op. 14.

Bernstein, Leonard (Modern) 8/25/1918– 10/14/1990; Mass, *Chichester Psalms*.

Boccherini, Luigi (Classical) 2/19/1743– 5/28/1805; Quintets for Guitar and Strings.

Borodin, Alexander (Romantic) 11/12/1833– 2/27/1887; Quartets.

Brahms, Johannes (Romantic) 5/07/1833– 4/03/1897; Serenades for Orchestra, Symphonies, Trios for Piano and Strings.

Britten, Benjamin (Modern) 11/22/1913– 12/04/1976; *Young Person's Guide to the Orchestra*.

Bruckner, Anton (Romantic) 9/04/1824– 9/11/1896; Symphonies.

Byrd, William (Renaissance) 1543–7/04/1623; Keyboard Music (Pavanes and Galliards), Sacred Choral Music (Mass in 4 Parts).

Chopin, Frederic (Romantic) 3/01/1810– 10/17/1849; Piano Music (Etudes and Nocturnes), Sonatas for Piano.

Copland, Aaron (Modern) 11/14/1900– 12/02/1990; *Appalachian Spring, Fanfare for the Common Man*.

Couperin, François (Baroque) 1626–8/26/1661; *Concerts royaux*, *Pièces de clavecin*.

Debussy, Claude (Romantic) 8/22/1862– 3/25/1918; *Clair de lune*, Preludes for Piano.

Dvořák, Antonin (Romantic) 9/08/1841– 5/01/1904; Concerto for Cello op. 104, Quartets, Quartets for Piano and Strings.

Elgar, Edward (Romantic) 6/02/1857– 2/23/1934; Concerto for Cello op. 85, Symphonies.

Fauré, Gabriel (Romantic) 5/12/1845– 11/04/1924; Chamber Music for Quartets and Quintets.

Franck, César (Romantic) 12/10/1822– 11/08/1890; Organ Music, Symphony in D Minor.

Gershwin, George (Modern) 9/26/1898– 7/11/1937; *An American in Paris, Rhapsody in Blue*.

Gibbons, Orlando (Renaissance) 12/25/1583– 6/05/1623; Church Music, Fantasias for Viol Consort.

Grieg, Edvard (Romantic) 6/15/1843–9/04/1907; Concerto for Piano op. 16, *Peer Gynt Suites*.

Handel, George Frideric (Baroque) 2/23/1685– 4/14/1759; *Messiah, Water Music, Concerti Grossi* op. 6.

Haydn, Franz Joseph (Classical) 3/31/1732– 5/31/1809; Concertos for Keyboard, Quartets, Symphonies.

Ives, Charles (Modern) 10/20/1874–5/19/1954; Piano Sonatas, *Three Places in New England*.

Lassus, Orlando de (Renaissance) 1532–6/14/1594; Madrigals.

Liszt, Franz (Romantic) 2/03/1809–11/04/1847; *Hungarian Rhapsodies*, Piano works. Symphonies.

Mahler, Gustav (Modern) 7/07/1860–5/18/1911; Symphonies 1, 9.

Mendelssohn, Felix (Romantic) 1809– 1847; Incidental music for *A Midsummer Night's Dream*, Symphonies; Concertos.

Monteverdi, Claudio (Renaissance) 5/15/1567–11/29/1643; Madrigals, Masses.

Mozart, Wolfgang Amadeus (Classical) 1/27/1756–12/05/1791; Concertos for Piano, Quintets for Strings, Symphonies.

Mussorgsky, Modest (Romantic) 3/21/1839–3/29/1881; *Pictures at an Exhibition, Night on the Bare Mountain.*

Offenbach, Jacques (Romantic) 6/20/1819–10/05/1880; *Orpheus in the Underworld Overture.*

Pachelbel, Johann (Baroque) 9/01/1653–3/09/1706; Canon, Organ Music (Choral Preludes and Fantasias).

Prokofiev, Sergei (Modern) 4/27/1891–3/04/1953; *Peter and the Wolf,* Sonatas for Piano.

Purcell, Henry (Baroque) 1659–11/21/1695; Trio Sonatas for Strings and Continuo.

Rachmaninov, Sergei (Romantic) 4/01/1873–3/28/1943; Concertos for Piano, *Rhapsody on a Theme of Paganini.*

Ravel, Maurice (Romantic) 3/07/1875–12/28/1937; Bolero for Orchestra, *Daphnis et Chloé.*

Rimsky-Korsakov, Nikolai (Romantic) 3/18/1844-6/21/1908; *Scheherazade* (Symphonic Suite).

Satie, Erik (Modern) 5/17/1866–7/01/1925; Piano music.

Scarlatti, Dominico (Baroque) 5/02/1660–10/22/1726; Sonatas for Harpsicord.

Schoenberg, Arnold (Modern) 9/10/1874–7/13/1951; Chamber Symphony No. 1, *Five Pieces for Children.*

Schubert, Franz (Romantic) 1/31/1797–11/19/1828; Quartets Nos. 12, 13, and 14, Symphonies.

Schuman, William (Modern) 8/04/1910–2/15/1992; *A Song of Orpheus.*

Schumann, Robert (Romantic) 6/08/1810–7/29/1856; *Carnaval for Piano* op. 9, Symphonies.

Shostakovich, Dmitri (Modern) 9/25/1906–8/09/1975; String Quartets, Symphonies.

Sibelius, Jean (Modern) 12/08/1865–9/20/1957; *Finlandia* op. 26, Symphonies.

Strauss, Johann II (Romantic) 10/25/1825–6/03/1899; Waltzes.

Strauss, Richard (Modern) 6/11/1864–9/08/1949; *Also Sprach Zarathustra* op. 30, *Four Last Songs* for Soprano and Orchestra.

Stravinsky, Igor (Modern) 6/17/1882–4/06/1971; *Firebird* (Ballet Suite), *Petrouchka* (Ballet).

Tallis, Thomas (Renaissance) 1505–11/23/1585; Sacred Choral Music.

Tchaikovsky, Pyotr Ilich (Romantic) 5/07/1840–11/06/1893; *Nutcracker Suite* op. 71, *1812 Overture, Swan Lake.*

Telemann, Georg Philipp (Baroque) 3/14/1681–6/25/1767; *Musique de Table,* Suite in A Minor for Flute and Strings.

Torelli, Giuseppe (Baroque) 4/22/1658–2/08/1709; Concerti Grossi op. 8.

Vaughan Williams, Ralph (Modern) 10/12/1872–8/26/1958; *The Lark Ascending* for Violin and Orchestra, Symphonies.

Vivaldi, Antonio (Baroque) 3/04/1678–7/28/1741; *Four Seasons,* Sonatas for Cello and Continuo op. 14.

DICTATORS AND DESPOTS, PRESENT DAY

Burundi Major Pierre Buyoya has been head of state since a 1996 coup.

Chad General Idriss Deby has been head of state since the 1990 coup when President Habre was overthrown.

Republic of Congo General Denis Sassou Nguesso has very recently overthrown former head of state Pascal Lissouba.

Cuba Fidel Castro has been the head of state and government since the 1959 coup of General Batista.

Iraq Saddam Hussein has been in power since seizing control of the government in 1979.

Kenya Daniel Arap Moi has been president since 1978.

Korea, North Kim II Jong took over control of the government after the death of his father on July 8, 1994.

Laos The Communist Nouhak Phoumsavan has been the head of state since 1992.

Liberia Former rebel leader Charles Taylor has been head of state since 1997.

Libya Colonel Muammar al-Qaddafi has held the reins of power in this North African country since 1969.

Myanmar General Tharu Shwe has suppressed opposition since 1992 in this land that was until recently known as Burma.

Sudan General Omer Hassan Ahmed al-Bashir has been the head of state and government since 1989.

Togo General Gnassingbe Eyadema has been the head of state since 1967.

Vietnam President Tran Duc Luong has been the head of state since 1997.

Yugoslavia Slobodan Milosovic was head of state until October 2000.

EGYPTIAN PHARAOHS

EARLY DYNASTIC PERIOD

1st and 2nd dynasties (3110–2780 BCE)

Menes, 1st dynasty. Upper and Lower Egypt united.

OLD KINGDOM

3rd–6th dynasties (2780–2258 BCE)

Snefru, 3rd dynasty. Step pyramid built.

Khufu (Cheops), Khafre, Menkaure, 4th dynasty. The great pyramids built.

Pepi I, Pepi II, 6th dynasty

FIRST INTERMEDIATE PERIOD

7th–11th dynasties (2258–2000 BCE)

Divided Egypt ruled by local monarchs until 2134 BCE
Mentuhotep II, 11th dynasty. Egypt reunified.

MIDDLE KINGDOM

12th dynasty (2000–1786 BCE)

Amenemhet I, Sesostris I, Amenemhet II, Sesostris II, Amenemhet III, Amenemhet IV.

SECOND INTERMEDIATE PERIOD

13th–17th dynasties (1786–1570 BCE)

Hyksos. Theban dynasty frees Egypt.

NEW KINGDOM

18th–30th dynasties (1570–341 BCE)

Amenhotep I, Thutmose I, Thutmose II,

Hatshepsut, Thutmose III, Thutmose IV, Akhenaton, Tutankhamun, 18th dynasty. Empire extended.

Seti I, Ramses I, Ramses II, 19th dynasty

Ramses III, 20th dynasty

Ramses XI, 21st dynasty. Civil war.

Sheshonk I, Sheshonk II, 22nd dynasty. Libyan dynasty; Jerusalem conquered.

Taharka, 25th dynasty. Invaded by Assyria.

Necho, 26th dynasty

Darius II, 27th dynasty. Egypt under Persian rule.

Nekhtnebf I, 28th dynasty

Alexander the Great conquers Egypt, ending the 30th dynasty.

DYNASTY OF THE PTOLEMIES

(323–31 BCE)

Ptolemy Soter, Cleopatra VII

FEUDAL RANK

Feudalism, as a political institution, entered England via Western Europe in the 10th and 11th centuries. In essence it was a system of protection and a way to ensure loyalty and service in time of war—which was often. The feudal pyramid was surmounted by the king, to whom all ultimately paid homage, but between one level and the next loyalty was bought and sold frequently.

King He owned all the land, which he granted as fiefs (contracts of future service), in the form of parcels of land.

Lords/Overlords They held the land given by the king, which they then leased to lesser ranks, who in return promised to furnish their lords with knights or monetary aid, when needed.

Vassals Barons who paid homage to the overlords. They leased land to knights.

Knights They may sometimes have been subtenants of vassals, leasing land for services rendered.

Squires Trainee knights, 14 to 21 years old.

Seigneurs/Suzerains The lords of a manor (the smallest parcel of land).

Villeins/Serfs They lived on and were bound to the manor or fief, working for the lord and paying him rent.

Servants They were owned by the nobility and wealthy merchants.

LITERARY VILLAINS

Angelo The potentate who will release Isabella's brother if she gives herself to him. From William Shakespeare's *Measure for Measure*.

Big Brother The nameless dictator of Oceania in George Orwell's *1984*.

Bluebeard The murderous husband whose wife finds skeletons of his former wives in their closet, from Charles Perrault's 1697 *Tales of Mother Goose*.

Captain Ahab Herman Melville's monomaniacal captain intent on killing the white whale in *Moby-Dick; or, The Whale*.

Captain Hook Peter Pan's nemesis from J. M. Barrie's 1911 *Peter Pan and Wendy*.

Cassius Caesar's political opponent who hatches a plot to have him killed in William Shakespeare's play *Julius Caesar*.

Circe The sorceress who turned Ulysses' crew to swine in Homer's *The Odyssey*.

Citizen Chauvelin A cunning agent of Robespierre who plagues the heroic Scarlet Pimpernel in the book by Emmuska, Baroness Orczy, *The Scarlet Pimpernel*.

Cowperwood, Frank The ruthless, power-hungry businessman in Theodore Dreiser's novels *The Financier* and *The Titan*.

Cyclops A giant one-eyed monster who ate some of Ulysses' crew in Homer's *The Odyssey*.

DeFarge, Madame The vindictive, constantly knitting leader of the mob that storms the Bastille in Charles Dickens's novel *A Tale of Two Cities*.

Dimmesdale The young minister who brands Hester Prynne with the "A" for adulteress in Nathaniel Hawthorne's *The Scarlet Letter*.

Dorian Gray Oscar Wilde's never-ageing murderer from his 1890 *The Picture of Dorian Gray*.

Dr. No The nemesis of James Bond who plans world chaos and conquest in Ian Fleming's 1958 *Dr. No*.

Dracula Bram Stoker's blood-drinking vampire, the prototype of all that followed, from his 1897 *Dracula*.

Fagin Charles Dickens's chief thief from his *Oliver Twist*.

Frollo The Archdeacon who kills Captain Pheobus in Victor Hugo's *The Hunchback of Notre Dame*.

Fu Manchu, Doctor The head of the Chinese secret society known as Si-Fan. Created by Sax Rohmer in *The Mystery of Fu Manchu*.

Godunov, Boris The murdering privy councillor of the Czar in Alexander Pushkin's novel *Boris Godunov*.

Grendel The grim demon from the old English epic *Beowulf*.

HAL Arthur C. Clarke's malfunctioning computer from *2001: A Space Odyssey*.

Iago Shakespeare's lecherous back-stabbing villain from *Othello*.

Injun Joe Tom Sawyer's dark-hearted murderous nemesis from Mark Twain's *The Adventures of Tom Sawyer*.

Jack The cruel and power-hungry redheaded youth leader in William Golding's novel *The Lord of the Flies*.

Jasper, John The presumed villain from Charles Dickens's unfinished work *The Mystery of Edwin Drood*.

King Claudius Hamlet's uncle who kills the king, and takes his wife and kingdom in Shakespeare's *Hamlet*.

Kurtz, Mr. The tortured villain of Joseph Conrad's novella *Heart of Darkness*.

Lime, Harry Graham Greene's villain who runs a medical racket in postwar Vienna in *The Third Man*.

Macbeth and Lady Macbeth The power couple who murder their way to the Scottish throne in Shakespeare's *Macbeth*.

Mephistopheles Faustus's tempter in Johann Wolfgang von Goethe's 1801 *Faust*.

Merrick, Ronald The villainous British officer in Paul Scott's *The Raj Quartet,* about the last days of British rule in India.

Montoni The satanic hero-villain of Mrs. Radcliffe's Gothic novel *The Mysteries of Udolpho.*

Mordred, Sir King Arthur's nephew, who wanted to marry his stepmother, from *Le Morte D'Arthur.*

Moriarty, Professor Sherlock Holmes's nemesis in Sir Arthur Conan Doyle's 1893 *The Final Problem.*

Mr. Hyde The crazed murderer from Robert Louis Stevenson's 1888 *The Strange Case of Dr. Jekyll and Mr. Hyde.*

Napoleon The dictator who takes over the barnyard in George Orwell's cautionary tale *Animal Farm.*

Nikola, Doctor An urbane, cat-loving villain in Guy Boothby's *A Bid for Fortune.*

Raskolnikov The student murderer from Fyodor Dostoyevsky's 1866 *Crime and Punishment.*

Richard III The scheming duke of Gloucester who kills his way to the throne in Shakespeare's *Richard III.*

The Ringer The master criminal who is a supreme expert in the art of disguise in Edgar Wallace's *The Gaunt Stranger.*

Satan The ruler of hell in John Milton's 1667 *Paradise Lost.*

Sauron The Dark Lord in J. R. R. Tolkien's *The Lord of the Rings.*

Scrooge, Ebenezer The villain turned hero in Charles Dickens's *A Christmas Carol.*

Sikes, Bill The villain with whom Oliver Twist comes into contact in Charles Dickens's *Oliver Twist.*

Silver, Long John A one-legged pirate who masquerades as a sea-cook in Robert Louis Stevenson's *Treasure Island.*

Svengali The musician who uses his sinister hypnotic powers to control a young singer in George du Maurier's *Trilby.*

Todd, Sweeney The "Demon Barber" who slits customers' throats first appeared in print in Thomas Peckett's novel *The String of Pearls.*

Villefort, M. The deputy prosecutor who plagues the heroic Edmond Dantes in Alexander Dumas's *The Count of Monte Cristo.*

GANGSTERS (AMERICAN)

Accardo, Anthony Joseph Known as "Joe Batters" for his adept use of a baseball bat for the Capone gang.

Adonis, Joe a.k.a. Giuseppe Doto. One of the premier members of the national crime syndicate, Adonis originally headed the Prohibition-era Broadway mob. He was deported to Italy in 1956.

Alterie, Louis "Two Gun" ran with the O'Banion gang in Chicago in the 1920s and early 1930s. He was killed in 1935.

Bonanno, Joe "Joe Bananas" began his career in New York in the 1930s, eventually headed a crime family, and was jailed in the mid-1980s after a forced retirement.

Brooklier, Dominic Brooklier ran the Los Angeles mob and was eventually jailed. He died in 1984.

Buccieri, Fiore "Fifi" was an employed killer for Mafia boss Sam Giancana until his death from cancer in 1973.

Capone, Alphonse "Scarface Al" led the Chicago mob during Prohibition. He was convicted of tax evasion in 1929 and died at his estate in Florida in 1947.

Cohen, Mickey A California gangster who served as Bugsy Siegel's bodyguard. He was twice convicted of tax evasion and died peacefully in 1976.

Coli, Eco James Coli worked as a murderer for the Chicago crime syndicate.

Coll, Vincent "Mad Dog" muscled in on Dutch Schultz's liquor racket in New York. He was eventually gunned down in a telephone booth in 1932.

Dragna, Louis Tom Reputedly the head of the Mafia in Southern California, Dragna was convicted on conspiracy charges in 1980 but served little time.

Drucci, Vincent "Schemer" headed Chicago's O'Banion gang and was one of Capone's chief rivals. Killed in 1927.

Galante, Carmine "The Cigar" moved through the Bonanno crime family until he was shot to death in 1979 after a meal in Brooklyn, his cigar still clenched in his mouth.

Genovese, Vito Reputedly the boss of bosses, "Don Vito" was sentenced to 15 years on conspiracy charges and died in jail in 1969.

Giancana, Sam "Momo" was one of the most powerful and ruthless Mafia members west of the Mississippi until he was killed in 1975.

Gigante, Vincent "The Chin" rose from petty killer to head of the Genovese crime family. His feigned mental illness did not preclude him from conviction and jail time.

Gotti, John The flamboyant "dapper don" acted as head of the Gambino crime family until a confession by "Sammy the Bull" Gravano, his consigliere, sent him to jail.

Gravano, Salvatore "Sammy the Bull" was John Gotti's right-hand man until he traded jail time for information on the "dapper don."

Humphreys, Murray "The Camel" was actually a Welshman who pulled a number of capers in the Chicago mob until his arrest and untimely death by seizure in 1965.

Karpis, Alvin "Creepy" was a public enemy when he was wooed by Capone to join his gang. He refused, was eventually convicted in 1936, and was released in 1962.

Langella, Gennaro "Jerry Lang" took over the Colombo crime family in the mid-1980s.

Lansky, Meyer Maier Suchowljansky was notable for being Jewish and for being arguably the most powerful gangster in a line of business dominated by Italians.

Larocca, John Sebastian Head of the Pittsburgh Mafia, Larocca eluded much jail time until his death of natural causes in 1984.

Lepke, Louis Labelled the "most dangerous criminal in the U.S." by J. Edgar Hoover, Lepke was chief of the American rackets until his execution in 1944.

Licata, Nick Licata killed his way through the Chicago syndicate until he became a Los Angeles crime family boss in 1968. He died in 1974.

Licavoli, James T. "Blackie," a Cleveland crime family head, was one of the first gangsters to be convicted under the RICO statute. He died in prison in 1985.

Lovett, William "Wild Bill" ran rackets in Brooklyn until his untimely demise in 1923 from gunfire and a cleaver.

Lucchese, Thomas "Three-Finger Brown" was a popular crime boss until his death in 1967 of the effects of heart disease and a brain tumour.

Luciano, Charles "Lucky" created the American Mafia in 1931 and was the most successful and influential Italian in the mob until his death of natural causes in 1962.

Lupo the Wolf This leader of the Morello crime family in New York struck fear into the hearts of other mobsters for his brutality. He died a few years after release from prison.

McGurn, Jack "Machine Gun Jack" became adept with a tommy gun in the Capone gang until he was killed in 1936 in a bowling alley.

Madden, Owney "The Killer" was actually an English-born killer who ran casinos in Hot Springs, Arkansas, after leaving the New York rackets.

Magaddino, Stefano Magaddino ran the Buffalo Mafia until his death in 1974.

Maranzano, Salvatore Considered the boss of bosses, this Sicilian built up what we now consider the Mafia in New York until he was murdered in 1931.

Marcello, Carlos A tightfisted boss of the New Orleans Mafia, Marcello is mainly known for the rumour that he was involved in the murder of JFK.

Masseria, Giuseppe "Joe the Boss," or "Joe the Glutton," was a Sicilian who worked out of New York until he was killed by Lucky Luciano's men in 1931.

Matranga, Charles An early New Orleans crime boss. He died in 1943 at the age of 86.

Mirabella, John This tough was a hit man in the Midwest until cirrhosis of the liver curtailed his activities.

Moran, George "Bugs" vied for control in Chicago with Capone but wound up dying in Leavenworth Prison of cancer in 1957.

Moretti, Willie After providing levity at the Kefauver mob hearings, the syphilis-suffering Moretti was gunned down at a diner in 1951.

Morton, Samuel J. "Nails" worked as a killer for the O'Banion mob in Chicago until he was thrown and kicked to death in 1924. Bugs Moran led the execution on a horse.

Nardi, John This Cleveland gangster was involved in the Teamsters Union until his death in 1977.

Nitti, Frank Nitti ran the Capone organization after Capone went to jail. He killed himself in 1943 instead of returning to jail himself.

Noland, John T. After earning the nickname "Legs Diamond" for his speed as a petty thief, Noland ran his own New York gang until he was gunned down in 1931.

O'Banion, Charles Dion "Deanie" ran a florist shop and was Capone's biggest competitor in the crime world until his death in 1924.

Patriarca, Raymond L. S. This ruthless New England Mafia boss spent few years in jail and died peacefully in 1984.

Prio, Ross This Sicilian native ran the syndicate in Chicago until his death of natural causes in 1972.

Profaci, Joseph Profaci ran the crime family of his name for over three decades until he died in 1962 of cancer.

Reina, Tom Reina was a New York crime family head until his death by shotgun in 1930.

Reles, Abe "Kid Twist" was a prime player in the so-called Murder, Inc., until he sang to the police. He fell from a window in 1941.

Riccobene, Harry Riccobene vied for control of the Philadelphia Mafia until jailed in the 1980s.

Roberts, Johnny Roberts was a hit man, known primarily for his assassination of New Jersey crime kingpin Willie Moretti. Roberts was himself hit in 1958.

Salerno, Anthony "Fat Tony" is known to be a boss of the Genovese crime family.

Schultz, Dutch Born Arthur Glegenheimer, Schultz was a notorious killer and gang leader in New York before being gunned down in Newark in 1935.

Siegel, Benjamin "Bugsy" worked the East Side of Manhattan with his pal Meyer Lansky, eventually building a casino in Las Vegas before dying of gunshot wounds in 1947.

Squillante, Jimmy Squillante was the boss of the garbage collection racket in New York until he was indicted in 1960, when he quietly "disappeared."

Stevens, Walter Stevens was suspected of killing over 60 men, some by contract from Capone, until his retirement from the profession.

Teresa, Vincent Charles "Fat Vinnie" entered the Federal Witness Protection Program after ratting on his fellow New England Mafia members.

Testa, Philip "Chicken Man" was an underboss of a Philadelphia Mafia family until he was blown up by a remote-control bomb in 1981.

Tieri, Frank "Funzi" headed the Luciano-Genovese crime family until he died in 1981 at age 77, two months after being convicted for the first time.

Torrio, John Torrio moved to Chicago after finding Brooklyn too small for his hijacking, prostitution, and narcotics schemes. He helped begin Capone's career.

Touhy, Roger Hawk-nosed and beady-eyed, "Terrible" struck fear into even Capone's heart as he ran the liquor syndicate in Chicago. He was killed in 1959 after spending 25 years in jail.

Trafficante, Santo This Sicilian immigrant ran the Tampa crime syndicate from the late 1930s until his death in 1954.

Valenti, Rocco A New York–New Jersey tough in the 1910s until his murder in 1922.

Weiss, Hymie Born Earl Wajciechowski, Weiss was a boss in the O'Banion mob in Chicago in the 1920s until he was rubbed out by Capone's men.

Zerilli, Joseph Zerilli cut his teeth in Detroit in the 1920s with the Purple Gang, eventually becoming a crime boss.

Ziegler, George "Shotgun" was a well-educated member of the Capone organization. He was killed by a shotgun blast in 1934.

GANGSTERS (UK)

The Kray brothers - Reggie, Ronnie and Charlie

Frankie Fraser

Jack 'The Hat' McVitie

Tony Lambrianou

Ronnie Biggs

Ronnie Knight

Charlie Richardson

Freddie Foreman

Dave Courtney

Buster Edwards

GODS AND GODDESSES: GREEK, ROMAN, NORSE, AND HINDU

GREEK GODS AND GODDESSES

Zeus chief god, sky god
Hera chief goddess, goddess of marriage
Hestia hearth goddess
Demeter vegetation, harvest goddess
Hades underworld god
Persephone underworld goddess
Poseidon sea god
Aphrodite goddess of love, beauty
Athena wisdom, war goddess
Ares war god
Dionysus wine, fertility god
Hermes messenger god, god of cunning
Hebe youth goddess
Hephaestus fire god
Artemis moon, hunting, fertility goddess
Apollo sun, healing god
Aeolus god of winds
Pan god of herds, shepherds
Nike goddess of victory
Nemesis goddess of vengeance
Thanatos god of death
Hypnos god of sleep
Morpheus god of dreams
Iris messenger goddess, goddess of rainbows
Kronos god of fertility
Dike goddess of justice
Adikia goddess of injustice
Hyperion god of light
Selena moon goddess
Gaia earth goddess
Nyx goddess of night
Kratos god of strength
Hygieia goddess of health
Mnemosyne goddess of memory

Horkos god of oaths
Logos god of reason
Irene goddess of peace
Hecate moon goddess, goddess of pathways

ROMAN GODS AND GODDESSES

Jupiter chief god, sky god
Juno chief goddess, goddess of marriage
Vesta hearth goddess
Ceres goddess of grain, fertility
Neptune sea god
Pluto underworld god
Proserpine underworld goddess
Minerva goddess of wisdom, arts
Diana moon, fertility, hunting goddess
Apollo sun, healing god
Venus goddess of love, beauty
Bacchus wine, fertility god
Mercury messenger god, god of trade
Mars god of war
Vulcan god of fire
Flora goddess of flowers
Boreas god of the north wind
Aquilo god of the west wind
Eurus god of the east wind
Zephyrus god of the south wind
Victoria victory goddess
Honus god of martial honor
Abeona goddess of safe travel
Luna moon goddess
Aurora goddess of dawn
Pomona goddess of fruit
Maia earth goddess
Fortuna goddess of good fortune
Abundantia goddess of abundance
Edusa god of infants
Promitor god of crops
Egeria fertility goddess
Occator harvest god
Mors god of death
Meditrina goddess of healing
Fauna goddess of woods and plants
Faunus god of woods and plants
Silvanus forest god
Discordia goddess of dissent
Pax goddess of peace
Amor god of love

Fides god of loyalty
Unxia goddess of marriage

NORSE GODS AND GODDESSES

Odin chief god, sky god
Frigg chief goddess, goddess of marriage
Balder sun god
Freya goddess of love, fertility
Thor thunder god
Heimdall warden god
Tyr war god
Loki god of mischief
Hel underworld goddess
Mimir god of wisdom
Weland god of crafts
Hoenir god of foretelling
Donar storm god
Heimdall guardian god
Idunn goddess of immortality
Sif grain goddess
Gefjon goddess of agriculture
Fjorgyn fertility goddess
Hermod messenger god
Bragi god of poetry
Mimir god of wisdom
Iord earth goddess
Nanna vegetation goddess
Mani moon god
Njord god of sea, winds
Ran storm goddess
Sol sun goddess
Ull god of justice
Vor goddess of oaths, pacts

HINDU GODS AND GODDESSES

Brahma creator of the world
Vishnu chief god, preserver
Shiva storm god, god of healing
Parvati goddess of fertility
Lakshmi goddess of beauty, fortune
Kali goddess of power, destruction
Krishna god of love
Indra war god, god of weather
Durga war goddess
Varuna sea god, god of order

Rudra god of disease, healing
Surya sun god
Agni fire god
Soma moon god, god of crops
Ganesh god of luck
Hiranyagarbha creator god
Hanuman monkey god
Indrani goddess of wrath
Abhijit goddess of fortune
Aditi mother goddess, guardian goddess
Vivasvan sun god
Vrta god of chaos
Hardaul god of plague
Didi Thakrun goddess of plague
Hotra goddess of sacrifice
Ardra goddess of misfortune
Dhara god of support
Candika goddess of desire
Dipti goddess of brightness
Dhatar sun god
Surya god of sun, knowledge
Siddhi goddess of success
Pusan god of journeys
Candra moon god
Narada music god
Manasa snake goddess
Vijaya victory god
Malhal Mata goddess of disease
Kaumudi goddess of moonlight
Dharma goddess of justice

JAPANESE EMPERORS

Name (Reign)	Reign began (Coronation)	Reign ended
Jimmu	(660)	585 BCE
Suizei	581	549
Annei	549	511
Itoku	510	477
Kosho	475	393
Koan	392	291
Korei	290	215
Kogen	214	158
Kaika	158	98
Sujin	(97)	30
Suinin	29 BCE	70 CE
Keiko	(71)	130
Seimu	(130)	190
Jingu Kogo	201–69 (Regent)	
Chuai	(192)	210
Ojin	(270)	310
Nintoku	(313)	399
Richu	(400)	405
Hanzei	(406)	410
Ingyo	(412)	453
Anko	453	456
Yuryaku	456	479
Seinei	(480)	484
Kenzo	(485)	487
Ninken	(488)	498
Buretsu	498	506
Keitai	(507)	531
Ankan	531	535
Senka	535	539
Kimmei	539	571
Bidatsu	(572)	585
Yomei	585	587
Sushun	587	592
Empress Suiko	592	628
Jomei	(629)	641
Empress Kogyoku	(642)	645
Kotoku	645	654
Empress Saimei	(655)	661
Tenji	(662)	671
Kobun	671	672

Name (Reign)	Reign began (Coronation)	Reign ended	Name (Reign)	Reign began (Coronation)	Reign ended
Temmu	(673)	686	Gohorikawa	1221	1232
Empress Jito	(690)	697	Shijo	1232	1242
Mommu	697	707	Gosaga	1242	1246
Empress Gemmei	707	715	Gofukakusa	1246	1259
Empress Gensho	715	724	Kameyama	1259	1274
Shomu	724	749	Go-uda	1274	1287
Empress Koken	749	758	Fushimi	(1288)	1298
Junnin	758	764	Gofushimi	1298	1301
Empress Shotoku	764	770	Gonijo	1301	1308
Konin	770	781	Hanazono	1308	1318
Kammu	781	806	Godaigo	1318	1339
Heizei	806	809	Gomurakami	1339 (?)	1368
Saga	809	823	Chokei	1368 (?)	1383
Junna	823	833	Gokameyama	1383	1392
Nimmyo	833	850	Gokomatsu	1392	1412
Montoku	850	858	Shoko	1412 (1414)	1428
Seiwa	858	876	Gohanazono	1429? (1429)	1464
Yozei	876 (877)	884	Gotsuchimikado	1465? (1465)	1500
Koko	884	887	Gokashiwabara	1500 (1521)	1526
Uda	887	897	Gonara	1526 (1536)	1557
Daigo	897	930	Ogimachi	1557 (1560)	1586
Suzaku	930	946	Goyozei	1586	1611
Murakami	946	967	Gomizuno-o	1611	1629
Reizi	967	969	Empress Meisho	1630	1643
En-yu	969	984	Gokomyo	1643	1654
Kazan	984	986	Gosai	1656	1663
Ichijo	986	1011	Reigen	1663	1687
Sanjo	1011	1016	Higashiyama	1687	1709
Go-ichijo	1016	1036	Nakamikado	1710	1735
Gosuzaku	1036	1045	Sakuramachi	1735	1747
Goreizi	1045	1068	Momozono	1747	1762
Gasanjo	1068	1072	Gosakuramachi	1763	1770
Shirakawa	1072	1086	Gomomozono	1771	1779
Horikawa	1086	1107	Kokaku	1780	1817
Toba	1107	1123	Ninko	1817	1846
Sutoku	1123	1141	Komei	1847	1866
Konoe	1141	1155	Meiji	1866 (1868)	1912
Goshirakawa	1155	1158	Taisho	1912 (1915)	1926
Nijo	1158	1165	Hirohito (Showa)	1926 (1928)	1989
Rokujo	1165	1168	Akihito (Heisei)	1989 (1990)	present
Takakura	1168	1180			
Antoku	1180	1183			
Gotoba	1183 (1184)	1198			
Tsuchimikado	1198	1210			
Juntoku	1210	1221			
Chukyo	1221	1221			

MILITARY RANKS

ROYAL NAVY	US NAVY
Officers	
Admiral of the Fleet	Fleet Admiral
Admiral	Admiral
Vice Admiral	Vice Admiral
Rear Admiral	Rear Admiral (upper half)
Commodore	Rear Admiral (lower half)
Captain	Captain
Commander	Commander
Lieutenant Commander	Lieutenant Commander
	Chief Warrant Officer
Lieutenant	Lieutenant
	Lieutenant Junior Grade
Sub-Lieutenant	Ensign
Midshipman	Warrant Officer
Enlisted	
	Master Chief Petty Officer of the Navy
Warrant Officer	Master Chief Petty Officer
	Senior Chief Petty Officer
	Chief Petty Officer
Chief Petty Officer	Petty Officer First Class
Petty Officer	Petty Officer Second Class
Leading Seaman	Petty Officer Third Class
	Seaman
Able Seaman	Seaman Apprentice
Ordinary Seaman	Seaman Recruit

RAF	USAF
Officers	
Marshal of the Royal Air Force	General of the Air Force
Air Chief Marshal	General
Air Marshal	Lieutenant General
Air Vice-Marshal	Major General
Air Commodore	Brigadier General
Group Captain	Colonel
Wing Commander	Lieutenant Colonel
Squadron Leader	Major
Flight Lieutenant	Captain
Flying Officer	First Lieutenant
Pilot Officer	Second Lieutenant
Acting Pilot Officer	
Enlisted	
	Chief Master Sergeant of the Air Force
Warrant Officer	Chief Master Sergeant
	Senior Master Sergeant
	Master Sergeant
Flight Sergeant/Chief Technician	Technical Sergeant
Sergeant	Staff Sergeant
Corporal	Senior Airman
	Airman First Class
Junior Technician/Senior aircraftman/Leading aircraftman	Airman
Aircraftman	Airman Basic

BRITISH ARMY	US ARMY
Officers	
Field Marshal	General of the Army
General	General
Lieutenant General	Lieutenant General
Major General	Major General
Brigadier	Brigadier General
Colonel	Colonel
Lieutenant Colonel	Lieutenant Colonel
	Master Warrant Officer
Major	Major
	Chief Warrant Officer
Captain	Captain
Lieutenant	First Lieutenant
Second Lieutenant	Second Lieutenant
	Warrant Officer
Enlisted	
	Commander Sergeant Major of the Army
Warrant Officer Class 1	Sergeant Major
	Command Sergeant Major
	Master Sergeant
	First Sergeant

Warrant Officer Class 2	Platoon Sergeant
	Sergeant First Class
Staff Sergeant	Staff Sergeant
Sergeant	Sergeant
Corporal	Corporal
	Specialist
Lance Corporal	Private First Class
Private	Private

ROYAL MARINES

Officers
General
Lieutenant General
Major General
Brigadier
Colonel
Lieutenant Colonel

Major
Captain
Lieutenant
Second Lieutenant

Enlisted

Warrant Officer Class 1

Warrant Officer Class 2
Colour Sergeant
Sergeant
Corporal
Lance Corporal

Marine

US MARINE CORPS

General
Lieutenant General
Major General
Brigadier General
Colonel
Lieutenant Colonel
Chief Warrant Officer
Major
Captain
First Lieutenant
Second Lieutenant
Warrant Officer

Sergeant Major of the
Marine Corps
Master Gunnery
Sergeant
Sergeant Major
Master Sergeant
First Sergeant
Gunnery Sergeant
Staff Sergeant
Sergeant
Corporal
Lance Corporal
Private First Class
Private

MONARCHS OF ENGLAND, FRANCE, SPAIN

BRITISH MONARCHS

Saxons and Danes
Egbert, 802–839
Ethelwulf, 839–858
Ethelbald, 858–860
Ethelbert, 860–865
Ethelred, 865–871
Alfred the Great, 871–899
Edward the Elder, 899–924
Athelstan, 924–939
Edmund, 939–946
Edred, 946–955
Edwy, 955–959
Edgar, 959–975
Edward the Martyr, 975–978
Ethelred II, the Unready, 978–1016
Edmund Ironside, 1016
Canute, 1016–1035
Harold I, 1037–1040
Hardacnute, 1040–1042
Edward the Confessor, 1042–1066
Harold II, 1066

House of Normandy
William the Conqueror, 1066–1087
William II, 1087–1100
Henry I, 1100–1135

House of Blois
Stephen, 1135–1154

House of Plantagenet
Henry II, 1154–1189
Richard the Lionheart, 1189–1199
John, 1199–1216
Henry III, 1216–1272
Edward I, 1271–1307
Edward II, 1307–1327
Edward III, 1327–1377
Richard II, 1377–1399

House of Lancaster
Henry IV, 1399–1413
Henry V, 1413–1422
Henry VI, 1422–1461 / 1470–1471

House of York
Edward IV, 1461–1470 / 1471–1483
Edward V, 1483
Richard III, 1483–1485

House of Tudor
Henry VII, 1485–1509
Henry VIII, 1509–1547
Edward VI, 1547–1553
Mary I, 1553–1558
Elizabeth I, 1558–1603

House of Stuart
James I, 1603–1625
Charles I, 1625–1649

Commonwealth
Oliver Cromwell, 1653–1658
Richard Cromwell, 1658–1659

House of Stuart
Charles II, 1660–1685
James II, 1685–1688
Mary II, 1689–1694
William III, 1689–1702
Anne, 1702–1714

House of Hanover
George I, 1714–1727
George II, 1727–1760
George III, 1760–1820
George IV, 1820–1830
William IV, 1830–1837
Victoria, 1837–1901

House of Saxe-Coburg
Edward VII, 1901–1910

House of Windsor
George V, 1910–1936
Edward VIII, 1936
George VI, 1936–1952
Elizabeth II, 1952–present

FRENCH MONARCHS

Carolingians
Charlemagne, 768–814
Louis I, the Pious, 814–840
Charles I, the Bald, 840–877
Louis II, the Stammerer, 877–879
Louis III, 879–882
Carloman, 879–884
Charles II, the Fat, 884–887
Eudes (Odo), 888–898
Charles III, the Simple, 898–922
Robert I, 922–923
Raoul, 923–936
Louis IV, 936–954
Lothair, 954–986
Louis V, the Sluggard, 986–987

Capets
Hugh Capet, 987–996
Robert II, the Wise, 996–1031
Henri I, 1031–1060
Philippe I, the Fair, 1060–1108
Louis VI, the Fat, 1108–1137
Louis VII, the Younger, 1137–1180
Philippe II, 1180–1223
Louis VIII, the Lion, 1223–1226
Louis IX, 1226–1270
Philippe III, the Hardy, 1270–1285
Philippe IV, the Fair, 1285–1314
Louis X, the Quarrelsome, 1314–1316
Philippe V, the Tall, 1316–1322
Charles IV, the Fair, 1322–1328

House of Valois
Philippe VI, 1328–1350
Jean II, the Good, 1350–1364
Charles V, the Wise, 1364–1380
Charles VI, 1380–1422
Charles VII, 1422–1461
Louis XI, 1461–1483
Charles VIII, the Affable, 1483–1498
Louis XII, 1498–1515
Francois I, 1515–1547
Henri II, 1547–1559
Francois II, 1559–1560
Charles IX, 1560–1574

Henri III, 1574–1589

House of Bourbon
Henry IV, 1589–1610
Louis XIII, 1610–1643
Louis XIV, 1643–1715
Louis XV, 1715–1774
Louis XVI, 1774–1793

First Republic 1792–1804

First Empire
Napoleon I, 1804–1814

Restoration of Monarchy
Louis XVIII, 1814–1824
Charles X, 1824–1830
Louis-Philippe, 1830–1848

Second Republic
Louis Napoleon, 1848–1851

Second Empire
Napoleon III, 1852–1870

Restoration of Republic 1870

SPANISH MONARCHS

Isabella I, 1474–1504
Ferdinand I, 1474–1516
Charles I, 1516–1556
Philip II, 1556–1598
Philip III, 1598–1621
Philip IV, 1621–1665
Charles II, 1665–1700
Philip V, 1700–1746
Ferdinand VI, 1746–1759
Charles III, 1759–1788
Charles IV, 1788–1808
Joseph Bonaparte, 1808–1813
Ferdinand VII, 1814–1833
Isabella II, 1833–1868
Amadeo, 1870–1873

First Republic 1873–1874

Restoration of Monarchy
Alfonso XII, 1875–1885
Alfonso XIII, 1886–1931

Second Republic 1931–1939

Franco Dictatorship 1939–1975

Restoration of Monarchy
Juan Carlos, 1975–present

NATIVE AMERICAN TRIBES

Abitibi
Abnaki
Achomawi
Acolapissa
Acoma
Adirondack
Ahtena
Ais
Alabama
Aleut
Algonkin
Alibamu
Alsea
Apache
Apalachee
Arapaho
Aravaipa Apache
Arikara
Assiniboin
Assiniboin (Stoney)
Atakapa
Athapaskan
Atsina
Bannock
Basinai
Bella Bella
Bella Coola

Beothuk	Comanche
Bidai	Comox
Biloxi	Conestoga
Blackfoot	Coos
Blood	Coos Bay
Brule	Costano
Caddo	Costanoan
Cahuilla	Cowichan
Calusa	Cowlitz
Carrier	Coyotera Apache
Catawba	Cree
Cayuga	Creek
Cayuse	Crow
Chakchiuma	Cupeno
Chastacosta	Cusabo
Chatot	Dakota
Chaui	Delaware
Chawasha	Diegueno
Chehalis	Dogrib
Chelan	Duwamish
Chemehuevi	Eastern Dakota
Cheraw	Eno
Cherokee	Erie
Cheyenne	Eskimo
Chiaha	Eyak
Chickahominy	Flathead
Chickasaw	Flathead (Salish)
Chilcotin Beaver	Fox
Chimakum	Gabrielino
Chinook	Gitksan
Chinookan	Gosiute
Chipewyan	Gros Ventre
Chippewa	Gros Venture (Atsina)
Chippewa-Munsee	Guale
Chiricahua Apache	Haida
Chitimacha	Haisla
Choctaw	Halchidhoma
Chumash	Han
Clallam	Hano
Clatskanie	Hare
Clatsop	Hasinai
Coahuiltec	Hatteras
Coast Miwok	Havasupai
Coast Salish	Heiltsuk
Cochiti	Hidatsa
Cocopa	Hitchiti
Coeur d'Alene	Hopi
Columbia	Houma
Colville	Hualapai

Humptulips	Maidu
Hunkpapa	Makah
Hupa	Malecite
Huron	Mandan
Huron (Wyandot)	Maricopa
Illinois	Massachuset
Ingalik	Meherrin
Iowa	Menominee
Isleta	Mescalero Apache
Jemez	Methow
Jicarilla	Metoac
Jicarilla Apache	Miami
Juaneno	Micmac
Kalapuya	Mimbreno Apache
Kalispel	Miniconjou
Kamia	Mission Indians
Kansa	Missouri
Karankawa	Mistassini
Karok	Miwok
Kaska	Mobile
Kaskaskia	Modoc
Kato	Mohave
Kawaiisu	Mohawk
Keres	Mohegan
Keresan Pueblo	Mojave
Kern River Tribes	Molala
Kichai	Monacan
Kickapoo	Mono
Kiowa	Montagnais
Kiowa-Apache	Montauk
Kitkehahki	Mosopelea
Klallam	Mountain
Klamath	Munsee
Klikatat	Muskogee
Koasati	Nabesna
Kootenay	Nambe
Koowan	Nanaimo
Koyukon	Nanticoke
Kutchin	Napochi
Kutenai	Narraganset
Kwakiutl	Naskapi
Kwalhioqua	Natchez
Laguna	Navajo
Lake	Neutral Erie
Lillooet	Neutrals
Lipan Apache	Nez Percé
Luiseno	Nicola
Lumni	Nipissing
Mahican	Nipmuc

Niska
Nisqually
Nooksack
Nootka
Nottaway
Ntlakyapamuk
Ofo
Oglala
Ojibway
Okanagan
Omaha
Oneida
Onondaga
Osage
Oto
Ottawa
Owens Valley
Paiute
Palouse
Pamlico
Panamint
Papago
Passamaquoddy
Paviotso
Pawnee
Pecos
Pedee
Pend d'Oreille (Kalispel)
Pennacook
Penobscot
Pensacola
Peoria
Pequot
Piankashaw
Picuris
Piegan
Pima
Piro
Pitahauerat
Plains Cree
Podunk
Pojoaque
Pomo
Ponca
Poosepatuck
Potawatomi
Potomac
Powhatan
Pueblo

Puntlatch
Puyallup
Quapaw
Quileute
Salina
Salinan
Salishan
San Felipe
San Ildefonso
San Juan
Sandia
Sanpoil
Sans Arc
Santa Ana
Santa Clara
Sante Sioux
Santee
Santo Doming
Saponi
Saschutkennie
Sauk
Sauk and Fox
Saulteaux
Secotan
Seechelt
Sekani
Semiahmoo
Seminole
Seneca
Serrano
Shahaptin
Shasta
Shawnee
Shennecock
Shoshoni
Shuswap
Sia
Siletz
Simonole
Sioux
Sisseton
Siuslaw
Skagit
Skidi
Skokomish
Slave
Snoqualmie
Spokan
Squamish

Sugeree
Susquehanna
Susquehannock
Swampy Cree
Taensa
Tagish
Tahltan
Takelma
Talelma
Tamathli
Tanaina
Tanoan
Tanoan Pueblo
Taos
Tawakoni
Tekesta
Tenino
Tesuque
Tete De Boule Cree
Teton
Teton Sioux
Tewa
Tillamook
Timucua
Tiwa
Tlatskanai
Tlingit
Tobacco
Tohome
Tolowa
Tongass
Tonkawa
Towa Pecos
Tsetsaut
Tsimshian
Tubatulabal
Tunica
Tuscarora
Tuskegee
Tutchone
Tutelo
Tututni
Twana
Two-Kettle
Umatilla
Umpqua
Ute
Waccamaw
Waco

Wailaki
Walapai
Walla Walla
Wanapam
Wappinger
Wappo
Warm Springs
Wasco
Washo
Watcree
Wea
Weapemeoc
Wenatchee
Western Wood Cree
White Mountain Apache
Wichita
Wind River
Wind River Shoshoni
Winnebago
Winturn
Wishram
Wiyot
Woccon
Yakima
Yamassee
Yana
Yani
Yanktonai Sioux
Yaquina
Yavapai
Yayuse
Yazoo
Yellowknife
Yokuts
Yuchi
Yuki
Yuki-Wappo
Yuma
Yurok
Zuni

NEW TESTAMENT FIGURES

Aeneas This man of Lydda was cured of his palsy by Peter. (Acts 9)

Agabus A prophet in Antioch who foresaw Paul's arrest by the Jews. (Acts 21)

Agrippa I (a.k.a. Herod Agrippa) King of Judaea from 37 to 44 CE.

Agrippa II The king of the Roman province of Syria from 48 to 100 CE.

Ananias Although three figures with this name appear in the New Testament, the most recognized is the Jerusalem high priest who ordered bystanders to strike Paul. (Acts 23)

Andrew A fisherman in Bethsaida who was the first of Jesus' apostles. (Matt. 10; Mark 3, 13; Luke 6; John 6, 12; Acts 1)

Anna A prophetess in Jerusalem who served God through prayer and fasting. (Luke 2)

Annas A high priest in Jerusalem who was instrumental in suppressing Jesus. (John 18, 24)

Antipas (a.k.a. Herod Antipas) The tetrarch of Galilee who was responsible for the death of John the Baptist. (Luke 3, 23)

Barabbas This murderer was released by Pilate instead of Jesus, according to custom. (Matt. 27; Mark 15; Luke 23; John 18)

Barnabas This Levite from Cyprus was a close friend of Paul. (Acts 4, 11–15; 1 Cor. 9; Gal. 2, 13; Col. 4)

Bartholomew Called Nathanael by John, Bartholomew was one of the orginal twelve apostles. (Matt. 10; Mark 3; Luke 6; Acts 1)

Bartimaeus A beggar who had his sight restored by Jesus. (Mark 10)

Caiaphas A high priest in Jerusalem from 18 to 36 CE. (Matt. 26; Luke 3; John 11, 18)

Candace Queen of Ethiopia. (Acts 8)

Claudius Lysias Chief captain of the Roman guard in Jerusalem who hustled Paul out of the city to avoid persecution. (Acts 23)

Cleopas One of the disciples joined by Jesus on the road to Emmaus after the Resurrection. (Luke 24)

Cornelius A centurion who went to Joppa to get Peter in accordance with a dream he had. (Acts 10)

Damaris A woman of Athens converted by Paul. (Acts 17)

Demetrius A silversmith of Ephesus who incited a mob against Paul. (Acts 19)

Dionysius This member of the court in Athens was converted by Paul. (Acts 17)

Epaphas A companion of Paul while in prison. (Col. 1, 4)

Epaphroditus This man from Philippi was a close friend of Paul. (Phil. 2, 4)

Felix Governor of Judaea from 52 to 60 CE who kept Paul in prison.

Gamaliel A Pharisee who advised his fellow Jews to leave the apostles alone. (Acts 5)

Herod the Great Governor of Galilee from 47 BCE and king of Judaea from 40 to 4 BCE who ordered the massacre of innocents. (Matt. 2, 14; Mark 6; Luke 1)

Jairus A synagogue elder whose daughter was brought back to life by Jesus. (Mark 5; Luke 8)

James This son of Zebedee was a fisherman and one of the twelve apostles. (Matt. 4, 10, 17; Mark 1, 3, 5, 9, 10, 13, 14; Luke 5, 8; Acts 1, 12; 1 Cor. 15)

James Son of Alphaeus and one of the twelve apostles. (Matt. 10; Mark 3; Luke 6; Acts 1)

James the Less A respected member of the Christian community in Jerusalem. (Matt. 13; Mark 6, 15, 16, 24; Acts 15, 21; Gal. 1, 2)

Jason A friend of Paul's in Thessalonica whose house was assaulted. (Acts 17)

Jesus Called the Christ, Jesus was born of Mary of Nazareth in Bethlehem. His empty grave was found by Mary Magdalene.

John the Baptist This son of Zacharias and Elizabeth was a cousin of Jesus and was killed by Herod Antipas. (Matt. 3, 4, 9, 11, 14, 21; Mark 1, 2, 6, 11; Luke 1, 3, 5, 7, 9, 20; John 1, 3, 5, 10; Acts 1, 13)

John Like James, John was a son of Zebedee, a fisherman, and one of the twelve apostles. (Matt. 4, 10, 17, 26; Mark 9–14; Luke 5, 6; John 20, 21; Acts 1)

John Author of the Fourth Gospel who lived to an old age in Ephesus.

John Author of the Book of Revelation who lived on the island of Patmos.

John Mark Accompanied Paul and Barnabas to Antioch. (Acts 4, 12, 13; Col. 4; Philem.; 2 Tim. 4)

Joseph This carpenter in Nazareth was the husband of Mary. (Matt. 1, 3; Luke 112; John 6)

Joseph of Arimathea A rich follower of Jesus who petitioned Pilate for Jesus' body after the Crucifixion. (Matt. 27; Mark 15; Luke 23; John 19)

Judas Iscariot The apostle who betrayed Jesus. (Matt. 10, 26, 27; Mark 3, 14; John 6, 12, 13, 18; Acts 1, 3, 4, 8)

Lazarus The brother of Martha and Mary lived in Bethany and was raised from the dead by Jesus. (John 11,12)

Luke A Greek Gentile, physician, and author of the Third Gospel.

Mark This evangelist and saint wrote the Second Gospel.

Martha The sister of Mary and Lazarus of Bethany. (Matt. 26; Mark 14; Luke 10; John 11, 12)

Mary The virgin mother of Jesus. (Matt. 1, 2, 27, 28; Mark 15, 16; Luke 1, 2, 24; John 19; Acts 1)

Mary of Bethany Sister of Martha and Lazarus. (Matt. 27, 28; Mark 15, 16; Luke 8; John 19, 20)

Matthew A tax collector and one of Jesus' twelve apostles. (Matt. 10; Mark 3; Luke 6; Acts 1)

Matthew This Greek-speaking Syrian Jew was not an apostle, but was an evangelist and saint who wrote the First Gospel.

Matthias Succeeded Judas as one of the twelve apostles. (Acts 1)

Nicodemus A Pharisee who went to see Jesus under the cover of darkness. (John 3, 7, 19)

Paul Originally named Saul, this missionary became a follower of Christ on the road to Damascus, and was instrumental in preaching the gospel. (Acts 2, 8)

Peter Originally known as Simon, Peter was a fisherman who eventually founded the church in Rome.

Philemon A person who had authority in the Christian community in Asia Minor. (Philem.)

Phillip One of Jesus' twelve apostles. (Matt. 10; Mark 3; Luke 6; John 6, 12, 14; Acts 1)

Pontius Pilate The Roman governor of Judaea who was forced by the local priests in Jerusalem to put Jesus to death. (Matt. 27; Mark 15; Luke 3, 23; John 18,19)

Silas One of Paul's missionary companions. (Acts 15)

Simeon A devout man in Jerusalem to whom it was revealed that the child Jesus was the Saviour. (Luke 2)

Simon the Zealot One of the twelve apostles of Jesus, from Canaan. (Matt. 10; Mark 3; Luke 6; Acts 1)

Simon of Cyrene He helped carry the cross of Jesus. (Mark 15; Luke 23)

Sosthenes Head of a synagogue in Corinth who welcomed Paul. (Acts 18; 1 Cor. 1)

Stephen The first Christian martyr, who was stoned to death. (Acts 6, 7)

Tabitha A woman of Joppa who was restored to life by Peter. (Acts 9)

Thaddeus One of the twelve apostles. In Acts he is called Judaeus. (Matt. 10; Mark 3; Acts 1)

Theophilus A friend of Luke's, to whom Luke's gospel is addressed. (Luke 1; Acts 1)

Thomas A twin who is one of Jesus' disciples. (Matt. 10; Mark 3; Luke; John 11, 14, 20, 21; Acts 1)

Timothy A companion of Paul (Acts 16–18; 1 Cor. 1; 1 Thess. 1, 3; 2 Thess. 1; Col. 1; Phil. 2; Philem. 1; 1 and 2 Tim.)

Titus A Gentile of Antioch who accompanied Paul on a missionary trip. (2 Cor. 2, 8, 12; Gal. 2; 2 Tim. 4)

Tychichus A companion of Paul on a journey to Jerusalem. (Acts 20; Col. 4; Eph. 6; 2 Tim. 4, 21; Titus 3)

Zacharias A priest, husband of Elizabeth and father of John the Baptist. (Matt. 24; Luke 1, 11)

Zacchaeus A rich publican from Jericho who had to stand in a tree to see Jesus. (Luke 19)

Zebedee The father of two apostles, James and John. (Matt. 4, 10, 20, 28; Mark 1, 3, 15, 16)

NOBEL PEACE PRIZE WINNERS

1901	Henri Dunant	Switzerland
	Frederick Passy	France
1902	Elie Ducommun	Switzerland
	Albert Gobat	Switzerland
1903	Sir William R. Cremer	United Kingdom
1904	Institut de Droit International	Belgium
1905	Bertha von Suttner	Austria
1906	Theodore Roosevelt	United States
1907	Ernesto T. Moneta	Italy
	Louis Renault	France
1908	Klas P. Arnoldson	Sweden
	Frederick Bajer	Denmark
1909	August M. F. Beernaert	Belgium
	Baron Paul H. B. B. d'Estournelles de Constant de Rebecque	France
1910	Bureau International Permanent de la Paix	Switzerland
1911	Tobias M. C. Asser	Holland
	Alfred H. Fried	Austria
1912	Elihu Root	United States
1913	Henri La Fontaine	Belgium
1914	*no award*	
1915	*no award*	
1916	*no award*	
1917	International Red Cross	
1918	*no award*	
1919	Woodrow Wilson	United States
1920	Léon Bourgeois	France
1921	Karl H. Branting	Sweden
	Christian L. Lange	Norway
1922	Fridtjof Nansen	Norway
1923	*no award*	

1924	*no award*	
1925	Sir Austen Chamberlain	United Kingdom
	Charles Dawes	United States
1926	Aristide Briand	France
	Gustav Stresemann	Germany
1927	Ferdinand Buisson	France
	Ludwig Quidde	Germany
1928	*no award*	
1929	Frank B. Kellogg	United States
1930	Lars O. J. Söderblom	Sweden
1931	Jane Addams	United States
	Nicholas M. Butler	United States
1932	*no award*	
1933	Sir Norman Angell	United Kingdom
1934	Arthur Henderson	United Kingdom
1935	Karl von Ossietzky	Germany
1936	Carlos de S. Lamas	Argentina
1937	Lord Cecil of Chelwood	United Kingdom
1938	Office International Nansen pour les Réfugiés	Switzerland
1939	*no award*	
1940	*no award*	
1941	*no award*	
1942	*no award*	
1943	*no award*	
1944	International Red Cross	
1945	Cordell Hull	United States
1946	Emily G. Balch	United States
	John Mott	United States
1947	Americans Friends Service Committee	United States
	British Society of Friends' Service Council	United Kingdom
1948	*no award*	

1949	Lord John Boyd Orr	Scotland
1950	Ralph J. Bunche	United States
1951	Léon Jouhaux	France
1952	Albert Schweitzer	French Equatorial Africa
1953	George C. Marshall	United States
1954	Office of United Nations High Commission for Refugees	
1955	*no award*	
1956	*no award*	
1957	Lester B. Pearson	Canada
1958	Reverend Dominique Georges Henry Pire	Belgium
1959	Philip John Noel-Baker	United Kingdom
1960	Albert John Luthuli	South Africa
1961	Dag Hammarskjöld	Sweden
1962	Linus Pauling	United States
1963	International Committee of the Red Cross	Geneva
	League of Red Cross Societies	Geneva
1964	Reverend Dr. Martin Luther King Jr.	United States
1965	UNICEF (United Nations Children's Fund)	
1966	*no award*	
1967	*no award*	
1968	René Cassin	France
1969	International Labour Organization	
1970	Norman E. Borlaug	United States
1971	Willy Brandt	West Germany
1972	*no award*	
1973	Henry Kissinger	United States
	Le Duc Tho	North Vietnam
1974	Eisaku Sato	Japan
	Sean McBride	Ireland

1975	Andrei D. Sakharov	U.S.S.R.
1976	Mairead Corrigan	Northern Ireland
	Betty Williams	Northern Ireland
1977	Amnesty International	
1978	Menachem Begin	Israel
	Anwar el-Sadat	Egypt
1979	Mother Teresa of Calcutta	India
1980	Adolfo Perez Esquivel	Argentina
1981	Office of the United Nations Commissioner for Refugees	
1982	Alva Myrdal	Sweden
	Alfonso García Robles	Mexico
1983	Lech Walesa	Poland
1984	Bishop Desmond Tutu	South Africa
1985	International Physicians for the Prevention of Nuclear War	
1986	Elie Wiesel	United States
1987	Oscar Arias Sánchez	Costa Rica
1988	United Nations Peacekeeping Forces	
1989	Dalai Lama	Tibet
1990	Mikhail S. Gorbachev	U.S.S.R.
1991	Daw Aung San Suu Kyi	Burma
1992	Rigoberto Menchu	Guatemala
1993	F. W. de Klerk	South Africa
	Nelson Mandela	South Africa
1994	Yasir Arafat	Palestine
	Yitzhak Rabin	Israel
1995	Joseph Roblat and Pugwash Conference on Science and World Affairs	United Kingdom
1996	Carlos Felipe Ximenes Belo	East Timor
	José Ramos-Horta	East Timor
1997	International Campaign to Ban Landmines	
	Jody Williams	U.S.A.
1998	David Trimble	Northern Ireland
	John Hume	Northern Ireland

1999	Médecins sans Frontières	France
2000	Kim Dae Jung	South Korea
	(awarded in October)	

OLD TESTAMENT FIGURES

Adam The first man created by God. (Gen. 1–5)

Eve The first woman created by God. (Gen. 2, 3)

Cain The farmer son of Adam and Eve. (Gen. 4)

Abel The second son of Adam, murdered by Cain. (Gen. 4)

Noah This righteous man built the ark and was saved from the flood along with his family. (Gen. 6–9)

Abraham The name means "father of multitude." Abraham was a faithful man in God's eyes. (Gen. 11:26–25:11)

Isaac Son of Abraham. (Gen. 21–28)

Jacob The younger son of Isaac and Rebekah; inherited the covenant given to Abraham. (Gen. 25–49)

Joseph Son of Jacob. He was sold into slavery, but went on to become a second son to Pharaoh in Egypt. (Gen. 37–50)

Moses Delivered God's people from Egypt. (Exod.; Lev.; Num.; Deut.)

Joshua Renamed "God, saved" by Moses, from whom he took command of the Israelites. (Josh.)

Samson Known for his great strength, he was betrayed by Delilah. (Judg. 13–16)

Delilah She cut Samson's hair to render him powerless. (Judg. 13–16)

Ruth A Moabite woman who became an Israelite through marriage and was blessed by God. (Ruth)

Samuel He appointed Saul king, and also anointed David as Saul's successor. (1, 2 Sam.)

Saul The first, flawed king of Israel. (1 Sam. 9–31)

David The greatest king of Israel. (1, 2 Sam.; 1 Chron.)

Solomon The son and successor of David. (1 Kings 1–11; 2 Chron. 1–9)

Elijah Kept King Ahab from establishing Baal worship as Israel's religion. (1 Kings 17–19; 2 Kings 1, 2)

Elisha The successor of Elijah, and leading prophet of Israel. (2 Kings 1–9, 13)

Judith A pious woman who saved Israel by killing an opposing general. (Jth.)

Esther A Jewish heroine who was able to stop a massacre of her people. (Esther)

Job A man faithful to God despite the direst circumstances. (Job)

Daniel An exiled Jew in Babylon who resisted temptation and stayed faithful to God. (Dan.)

Aaron Moses' older brother and companion during the Exodus. (Exod. 4–40; Lev., Num., Deut. 9, 10)

Abigail The wife of Nabal, then married to David. (1 Sam. 25, 27, 30; 2 Sam. 2, 3)

Abner Commander of Saul's army. (1, 2 Sam.)

Absalom Son of David who threatened his father's house. (2 Sam. 13–20)

Achan He betrayed God's command and took treasure from Jericho. (Josh. 7, 8)

Ahab One of Israel's most wicked kings. (1 Kings 16–22; 2 Chron. 18)

Alexander the Great The king of Macedon who conquered the Persian empire. (Dan.)

Amaziah The eighth king of Judah, who was assassinated. (2 Kings 14; 2 Chron. 25)

Bathsheba She married David and had four sons. (2 Sam. 11, 12; Kings 1, 2)

Caleb One of two spies who urged Israel to attack Canaan. (Num. 14; Josh. 14, 15; Judg. 1:12–20)

Darius The name of three Persian rulers in the Old Testament.

Enoch Son of Cain. (Gen.)

Gideon The fifth judge of Israel. (Judg. 6–8)

Hagar A servant given to Abraham to bear him children. (Gen. 16:1–16; 21:8–21)

Ham The second son of Noah. (Gen.)

Hannah The mother of Samuel, Israel's last judge. (1 Sam. 1:1–2:11)

Hosea The name means "he has saved." Hosea was the son of Beeri from the Northern Kingdom. (Hos.)

Ismael Son born to Abraham and Hagar. (Gen. 16, 17, 21, 25; 1 Chron. 1)

Japeth Noah's son, ancestor of the Philistines.

Jehoshaphat Fourth king of Judah. (2 Chron. 17:6)

Jeroboam A rebel who founded the Northern Kingdom of Israel. (1 Kings 11–14)

Jeremiah Seventh-century BCE prophet.

Jehu A king of Israel in the 9th century BCE. (2 Kings 9:20)

Jesse King David's father and progenitor of the line of Jesus. (Isa.)

Jeroboam II A politically and militarily successful 13th-century king of Israel. (2 Kings 14:23–29)

Jezebel An opponent of Elijah and murderer of many prophets. (1 Kings 16–22; 2 Kings 9, 10)

Joel He penned the prophetic book that describes plagues. (Joel)

Jonathan Son and heir of King Saul. (1 Sam. 14, 18–20)

Josiah The pious 17th king of Judah. (Kings 21–24; 2 Chron. 33–35)

Judah Jacob's fourth son by his first wife, Leah. (Gen.)

Korah A Levite who led a rebellion against Moses. (Num. 16)

Laban The deceitful uncle and father-in-law of Jacob. (Gen. 29–31)

Lamech A descendant of Cain. (Gen. 4:18–26)

Levi The third son of Jacob and Leah, father of one of the tribes of Israel. (Gen. 34:25–29)

Lot Abraham's nephew who settled in Sodom. (Gen. 11–14, 19)

Melchizedek A king and priest of Jerusalem who blessed Abraham. (Gen. 1, 4:18–20)

Methuselah A patriarch who lived 969 years. (Gen.)

Micaiah A prophet who predicted the death of King Ahab. (1 Kings 22; 2 Chron. 18)

Mephibosheth The crippled grandson of Saul. (2 Sam 4:4)

Michal The younger daughter of Saul who married David. (1 Sam. 18, 19; 2 Sam. 3, 6)

Miriam The prophetess sister of Moses and Aaron. (Exod. 2, 15; Num. 12)

Mordecai The Jewish vizier of the Persian empire. (Esther)

Naaman A leper who commanded Syria's army. (2 Kings 5)

Naomi Ruth's mother-in-law. (Ruth)

Nathan A prophet at David's court. (2 Sam. 7, 12; 1 Kings 1)

Bed The son born of the union between Ruth and Boaz. (Ruth)

Nebuchadnezzar II The ruler of Babylon who exiled the Jews from their land. (Dan.)

Nehemiah He rebuilt Jerusalem in the 5th century BCE and became its governor. (Neh.)

Obadiah Ahab's majordomo. (Obad.)

Og The king of Bashan, defeated by Moses. (Num. 21; Deut. 1, 3, 4, 29, 31)

Phineas II Son of Eli and priest of the sanctuary at Shiloh. (1 Sam.)

Pothipar The rich Egyptian whose wife tried to seduce Joseph. (Gen.)

Queen of Sheba The queen of the Arabian Peninsula who visited Solomon. (2 Chron.)

Rachel The favourite wife of Jacob. (Gen. 29–35)

Rahab The prostitute in Jericho who helped two Israelite spies escape. (Josh. 2, 6)

Rebekah Isaac's wife who plotted with her son Jacob to get his father's special blessing. (Gen. 24–28)

Rehoboam The son of Solomon who divided his father's kingdom. (1 Kings 12, 14, 15; 2 Chron. 10–12)

Sarah The wife of Abraham who gave birth to Isaac. (Gen. 12, 22)

Seth The son of Adam and Eve after Cain and Abel. (Gen.)

Sihon An amorite king defeated by Moses. (Num. 21, 32; Deut. 1; Josh. 2, 9)

Sheba The leader of a revolt against David. (2 Sam.)

Shen Noah's son and ancestor of the Semites. (1 Sam. 7)

Shechen Hamor's son who raped Jacob's daughter. (Gen. 33; Josh. 24; Judg. 9)

Simeon The son of Jacob and Leah and ancestor of one of the twelve tribes. (Josh. 19; Judg. 1)

Sisera The leader of the Canaanite troops, killed by Gaiele. (Judg. 4; 1 Sam. 12)

Susanna The wife of Jehoiachim who was accused of adultery. (Dan.)

Tamor David's daughter who was raped by her half-brother Amnon. (2 Sam.)

Uriah Bathsheba's husband who was sent into combat by King David. (2 Sam.)

Vashti Ahasuerus' first wife who was eventually replaced by Esther. (Esther 1, 2, 4)

Xerxes Greek name for Ahasuerus, Persian emperor and husband of Esther. (Esther)

Zabulon The son of Jacob and Leah and ancestor of one of the twelve tribes. (Gen.)

Zepporah Jethro's daughter and Moses' wife. (Exod.)

Zephaniah This man, whose name means "God has preserved," predicted divine judgment for the land of Israel. (Zeph.)

Zillpah A descendant of Cain who was married to Lamech I. (Gen. 4)

Zophar A friend and confidant of Job. (Job)

ORGANIZED CRIME FAMILIES

Bonanno Begun by Joe Bonanno in the early 1930s, this New York crime family was also headed by Natale Evola and Phil Rastelli.

Chicago This syndicate was run by the famous Al Capone until he went to jail. The reins of leadership then went to Paul Ricca, who ran it until 1972.

Cleveland This crime family was run by James "Blackie" Licavoli, who controlled the teamsters in that city as well as penetrating the local FBI.

Columbo Columbo took over and renamed the Profaci crime family syndicate after the so-called Banana War between 1964 and 1969.

Gambino The richest and most lucrative of New York crime families was taken over by Carlo Gambino in the late 1950s. Paul Castellano and John Gotti were notable members.

Genovese Located in New York, this crime family was run by Vito Genovese, who watched it weaken from his jail cell until it was taken over and run by such bosses as Frank Tieri and Vinnie "the Chin" Gigante.

Los Angeles The "Mickey Mouse" crime family was so named because of the second-rate reputation it developed in both law enforcement and Mafia circles.

Luchese Tommy Luchese took over this gang, which was originally the outfit of Joe Masseria in 1953. He dominated the New York garment industry with it.

Luciano This family was run by Lucky Luciano in New York until Vito Genovese won control of it in 1957, shortly before he went to jail.

Mangano Vincent Mangano ran this family, which specialized in the New York waterfront rackets, until he was murdered. It then became the Anastasia family in 1951.

New Orleans This family was run by the iron-fisted Carlos Marcello, who took it as a slight if other crime family members visited New Orleans without his say-so.

Morello A true family consisting of brothers and half brothers from Corleone, Italy, that operated in New York in the late 19th century.

O'Banion More a gang than a Mafia family, this operation was run by the charming psychopath Dion O'Banion until Capone forces killed him in 1924.

Pillow Gang This St. Louis family was so named because its leader, Carmelo Fresina, had been shot in the backside and needed a pillow to sit.

Pittsburgh This family, begun by John Larocca, was never considered to be in the major leagues within the Mafia. Michael Genovese took over operations in 1984.

Profaci This was one of the famous five Mafia families in New York until Joseph Profaci died in 1962. It then became the Columbo crime family.

Purple Gang This nearly all-Jewish mob, known for its viciousness, specialized in booze distribution during Prohibition in Detroit. The name was revived in the 1970s by what is now considered the sixth New York crime family.

Reina The Reina family operated in New York in the early 20th century until Tom Reina's death, when it was divided up between competing mobsters.

Scarfo This Philadelphia organization is named after "Little Nicky" Scarfo, who wrested control of the city's operations in the mid-1980s.

Tampa This Florida family was run by Santo Trafficante until his death in 1954, when the family was taken over by his son, Santo Jr.

Zerrilli This Detroit crime family was run by Joseph Zerilli after the Purple Gang disbanded.

PIRATES

Aragona, Ferdinando A corsair from Naples who plundered the Mediterranean at the beginning of the 17th century.

Barbarossa, Ariz a.k.a. Red Beard. This Barbary corsair plundered the western Mediterreanean until he was killed by the Spanish.

Barker, Andrew This Englishman pirated the Caribbean before the Spanish ended his career and his life.

Baughe, William An English pirate known for his ruthlessness.

Bellamy, Samuel Bellamy, an Englishman, is famous for having seized the iron- and gold-laden *Whydah* in 1717. He was killed the same year.

Bishop, Richard This Englishman plundered the Mediterranean in the early 17th century. He was also elected "admiral" by a confederation of Atlantic pirates.

Bodulgate, Thomas Bodulgate was under commission by the English to stop pirates when he did most of his own piracy. He died in 1471.

Boggs, Eli This effeminate American once quartered a man to speed up negotiations in the South China Sea, where he did most of his pirating until he was imprisoned in 1857.

Bonnet, Steve Although rumoured, there is no proof that this dandy was the creator of walking the plank.

Bonnet, Stede This British pirate prowled the Caribbean and the Atlantic Ocean until he was hanged in Charleston in 1718.

Bonny, Anne This American girl took up with Jack Rackham and together they plundered the Caribbean. She was saved from execution in 1702 because she was pregnant.

Bontemps, Jean Bontemps was a Frenchman who plundered the West Indies until he was killed by the Spanish in 1570.

Browne, James A Scot, Browne pirated the Caribbean until he was hanged by the Jamaican governor in 1677.

Callice, John Callice plundered the Welsh and Irish coasts before sailing to the Mediterranean, where he was killed in 1587.

Kidd, William a.k.a. Captain Kidd. A fairly inconsequential pirate whose exploits were exaggerated by the writer Daniel Defoe. Kidd was hanged in 1701.

Cheng 1 This Chinese pirate was born into a pirate family that operated in the South China Sea. He led a large confederation of pirates until his death in 1807.

Chevalier de Grammant An impoverished nobleman who sought to repair his fortune by piracy in the 1680s.

Clifford, George The third earl of Cumberland, Clifford financed a number of pirate missions but wound up losing more than he ever stole.

Easton, Peter This Englishman acted as "admiral" of a confederation of pirates who plundered the West African coast until he surrendered to an Italian courtier in the early 17th century.

England, Edward England plundered ships in the Caribbean until the British silenced him in 1718.

Every, Henry a.k.a. John Avery or Long Ben Avery. This Englishman plundered ships in the Red and other eastern seas around 1895.

Francois, Pierre Francois, a Frenchman, captured a boat full of pearls but was caught and sent to trial in Spain around 1665.

Gibbs, Charles This American, who was active in the Caribbean, was said to have cut off a captain's arms and legs. He was hanged in 1831.

Grillo, Diego a.k.a. El Mulato. This pirate of African and Spanish descent preyed on Spanish ships until he was captured and killed in 1673.

Hawkins, Sir John Hawkins was an Englishman who trafficked in pirated or captured slaves in the Caribbean.

Herriot, David Herriot joined up with pirate Edward Teach. Together they prowled the Caribbean until he died in 1718.

Howell, Davis Davis occasionally posed as a merchant or pirate hunter to lure his prey closer. He was eventually killed by the Portuguese in 1720.

Lewis, William This Englishman was hanged after he raided New Providence Island in the Bahamas in 1718.

L'Olonnais, François Hatred of the Spanish is what this vicious Frenchman was known for until his death in Central America in 1668.

Low, Edward The cruel Low was probably marooned by fellow pirates in 1724 after his pirating career in the Caribbean and off the American coast.

Mesmyn, Guillame Mesmyn was a French pirate whose career in the Caribbean spanned from 1556 to 1569.

North, Nathaniel This Englishman preyed on Indian ships in the Red Sea and Indian Ocean until he was killed by tribesmen in Madagascar in 1707.

Portugues, Bartholomew This Portuguese pirate is famous for having attacked a Spanish ship off Cuba in the mid-1600s.

Rackham, John a.k.a. Calico Jack. Named for his flamboyant clothing, Rackham is best remembered for his romance with lady pirate Anne Bonny, until he was captured in 1720.

Read, Mary Along with Jack Rackham and Anne Bonny, Read pirated the Caribbean. She eluded a death sentence by pleading pregnancy.

Roberts, Bartholomew a.k.a. Black Bart. One of the greatest of pirates, Roberts plundered the Caribbean and African coasts till caught by the British in 1722.

Sao, Cheng 1 This Chinese wife of Cheng 1 took over her husband's pirate fleet upon his death in the South China Sea.

Shalay, Sherip Shalay was a Malay pirate who prowled the South China Sea in the 1840s.

Smith, James This captain of the *Cygnet* plundered the South China Sea. His career lasted from 1683 to 1689.

Teach, Edward a.k.a. Blackbeard. Teach actually had only a short pirating career (15 months). His reputation was exaggerated by the writer Daniel Defoe.

Tucker, Thomas Tucker was an English pirate who was active in the Atlantic and the Mediterranean from 1611 to 1615.

Valentine, William Valentine ended up being killed by fellow Englishmen after being tortured in London in 1583.

Vane, Charles Vane terrorized the eastern coast of America as well as Bermuda and the Bahamas in the early 1700s.

Wake, Thomas Wake was an Englishman who teamed up with Henry Every to pirate the Red Sea until his death of disease in 1696.

Walden, John This Englishman prowled the Atlantic and Caribbean. He was accused of burning alive over 80 African slaves, whereupon he was tried and hanged in 1723.

Wall, George This American was active in the Atlantic in the 1780s. He lured ships to his own by having his wife alone topside, as though she were the sole survivor of a storm.

Ward, John Ward was an Englishman who preyed upon ships in the Caribbean and Mediterranean in the early 17th century.

Williams, Paul Active from 1716 to 1717, this Englishman pirated the Atlantic and the Caribbean.

Worley, Captain Americans sent four ships to capture the British Worley after he plundered a ship on the Delaware River. He was hanged in South Carolina.

Yallahs, Captain This Dutchman was active in the Caribbean in the late 17th century.

Yeats, Captain Yeats was an Englishman who pirated the Caribbean and Atlantic around 1718.

POPES

Pope	Reign	Given name
St. Peter the Apostle	died c. 64	
St. Linus	c. 66–c. 78	
St. Anacletus (Cletus)	c. 79–c. 91	
St. Clement I	c. 91–c. 100	
St. Evaristus	c. 100–c. 109	
St. Alexander I	c. 109–c. 16	
St. Sixtus I	c. 116–c. 125	
St. Telesphorus	c. 125–c. 136	
St. Hyginus	c. 136–c. 142	
St. Pius	c. 142–c. 155	
St. Anicetus	c. 155–c. 166	
St. Soter	c. 166–c. 174	
St. Eleutherius	c. 174–89	
St. Victor I	189–98	
St. Zephyrinus	198–17	
St. Callistus (Calixtus) I	217–22	
St. Urban I	222–30	
St. Pontianus (Pontian)	230–35	
St. Anterus	235–36	
St. Fabian	236–50	
St. Cornelius	251–53	
St. Lucius I	253–54	
St. Stephen I	254–57	
St. Sixtus II	257–58	
St. Dionysius	260–68	
St. Felix I	269–74	
St. Eutychian	275–83	
St. Gaius (Caius)	283–96	
St. Marcellinus	296–304	
St. Marcellus I	306–08	
St. Eusebius	310 April–Oct.	
St. Militiades (Melchiades)	311–14	
St. Silvester I	314–35	
St. Mark	336 Jan.–Oct.	
St. Julius I	337–52	
Liberius	352–66	
St. Damasus I	366–84	
St. Siricius	384–99	
St. Anastasius I	399–401	
St. Innocent I	401–17	
St. Zosimus	417–18	
St. Boniface I	418–22	
St. Celestine I	422–32	

Pope	Reign	Given name
St. Sixtus III	432–40	
St. Leo I	440–61	
St. Hilary (Hilarus)	461–68	
St. Simplicius	468–83	
St. Felix III (II)	483–92	
St. Gelasius I	492–96	
Anastasius II	496–98	
St. Symmachus	498–514	
St. Hormisdas	514–23	
St. John I	523–26	
St. Felix IV (III)	526–30	
Boniface II	530–32	
John II	533–35	
St. Agapitus I	535–36	
St. Silverius	536–37	
Vigilius	537–55	
Pelagius I	556–61	
John III	561–74	
Benedict I	575–79	
Pelagius II	579–90	
St. Gregory I	590–604	
Sabinian	604–06	
Boniface III	607 Feb.–Nov.	
St. Boniface IV	608–15	
St. Deusdedit I	615–18	
Boniface V	619–25	
Honorius I	625–38	
Severinus	640 May–Aug.	
John IV	640–42	
Theodore I	642–49	
St. Martin I	649–53	
St. Eugene I	654–57	
St. Vitalian	657–72	
Deusdedit III	672–76	
Donus	676–78	
St. Agatho	678–81	
St. Leo II	682–83	
St. Benedict II	684–85	
John V	685–86	
Conon	686–87	
St. Sergius I	687–701	
John VI	701–05	
John VII	705–07	
Sissinius	708 Jan.–Feb.	
Constantine	708–15	
St. Gregory II	715–31	
St. Gregory III	731–41	

Pope	Reign	Given name
St. Zachary	741–52	
Stephen	752 March	
Stephen II (III)	752–57	
St. Paul I	757–67	
Stephen III (IV)	768–72	
Adrian I (Hadrian I)	772–95	
St. Leo III	795–816	
Stephen IV (V)	816–17	
St. Paschal I	817–24	
Eugene II	824–27	
Valentine	827 Aug.–Sept.	
Gregory IV	827–44	
Sergius II	844–47	
St. Leo IV	847–55	
Benedict III	855–58	
St. Nicholas I	858–67	
Adrian II (Hadrian II)	867–72	
John VIII	872–82	
Marinus I	882–84	
St. Adrian III (St. Hadrian III)	884–85	
Stephen V (VI)	885–91	
Formosus	891–96	
Boniface VI	896 April	
Stephen VI (VII)	896–97	
Romanus	897 Aug.–Nov.	
Theodore II	897 Nov.–Dec.	
John IX	898–900	
Benedict IV	900–903	
Leo V	903 Aug.–Sept.	
Sergius III	904–11	
Anastasius III	911–13	
Lando	913–14	
John X	914–28	
Leo VI	928 May–Dec.	
Stephen VII (VIII)	928–31	
John XI	931–35	
Leo VII	936–39	
Stephen VIII (IX)	939–42	
Marinus II	942–46	
Agapetus II	946–55	
John XII	955–63	Octavian
Leo VIII	963–64	
Benedict V	964 May–June	
John XIII	965–72	
Benedict VI	973–74	
Benedict VII	974–83	
John XIV	983–84	Peter Canepanova

Pope	Reign	Given name
John XV	985–96	
Gregory V	996–99	Bruno
Silvester II	999–1003	Gerbert
John XVII	1003 May–Nov.	John Sicco
John XVIII	1003–9	John Fasanus
Sergius IV	1009–12	Peter
Benedict VIII	1012–24	Theophylact
John XIX	1024–32	Romanus
Benedict IX	1032–45	Theophylact
Silvester III	1045 Jan.–March	John of Sabina
Benedict IX	1045 April–May	
Gregory VI	1045–46	John Gratian
Clement II	1046–47	Suidger
Benedict X	1047–48	
Damasus II	1048 July–Aug.	Poppo
St. Leo IX	1049–54	Bruno
Victor II	1055–57	Gebhart
Stephen IX (X)	1057–58	Frederick of Lorraine
Nicholas II	1058–61	Gerard
Alexander II	1061–73	Anselm
St. Gregory VII	1073–85	Hildebrand
Victor III	1086–87	Daufer
Urban II	1088–99	Odo
Paschal II	1099–1118	Rainerius
Gelasius II	1118–19	John of Gaeta
Calistus II	1119–24	Guido
Honorius	1124–30	Lamberto of Ostia
Innocent II	1130–43	Gregorio Papareschi
Celestine II	1143–44	Guido of Citta de Castello
Lucius II	1144–45	Gherardo Caccianemici
Eugene III	1145–53	Bernardo Pignatelli
Anastasius IV	1153–54	Corrado
Adrian IV (Hadrian IV)	1154–59	Nicholas Breakspear
Alexander III	1159–81	Orlando Bandinelli
Lucius III	1181–85	Ubaldo Allucingoli
Urban III	1185–87	Umberto Crivelli
Gregor VII	1187 Oct.–Dec.	Alberto de Morra
Clement III	1187–91	Paulo Scolari
Celestine III	1191–98	Giacinto Bobo
Innocent III	1198–1216	Lotario
Honorius III	1216–27	Cencio Savelli
Gregory IX	1227–41	Ugo (Ugolino)
Celestine IV	1241 Oct.–Nov.	Golffredo da Castiglione
Innocent IV	1243–54	Sinibaldo Fieschi
Alexander IV	1254–61	Rinaldo, Count of Segni
Urban IV	1261–64	Jacques Pantaléon
Clement IV	1265–68	Guy Foulques

Pope	Reign	Given name
Gregory X	1271–76	Tedaldo Visconti
Innocent V	1276 Jan.–June	Pierre of Tarentaise
Adrian V (Hadrian V)	1276 July–Aug.	Ottobono Fieschi
John XXI	1276–77	Pedro Julião (Peter of Spain)
Nicholas III	1277–80	Giovanni Gaetano
Martin IV	1281–85	Simon de Brie (Brion)
Honorius IV	1285–87	Giacomo Savelli
Nicolas IV	1288–92	Girolamo Masci
St. Celestine V	1294 July–Dec.	Pietro del Morrone
Boniface VIII	1294–1303	Benedetto Caetani
Benedict XI	1303–04	Niccolo Boccasino
Clement V	1305–14	Bertrand de Got
John XXII	1316–34	Jacques Duese
Benedict XII	1334–42	Jacques Fournier
Clement VI	1342–52	Pierre of Rosier d'Egleton
Innocent VI	1352–62	Étienne Aubert
Urban V	1362–70	Guillaume de Grimoard
Gregory XI	1370–78	Pierre Roger de Beaufort
Urban VI	1378–89	Bartolomeo Prignano
Boniface IX	1389–1404	Pietro Tomacelli
Innocent VII	1404–6	Cosimo Gentile
Gregory XII	1406–15	Angelo Correr
Martin V	1417–31	Oddo Colonna
Eugene IV	1431–47	Gabriele Condulmaro
Nicholas V	1447–55	Tommaso Parentucelli
Callistus III	1455–58	Alfonso de Borja (Borgia)
Pius II	1458–64	Enea Silvo
Piccolomini (Paul II)	1464–71	Pietro Barbo
Sixtus IV	1471–84	Francesco della Rovere
Innocent VIII	1484–92	Giovanni Battista Cibo
Alexander VI	1492–1503	Rodrigo de Borya y Borya (Borgia)
Pius III	1503 Sept.–Oct.	Francesco Todeschini
Julius II	1503–13	Giuliano dell Rovere
Leo X	1513–21	Giovanni de Medici
Adrian VI (Hadrian VI)	1522–23	Adrian Florensz Dedal
Clement VII	1523–34	Giulio de Medici
Paul III	1534–49	Alessandro Farnese
Julius III	1550–55	Giovanni Maria Ciocchi del Monte
Marcellus II	1555 April–May	Marcello Cervini
Paul IV	1555–59	Giampietro Carafa
Pius IV	1559–65	Giovanni AngeloMedici
St. Pius V	1566–72	Michele Ghislieri
Gregory XIII	1572–85	Ugo Boncompagni
Sixtus V	1585–90	Felice Peretti
Urban VII	1590 Sept.	Giambattista Castagna
Gregory XIV	1590–91	Niccolo Sfondrati
Innocent IX	1591 Oct.–Dec.	Giovanni Antonio Fachinetti

Pope	Reign	Given name
Clement VIII	1592–1605	Ippolito Aldobrandini
Leo XI	1605 April	Alessandro Ottaviano de Medici
Paul V	1605–21	Camillo Borghese
Gregory XV	1621–23	Alessandro Ludovisi
Urban VIII	1623–44	Mafeo Barberini
Innocent X	1644–55	Giambattista Pamfili
Alexander VII	1655–67	Fabio Chigi
Clement IX	1667–69	Giulio Rospigliosi
Clement X	1670–76	Emilio Altieri
Innocent XI	1676–89	Benedetto Odescalchi
Alexander VIII	1689–91	Pietro Ottoboni
Innocent XII	1691–1700	Antonio Pignatelli
Clement XI	1700–1721	Giovanni Francesco Albani
Innocent XIII	1721–24	Michelangelo dei Conti
Benedict XIII	1724–30	Pietro Francesco Orsini
Clement XII	1730–40	Lorenzo Corsini
Benedict XIV	1740–58	Prospero Lorrenzo
Clement XIII	1758–69	Carlo dela Torre Rezzonico
Clement XIV	1769–74	Lorenzo Ganganelli
Pius VI	1775–99	Giovanni Angelo Brachi
Pius VII	1800–1823	Luigi Barnaba Chiaramonte
Leo XII	1823–29	Annibale Sermattei della Genga
Pius VIII	1829–30	Francesco Saverio Castiglione
Gregory XVI	1831–46	Bartolomeo Albert Cappellari
Pius IX	1846–78	Giovanni Maria Mastai-Ferretti
Leo XIII	1878–1903	Gioacchino Vincenzo Pecci
St. Pius X	1903–14	Giuseppe Melchiorre Sarto
Benedict XV	1914–22	Giacomo dela Chiesa
Pius XI	1922–39	Ambrogio Damiano Achille Ratti
Pius XII	1939–58	Eugenio Maria Giuseppe Giovanni Pacelli
John XXIII	1958–63	Angelo Giuseppe Roncalli
Paul VI	1963–78	Giovanni Battista Montini
John Paul I	1978 Aug.–Sept.	Albino Luciani
John Paul II	1978–present	Karol Wojtyla

PRESIDENTS, VICE PRESIDENTS, & PRESIDENTIAL CANDIDATES

Presidents of the United States/ Vice Presidents of the United States	Years in office
George Washington John Adams	1789–97
John Adams Thomas Jefferson	1797–1801
Thomas Jefferson Aaron Burr (1801–05) George Clinton (1805–09)	1801–09
James Madison George Clinton (1809–12) *No vice president April 1812–13* Elbridge Gerry (1813–14) *No vice president Nov. 1814–17*	1809–17
James Monroe Daniel D. Tompkins	1817–25
John Quincy Adams John C. Calhoun	1825–29
Andrew Jackson John C. Calhoun (1829–32) *No vice president Dec. 1832–33* Martin Van Buren (1833–37)	1829–37
Martin Van Buren Richard M. Johnson	1837–41
William Henry Harrison John Tyler	1841
John Tyler *No vice president*	1841–45
James Knox Polk George M. Dallas	1845–49

Presidents of the United States/ Vice Presidents of the United States	Years in office
Zachary Taylor Millard Fillmore	1849–50
Millard Fillmore *No vice president*	1850–53
Franklin Pierce William R. King (1853) *No vice president April 1853–57*	1853–57
James Buchanan John C. Breckinridge	1857–61
Abraham Lincoln Hannibal Hamlin (1861–65) Andrew Johnson (1865)	1861–65
Andrew Johnson *No vice president*	1865–69
Ulysses Simpson Grant Schuyler Colfax (1869–73) Henry Wilson (1873–75) *No vice president Nov. 1875–77*	1869–77
Rutherford B. Hayes William A. Wheeler	1877–81
James A. Garfield Chester Alan Arthur	1881
Chester Alan Arthur *No vice president*	1881–85
Grover Cleveland Thomas A. Hendricks (1885) *No vice president Nov. 1885–89*	1885–89
Benjamin Harrison Levi P. Morton	1889–93
Grover Cleveland Adlai E. Stevenson	1893–97
William McKinley Garret A. Hobart (1897–99) *No vice president Nov. 1899–01* Theodore Roosevelt (1901)	1897–1901
Theodore Roosevelt *No vice president Sept. 1901–05* Charles W. Fairbanks (1905–09)	1901–09

Presidents of the United States/ Vice Presidents of the United States	Years in office
William Howard Taft James S. Sherman (1909–1912) *No vice president Oct. 1912–13*	1909–13
Woodrow Wilson Thomas R. Marshall	1913–21
Warren Gamaliel Harding Calvin Coolidge	1921–23
Calvin Coolidge *No vice president 1923–25* Charles G. Dawes (1925–29)	1923–29
Herbert Hoover Charles Curtis	1929–33
Franklin D. Roosevelt John Nance Garner (1933–41) Henry A. Wallace (1941–45) Harry S. Truman (1945)	1933–45
Harry S. Truman *No vice president 1945–49* Alben W. Barkley (1949–53)	1945–53
Dwight D. Eisenhower Richard M. Nixon	1953–61
John F. Kennedy Lyndon B. Johnson	1961–63
Lyndon B. Johnson *No vice president Nov. 1963–65* Hubert H. Humphrey (1965–1969)	1963–69
Richard M. Nixon Spiro T. Agnew (1969–73) Gerald R. Ford (1973–74)	1969–74
Gerald R. Ford Nelson A. Rockefeller	1974–77
Jimmy Carter Walter F. Mondale	1977–81
Ronald Reagan George Bush	1981–89
George Bush Dan Quayle	1989–93
William J. Clinton Albert A. Gore	1993–2000
George W. Bush Richard B. Cheney	2000–present

U.S. PRESIDENTIAL ELECTION OPPONENTS

Year	Elected	Major opponents
1789	George Washington	*Unopposed*
1792	George Washington	*Unopposed*
1796	John Adams	Thomas Jefferson
1800	Thomas Jefferson	John Adams, Aaron Burr, Charles C. Pinckney
1804	Thomas Jefferson	Charles C. Pinckney
1808	James Madison	Charles C. Pinckney
1812	James Madison	DeWitt Clinton
1816	James Monroe	Rufus King
1820	James Monroe	John Quincy Adams
1824	John Quincy Adams	Andrew Jackson, William H. Crawford, Henry Clay
1828	Andrew Jackson	John Quincy Adams
1832	Andrew Jackson	Henry Clay
1836	Martin Van Buren	William H. Harrison
1840	William H. Harrison	Martin Van Buren
1844	James K. Polk	Henry Clay
1848	Zachary Taylor	Lewis Cass
1852	Franklin Pierce	Winfield Scott
1856	James Buchanan	John C. Fremont, Millard Fillmore
1860	Abraham Lincoln	Stephen A. Douglas, John C. Breckinridge, John Bell
1864	Abraham Lincoln	George B. McClellan
1868	Ulysses S. Grant	Horatio Seymour

1872	Ulysses S. Grant	Horace Greeley
1876	Rutherford B. Hayes	Samuel J. Tilden
1880	James A. Garfield	Winfield S. Hancock
1884	Grover Cleveland	James G. Blaine
1888	Benjamin Harrison	Grover Cleveland
1892	Grover Cleveland	Benjamin Harrison, James Weaver
1896	William McKinley	William Jennings Bryan
1900	William McKinley	William Jennings Bryan
1904	Theodore Roosevelt	Alton B. Parker
1908	William Howard Taft	William Jennings Bryan
1912	Woodrow Wilson	William Howard Taft, Theodore Roosevelt
1916	Woodrow Wilson	Charles E. Hughes
1920	Warren Gamaliel Harding	James M. Cox
1924	Calvin Coolidge	John W. Davis, Robert M. La Follette
1928	Herbert Hoover	Alfred E. Smith
1932	Franklin D. Roosevelt	Herbert Hoover
1936	Franklin D. Roosevelt	Alfred M. Landon
1940	Franklin D. Roosevelt	Wendell L. Willkie
1944	Franklin D. Roosevelt	Thomas E. Dewey
1948	Harry S. Truman	Thomas E. Dewey
1952	Dwight D. Eisenhower	Adlai Stevenson
1956	Dwight D. Eisenhower	Adlai Stevenson
1960	John F. Kennedy	Richard M. Nixon
1964	Lyndon B. Johnson	Barry M. Goldwater
1968	Richard M. Nixon	Hubert H. Humphrey, George Wallace
1972	Richard M. Nixon	George S. McGovern
1976	Jimmy Carter	Gerald R. Ford
1980	Ronald Reagan	Jimmy Carter, John B. Anderson
1984	Ronald Reagan	Walter F. Mondale
1988	George Bush	Michael S. Dukakis
1992	William J. Clinton	George Bush, Ross Perot
1996	William J. Clinton	Robert Dole
2000	George W. Bush	Albert A. Gore

BRITISH PRIME MINISTERS, 1721–2001

Robert Walpole (Whig)	1721–1742
Earl of Wilmington (Whig)	1742–1743
Henry Pelham (Whig)	1743–1754
Duke of Newcastle (Whig)	1754–1756
Duke of Devonshire (Whig)	1756–1757
Duke of Newcastle (Whig)	1757–1762
Earl of Bute (Tory)	1762–1763
George Grenville (Whig)	1763–1765
Marquess of Rockingham (Whig)	1765–1766
Duke of Grafton (Whig)	1766–1770
Lord North (Tory)	1770–1782
Marquess of Rockingham (Whig)	1782
Earl of Shelburne (Whig)	1782–1783
Duke of Portland (Coalition)	1783
William Pitt (Tory)	1783–1801

Henry Addington (Tory)	1801–1804	Henry Campbell-Bannerman (Lib)	1905–1908
William Pitt (Tory)	1804–1806	Herbert Henry Asquith (Lib)	1908–1915
Lord Grenville (Whig)	1806–1807	Herbert Henry Asquith (Coalition)	1915–1916
Duke of Portland (Tory)	1807–1809	David Lloyd George (Coalition)	1916–1922
Spencer Perceval (Tory)	1809–1812	Andrew Bonar Law (Con)	1922–1923
Earl of Liverpool (Tory)	1812–1827	Stanley Baldwin (Con)	1923–1924
George Canning (Tory)	1827	James Ramsey MacDonald (Lab)	1924
Viscount Goderich (Tory)	1827–1828	Stanley Baldwin (Con)	1924–1929
Duke of Wellington (Tory)	1828–1830	James Ramsey MacDonald (Lab)	1929–1931
Earl Grey (Whig)	1830–1834	James Ramsey MacDonald (National coalition)	1931–1935
Viscount Melbourne (Whig)	1834		
Robert Peel (Con)	1834–1835	Stanley Baldwin (National coalition)	1935–1937
Viscount Melbourne (Whig)	1835–1841	Arthur Neville Chamberlain (National coalition)	1937–1940
Robert Peel (Con)	1841–1846	Winston Churchill (Coalition)	1940–1945
Lord John Russell (Lib)	1846–1852	Clement Atlee (Lab)	1945–1951
Earl of Derby (Con)	1852	Winston Churchill (Con)	1951–1955
Lord Aberdeen (Peelite)	1852-1855	Anthony Eden (Con)	1955–1957
Viscount Palmerston (Lib)	1855–1858	Harold Macmillan (Con)	1957–1963
Earl of Derby (Con)	1958–1859	Alec Douglas-Home (Con)	1963–1964
Viscount Palmerston (Lib)	1859–1865	Harold Wilson (Lab)	1964–1970
Lord John Russell (Lib)	1865–1866	Edward Heath (Con)	1970–1974
Earl of Derby (Con)	1866–1868	Harold Wilson (Lab)	1974–1976
Benjamin Disraeli (Con)	1868	James Callaghan (Lab)	1976–1979
William Ewart Gladstone (Lib)	1868–1874	Margaret Thatcher (Con)	1979–1990
Benjamin Disraeli (Con)	1874–1880	John Major (Con)	1990–1997
William Ewart Gladstone (Lib)	1880–1885	Tony Blair (Lab)	1997–present
Marquess of Salisbury (Con)	1885–1886		
William Ewart Gladstone (Lib)	1886		
Marquess of Salisbury (Con)	1886–1892		
William Ewart Gladstone (Lib)	1892–1894		
Earl of Roseberry (Lib)	1894–1895		
Marquess of Salisbury (Con)	1895–1902		
Arthur James Balfour (Con)	1902–1905		

TWO HUNDRED GREAT PROTAGONISTS FROM LITERATURE

Jack Absolute *The Rivals,* Richard Brinsley Sheridan

Frankie Addams *The Member of the Wedding,* Carson McCullers

Captain Ahab *Moby-Dick; or, The Whale,* Herman Melville

Alceste *The Misanthrope,* Molière

Harry Angstrom *Rabbit, Run,* John Updike

Isabel Archer *A Portrait of a Lady,* Henry James

Newland Archer *The Age of Innocence,* Edith Wharton

Florentino Ariza *Love in the Time of Cholera,* Gabriel García Márquez

D'Artagnan *The Three Musketeers,* Alexandre Dumas

Bilbo Baggins *The Hobbit,* J. R. R. Tolkien

Sophia Baines *The Old Wives' Tale,* Arnold Bennett

David Balfour *Kidnapped,* Robert Louis Stevenson

Jake Barnes *The Sun Also Rises,* Ernest Hemingway

Lily Bart *The House of Mirth,* Edith Wharton

Paul Baumer *All Quiet on the Western Front,* Erich Maria Remarque

Jody Baxter *The Yearling,* Marjorie Kinnan Rawlings

William Sylvanus Baxter *Seventeen,* Booth Tarkington

Elizabeth Bennet *Pride and Prejudice,* Jane Austen

Alexandra Bergson *O Pioneers!,* Willa Cather

Pierre Besukov *War and Peace,* Leo Tolstoy

Bibi *Letters from a Student Revolutionary,* Elizabeth Wong

Rupert Birkin *Women in Love,* D. H. Lawrence

Percy Blakeney *The Scarlet Pimpernel,* Baroness Orczy

Leopold Bloom *Ulysses,* James Joyce

Caithleen Brady *The Country Girls,* Edna O'Brien

Dorothea Brooke *Middlemarch,* George Eliot

Buck *The Call of the Wild,* Jack London

Natty Bumppo *The Deerslayer,* James Fenimore Cooper

Jack Burden *All the King's Men,* Robert Penn Warren

Philip Carey *Of Human Bondage,* W. Somerset Maugham

Henry Carr *Travesties,* Tom Stoppard

Nick Carraway *The Great Gatsby,* F. Scott Fitzgerald

Sydney Carton *A Tale of Two Cities,* Charles Dickens

Pompey Casmilus *Novel on Yellow Paper,* Stevie Smith

Hans Castorp *The Magic Mountain,* Thomas Mann

Jessie Cates *Night, Mother,* Marsha Norman

Holden Caulfield *Catcher in the Rye,* J. D. Salinger

Celie *The Colour Purple,* Alice Walker

Charlie Citrine *Humboldt's Gift,* Saul Bellow

Clay *Dutchman,* Amiri Baraka

Hugh Conway *Lost Horizon,* James Hilton

Antoinette Cosway *Wide Sargasso Sea,* Jean Rhys

Frank Algernon Cowperwood *The Titan,*

Theodore Dreiser

Sarah Crewe *The Little Princess*, Frances Hodgson Burnett

Edmund Dantes *The Count of Monte Cristo*, Alexandre Dumas

Larry Darrell *The Razor's Edge*, W. Somerset Maugham

Clarence Day *Life with Father*, Clarence Day Jr.

Stephen Dedalus *A Portrait of the Artist as a Young Man*, James Joyce

Fabrizio del Dongo *The Charterhouse of Parma*, Stendhal

Dick Diver *Tender Is the Night*, F. Scott Fitzgerald

Eliza Doolittle *Pygmalion*, George Bernard Shaw

Blanche DuBois *Streetcar Named Desire*, Tennessee Williams

Anne Elliot *Persuasion*, Jane Austen

Julian English *Appointment in Samarra*, John O'Hara

Fanny Farelly *Watch on the Rhine*, Lillian Hellman

Jude Fawley *Jude the Obscure*, Thomas Hardy

Scout (Jean Louise) Finch *To Kill a Mockingbird*, Harper Lee

Henry Fleming *The Red Badge of Courage*, Stephen Crane

Phineas Fogg *Around the World in Eighty Days*, Jules Verne

Soames Forsythe *The Man of Property*, John Galsworthy

Rene Gallimard *M. Butterfly*, David Henry Hwang

Eugene Gant *Look Homeward Angel*, Thomas Wolfe

Holly Golightly *Breakfast at Tiffany's*, Truman Capote

Helen Graham *The Tenant of Wildfell Hall*, Anne Brontë

Esther Greenwood *The Bell Jar*, Sylvia Plath

Griffin *The Invisible Man*, H. G. Wells

Clyde Griffiths *An American Tragedy*, Theodore Dreiser

Lemuel Gulliver *Gulliver's Travels*, Jonathan Swift

Margaret Hale *North and South*, Elizabeth Gaskell

Henry Haller *Steppenwolf*, Hermann Hesse

Richard Hannay *The Thirty-Nine Steps*, John Buchan

Harpagon *The Miser*, Molière

Kate Hardcastle *She Stoops to Conquer*, Oliver Goldsmith

Septimus Harding *The Warden*, Anthony Trollope

Ralph Hartsook *The Hoosier Schoolmaster*, Edward Eggleston

Jim Hawkins *Treasure Island*, Robert Louis Stevenson

Heathcliff *Wuthering Heights*, Emily Brontë

Nora Helmer *A Doll's House*, Henrik Ibsen

Michael Henchard *The Mayor of Casterbridge*, Thomas Hardy

Frederick Henry *A Farewell to Arms*, Ernest Hemingway

Axel Heyst *Victory*, Joseph Conrad

Katherine Hilbery *Night and Day*, Virginia Woolf

Heidi Holland *The Heidi Chronicles*, Wendy Wasserstein

Lucy Honeychurch *A Room with a View*, E. M. Forster

Sam Hughes *In Country*, Bobbie Ann Mason

Humbert Humbert *Lolita*, Vladimir Nabokov

Matty Jenkyns *Cranford*, Elizabeth Gaskell

Sasha Jensen *Good Morning, Midnight*, Jean Rhys

Gulley Jimson *The Horse's Mouth*, Joyce Cary

Tom Joad *The Grapes of Wrath*, John Steinbeck

Brutus Jones *The Emperor Jones*, Eugene O'Neill

Robert Jordan *For Whom the Bell Tolls*, Ernest Hemingway

Julia *The Wedding Band*, Alice Childress

K *The Castle*, Franz Kafka

Carol Kennicott *Main Street*, Sinclair Lewis

Ko-Ko *The Mikado*, W. S. Gilbert

Stephen Kumalo *Cry, the Beloved Country*, Alan Paton

Etienne Lantier *Germinal*, Emile Zola

Macon Leary *The Accidental Tourist*, Anne Tyler

Lorelei Lee *Gentlemen Prefer Blondes*, Anita Loos

Nina Leeds *Strange Interlude*, Eugene O'Neill

Mary Lennox *The Secret Garden*, Frances Hodgson Burnett

Jeeter Lester *Tobacco Road*, Erskine Caldwell

Dolly Levi *The Matchmaker*, Thornton Wilder

Willy Loman *Death of a Salesman*, Arthur Miller

Harold Loomis *Joe Turner's Come and Gone*, August Wilson

Lucius *The Golden Ass*, Lucius Apuleius

Christy Mahon *The Playboy of the Western World*, John Millington Synge

Lavinia Mannon *Mourning Becomes Electra*, Eugene O'Neill

Josephine March *Little Women*, Louisa May Alcott

Rose Maurrant *Street Scene*, Elmer Rice

Maurya *Riders to the Sea*, John Millington Synge

Troy Maxon *Fences*, August Wilson

Wiletta Mayer *Trouble in Mind*, Alice Childress

Randall Patrick McMurphy *One Flew over the Cuckoo's Nest*, Ken Kesey

Laura McRaven *Delta Wedding*, Eudora Welty

Augustin Meaulnes *The Grand Meaulnes*, Alain-Fournier

Gregor Melekhov *And Quiet Flows the Don*, Mikhail Sholokhov

Sybylla Melvyn *My Brilliant Career*, Miles Franklin

Robert Merivel *Restoration*, Rose Tremain

Guy Montag *Fahrenheit 451*, Ray Bradbury

Father Montez *The Power and the Glory*, Graham Greene

Frederic Moreau *A Sentimental Education*, Gustave Flaubert

Paul Morel *Sons and Lovers*, D. H. Lawrence

Huw Morgan *How Green Was My Valley*, Richard Llewellyn

Hazel Motes *Wise Blood*, Flannery O'Connor

Mowgli *The Jungle Book*, Rudyard Kipling

Prince Myshkin *The Idiot*, Fyodor Dostoyevsky

Francie Nolan *A Tree Grows in Brooklyn*, Betty Smith

Gypo Nolan *The Informer*, Liam O'Flaherty

Offred *The Handmaid's Tale*, Margaret Atwood

Scarlett O'Hara *Gone with the Wind*, Margaret Mitchell

Pao-yu *Dream of the Red Chamber*, Tsao Hsueh-chin

Willoughby Patterne *The Egoist*, George Meredith

Paul Pennyfeather *Decline and Fall*, Evelyn Waugh

Billy Pilgrim *Slaughterhouse Five*, Kurt Vonnegut

Pip (Philip Pirrip) *Great Expectations*, Charles Dickens

Maggie Pollitt *Cat on a Hot Tin Roof*, Tennessee Williams

Edna Pontellier *The Awakening*, Kate Chopin

Ernest Pontifex *The Way of All Flesh*, Samuel Butler

Jimmy Porter *Look Back in Anger*, John Osborne

Flora Poste *Cold Comfort Farm,* Stella Gibbons

Fanny Price *Mansfield Park,* Jane Austen

Dr. Primrose *The Vicar of Wakefield,* Oliver Goldsmith

Prospero *The Tempest,* William Shakespeare

Hester Prynne *The Scarlet Letter,* Nathaniel Hawthorne

Allan Quatermain *King Solomon's Mines,* H. Rider Haggard

Portia Quayne *The Death of the Heart,* Elizabeth Bowen

Quasimodo *The Hunchback of Notre Dame,* Victor Hugo

Thady Quirk *Castle Rackrent,* Maria Edgeworth

Laura Rambotham *The Getting of Wisdom,* Henry Handel Richardson

Madame Ranevskaya *The Cherry Orchard,* Anton Chekov

Raskolnikov *Crime and Punishment,* Fyodor Dostoyevsky

Rudolf Rassendyll *The Prisoner of Zenda,* Anthony Hope

Bernard Rieux *The Plague,* Albert Camus

Antoine Roquentin *Nausea,* Jean-Paul Sartre

Rosalind *As You Like It,* William Shakespeare

Jurgis Rudkus *The Jungle,* Upton Sinclair

Charles Ryder *Brideshead Revisited,* Evelyn Waugh

Santiago *The Old Man and the Sea,* Ernest Hemingway

Prudence Sarn *Precious Bane,* Mary Webb

Arthur Seaton *Saturday Night and Sunday Morning,* Alan Sillitoe

Ebenezer Scrooge *A Christmas Carol,* Charles Dickens

Sethe *Beloved,* Toni Morrison

Lily Shane *The Green Bay Tree,* Louis Bromfield

Becky Sharp *Vanity Fair,* William Makepeace Thackeray

George Sherston *Memoirs of a Fox-Hunting Man,* Siegfried Sassoon

Anne Shirley *Anne of Green Gables,* L. M. Montgomery

Catherine Sloper *Washington Square,* Henry James

Winston Smith *1984,* George Orwell

Lucy Snowe *Villette,* Charlotte Brontë

Julian Sorel *The Red and the Black,* Stendhal

Sam Spade *The Maltese Falcon,* Dashiell Hammett

Stevens *The Remains of the Day,* Kazuo Ishiguro

Thomas Stockmann *An Enemy of the People,* Henrik Ibsen

Denis Stone *Chrome Yellow,* Aldous Huxley

Lambert Strether *The Ambassadors,* Henry James

Esther Summerson *Bleak House,* Charles Dickens

Charles Surface *The School for Scandal,* Richard Brinsley Sheridan

Christopher Tietjens *Parade's End,* Ford Madox Ford

Bigger Thomas *Native Son,* Richard Wright

Phoebe Throssel *Quality Street,* James M. Barrie

Nell Trent *The Old Curiosity Shop,* Charles Dickens

Maggie Tulliver *The Mill on the Floss,* George Eliot

Jean Valjean *Les Misérables,* Victor Hugo

Alice Vavasor *Can You Forgive Her?,* Anthony Trollope

Maggie Verver *The Golden Bowl,* Henry James

Rachel Vinrace *The Voyage Out,* Virginia Woolf

Viola *Twelfth Night,* William Shakespeare

Gustave von Aschenbach *Death in Venice,*
Thomas Mann

William Wallace *The Scottish Chiefs,* Jane Porter

Prior Walter *Angels in America,* Tony Kushner

Wang Lung *The Good Earth,* Pearl Buck

Frank Ware *A Man's World,* Rachel Crothers

George Webber *You Can't Go Home Again,*
Thomas Wolfe

Sayward Wheeler *The Fields,* Conrad Richter

Isadora Wing *Fear of Flying,* Erica Jong

Amanda Wingfield *The Glass Menagerie,*
Tennessee Williams

Janie Woods *Their Eyes Were Watching God,*
Zora Neale Hurston

John Worthing *The Importance of Being Earnest,*
Oscar Wilde

Anna Wulf *The Golden Notebook,* Doris Lessing

Yank (Robert Smith) *The Hairy Ape,* Eugene
O'Neill

Clym Yeobright *The Return of the Native,*
Thomas Hardy

Yossarian *Catch-22,* Joseph Heller

Walter Younger *A Raisin in the Sun,* Lorraine
Hansberry

Mr. Zero *The Adding Machine,* Elmer Rice

ROMAN EMPERORS

BEFORE THE COMMON ERA (BCE)

27	Augustus (Gaius Julius Caesar Octavianus)

OF THE COMMON ERA (CE)

14	Tiberius I
37	Gaius Caesar (Caligula)
41	Claudius I
54	Nero
68	Galba
69	Galba; Otho; Vitellius
69	Vespasianus
79	Titus
81	Domitianus
96	Nerva
98	Trajanus
117	Hadrianus
138	Antoninus Pius
161	Marcus Aurelius and Lucius Verus
169	Marcus Aurelius *(alone)*
180	Commodus
193	Pertinax; Julianus I
193	Septimius Severus
211	Caracalla and Geta
212	Caracalla *(alone)*
217	Macrinus
218	Elagabalus (Heliogabalus)
222	Alexander Severus
235	Maximinus I (the Thracian)
238	Gordianus I and Gordianus II; Pupienus and Balbinus
238	Gordianus III
244	Philippus (the Arab)
249	Decius
251	Gallus and Volusianus
253	Aemilianus
253	Valerianus and Gallienus
258	Gallienus *(alone)*
268	Claudius Gothicus
270	Quintillus

270	Aurelianus
275	Tacitus
276	Florianus
276	Probus
282	Carus
283	Carinus and Numerianus
284	Diocletianus
286	Diocletianus and Maximianus
305	Galerius and Constantius I
306	Galerius, Maximinus II, Severus I
307	Galerius, Maximinus II, Constantinus I, Licinius, Maxentius
311	Maximinus II, Constantinus I, Licinius, Maxentius
314	Maximinus II, Constantinus I, Licinius
314	Constantinus I and Licinius
324	Constantinus I (the Great)
337	Constantinus II, Constans I, Constantius II
340	Constantius II and Constans I
350	Constantius II
361	Julianus II (the Apostate)
363	Jovianus

WEST (ROME) AND EAST (CONSTANTINOPLE)

364	Valentinianus I (W) and Valens (E)
367	Valentinianus I with Gratianus (W) and Valens (E)
375	Gratianus with Valentinianus II (W) and Valens (E)
378	Gratianus with Valentinianus II (W) and Theodosius I (E)
383	Valentinianus II (W) and Theodosius I (E)
394	Theodosius I (the Great)
395	Honorius (W) and Arcadius (E)
408	Honorius (W) and Theodosius II (E)
423	Valentinianus III (W) and Theodosius II (E)
450	Valentinianus III (W) and Marcianus (E)
455	Maximus (W), Avitus (W); Marcianus (E)
456	Avitus (W), Marcianus (E)
457	Majorianus (W), Leo I (E)
461	Severus II (W), Leo I (E)
467	Anthemius (W), Leo I (E)

472	Olybrius (W), Leo I (E)
473	Glycerius (W), Leo I (E)
474	Julius Nepos (W), Leo II (E)
475	Romulus Augustulus (W) and Zeno (E)
476	End of Western empire; Byzantine empire rises from Constantinople

ROYALTY, PRESENT DAY

Bahrain Sheik Hamed bin Isa al-Khalifa
Belgium King Albert II, Queen Paola
Bhutan King Jigme Singye Wangchuk
Brunei Sultan Sir Muda Hassanal Bolkiah Muvizzadin
Cambodia Prince Norodom Sihanouk
Denmark Queen Margrethe II
Greece King Constantine
Japan Emperor Akihito
Jordan King Abdulla II
Kuwait Emir Sheik Jaber al-Ahmad al-Jaber a-Sabah
Lesotho King Letsie III
Liechtenstein Prince Hans-Adam II
Luxembourg Grand Duke Jean, Grand Duchess Josephine-Charlotte
Malaysia Paramount Ruler Tuanku Jaafar ibni Al-Marhum Tuanku Abdul Rahman
Monaco Prince Rainier III
Morocco King Muhammad VI
Nepal King Gyanendra Bir Bikram Shah Dev
Netherlands Queen Beatrix
Norway King Harald V, Queen Sonja
Oman Sultan Qabus bin Said
Qatar Emir Hamad bin Khalifa al-Thani
Saudi Arabia King Fahd bin Abdulaziz
Spain King Juan Carlos I, Queen Sofia
Swaziland King Mswati III
Sweden King Carl Gustav XVI, Queen Silvia
Thailand King Bhumibol Adulyadej
Tonga King Taufa'ahau Tupou IV
United Kingdom Queen Elizabeth II

RUSSIAN CZARS

Czar	Reign
House of Riurik	
Ivan IV, the Terrible	1547–84
Fyodor I	1584–98
Boris Godunov	1598–1605
Fyodor II	1605
Dmitri II, the false Dmitri	1605–06
Vasily IV Shuisky	1606–10
Civil War 1610–13	
House of Romanov	
Mikhail (Michael Romanov)	1613–45
Alexei I Mikhailovitch	1645–76
Fyodor III	1676–82
Peter, the Great 1682–1725 *(joint ruler to 1696)*	
Ivan V	1682–96 *(joint ruler)*
Catherine I	1725–27
Peter II	1727–30
Anna Ivovna	1730–40
Ivan VI	1740–41
Elizabeth Petrovna	1741–62
Peter III	1762
Catherine, the Great	1762–96
Paul	1796–1801
Alexander I	1801–25
Nicholas I	1825–55
Alexander II, the Liberator	1855–81
Alexander III	1881–94
Nicholas II	1894–1917

SAINTS

SAINTS AS PATRONS AND INTERCESSORS

Adelard gardeners
Adjutor yachtsmen
Adrian butchers; soldiers
Aedh Mac Bricc headache sufferers
Agatha nurses
Agnes girls
Albert the Great medical technicians; scientists
Alexus beggars
Aloysius Gonzaga youth
Alphonsus vocations
Alphonsus Liguori theologians; confessors
Amand wine merchants
Ambrose learning
Anastasia weavers
Anastasius goldsmiths; weavers
Andrew fishermen
Andronicus silversmiths
Anne cabinetmakers; housewives; women in labour
Anthony brushmakers
Anthony of Padua poor; barren women; lost articles; travellers
Antony butchers; domestic animals; grave diggers
Apollonia dentists
Armand hotelkeepers
Arnulph millers
Augustine brewers; printers; theologians
Barbara architects; builders; dying; fire prevention; founders; prisoners; stonemasons
Bartholomew plasterers
Basil the Great hospital administrators
Benedict poisoning; speleologists
Bernadine of Siena advertising
Bernard skiers
Bernard of Clairvaux candlemakers
Bernard of Montjoux mountaineers
Bernardino of Siena communications personnel; public relations
Bl. **Contardo Ferrini** universities
Blaise throat
Brendan sailors
Brigid scholars
Camillus de Lellis hospitals; nurses; sick

Cassian of Tangiers stenographers
Catherine maidens
Catherine of Alexandria philosophers; preachers; students
Catherine of Bologna art
Catherine of Siena fire prevention; nursing service
Cecilia musicians; poets; singers
Charles Borromeo catechists; seminarians
Christopher motorists; porters; sailors; travellers
Clare of Assisi television
Claude sculptors
Clement stonecutters
Cosmas and Damian barbers; druggists; pharmacists; physicians; surgeons
Crispin and Crispinian tanners; leather workers; saddlers; shoemakers
Cuthbert sailors
David poets
Dismas funeral directors; prisoners
Dominic astronomers
Dominic Savio choirboys
Dorothy gardeners
Drogo shepherds
Dunstan blacksmiths; goldsmiths; jewellers; lighthouse keepers; locksmiths; musicians; silversmiths
Dymphna epileptics; mentally ill
Eligius jewellers; metalworkers
Elizabeth of Hungary bakers; nursing service; tertiaries
Elmo sailors
Emygdius earthquakes
Erasmus sailors
Eulalia sailors
Eustachius hunters
Felicity barren women
Ferdinand III engineers
Fiacre cab drivers; gardeners
Florian firemen
Frances of Rome motorists
Francis de Sales journalists; authors; Catholic press; deaf; writers
Francis of Assisi Catholic action; ecologists; merchants
Francis Xavier missions
Francis Xavier Cabrini emigrants; hospital administrators
Gabriel clerics; messengers; postal workers; radio workers; telecommunications workers; television workers
Gabriel Possenti youth
Genesius actors; lawyers; printers; secretaries; stenographers
George Boy Scouts; farmers; soldiers
Gerard Majella childbirth; pregnant women
Gertrude of Nivelles gardeners; travellers
Gervase and Protase haymakers
Giles beggars; cripples
Gregory singers
Gregory of Neocaesarea desperate situations
Gregory the Great musicians; teachers
Herve eye trouble
Holy Innocents foundlings
Homobonus tailors
Honoratus bakers
Hubert hunters
Ignatius Loyola retreats; soldiers
Isidore labourers
Isidore the Farmer farmers
Ivo lawyers
James labourers; pilgrims
James the Greater pharmacists; rheumatism
James the Less druggists; hatters
Januarius blood banks
Jerome Emiliani abandoned children; orphans
Joan of Arc soldiers
John Baptist de la Salle teachers
John Baptist Vianney parish priests
John Berchmans altar boys
John Berchmas youth
John Bosco editors; labourers
John Capistran jurists
John Chrysostom orators; preachers
John Gaulbert foresters
John Nepomucen confessors
John of God heart patients; hospitals; nurses; printers; sick
John Thwing women in difficult labour
Joseph carpenters; the church; dying; fathers of families; social justice; workingmen
Joseph Cafasso prisons
Joseph of Arimathea funeral directors
Joseph of Cupertino air travellers; pilots
Jude desperate situations
Jude Thaddeus hospitals
Julian the Hospitaler boatmen; hotelkeepers; travellers

Justin philosophers
Lawrence cooks; poor
Leonard prisoners of war
Leonard of Port Maurice (parish) missions
Lidwina skaters
Louis barbers; tertiaries
Louise de Marillac social workers
Lucy eye trouble; writers
Luke artists; brewers; butchers; glassworkers; notaries; painters; physicians; surgeons
Marculf skin diseases
Margaret pregnant women
Mark notaries
Martha cooks; hospital dietitians; servants
Martin de Porres hairdressers; interracial justice
Martin of Tours soldiers
Matrona dysentery sufferers
Matthew accountants; bankers; bookkeepers; tax collectors
Maurice infantrymen; swordsmiths
Maurice and Lydia Purpuraria dyers
Maurus coppersmiths
Michael grocers; mariners; paratroopers; policemen; radiologists; sick
Monica married women; mothers
Morandi winegrowers
Nicholas bakers; sailors
Nicholas of Myra brewers; brides; children; merchants; pawnbrokers; travellers
Nicholas of Tolentine mariners
Odilia the blind
Pachal Baylon Eucharistic congresses and societies
Pantaleon physicians
Paul public relations for hospitals
Paul the Hermit weavers
Paula widows
Peregine Laziosi cancer victims
Peter Gonzales sailors
Peter of Alcantara watchmen
Phocas gardeners
Raphael lovers; nurses; physicians; the blind; travellers
Raymond Nonnatus falsely accused; midwives; pregnant women
Raymond of Penafort canonists
Reinold stonemasons
Rene Goupil anaesthetists
Rita of Cascia desperate situations

Robert Bellarmine catechists
Roch invalids; plague
Scholastica convulsive children
Sebastian archers; athletes; soldiers
Simon tanners
Sryphon gardeners
Stephen bricklayers; stonemasons
Swithbert angina sufferers
Tarcisius first communicants
Teresa of Avila headache sufferers
Therese of Lisieux aviators; florists; missions
Thomas Aquinas students
Thomas More lawyers
Thomas the Apostle architects
Three Magi (Caspar, Melchior, Balthasar) travellers
Valentine greetings; lovers
Victor millers
Vincent Ferrer builders
Vincent de Paul charitable societies
Vincent winegrowers
Vitus actors; comedians; dancers; epileptics
Zita servants

SAINTS OF COUNTRIES AND PLACES

Adalbert Prussia
Alexander Sauli Corsica
Andrew Greece; Russia; Scotland
Anne Canada
Ansgar Denmark; Scandinavia; Sweden
Augustine of Canterbury England
Barnabas Cyprus
Benedict Europe
Bernardio of Siena Italy
Bl. Astericus Hungary
Bl. Cunegund Lithuania
Boniface Germany
Boris Moscow
Bridget Sweden
Brigid Ireland
Bruno Ruthenia
Bruno of Querfurt Prussia
Canute Denmark
Casimir Lithuania; Poland
Catherine of Siena Italy
Columba Scotland
Columbia Ireland

Cunegund Poland
Cyril and Methodius Moravia
David Wales
Denis France
Dominic Dominican Republic
Eric Sweden
Euphrasius Spain
Felix Spain
Francis Borgia Portugal
Francis of Assisi Italy
Francis Xavier East Indies; Japan
Frumentius Ethiopia
Gall Sweden; Switzerland
Genevieve Paris
George Aragon; England; Genoa; Portugal
Gerard Hungary
Gertrude West Indies
Gregory the Great England
Gregory the Illuminator Armenia
Hedwig Silesia
Henry of Uppsala Finland
Hyacinth Poland
Immaculate Conception Brazil; Corsica; Portugal; United States
Isaac Jogues and companions North America
Isidore the Farmer Madrid
James Chile; Spain
Joan of Arc France
John Cantius Lithuania; Poland
John Nepomucen Czechoslovakia
John of Avila Spain
John the Evangelist Asia Minor
Joseph Belgium; Canada; China; Peru
Julia of Corsica Corsica
Kilian Bavaria
Lawrence Sri Lanka
Louis Bertrand Colombia
Ludmilla Bohemia
Margaret of Scotland Scotland
Martin of Tours France
Maruthas Persia
Michael Germany
Nicetas Romania
Nicholas of Myra Greece; Russia; Sicily
Nino Georgia (Russia)
Odilia Alsace
Olaf Norway
Our Lady Help of Christians Australia; New Zealand

Our Lady of Czestochowa Poland
Our Lady of Guadalupe Mexico
Our Lady of High Grace Dominican Republic
Our Lady of Lujan Argentina; Uruguay
Our Lady of Mount Carmel Chile
Our Lady of the Assumption France; India; Paraguay; Slovakia; South Africa
Palladius Scotland
Patrick Ireland
Peter Baptist Japan
Peter Canisius Germany
Peter Claver Colombia
Peter of Alcantara Brazil
Philip Neri Rome
Plechelm Holland
Procopius Czechoslovakia
Remigius France
Rose of Lima Americas; South America
Sacred Heart Ecuador
Sacred Heart of Mary Philippines
Sigfrid Sweden
Stanislaus Poland
Stephen Hungary
Teresa of Avila Spain
Therese of Lisieux Russia
Thomas East Indies
Titus Crete
Vincent Portugal
Vladimir I of Kiev Russia
Wenceslaus Bohemia; Czechoslovakia
Willehad Saxony
Willibrord Holland

SAINTS' SYMBOLS IN ART

Agatha tongs; veil
Agnes lamb
Ambrose bees; dove; ox; pen
Andrew transverse cross
Angela Merici ladder; cloak
Anne door
Anthony of Padua Christ child; book; bread; lily
Antony bell; hog
Augustine child; dove; pen; shell
Barbara cannon; chalice palm; tower
Barnabas axe; lance; stones
Bartholomew flayed skin; knife
Benedict bell; broken cup; bush; crozier; raven

Bernard bees; pen
Bernardio of Siena chrism; sun inscribed with HIS; tablet
Blaise iron comb; wax candle
Bonaventure cardinal's hat; ciborium
Boniface axe; book; fox; fountain; oak; raven; scourge; sword
Bridget of Sweden book; pilgrim's staff
Brigid candle; cross; flame over her head
Bruno chalice
Catherine of Alexandria lamb; sword wheel
Catherine di Ricci crown; crucifix; ring
Catherine of Siena cross; lily; ring; stigmata
Cecilia organ
Charles Borromeo Eucharist
Christopher Christ child; giant; torrent; tree
Clare monstrance
Colette birds; lamb
Cosmas and Damian box of ointment; vial
Cyril of Alexandria pen
Cyril of Jerusalem book; purse
Dominic rosary; star
Dorothy flowers; fruit
Edmund arrow; sword
Elizabeth of Hungary bread; flowers; pitcher
Francis of Assisi birds; deer; fish; skull; stigmata; wolf
Francis Xavier bell; crucifix; ship
Genevieve bread; candle; herd; keys
George dragon
Gertrude crown; lily; taper
Gervaise and Protase club; scourge; sword
Giles crozier; hermitage; hind
Gregory the Great crozier; dove tiara
Helena cross
Hilary child; pen; stick
Ignatius Loyola book; chasuble; Eucharist
Isidore bees; pen
James the Greater key; pilgrim's staff; shell; sword
James the Less club; halberd; square rule
Jehosaphat chalice; crown; winged deacon
Jerome lion
John the Baptist head on platter; lamb; skin of animal
John Berchmans cross; rosary
John Chrysostom bees; dove; pen
John Climacus ladder
John the Evangelist armour; chalice; eagle; kettle

John of God alms; crown of thorns; heart
Joseph carpenter's square; infant Jesus; lily; plane; rod
Jude club; square rule
Justin Martyr axe; sword
Lawrence book of gospels; cross; gridiron
Leander pen
Liborius pebbles; peacock
Longinus lance
Louis crown of thorns; nails
Lucy cord; eyes
Luke book; bush; ox; palette
Margaret dragon
Mark book; lion
Martha dragon; holy water; sprinkler
Mary Magdalen alabaster box of ointment
Matilda alms; purse; winged man
Matthias lance
Maurus crutch; scales; spade
Michael banner; dragon; scales; spade; sword
Monica girdle; tears
Nicholas anchor; boat; boy in boat; three purses
Patrick baptismal font; cross; harp; serpent; shamrock
Paul book; scroll; sword
Peter boat; cock; keys
Philip column
Philip Neri altar; chasuble; vial
Rita crucifix; rose; thorn
Roch angel; bread; dog
Rose of Lima anchor; city; crown of thorns
Sebastian arrows; crown
Sergius and Bacchus military uniform; palm
Simon cross; saw
Simon Stock scapular
Teresa of Avila arrow; book; heart
Therese of Lisieux roses entwining a crucifix
Thomas axe; lance
Thomas Aquinas chalice; dove; monstrance; ox
Ursula arrow; clock; ship
Vincent boat; gridiron
Vincent de Paul children
Vincent Ferrer captives; cardinal's hat; pulpit; trumpet

SIGNERS OF THE DECLARATION OF INDEPENDENCE

Connecticut Roger Sherman, Samuel Huntington, William Williams, Oliver Wolcott

Delaware Caesar Rodney, George Read, Thomas McKean

Georgia Button Gwinnett, Lyman Hall, George Walton

Maryland Samuel Chase, William Paca, Thomas Stone, Charles Carroll

Massachusetts John Hancock, Samuel Adams, John Adams, Robert Treat Paine, Elbridge Gerry

New Hampshire Josiah Bartlett, William Whipple, Matthew Thornton

New Jersey Richard Stockton, John Witherspoon, Francis Hopkinson, John Hart, Abraham Clark

New York William Floyd, Philip Livingston, Francis Lewis, Lewis Morris

North Carolina William Hooper, Joseph Hewes, John Penn

Pennsylvania Robert Morris, Benjamin Rush, Benjamin Franklin, John Morton, George Clymer, James Smith, George Taylor, James Wilson, George Ross

Rhode Island Stephen Hopkins, William Ellery

South Carolina Edward Rutledge, Thomas Heyward, Thomas Lynch, Arthur Middleton

Virginia George Wythe, Richard Henry Lee, Thomas Jefferson, Benjamin Harrison, Thomas Nelson, Francis Lightfoot Lee, Carter Braxton

SUPERHEROES

Aquaman This citizen of the underwater world of Atlantis was introduced by Mort Weisinger and artist Paul Norris in the 1941 *More Fun Comics*.

The Atom This tiny powerhouse, the alter ego of scientist Ray Palmer, was introduced in DC Comics in 1962.

Batman This caped crusader first appeared in 1940 in Detective Comics, created by Bob Kane and Bill Finger.

Captain Action Archaeologist Clive Arno was first transformed into this superhero via ancient coins in a 1968 edition of DC Comics.

Captain America Lightweight Steve Rogers takes a top secret military serum and begins fighting Nazis in 1941, along with his sidekick, Bucky. Created by Jack Kirby and Joe Simon.

Captain Atom This radiation-exuding superhero was introduced by Charlton Comics in 1965.

Captain Marvel Newsboy Billy Batson became a crime-fighting superhero after shouting the name "Shazam!" in the 1940s.

Daredevil Matt Murdock is blinded by radioactive waste as a child but develops into this superhero in the 1964 premiere edition of this Marvel Comic.

Falcon A politically correct superhero starring Captain America's former partner, introduced by Marvel Comics in 1983.

Fighting American Nelson Flagg is aided by military superscience to improve his body so that he can fight the Commies who killed his brother. Introduced by Headline Comics in 1954.

Firestorm High-school student Ronnie Raymond becomes this DC Comics superhero after being caught next to a detonated nuclear bomb in 1978.

Flash Superspeedy Barry Allen began his popular streak as a superhero in the 1940s *Flash Comics*.

Green Arrow DC Comics created Oliver Queen, wealthy adventurer and great archer, and his alter ego, Green Arrow, in 1941.

Green Lantern Hal Jordan becomes a superhero via his power ring that must be recharged by a green lantern every 24 hours in this comic introduced in the 1940s.

Incredible Hulk Scientist Bruce Banner, pelted by gamma rays, becomes the unsightly hero in this famous Marvel Comics series.

Isis Professor Andrea Thomas transforms herself into this Egyptian goddess in the DC Comics series.

Human Torch Although introduced by creator Carl Burgos for Timely Comics in 1940, this flaming hero did not gain much attention until he became a member of Marvel's Fantastic Four.

Martian Manhunter This second-string founding member of the Justice League started fighting evil in the beginning of the 1950s

The Phantom This lineage of pirate- and crime-fighting superheroes began as a newspaper strip by Lee Falk in 1934.

The Ragman Rory Reagan, pawnshop owner, became a superhero of the ghettos beginning in the 1976 DC Comic.

Robin This ward of Bruce Wayne (a.k.a. Batman) began fighting criminals along with his mentor in 1940.

Silver Surfer Jack Kirby and editor Stan Lee created this surfing alien in a Marvel Comics edition of *Fantastic Four*.

Spectre Policeman Jim Corrigan returns to Earth after he has been murdered, first as a vengeful spirit in the 1940s and then as a superhero in the 1960s DC Comics.

Spiderman Stan Lee's famous creation for Marvel Comics traces the crime-fighting career of student Peter Parker who was bitten by a radioactive spider.

Sub-Mariner (a.k.a. Prince Namor of Atlantis) Beginning as a rather amoral citizen of Atlantis in the 1940s, this superhero went on to fight evil for Marvel Comics in the late 1960s.

Superboy This superhero began in stories of the youthful Superman in 1945.

Superman Hailing from the planet Krypton, this quintessential American superhero was created by Jerry Siegel and Joe Shuster for *Action Comics*.

The Mighty Thor Stan Lee and Jack Kirby created this hammer-wielding superhero from Norse myths for Marvel Comics.

Wonder Woman Initiated in 1941 by creator William Marston and artist Harry G. Peter as an alternative to the violent, masculine comic books of the time, Wonder Woman hailed from the Amazon and had a magic lasso to get the truth out of criminals.

X-Men Mutant heroes who began life in Marvel comics in 1963; they made it onto the big screen in 2000.

BRITISH TITLES OF NOBILITY

King
Queen
Prince
Princess
Marquess
Marchioness
Duke
Duchess
Earl
Countess
Viscount
Viscountess
Baron
Baroness
Life Baron
Life Baroness

WORLD LEADERS

Afghanistan Mohammad Oman (96), president

Albania Rexhep Mejdani, president (97); Ilir Meta, prime minister (99)

Algeria Abdel-Aziz Bouteflika, president (99); Ahmed Benbitour, prime minister (99)

Andorra Don Marc Forné Molné, prime minister (94)

Angola José Eduardo dos Santos, president (79); Fernando van Dunem, prime minister

Antigua and Barbuda Lester B. Bird, prime minister (94)

Argentina Fernando de la Rúa, president (99)

Armenia Robert Kocharian, president (98); Andranik Markanian, prime minister (00)

Australia Sir William Deane, governor-general (96); John Howard, prime minister (96)

Austria Thomas Klestil, president (92); Wolfgang Schüssel, Chancellor (00)

Azerbaijan Heydar Aliyev, president (93); Artur Rasizade, prime minister (96)

Bahamas Sir Orville Turnquest, governor-general (95); Hubert A. Ingraham, prime minister (92)

Bahrain Isa bin Sulman al-Khalifa, prime minister

Bangladesh Shahbuddin Ahmed, president (96); Ms Sheik Hasina Wazed, prime minister (96)

Barbados Sir Clifford Husbands, governor-general (96); Owen Arthur, prime minister (94)

Belarus Aleksander Lukashenko, president (94); Uladzimir Yarmoshyn, prime minister (00)

Belgium King Albert II; Guy Verhofstadt, prime minister (99)

Belize Sir Corville Norbert Young, governor-general (93); Said Musa, prime minister (98)

Benin Matthieu Kérékou, head of state

Bhutan King Jigme Singye Wangchuk

Bolivia Hugo Banzer Suarez, president (97)

Bosnia and Herzegovina Ante Jelavic, president (99); Alija Izetbegovic and Zivko Radisic, co-prime ministers (99)

Botswana Festus Mogae, president (98)

Brazil Fernando Henrique Cardoso, president (95)

Brunei Sir Hassanal Bolkiah, sultan and prime minister (67)

Bulgaria Petar Stoyanov, president (97); Ivan Kostov, prime minister (97)

Burkina Faso Blaise Compaore, president (91); Paramanga Ernest Yonli, prime minister (00)

Burma (See Myanmar)

Burundi Pierre Buyoya, president (96); Frederic Bamvuginyumvira, prime minister (98)

Cambodia Prince Norodom Sihanouk; Hun Sen, premier (93)

Cameroon Paul Biya, president (88); Peter Manfay Musonga, prime minister (96)

Canada Jean Chrétien, prime minister (93); Adrienne Clarkson, governor-general (99)

Cape Verde Antonio M. Monteiro, president; José Maria Neves, prime minister (01)

Central African Republic Ange Felixe Patassé, head of state (93); Anicet Georges Dologuele, prime minister (99)

Chad Idriss Déby, president (90); Nagoum Yamassoum, prime minister (99)

Chile Ricardo Lagos, president (00)

China Jiang Zemin, president (93); Zhu Rongj, premier (98)

Colombia Andrés Pastrana Arango, president (98)

Comoros Col. Azaly Assoumani, president (99)

Congo, Rep of Denis Sassou-Nguesso, president (97)

Congo, Dem Rep Joseph Kabila, president (01)

Costa Rica Miguel Angel Rodriguez , president (98)

Cote d'Ivoire Gen. Robert Guei, president (99); Seydou Elimane Diarra, prime minister (00)

Croatia Stipe Mesic, president (00); Ivica Racan, prime minister (00)

Cuba Fidel Castro, president and prime minister

Cyprus Glafcos Clerides, president (93)

Czech Republic Vaclav Havel, president (93); Milos Zeman, prime minister (98)

Denmark Queen Margrethe II (72); Poul Nyrup Rasmussen, prime minister (93)

Djibouti Ismail Omar Guellah, president (99); Barkat Gourad Hamadou, prime minister (78)

Dominica Vernon Shaw, president (98); Pierre Charles, prime minister (00)

Dominican Republic Hipolito Mejia, president (00)

Ecuador Gustavo Noboa, president (00)

Egypt Muhammad Hosni Mubarak, president (81); Atef Ebeid, prime minister (99)

El Salvador Francisco Guillermo Flores Pérez, president (99)

Equatorial Guinea Col. Teodoro Obiang Neguema Mbasogo, president (79); Don Agnel-Serafin Seriche Dougan, prime minister (96)

Eritrea Issaias Afwerki, president (93)

Estonia Lennart Meri, president (92); Mart Laar, prime minister (99)

Ethiopia Negasso Gidada, president (95); Meles Zenawi, prime minister (95)

Fiji Commodore Josaia Voreque Bainimarama (Head Interim Military Govt); Ratu Josefa Iloilo, president (interim) (00)

Finland Tarja Halonen, president (00)

France Jacques Chirac, president (95); Lionel Jospin, prime minister (97)

Gabon El Hadj Omar Bonjo, president (67); Jean-François Ntoutoume, premier (99)

The Gambia Col. Yahya Jammeh, president (97)

Georgia Eduard A. Shevardnadze, president (92); Giorgi Arsenistivili, Sec. of state (00)

Germany Johannes Rau, president (99); Gerhard Schroder, chancellor (98)

Ghana John Agyekum Kufuor, president (01)

Greece Constantinos Stephanopoulos, president (95); Costas Simitas, prime minister (96)

Grenada Sir Daniel C. Williams, governor-general (96); Dr. Keith C. Mitchell, prime minister (95)

Guatemala Alfonso Portillo Cabrera, president (00)

Guinea Lansana Conté, president (84); Lamine Sidime, premier (99)

Guinea-Bissau Kumba Yala, president (00); Caetano N'Tchama, prime minister (00)

Guyana Bharrat Jagdeo, president (99); Samuel Hinds, prime minister (97)

Haiti René Preval, president (96); Jacques-Edouard Alexis, prime minister (99)

Honduras Carlos Roberto Flores Facusse, president (98)

Hungary Ferenc Madl, president (00); Viktor Orban, premier (98)

Iceland Olafur Ragnar Grimsson, president (96); David Oddsson, prime minister (91)

India K.R. Narayanan, president (97); Alal Bihari Vajpayee, prime minister (98)

Indonesia Abdurrham Wahid, president (98)

Iran Ayatollah Khameni, Chief of State (89); Seyed Mohammed Khatami, president (97)

Iraq Saddam Hussein, president (79); Ahmed Hussein Khudair, prime minister

Ireland Mary McAleese, president (97); Bertie Ahern, prime minister (97)

Israel Moshe Katzav, president (00; Ariel Sharon, prime minister (01)

Italy Carlo Azeglio Ciampi, president (99); Guiliano Amato, prime minister (00)

Jamaica Howard F.H. Cooke, governor-general (91); Percival James Patterson, prime minister (92)

Japan Emperor Akihito; Yoshiro Mori (00)

Jordan King Abdulla II (99); Ali abu al-Ragheb, prime minister (00)

Kazakhstan Nursultan A. Nazarbaev, president (90); Kasymzhomart Tokayev, prime minister (99)

Kenya Daniet T. Arap Moi, president (78)

Kiribati Terburo Tito, president (94)

Korea, North Kim Il Jong, head of state (94); Hong Song Nam, premier (97)

Korea, South Kim Dae Jung, president (98); Lee Han Dong, prime minister (00)

Kuwait Emir Jaber al-Ahmad al-Javer al-Sabah (77); Saad as-Abdulla al-Salem al-Sabah, prime minister (78)

Krygyzstan Askar A. Akayev, president (90); Kurmanbek Bakiyev, prime minister (00)

Laos Khamtai Siphandon, president (98) Sisavat Keobounphan, prime minister (98)

Latvia Vaira Vike-Freiberga, president (99); Andris Berzins, prime minister (00)

Lebanon Emile Lahoud, president (98); Selim al-Hoss, prime minister (98)

Lesotho King Letsie III (90); Pakalitha Mosisili, prime minister (98)

Liberia Charles Taylor, president (97)

Libya Col. Muammar al-Qaddafi, head of state (69); Mubarek Abdallah al-Shamikh, sec of general people's committee (00)

Liechtenstein Prince Hans-Adam II (89); Mario Frick, prime minister (93)

Lithuania Valdas Adamkus, president (98); Andrius Kubilius, prime minister (99)

Luxembourg Grand Duke Henri (00); Jean-Claude Juncher, premier (95)

Macedonia Boris Trajkovski, president (99); Ljupco Georgievski, prime minister (98)

Madagascar Didier Ratsiraka, president (97); Tantely Andrianarivo, premier (98)

Malawi Elson Bakili Mululizi, president (94

Malaysia Dr. Mahathir Mohamad, prime minister (81)

Maldives Maumoon Abdul Gayoon, president (78)

Mali Alpha Oumar Konaré, president (92); Mande Didibe, prime minister (00)

Malta Guido de Marco, president (00); Eddie Fenech Adami, prime minister (98)

Marshall Islands Kessai H. Note, president (00)

Mauritania Col. Maaouya Ould Sid Ahmed Taya, president (84); Cheikh El Avia Ould Mohamed Khouna, prime minister (96)

Mauritius Cassem Uteem, president (92); Sir Anerood Jugnauth, prime minister (00)

Mexico Vicente Fox Quesada, president (00)

Micronesia Leo A. Falcam, president (99)

Moldova Petro Lucinschi, president (97); Dumitru Braghis, prime minister (99)

Monaco Prince Rainier III (49); Patrick Leclecq, minister of state (00)

Mongolia Natsagiin Bagabandi, president (97); Nambaryn Enkhbayar, prime minister (00)

Morocco King Muhammad VI (99); Abderrahmane El Youssoufi, prime minister (98)

Mozambique Joachim Alberto Chissano, president (86); Dr. Pascoal Manuel Mocumbi, prime minister (94)

Myanmar Gen. Than Shwe, chairman (92)

Namibia Sam Mujoma, president (90); Hage G. Geingob, prime minister (90)

Nauru Bernard Dowiyogo, president (00)

Nepal King Gyanendra Bir Bikram Shah Dev (01); Girija Prasad Koirala, prime minister (00)

Netherlands Queen Beatrix Wilhemina Armgard (80); Wim Kok, prime minister (94)

New Zealand Sir Michael Hardie Boys, governor-general (96); Helen Clark, prime minister (99)

Nicaragua Arnoldo Aleman, president (97)

Niger Tandja Mamadou, president (99); Hama Amadou, prime minister (99)

Norway King Harald V; Jens Stoltenberg, prime minister (00)

Oman Qabus bin Said, sultan and prime minister (70)

Pakistan Gen. Pervez Musharraf, head of state (99); Mohammad Rafiz Tarar, prime minister (98)

Palau Tommy Remengesau, president (01)

Panama Mireya Moscosa, president (99)

Papua New Guinea Silas Atopare, governor-general (97); Mekere Morauta, prime minister (99)

Paraguay Luis Angel Gonzalez Macchi, president (99)

Peru Alberto Fujimori, president (90); Federico Salas Guevara, prime minister (00)

Philippines Gloria Macapagal-Arroyo, president (01)

Poland Aleksander Kwasniewski, president (95); Jerry Buzek, prime minister (97)

Portugal Jorge Sampaio, president (96); Antonio Guterres, prime minister (95)

Qatar Emir Hamad bin Khalifa al-Thani

Romania Ion Iliescu, president (00); Adrian Nastase, prime minister (00)

Russia Vladimir Putin, president (00); Mikhail Kasyanov, prime minister (00)

Rwanda Paul Kagame, president (00); Bernard Makuza, prime minister (00)

Saint Kitts and Nevis Cuthbert Sebastian, governor-general (96); Denzil Douglas, prime minister (95)

Saint Lucia Pearlette Louisy, governor-general (97); Kenny D. Anthony, prime minister (97)

Samoa Malietoa Tanumafili, head of state (62); Tuilaepa Saielele Malielegaoi, prime minister (98)

San Marino Gian Franco Terenzi and Enqo Colombini, Captains Regent (00)

Sao Tome and Principe Miguel dos Anjos da Cunha Trovoada, president; Guilherme Posser da Costa, prime minister (99)

Saudi Arabia King Fahd ibn Abdul-aziz, president

Senegal Abdoulaye Wade, president (00); Mame Madior Boye, prime minister (01)

Serbia and Montenegro (see Yugoslavia)

Seychelles France Albert René, president (82)

Sierra Leone Alhaj Ahmed Tejan Kabbah, president (98)

Singapore S.R. Nathan, president (99); Goh Chok Tong, prime minister (90)

Slovakia Rudolf Schuster, president (99); Mikulas Dzurinda, prime minister (98)

Slovenia Milan Kucan, president of Presidency (90);Andrej Bajuk, prime minister (00)

Solomon Islands John Lapli, governor-general (99); Manasseh Sogavare, prime minister (00)

Somalia Abdiqasim Salad Hassan, president; Ali Khalif Galaid, prime minister (00)

South Africa Thabo Mbeki, president (99)

Spain King Juan Carlos I (75); José Maria Aznar, prime minister (96)

Sri Lanka Chandrika Bandaranaike Kumaratunga, president (94); Ratnasiri Wickremanayake, prime minister (00)

Sudan Lt. Gen. Omer Hassan Ahmed Al Bashir, president (93)

Suriname Ronald Venetiaan, president (00); Jules Ajodhia, prime minister (00)

Swaziland King Mswati III (86); Barbabas Sibusiso Dlamini, prime minister (96)

Sweden King Carl XVI Gustaf (73); Goran Persson, prime minister (96)

Switzerland Moritz Leuenberger, president (01)

Syria Bashar al-Assad, president (00); Muhammad Mustafa Miro, prime minister (00)

Taiwan Chen Shui-bian, president (00); Chan Chun-hsiung, prime minister (00)

Tajikstan Imomali Rakhmonov, president (92); Akil Akilov, prime minister (99)

Tanzania Benhamin William Mkapa, president (95); Frederick Tluway Sumaye, prime minister (95)

Thailand King Bhumibol Adulyadej (46); Thaksin Shinawatra, prime minister (01)

Togo Gen. Gnassingbe Eyadema, president (67); Agbeyome Messan Kodjo, prime minister (00)

Tonga King Taufa'ahau Tupou IV (65); Prince Laraka Ata Ulukalala, prime minister (00)

Trinidad and Tobago A.N.R. Robinson, president (97); Basdeo Panday, prime minister (95)

Tunisia Zine El Abidine Ben Ali, president (87); Mohamed Ghannouchi, prime minister (99)

Turkey Ahmet Necdet Sezer, president (00); Bülent Ecevit, prime minister (99)

Turkmenistan Saparmurad A. Niyazov, president (90)

Tuvalu Tomasi Puapua, governor-general (98); Faimalaga Luka, prime minister (01)

Uganda Yoweri Musevani, president (86); Apolo Nsibambi, prime minister (99)

Ukraine Leonid D. Kuchma, president (94); Viktor Yuschchenko, prime minister (99)

United Arab Emirates Sheik Zayed Bin Sultan Al-Nahyan, president (71); Sheik Maktoum Bin Rashid al-Maktoum, prime minister (90)

United Kingdom Queen Elizabeth II (52); Tony Blair, prime minister (97)

United States George W. Bush, president (00); Richard B. Cheney, vice-president (00)

Uruguay Jorge Batlle, president (00

Uzbekistan Islam A. Karimov, president (90); Otkir Sultonov, prime minister (95)

Vanuatu John Bani, president (99); Barak Sopé, prime minister (99)

Vatican City (Holy See) John Paul II, Supreme Pontiff (78)

Venezuela Hugo Chavez, president (99)

Vietnam Tran Duc Luong, president (97); Phan Van Khai, prime minister (97)

Western Sahara No recognized head of state

Yemen Ali Abdullah Saleh, president; Abdul Karim al-Iryani, prime minister (98)

Yugoslavia Vojislav Kostunica, president (00); Zoran Zizic, prime minister (00)

Zambia Frederick T.J. Chiluba, president (91)

Zimbabwe Robert Mugabe, executive president (87)

PLACES

THE EARTH

DESERTS

AFRICA

Sahara: 3,500,000 square miles
Libyan Desert: 600,000 square miles
Nubian Desert: 100,000 square miles
Kalahari Desert: 200,000 square miles

ASIA

Arabian Desert: 500,000 square miles
    Rub al-Khali: 250,000 square miles
    Syrian Desert: 125,000 square miles
    An Nafud: 50,000 square miles
Gobi Desert: 400,000 square miles
Takla Makan: 125,000 square miles
Kara Kum (Garagum): 105,000 square miles
Thar Desert: 100,000 square miles
Kyzyl Kum (Qyzylqum): 70,000 square miles
Dasht-e-Lut: 20,000 square miles

NORTH AMERICA

Great Basin: 158,000 square miles
Chihuahuan Desert: 140,000 square miles
Sonoran Desert: 120,000 square miles
Mojave Desert: 25,000 square miles
Death Valley: 3,300 square miles

OCEANIA

Australian Desert: 600,000 square miles
    Great Sandy Desert: 160,000 square miles
    Great Victoria Desert: 125,000 square miles

Simpson Desert: 120,000 square miles
Gibson's Desert: 85,000 square miles

SOUTH AMERICA

Patagonian Desert: 260,000 square miles
Atacama Desert: 70,000 square miles

GEOLOGICAL ERAS AND PERIODS

Precambrian Eon: 4.6 billion–570 million
    years ago
Archean Era: 4.6 billion–2.5 billion years ago
Proterozoic Era: 2.5 billion–570 million years ago
Phanerozoic Eon: 570 million years ago–present
Paleozoic Era: 570 million–245 million years ago
Cambrian Period: 570 million–505 million
    years ago
Ordovician Period: 505 million–438 million
    years ago
Silurian Period: 438 million–408 million years ago
Devonian Period: 408 million–360 million years
    ago
Carboniferous Period: 360 million–286 million
    years ago
    Mississippian/Lower Carboniferous: 360
        million–320 million years ago
    Pennsylvanian/Upper Carboniferous: 320
        million–286 million years ago
Permian Period: 286 million–245 million years ago

Mesozoic Era: 245 million–66 million years ago
Triassic Period: 245 million–208 million years ago
  Scythian
  Anisian
  Ladinian
  Karnian
  Norian
  Rhaetian
Jurassic Period: 208 million–144 million years ago
  Hettangian
  Sinemurian
  Pliensbachian
  Toarcian
  Aalenian
  Bajocian
  Bathonian
  Callovian
  Oxfordian
  Kimmeridigian
  Tithonian
Cretaceous Period: 144 million–66 million
  years ago
Cenozoic Era: 66 million years ago–present
Tertiary Period: 66 million–1.6 million years ago
  Paleocene Epoch: 66 million–58 million
    years ago
  Eocene Epoch: 58 million–37 million years ago
  Oligocene Epoch: 37 million–24 million
    years ago
  Miocene Epoch: 24 million–5 million years ago
  Pliocene Epoch: 5 million–1 million years ago
Quaternary Period: 1 million years ago–present
  Pleistocene Epoch: 1 million years ago–10,000
    years ago
  Holocene Epoch: 10,000 years ago–present

ICE AGES

Ice ages listed from most recent to least recent.
Dates are approximate.

Pleistocene/Quaternary

Upper Pleistocene: 10,000–100,000 years ago
  Alps: Würm, Riss-Würm, Riss
  Northern Europe: Weischsel, Eemian, Saale
  North America: Sangamon, Illinoian

Middle Pleistocene: 100,000–450,000 years ago
  Northern and Central Europe: Mindel-Riss,
    Mindel, Günz-Mindel
  North America: Yarmouth, Kansan, Aftonian

Lower Pleistocene: 450,000–1 million years ago
  Northern and Central Europe: Günz, Donau-
    Günz, Donau
  North America: Nebraskan

Permo-Carboniferous: 280 million years ago

Ordovician: 420 million years ago

Precambrian

Varangian: 570 million years ago

Sturtian: 730 million years ago

Gnejso: 890 million years ago

Huronian: 1800–2000 million years ago

ISLANDS

Major islands or island groups with areas of more than 1,000 square miles.

AFRICA

Cape Verde (island group): 1,557 square miles
Madagascar 226,500 square miles

ASIA

Andaman India (island group): 2,500 square miles
Bali Indonesia: 2,171 square miles
Borneo Indonesia: 287,300 square miles
Flores Indonesia: 5,502 square miles
Hainan Dao China: 13,100 square miles
Hokkaido Japan: 32,245 square miles
Honshu Japan: 89,176 square miles
Java Indonesia: 51,038 square miles
Kyushu Japan: 17,129 square miles
Leyte Philippines: 2,785 square miles
Luzon Philippines: 40,420 square miles
Madura Indonesia: 2,113 square miles
Mindanao Philippines: 36,537 square miles
Mindoro Philippines: 3,759 square miles
Moluccas Indonesia: 32,307 square miles
Negros Philippines: 4,907 square miles
New Guinea Indonesia and Papua New Guinea: 316,000 square miles
Palawan Philippines: 4,550 square miles
Panay Philippines: 4,446 square miles
Sakhalin Russia: 29,500 square miles
Samar Philippines: 5,100 square miles
Shikoku Japan: 7,258 square miles
Seram (Ceram) Indonesia: 7,191 square miles
Sri Lanka: 24,900 square miles
Sulawesi (Celebes) Indonesia: 69,255 square miles
Sumatra Indonesia: 163,557 square miles
Taiwan: 13,900 square miles
Timor Indonesia: 5,743 square miles
Wrangel Island Russia: 2,800 square miles

EUROPE

Balearic Islands Spain (island group): 1,927 square miles
Canary Islands Spain (island group): 2,807 square miles
Corsica France: 3,367 square miles
Crete Greece: 3,189 square miles
Cyprus: 3,572 square miles
Euboea Greece: 1,411 square miles
Falkland Islands (island group) U.K.: 4,700 square miles
Franz Josef Land Russia: 8,000 square miles
Gotland Sweden: 1,159 square miles
Great Britain: 88,795 square miles
Greenland Denmark: 840,000 square miles
Hebrides (island group) U.K.: 2,744 square miles
Iceland: 39,800 square miles
Ireland: Irish Republic and Northern Ireland, U.K.: 32,375 square miles
New Caledonia France: 6,530 square miles
North East Land Norway: 6,350 square miles
Novaya Zemlya Russia: 31,900 square miles
Sardinia Italy: 9,301 square miles
Sicily Italy: 9,926 square miles
South Georgia Island U.K.: 1,450 square miles
Svalbard Norway (island group): 23,957 square miles
  Nordaustlandet: 5,410 square miles
  Spitsbergen: 15,260 square miles

NORTH AMERICA

Aleutian Islands U.S. (island group): 6,912 square miles
Anticosti Canada: 3,066 square miles
Axel Heiberg Canada: 16,671 square miles
Banks Island Canada: 27,038 square miles
Baffin Island Canada: 195,928 square miles
Bathurst Island Canada: 6,194 square miles
Cape Breton Island Canada: 3,981 square miles
Cuba: 42,800 square miles
Devon Island Canada: 21,331 square miles
Ellesmere Island Canada: 75,767 square miles
Greenland: 840,000 square miles
Hawaii U.S.: 4,034 square miles
Hispaniola Haiti and Dominican Republic: 29,979 square miles

Jamaica: 4,200 square miles
Kodiak Island U.S.: 3,670 square miles
Long Island U.S.: 1,377 square miles
Melville Island Canada: 16,274 square miles
Newfoundland Canada: 42,031 square miles
Prince Edward Island Canada: 2,185 square miles
Prince of Wales Island Canada: 12,872 square
    miles
Puerto Rico U.S.: 3,500 square miles
Somerset Island Canada: 9,570 square miles
Southampton Island Canada: 15,931 square miles
Unalaska Island U.S.: 1,051 square miles
Unimak Island U.S.: 1,571 square miles
Vancouver Island Canada: 12,079 square miles
Victoria Island Canada: 80,340 square miles

OCEANIA

Bougainville Papua New Guinea: 3,600 square
    miles
Fiji (island group): 7,083 square miles
    Vanua Levu: 2,128 square miles
    Viti Levu: 4,053 square miles
Guadalcanal Solomon Islands: 2,060 square miles
New Britain Papua New Guinea: 14,093 square
    miles
New Caledonia: 6,252 square miles
New Guinea Indonesia and Papua New Guinea:
    316,000 square miles
New Ireland Papua New Guinea: 3,500 square
    miles
North Island New Zealand: 44,332 square miles
Samoa Islands (island group): 1,177 square miles
South Island New Zealand: 58,093 square miles
Tasmania Australia: 26,200 square miles
Vanuatu: 4,707 square miles

SOUTH AMERICA

Galapagos Islands Ecuador (island group): 3,043
    square miles
Marajo Brazil: 15,444 square miles
Tierra del Fuego, Isla Grande de Chile and
    Argentina: 18,600 square miles
Trinidad Trinidad and Tobago: 1,864 square miles

LAKES

Due to seasonal fluctuations, areas may vary and
are approximate. Where area is not available,
length and width are given.

AFRICA

Lake Albert, Uganda, Zaire (also known as Albert
    Nyanza and Lake Mobutu Sese Seko)
Area: 2,065 square miles

Lake Chad, Chad, Cameroon, Nigeria, and Niger
Area: 4,000 to 10,000 square miles (depending on
    the season)

Lake Edward, Zaire, Uganda
Area: 830 square miles

Lake Kariba, Zambia, Zimbabwe (an artificial
    lake created by the Kariba dam)
Length: 175 miles
Maximum width: 25 miles

Lake Nyasa, Malawi, Tanzania, Mozambique
(also   known as Lake Malawi)
Area: 11,000 square miles

Lake Turkana, Kenya, Ethiopia (formerly Lake
    Rudolf)
Area: 2,500 square miles

Lake T'ana, Ethiopia
Area: 1,200 square miles

Lake Tanganyika, Burundi, Tanzania, Zambia,
    Zaire
Area: 12,700 square miles

Lake Victoria, Uganda, Kenya, Tanzania
Area: 26,828 square miles

ASIA

Lake Baikal, Siberian Russia (also known as **Lake Baykal**)
Area: 12,200 square miles

Lake Balqash, Kazakhstan
Area: 6,950 square miles

Laguna de Bay, Philippines
Area: 344 square miles

Lake Biwa, Japan
Area: 260 square miles

Caspian Sea, Azerbaijan, Russia, Kazakhstan, Turkmenistan, Iran (located in both Europe and Asia)
Area: 143,250 square miles

Dead Sea, Israel, Jordan
Area: 405 square miles

Lake Tiberias, Israel (also known as **Sea of Galilee**)
Area: 64 square miles

Lake Urmia, Iran
Area: 1,500 to 2,300 square miles

Van Golü, Turkey (also known as **Lake Van**)
Area: 1,453 square miles

EUROPE

Lake Balaton, Hungary
Area: 260 square miles

Caspian Sea, Azerbaijan, Russia, Kazakhstan, Turkmenistan, Iran (located in both Europe and Asia)
Area: 143,250 square miles

Lake Como, Italy
Area: 56 square miles

Lake Constance, Germany, Switzerland, Austria
Area: 208 square miles

Lake Garda, Italy
Area: 143 square miles

Lake Geneva, Switzerland, France (also known as **Lac Leman**, **Lake Leman**)
Area: 225 square miles

Ijsselmeer, Netherlands
Area: 850 square miles

Lake Inari, Finland
Area: 385 square miles

Loch Katrine, Scotland
Length: 8 miles
Width: 1 mile

Lakes of Killarney, Republic of Ireland
Three lakes: **Lough Leane**, **Muckross Lake**, **Upper Lake** (Lough Leane is the largest, 8 square miles)

Lake Ladoga, Russia
Area: 7,100 square miles

Loch Lomond, Scotland
Area: 27 square miles

Lake of Lucerne, Switzerland
Area: 44 square miles

Lake of Lugano, Switzerland, Italy
Area: 19 square miles

Lake Maggiore, Italy, Switzerland
Area: 82 square miles

Mälaren, Sweden
Area: 440 square miles

Lough Neagh, Northern Ireland
Area: 153 square miles

Loch Ness, Scotland
Area: 22 square miles

Lake of Neuchâtel, Switzerland
Area: 84 square miles

Neusiedler Lake, Austria, Hungary
Length: 20 miles
Width: 4–8 miles

Lake Onega, Russia
Area: 3,800 square miles

Lake Peipus, Russia, Estonia
Area: 1,400 square miles

Lake Saimaa, Finland
Area: 500 square miles

Lake Scutari, Albania, Montenegro
Area: 145 square miles

Lake Trasimeno, Italy (also known as **Lake of Perugia**)
Area: 50 square miles

Lake Vattern, Sweden (also known as **Lake Vatter**)
Area: 738 square miles

Lake of Zürich, Switzerland
Area: 34 square miles

NORTH AMERICA

Lake Athabasca, Canada
Area: 3,064 square miles

Lake Champlain, Canada, U.S.
Area: 431 square miles

Lake Chapala, Mexico
Area: 415 square miles

Crater Lake, U.S.
Area: 20 square miles

Lake Erie, Canada, U.S.
Area: 9,910 square miles

Finger Lakes, U.S. (includes **Lake Canandaigua**, **Lake Keuka**, **Lake Owasco**, **Lake Skaneateles**)
Area: ranges from 3.5 to 67 square miles

Lake George, U.S.
Area: 44 square miles

Great Bear Lake, Canada
Area: 12,028 square miles

Great Salt Lake, U.S.
Area: 1,700 square miles

Great Slave Lake, Canada
Area: 11,031 square miles

Lake Huron, Canada, U.S.
Area: 23,000 square miles

Lake of the Woods, Canada, U.S.
Area: 1,679 square miles

Lake Michigan, U.S.
Area: 22,300 square miles

Lake Misassini, Canada
Area: 902 square miles

Lake Nicaragua, Nicaragua
Area: 3,100 square miles

Lake Okeechobee, U.S.
Area: 730 square miles

Lake Ontario, Canada, U.S.
Area: 7,340 square miles

Reindeer Lake, Canada
Area: 2,568 square miles

Lake Saint Clair, Canada, U.S.
Area: 430 square miles

Salton Sea, U.S.
Area: 450 square miles

Lake Simcoe, Canada
Area: 287 square miles

Lake Superior, Canada, U.S.
Area: 31,700 square miles

Lake Tahoe, U.S.
Area: 193 square miles

Lake Winnipeg, Canada
Area: 9,417 miles

Lake Winnipegosis, Canada
Area: 2,075 square miles

Lake Winnipesaukee, U.S.
Area: 71 square miles

OCEANIA

Lake Eyre, Australia
Area: 3,600 square miles

Lake Taupo, New Zealand
Area: 234 square miles

SOUTH AMERICA

Lake Maracaibo, Venezuela
Area: 5,000 square miles

Lake Titicaca, Peru, Bolivia
Area: 3,500 square miles

LAYERS OF THE EARTH

Lithosphere: 70–100 km from Earth's surface
  Crust
    Upper crust
    Lower crust
  Moho (Mohorovicic discontinuity)
  Upper mantle
Athenosphere: 100–180 km from lithosphere
Mantle: 2900 km from crust
  Upper mantle
  Lower mantle
Core: 3470 km from lower mantle (extends to
    Earth's centre)
  Outer core
  Inner core

MOUNTAIN RANGES

AFRICA

Ahaggar: Algeria
Maximum elevation: 9,852 feet

Atlas: Tunisia, Morocco
Maximum elevation: 13,665 feet

Ruwenzori: Uganda, Zaire
Maximum elevation: 16,762 feet

Tibesti: Chad, Niger, Libya
Maximum elevation: 11,204 feet

ASIA

Altai: Russia, China, Mongolia
Maximum elevation: 14,783 feet

Caucasus: Georgia, Armenia, Azerbaijan, Russia
Maximum elevation: 18,510 feet

Elbruz: Iran
Maximum elevation: 18,376 feet

Himalayas: Pakistan, India, Tibet, Nepal, Bhutan
Maximum elevation: 29,028 feet

Hindu Kush: Afghanistan, Pakistan, Tajikistan
Maximum elevation: 25,230 feet

Karakorum (also known as Karakorum Shan):
 Afghanistan, India, Pakistan
Maximum elevation: 28,250 feet

Kunlun (also known as Kunlun Shan): China
Maximum elevation: 25,340 feet

Tien Shan: Kyrgyzstan, Kazakhstan, China
Maximum elevation: 22,949 feet

Urals: Russia
Maximum elevation: 6,214 feet

Zagros: Iran
Maximum elevation: 14,921 feet

EUROPE

Alps: France, Italy, Austria, Switzerland
Maximum elevation: 15,771 feet

Apennines: Italy
Maximum elevation: 9,560 feet

Balkans: Serbia, Romania, Bulgaria, Macedonia
Maximum elevation: 7,795 feet

Carpathians: Slovakia, Romania, Poland, Czech
 Republic
Maximum elevation: 8,711 feet

Caucasus: Georgia, Armenia, Azerbaijan, Russia
Maximum elevation: 18,510 feet

Pyrenees: France, Spain
Maximum elevation: 11,168 feet

Urals: Russia
Maximum elevation: 6,214 feet

NORTH AMERICA

Alaskan Range: U.S.
Maximum elevation: 20,030 feet

Appalachians: U.S., Canada
Maximum elevation: 6,684 feet

Brooks Range: U.S.
Maximum elevation: 9,020 feet

Cascade Range: U.S., Canada
Maximum elevation: 14,410 feet

Rocky Mountains (also known as the Rockies):
 U.S., Canada
Maximum elevation: 14,433 feet

Sierra Nevada: U.S.
Maximum elevation: 14,494 feet

SOUTH AMERICA

Andes: Argentina, Peru, Chile, Ecuador, Colombia,   Bolivia
Maximum elevation: 22,834 feet

MOUNTAINS

AFRICA

Cameroon, Cameroon: 13,435 feet
Elgon, Kenya–Uganda: 14,178 feet
Karisimbi, Congo–Rwanda: 14,787 feet
Kilimanjaro, Tanzania: 19,340 feet
Kenya (also known as **Kirinyaga**), Kenya: 17,058 feet
Margherita, Uganda–Congo: 16,763 feet
Meru, Tanzania: 14,979 feet
Ras Dashan, Ethiopia: 15,158 feet
Toubkal, Morocco: 13,661 feet

ANTARCTICA

Andrew Jackson: 13,750 feet
Kirkpatrick: 14,855 feet
Markham: 14,290 feet
Sidley: 13,720 feet
Vinson Massif: 16,060 feet
Wade: 13,400 feet

ASIA

Annapurna, Nepal: 26,504 feet
Api, Nepal: 23,399 feet
Ararat, Turkey: 16,804 feet
Chomo Lhari, Bhutan–China: 24,040 feet
Communism Peak, Tajikistan: 24,590 feet
Dhaulagiri, Nepal: 26,810 feet
Everest, Nepal: 29,028 feet
Fuji, Japan: 12,388 feet
Gasherbrum, China–Pakistan: 26,470 feet
Jaya, Indonesia: 16,500 feet
K2 (Qogir Feng), China–Pakistan: 28,250 feet
Kamet, China–India: 25,447 feet
Kanchenjunga, India–Nepal: 28,208 feet
Kerinci, Indonesia: 12,467 feet
Kinabalu, Malaysia: 13,455 feet
Kula Gangri, Bhutan: 24,748 feet
Lenin Peak, China: 23,405 feet
Makalu, China–Nepal: 27,825 feet

Muz Tagh Ata, China: 24,757 feet
Namcha Barwa, China: 25,445
Nanda Devi, India: 25,645 feet
Nanga Parbat, Pakistan: 26,660 feet
Semeru, Indonesia: 12,060 feet
Tirich Mir, Pakistan: 25,230 feet
Trikora, Indonesia: 15,585 feet
Ulugh Muz Tagh, China: 25,340 feet

EUROPE

Aneto, Spain: 11,168 feet
Dykh Tau, Russia: 17,054 feet
Ecrins, France: 13,461 feet
Elbrus, Russia: 18,841 feet
Etna, Italy: 10,902 feet
Finsteraarhorn, Switzerland: 14,022 feet
Jungfrau, Switzerland: 13,642 feet
Matterhorn, Switzerland: 14,692 feet
Mont Blanc, France–Italy: 15,771 feet
Olympus, Greece: 9,570 feet
Perdido, Spain: 11,007 feet
Teide, Canary Islands: 12,198 feet
Vesuvius, Italy: 4,190 feet
Weisshorn, Switzerland: 14,790 feet

NORTH AMERICA

Blanca, U.S.: 14,345 feet
Elbert, U.S.: 14,433 feet
Evans, U.S.: 14,264 feet
Fairweather, U.S.–Canada: 15,300 feet
Foraker, U.S.: 17,400 feet
Grand Teton, U.S.: 13,770 feet
Grays, U.S.: 14,270 feet
Gunnbjorn Fjeld, Greenland: 12,139 feet
Harvard, U.S.: 14,420 feet
Hood, U.S.: 11,239 feet
Iztaccíhuatl, Mexico: 17,343 feet
La Plata, U.S.: 14,361 feet
Logan, Canada: 19,524 feet
Longs, U.S.: 14,255 feet
Lucania, Canada: 17,147 feet
Massive, U.S.: 14,421 feet
Mauna Kea, U.S.: 14,692 feet
Mauna Loa, U.S.: 13,679 feet

McKinley, U.S.: 20,300 feet
Orizaba, Pico de, Mexico (also known as **Citlalte-**
petl): 18,406 feet
Pelée, Martinique: 4,583 feet
Pike's Peak, U.S.: 14,110
Popocatéptl, Mexico: 17,930 feet
Rainier, U.S.: 14,410 feet
Shasta, U.S.: 14,162 feet
Saint Elias, U.S.–Canada: 18,008 feet
Uncompahgre, U.S.: 14,309 feet
Washington, U.S.: 6,288 feet
Whitney, U.S.: 14,494 feet
Williamson, U.S.: 14,375 feet
Wrangel, U.S.: 14,163 feet

OCEANIA

Cook, New Zealand: 12,349 feet
Kosciusko, Australia: 7,310 feet
Wilhelm, Papua New Guinea: 14,793 feet

SOUTH AMERICA

Aconcagua, Argentina: 22,831 feet
Bonete, Argentina: 22,546 feet
Chimborazo, Ecuador: 20,702 feet
Cotopaxi, Ecuador: 19,347 feet
Huascarán, Peru: 22,204 feet
Illampu, Bolivia: 20,873 feet
Illimani, Bolivia: 21,201 feet
Liullaillaco, Argentina–Chile: 22,057
Ojos del Salado, Argentina–Chile: 22,572 feet
Sajama, Bolivia: 21,391 feet
Tupungato, Argentina–Chile: 22,310 feet
Yerupaja, Peru: 21,709 feet

OCEANS

Pacific Ocean	64,000,000 square miles
Atlantic Ocean	31,800,000 square miles
Indian Ocean	28,900,000 square miles
Arctic Ocean	5,400,000 square miles

RIVERS

All lengths are approximate.

AFRICA

Aruwimi, Zaire
Source: Ituri River
Outflow: Shari River
Length: 620 miles

Atbarah, Ethiopia–Sudan
Source: Ethiopian highlands
Outflow: Nile River
Length: 800 miles

Awash, Ethiopia
Source: the plateau on the northern scarp of the
Great Rift Valley, near Addis Ababa
Outflow: Lake Abe
Length: 500 miles

Benue, Cameroon–Nigeria
Source: Adamawa mountain range
Outflow: Niger River
Length: 870 miles

Congo, Zaire
Source: Lualaba River
Outflow: Atlantic Ocean
Length: 2,716 miles

Gambia, Senegal–Gambia
Source: Fouta Djallon mountain range in Senegal
Outflow: Atlantic Ocean
Length: 700 miles

Juba, Ethiopia–Somalia
Source: confluence of the Genale Dorya and the
    Dawa Rivers in the mountains of southern
    Ethiopia
Outflow: Indian Ocean
Length: 545 miles

Kasai, Angola–Zaire
Source: a plateau in northeastern Angola
Outflow: Congo River
Length: 1,338 miles

Limpopo, Zimbabwe–South Africa–Mozambique
Source: near Krugersdorp in South Africa
Outflow: Indian Ocean
Length: 1,100 miles

Lomami, Zaire
Source: the central region of the Katanga
    Highlands
Outflow: Congo River
Length: 800 miles

Niger, Guinea–Mali–Niger–Nigeria
Source: Fouta Djallon Mountains near the border
    of Sierra Leone
Outflow: Gulf of Guinea, Atlantic Ocean
Length: 2,590 miles

Nile, East Africa–North Africa
Source: Lake Victoria
Outflow: Mediterranean Sea
Length: 4,132 miles

Okavango, Angola–Namibia
Source: Bie Plateau in the central region of Angola
Outflow: Okovango Marshes near Lake Ngami
Length: 1,000 miles

Orange, South Africa
Source: Drakensberg Mountains
Outflow: Atlantic Ocean
Length: 1300 miles

Senegal, Mali–Mauritania–Senegal
Source: confluence of the Bafing and Bakoy Rivers
    at Bafoulabé
Outflow: Atlantic Ocean
Length: 1,015 miles

Shari, Chad
Source: junction of the Bamingui and Gubingui
    Rivers at the Ubangi–Shari Plateau
Outflow: Lake Chad
Length: 590 miles

Ubangi, Central African Republic–Zaire
Source: confluence of the Bomu and Uele Rivers
in   the highlands north of Lake Albert
Outflow: Congo River
Length: 1,400 miles (including the Uele River)

Volta, Upper Volta–Ghana
Source: confluence of the Black Volta and White
    Volta in northern Ghana
Outflow: Gulf of Guinea, Atlantic Ocean
Length: 710 miles

Zambezi, Angola–Zambia–Zimbabwe–
    Mozambique
Source: a corner of Angola, bordering Zaire and
    Zambia
Outflow: Indian Ocean
Length: 1,700 miles

ASIA

Adonis, Lebanon (also known as **Nahr Ibrahim**)
Source: Central Lebanon
Outflow: Mediterranean Sea
Length: 14 miles

Aldan, Siberia
Source: Stanovoi Range
Outflow: Lena River
Length: 1,767 miles

Amu Darya, central Asia–Afghanistan (known in the ancient world as the **Oxus**)
Source: confluence of the Pyandzh and Vaksh head-streams, which flow down from the Himalayas
Outflow: Aral Sea
Length: 872 miles

Amur, northeast Asia–China
Source: confluence of the Shilka and Argun Rivers
Outflow: Tatar Strait of the Sea of Okhotsk and the Sea of Japan
Length: 1,767 miles

Aras, Turkey
Source: Bingol Dag, in Turkish Armenia
Outflow: Kura River, and the Caspian Sea
Length: 550 miles

Brahmaputra, China–India–Bangladesh (also known as **Tsing Po**)
Source: a glacier near the Tibetan mountain pass of Mariam La
Outflow: Bay of Bengal
Length: 1,800 miles

Cagayan, Philippines
Source: mountains of northern Luzon
Outflow: Babuyan Channel of the Luzon Strait
Length: 220 miles

Cauvery, India (also known as **Kaveri**)
Source: Brahmagiri Hill in the Western Ghats
Outflow: Bay of Bengal
Length: 475 miles

Chambal, India
Source: Vindhya Range
Outflow: Yamuna (or Jumna) River
Length: 550 miles

Chao Phraya, Thailand
Source: hills of northern Thailand
Outflow: Gulf of Siam
Length: 140 miles

Chenab, Pakistan
Source: Great Himalayas
Outflow: Panjnad River
Length: 650 miles

Chindwin, Burma
Source: Patkai and Kumon mountain ranges
Outflow: Irrawaddy River
Length: 500 miles

Chulym, Siberia
Source: Kuznetsk Alatau Range
Outflow: Ob River
Length: 1,177 miles

Euphrates, western Asia
Source: mountains north of Erzurum, Turkey
Outflow: Persian Gulf
Length: 2,235 miles

Ganges, India
Source: town of Devaprayag in northern India
Outflow: Bay of Bengal
Length: 1,550 miles

Godavari, India
Source: Western Ghats
Outflow: Bay of Bengal
Length: 900 miles

Gogra, Tibet, Nepal, India (also known as the **Ghagra** or **Chagra**)
Source: Great Himalayas
Outflow: Ganges River
Length: 600 miles

Helmand, Afghanistan
Source: Paghman Mountains
Outflow: Sistan (or Seistan) Lake depression
Length: 700 miles

Hooghly, India (an arm of the **Ganges** delta)
Source: confluence of the Bhagirathi and Jalangi Rivers
Outflow: Bay of Bengal
Length: 160 miles

Huang Ho, China (also known as the **Hwang Ho**, **Hoang Ho**, or **Yellow River**)
Source: highlands of Tsinghai
Outflow: Gulf of Chihli, Yellow Sea
Length: 2,900 miles

Ili, China, Kazakhstan
Source: Tien Shan Mountains
Outflow: Lake Balkhash
Length: 540 miles

Indigirka, Siberia
Source: Oymyakon Plateau
Outflow: East Siberian Sea
Length: 1,113 miles

Indus, Tibet, Pakistan
Source: Kailas Range
Outflow: Arabian Sea
Length: 1,800 miles

Irrawaddy, Burma
Source: confluence of the Mali Hka and the Nmai
    Hka in the forests on the border between
    Burma and China
Outflow: Andaman Sea
Length: 1,300 miles

Irtysh, Siberia
Source: Altai Mountains in the Sinkiang Province
    of China
Outflow: Ob River
Length: 2,640 miles, including the Black Irtysh

Jordan, Israel
Source: various headstreams in the Hula Basin
Outflow: Dead Sea
Length: 200 miles

Kabul, Afghanistan, Pakistan
Source: Paghman Mountains
Outflow: Indus River
Length: 320 miles

Kan, China
Source: confluence of the Kung Shui and Chang
    Sui in Kiangsi Province
Outflow: Yangtze River
Length: 540 miles

Karun, Iran
Source: Zardeh Kuh Mountain
Outflow: Shatt al Arab, Persian Gulf
Length: 470 miles

Kerulen, Mongolia
Source: Henteyn Mountains
Outflow: Lake Dalai
Length: 785 miles

Kishon, Israel (also known as the **Qishon**)
Source: Mount Gilboa
Outflow: Bay of Haifa
Length: 45 miles

Kistna, India (also known as the **Krishna**)
Source: Western Ghats
Outflow: Bay of Bengal
Length: 800 miles

Kolyma, Siberia
Source: Cherskiy Range
Outflow: East Siberian Sea
Length: 1,335 miles

Kura, Turkey, Asian Russia
Source: eastern mountains of Turkey
Outflow: Caspian Sea
Length: 940 miles

Lena, Siberia
Source: Baykal Range
Outflow: Laptev Sea
Length: 2,650 miles

Luni, India
Source: Aravalli Range
Outflow: Arabian Sea
Length: 330 miles

Mahanadi, India
Source: Eastern Ghats
Outflow: Bay of Bengal
Length: 560 miles

Mahaweli Ganga, Sri Lanka
Source: Hatton Plateau
Outflow: Koddiyar Bay, Indian Ocean
Length: 206 miles

Mekong, Southeast Asia
Source: Tanglha Range in the province of Tsinghai
Outflow: South China Sea
Length: 2,500 miles

Menderes, Turkey
Source: Anatolian Plateau
Outflow: Aegean Sea
Length: 250 miles

Narmada, India
Source: Maikal Hills
Outflow: Arabian Sea
Length: 775 miles

Ob, Siberia
Source: Altai mountain range
Outflow: Ob Bay, Kara Sea, Atlantic Ocean
Length: 2,287 miles

Orhon, Mongolia
Source: Khangai Mountains
Outflow: Selenge River
Length: 700 miles

Orontes, Lebanon, Syria (also known as the **Nahr el Asi**)
Source: springs west of Baalbek in the Bekaa Valley
Outflow: Mediterranean Sea
Length: 355 miles

Salween, Tibet, China, Burma
Source: Tanglha Range in eastern Tibet
Outflow: Gulf of Martaban, Andaman Sea
Length: 1,750 miles

Sarda, Nepal, India
Source: Himalayas
Outflow: Gogra River
Length: 310 miles

Selenge, Mongolia
Source: confluence of the Ideriin and Mörön Rivers
Outflow: Lake Baykal
Length: 980 miles (including Ider River)

Subarnarekha, India
Source: Chotanagpur Plateau
Outflow: Bay of Bengal
Length: 290 miles

Sungari, China
Source: Changpai Mountains
Outflow: Amur River
Length: 1,150 miles

Sutlej, Pakistan
Source: Mount Kailas
Outflow: Panjnad River
Length: 850 miles

Syr Darya, Kyrgyzstan, Uzbekistan, Tajikistan, Kazakhstan
Source: Tien Shan Mountains
Outflow: Aral Sea
Length: 1,660 miles

Tapi, India
Source: Mahadeo Hills, Madhya Pradesh
Outflow: Gulf of Khambhat, Arabian Sea
Length: 450 miles

Tarim, China
Source: Karakoram mountain range
Outflow: Lop Nor Lake
Length: 1,300 miles

Tigris, southwestern Asia
Source: Lake Golcuk, Turkey
Outflow: Persian Gulf
Length: 1,180 miles

Tobol, Siberia
Source: Mugodzhary Mountains
Outflow: Irtysh River
Length: 1,042 miles

Tungabhadra, India
Source: Western Ghats
Outflow: Kistna River
Length: 400 miles

Tunguska, Lower, Siberia
Source: south Central Siberian Plateau
Outflow: Yenisey River
Length: 1,671 miles

Tunguska, Stony, Siberia
Source: Central Siberian Plateau
Outflow: Yenisey River
Length: 962 miles

Ural, Russia
Source: Ural Mountains
Outflow: Caspian Sea
Length: 1,575 miles

Yalu, China
Source: Changpai Mountains
Outflow: Korea Bay, Yellow Sea
Length: 500 miles

Yangtze, China
Source: Tanglha Range
Outflow: East China Sea
Length: 3,434 miles

Yenisey, Siberia
Source: confluence of the Bol'shoy (Great)
Yenisey   and Malyy (Little) Yenisey
Rivers at Kyzyl
Outflow: Kara Sea
Length: 2,566 miles

EUROPE

Aare, Switzerland
Source: Bernese Oberland
Outflow: Rhine River
Length: 180 miles

Adda, Italy
Source: Rhaetian Alps
Outflow: Po River
Length: 150 miles

Adige, Italy
Source: three small alpine lakes south of the
Passo di Resia where Italy, Switzerland,
and Austria meet
Outflow: Adriatic Sea
Length: 225 miles

Aisne, France
Source: western Lorraine
Outflow: Oise River
Length: 165 miles

Angerman, Sweden
Source: mountains near the Sweden–Norway
border
Outflow: Gulf of Bothnia
Length: 280 miles

Avon (Lower), Gloucestershire, England
Source: Northampton highlands
Outflow: Severn River
Length: 75 miles

Avon (Upper), Northamptonshire, England
Source: Cotswold Hills
Outflow: Severn River
Length: 95 miles

Berezina, Belarus
Source: Belarus uplands
Outflow: Dnepr River
Length: 365 miles

Blackwater, Ireland
Source: County Kerry
Outflow: Atlantic Ocean
Length: 90 miles

Boyne, Ireland
Source: near Edenderry in County Kildare
Outflow: Irish Sea
Length: 62 miles

Brenta, Italy
Source: two Alpine lakes, the Caldonazzo and
Levico
Outflow: Adriatic Sea
Length: 100 miles

Bug (Southern), Ukraine
Source: Volyno–Podolsk uplands
Outflow: Black Sea
Length: 533 miles

Bug (Western), Ukraine, Poland
Source: Volyno–Podolsk uplands
Outflow: Baltic Sea
Length: 484 miles

Cam, England
Source: northwestern Essex
Outflow: Great Ouse River
Length: 40 miles

Clyde, Scotland
Source: confluence of the Daer Water and the
  Potrail Water in the Scottish Borders
Outflow: Firth of Clyde
Length: 80 miles

Dal, Sweden
Source: confluence of the Osterdal and Vasterdal
  Rivers on the Norwegian border
Outflow: Gulf of Bothnia
Length: 330 miles

Danube, Europe
Source: confluence of the Brigach and Breg Rivers
  in southwestern Germany
Outflow: Black Sea
Length: 1,750 miles

Dart, England
Source: Dartmoor
Outflow: English Channel
Length: 46 miles

Dee, Scotland
Source: Pools of Dee in the Cairngorm mountain
  range
Outflow: North Sea
Length: 90 miles

Dee, Wales
Source: the base of Mount Dduallt
Outflow: Irish Sea
Length: 110 miles

Derwent, England
Source: Fylingdales Moor
Outflow: River Ouse
Length: 70 miles

Dnepr, Ukraine, Russia
Source: Valday Hills
Outflow: Black Sea
Length: 1,420 miles

Dnestr, Ukraine, Moldova
Source: Carpathian Mountains
Outflow: Black Sea
Length: 877 miles

Don, Russia
Source: Central Russian upland
Outflow: Sea of Azov
Length: 1,224 miles

Donets, Russia
Source: Central Russian upland
Outflow: Don River
Length: 631 miles

Dordogne, France
Source: Mont-Dore
Outflow: Garonne River
Length: 290 miles

Douro, Spain, Portugal
Source: Iberic mountain range
Outflow: Atlantic Ocean
Length: 490 miles

Dove, England
Source: Axe Edge, south of Buxton (border of
  Derbyshire and Staffordshire)
Outflow: Trent River
Length: 48 miles

Drava, central Europe
Source: Carnic Alps
Outflow: Danube River
Length: 450 miles

Dvina, Northern, northern European Russia
Source: confluence of Yug and Sukhona Rivers
Outflow: Dvina Gulf, White Sea
Length: 466 miles

Dvina, Western, Russia, Latvia (also known as the **Daugava**)
Source: Valday Hills
Outflow: Gulf of Riga, Baltic Sea
Length: 634 miles

Earn, Scotland
Source: western Perthshire
Outflow: Tay River
Length: 55 miles

Ebro, Spain
Source: Cantabrian Mountains
Outflow: Mediterranean Sea
Length: 580 miles

Elbe, central Europe
Source: Riesengebirge mountain range
Outflow: North Sea
Length: 706 miles

Elster, White, Czech Republic, Germany
Source: Smrciny region
Outflow: Saale River
Length: 153 miles

Erne, Republic of Ireland
Source: hills of central Country Cavan
Outflow: Atlantic Ocean
Length: 72 miles

Esk, Scotland, England
Source: confluence of the Black Esk and White Esk
Outflow: Solway Firth, Irish Sea
Length: 23 miles

Exe, England
Source: Somerset
Outflow: English Channel
Length: 54 miles

Forth, Scotland
Source: Ben Lomond
Outflow: North Sea
Length: 104 miles

Foyle, Northern Ireland, Republic of Ireland
Source: confluence of the Finn and Mourne Rivers near the town of Strabane
Outflow: Lough Foyle
Length: 24 miles

Garonne, Spain, France
Source: central Pyrenees Mountains
Outflow: Gironde Estuary
Length: 400 miles

Glåma, Norway (also known as the **Glomma**)
Source: east central Norway
Outflow: Skagerrak Strait
Length: 380 miles

Guadalquivir, Spain
Source: Sierra Morena
Outflow: Gulf of Cadiz, Atlantic Ocean
Length: 420 miles

Guadiana, Spain, Portugal
Source: La Mancha plateau
Outflow: Gulf of Cadiz, Atlantic Ocean
Length: 515 miles

Havel, Germany
Source: Mecklenburg Lake region
Outflow: Elbe River
Length: 215 miles

Inn, central Europe
Source: Graubünden, Switzerland
Outflow: Danube River
Length: 320 miles

Isar, Austria, Germany
Source: Karwendelgebirge, northern Austria
Outflow: Danube River
Length: 163 miles

Júcar, Spain
Source: Sierra de Albarracin
Outflow: Gulf of Valencia, Mediterranean Sea
Length: 310 miles

Kama, Russia
Source: central Ural Mountains
Outflow: Volga River
Length: 1,262 miles

Kemi, Finland
Source: confluence of the Kitinen, Kemihaara, and
    Luiro Rivers in the Lapland fells
Outflow: Gulf of Bothnia
Length: 300 miles

Kokemäen, Finland (also known as the
    Kokemäki)
Source: outlet for Nasijärvi Lake
Outflow: Gulf of Bothnia
Length: 90 miles

Kymi, Finland
Source: Paijanne lake system
Outflow: Gulf of Finland
Length: 90 miles

Lee, Ireland
Source: Derrynasagerat Mountains
Outflow: Laptev Sea, Atlantic Ocean
Length: 60 miles

Liffey, Ireland
Source: hills in County Wicklow
Outflow: Irish Sea
Length: 70 miles

Loire, France
Source: Massif Central
Outflow: Bay of Biscay
Length: 625 miles

Lune, England
Source: northern Pennines
Outflow: Irish Sea
Length: 55 miles

Main, Germany
Source: confluence of the Red and White Main
    Rivers at the town of Mainleus
Outflow: Rhine River
Length: 307 miles

Marne, France
Source: Plateau of Langres
Outflow: Seine River
Length: 325 miles

Medway, England
Source: the Weald
Outflow: Thomas Estuary
Length: 70 miles

Mersey, England
Source: confluence of the Goyt and Tame Rivers
Outflow: Irish Sea
Length: 70 miles

Mesta, Bulgaria, Greece
Source: Rila Mountains
Outflow: Aegean Sea
Length: 150 miles

Meuse, France, Belgium, Netherlands
Source: southern Lorraine
Outflow: North Sea
Length: 580 miles

Mezen, Russia
Source: Timan Hills
Outflow: White Sea
Length: 533 miles

Mures, Romania, Hungary (also known as the
    Marisus or **Maros**)
Source: Carpathian Mountains
Outflow: Tisza River
Length: 550 miles

Neckar, Germany
Source: Black Forest
Outflow: Rhine River
Length: 228 miles

Neisse, Glatzer, Czech Republic
Source: Sudeten Mountains
Outflow: Oder River
Length: 121 miles

Neisse, Lusatian, Czech Republic, Poland, Germany (also known as the **Gorlitzer Neisse**)
Source: Isergebirge, Czech Republic
Outflow: Oder River
Length: 140 miles

Neman, Belarus, Lithuania
Source: Belarus southwest of Minsk
Outflow: Baltic Sea
Length: 597 miles

Numedalslagen, Norway
Source: Hardangervidda
Outflow: Larvik Fjord, Skagerrak
Length: 190 miles

Oder, Czech Republic, Poland
Source: Oder Mountains
Outflow: Baltic Sea
Length: 563 miles

Oise, Belgium, France
Source: Ardennes plateau, Belgium
Outflow: Seine River
Length: 190 miles

Oka, western Russia
Source: south of Orël
Outflow: Volga River
Length: 918 miles

Onega, northwestern European Russia
Source: Lake Lacha
Outflow: White Sea
Length: 252 miles

Oulu, Finland
Source: Lake Oulu
Outflow: Gulf of Bothnia
Length: 65 miles

Ouse, England
Source: confluence of the Swale and Ure Rivers
Outflow: Humber River
Length: 61 miles

Pechora, northwestern European Russia
Source: Ural Mountains
Outflow: Pechora Gulf, Barents Sea
Length: 1,110 miles

Piniós, Greece
Source: Pindus Mountains
Outflow: Aegean Sea
Length: 135 miles

Po, Italy
Source: Cottian Alps
Outflow: Adriatic Sea
Length: 405 miles

Prut, Ukraine, Moldova, Romania
Source: Carpathian Mountains
Outflow: Danube River
Length: 600 miles

Rheidol, Wales
Source: hills in Cardiganshire
Outflow: Cardigan Bay, Irish Sea
Length: 24 miles

Rhine, Switzerland, Austria, France, Germany, Netherlands
Source: Hinter Rhine and Vorder Rhine in the Alps
Outflow: North Sea
Length: 820 miles

Rhône, France
Source: central Alps
Outflow: Mediterranean Sea
Length: 510 miles

Ribble, England
Source: Gayle Moor, North Yorkshire
Outflow: Irish Sea
Length: 100 miles

Ruhr, Germany
Source: northern slopes of the Sauerland
Outflow: Rhine at port of Ruhrort
Length: 130 miles

Saale, Saxonian, Germany
Source: Fichtelgebirge
Outflow: Elbe River
Length: 265 miles

Saar, France, Germany
Source: Vosges Mountains
Outflow: Moselle River
Length: 150 miles

Saône, France
Source: Vosges Mountains
Outflow: Rhône River at Lyons
Length: 300 miles

Sava, Slovenia, Croatia, Bosnia-Herzegovina,
    Serbia
Source: Julian Alps
Outflow: the Danube at Belgrade
Length: 583 miles

Scheldt, France, Belgium, Netherlands
Source: Picardy, France
Outflow: North Sea
Length: 270 miles

Seine, France
Source: Plateau of Langres
Outflow: English Channel
Length: 470 miles

Severn, Wales, England
Source: Plynlimon Fawr, central Wales
Outflow: Bristol Channel
Length: 200 miles

Shannon, Ireland
Source: County Cavan
Outflow: Atlantic Ocean
Length: 161 miles

Somme, France
Source: Picardy
Outflow: English Channel
Length: 150 miles

Spey, Scotland
Source: Monadhliath Mountains
Outflow: Moray Firth
Length: 100 miles

Spree, Germany
Source: Lusatian Mountains
Outflow: Havel River
Length: 250 miles

Struma, Bulgaria, Greece
Source: Vitosha Mountains
Outflow: Aegean Sea
Length: 215 miles

Taff, Wales
Source: confluence of the Great Taf and Little Taf
    in Breconshire
Outflow: Severn River at Cardiff
Length: 40 miles

Tagus, Spain, Portugal
Source: Teurel Province
Outflow: Atlantic Ocean
Length: 625 miles

Tay, Scotland
Source: Perthshire
Outflow: Firth of Tay
Length: 120 miles

Tees, England
Source: Pennine Mountains
Outflow: North Sea
Length: 96 miles

Teifi, Wales
Source: Cambrian Mountains
Outflow: Irish Sea
Length: 55 miles

Teviot, Scotland
Source: western Roxburghshire
Outflow: Tweed River
Length: 38 miles

Thames, England
Source: Seven Springs
Outflow: North Sea
Length: 209 miles

Tiber, Italy
Source: Etruscan Apennines
Outflow: Tyrrhenian Sea
Length: 251 miles

Tisza, Ukraine, Romania, Hungary, Serbia
Source: Carpathian Mountains
Outflow: Danube
Length: 800 miles

Torne, Finland, Sweden
Source: Lake Torne
Outflow: Gulf of Bothnia
Length: 250 miles

Towy, Wales (also known as the **Tywi**)
Source: Cambrian Mountains
Outflow: Bay of Carmarthen
Length: 65 miles

Trent, England
Source: Staffordshire
Outflow: Humber River
Length: 168 miles

Tweed, England, Scotland
Source: Tweed's Well
Outflow: North Sea
Length: 97 miles

Tyne, England
Source: Northumberland
Outflow: North Sea
Length: 80 miles

Vardar, Macedonia
Source: Shar Mountains
Outflow: Gulf of Salonika, Aegean Sea
Length: 230 miles

Vistula, Poland
Source: Beskid Mountains
Outflow: Baltic Sea
Length: 678 miles

Volga, Russia
Source: Valday Hills
Outflow: Caspian Sea
Length: 2,292 miles

Vuoski, Finland, Russia
Source: Lake Saimaa
Outflow: Lake Ladoga
Length: 93 miles

Warta, Poland, Germany
Source: Carpathian Mountains
Outflow: Oder River
Length: 445 miles

NORTH AMERICA

Alabama, U.S.
Source: confluence of the Coosa and Tallapoosa
    Rivers
Outflow: Tombigbee River
Length: 305 miles

Albany, Canada
Source: Lake St. Joseph
Outflow: James Bay
Length: 320 miles

Allegheny, U.S.
Source: Allegheny Plateau
Outflow: Ohio River
Length: 325 miles

Androscoggin, U.S.
Source: Rangelely, Richardson, and Umbagog
    Lakes
Outflow: Merrymeeting Bay
Length: 175 miles

Arkansas, U.S.
Source: Rocky Mountains
Outflow: Mississippi River
Length: 1,450 miles

Assiniboine, Canada
Source: eastern Saskatchewan
Outflow: Red River of the North
Length: 450 miles

Attawapiskat, Canada
Source: Lake Attawapiskat
Outflow: James Bay
Length: 465 miles

Back, Canada
Source: Contwoyto Lake
Outflow: Chantrey Inlet
Length: 600 miles

Balsas, Mexico
Source: Tlaxcala State
Outflow: Pacific Ocean
Length: 450 miles

Big Sioux, U.S.
Source: northeastern South Dakota
Outflow: Missouri River
Length: 420 miles

Bow, Canada
Source: Rocky Mountains
Outflow: South Saskatchewan River
Length: 315 miles

Brazos, U.S.
Source: confluence of the Salt and Double
       Mountain Forks
Outflow: Gulf of Mexico
Length: 870 miles

Canadian, U.S.
Source: Sangre de Cristo Mountains
Outflow: Arkansas River
Length: 900 miles

Cape Fear, U.S.
Source: confluence of the Deep and Haw Rivers
Outflow: Atlantic Ocean
Length: 200 miles

Catawba, U.S.
Source: south of Mount Mitchell
Outflow: Santee River
Length: 295 miles

Chagres, Panama
Source: Cordillera de San Blas
Outflow: Caribbean Sea
Length: 30 miles

Chattahoochee, U.S.
Source: Great Smoky Mountains
Outflow: Apalachicola River
Length: 436 miles

Cheyenne, U.S.
Source: eastern Wyoming
Outflow: Missouri River
Length: 527 miles

Churchill, Canada
Source: Methy Lake
Outflow: Hudson Bay
Length: 1,000 miles

Cimarron, U.S.
Source: northeastern New Mexico
Outflow: Arkansas River
Length: 692 miles

Clark Fork, U.S.
Source: near Butte, Montana, on the Continental
       Divide
Outflow: Pend Oreille Lake, then as the Pend
       Oreille River to the Columbia River
Length: 499 miles (including the Pend Oreille
       River)

Coco, Central America
Source: mountain ranges between Honduras and
       Nicaragua
Outflow: Caribbean Sea
Length: 300 miles

Colorado, U.S.
Source: Grand County, Colorado on the
       Continental Divide
Outflow: Gulf of California, Pacific Ocean
Length: 1,360 miles

Colorado (Texas), U.S.
Source: Llano Estacado
Outflow: Gulf of Mexico
Length: 970 miles

Columbia, U.S., Canada
Source: Rocky Mountains, British Columbia
Outflow: Pacific Ocean
Length: 1,200 miles

Conchos, Mexico
Source: Sierra Madre de Occidente
Outflow: Rio Grande
Length: 350 miles

Connecticut, U.S.
Source: Connecticut Lakes, New Hampshire
Outflow: Long Island Sound, Atlantic Ocean
Length: 345 miles

Coppermine, Canada
Source: Lac de Gras
Outflow: Coronation Gulf, Arctic Ocean
Length: 525 miles

Cumberland, U.S.
Source: Cumberland Plateau, Kentucky
Outflow: Ohio River
Length: 720 miles

Delaware, U.S.
Source: confluence of the East and West Branches in the Catskill Mountains
Outflow: Delaware Bay, Atlantic Ocean
Length: 390 miles

Des Moines, U.S.
Source: Lake Shetek, Minnesota
Outflow: Mississippi River
Length: 535 miles

Fraser, Canada
Source: near Mount Robson on the Continental Divide
Outflow: Georgia Strait, Pacific Ocean
Length: 850 miles

Gila, U.S.
Source: Elk Mountains, New Mexico
Outflow: Colorado River
Length: 630 miles

Great Whale, Canada
Source: Lake Bienville, Quebec
Outflow: Hudson Bay
Length: 230 miles

Green, U.S.
Source: Wind River Range on the Continental Divide
Outflow: Colorado River
Length: 730 miles

Grijalva, Guatemala, Mexico
Source: Sierra Madre
Outflow: Usumacinta River
Length: 200 miles

Hudson, U.S.
Source: Adirondack Mountains
Outflow: New York Bay, Atlantic Ocean
Length: 315 miles

Humboldt, U.S.
Source: Ruby Mountains
Outflow: Humboldt Sink
Length: 300 miles

Illinois, U.S.
Source: confluence of the Des Plaines and Kankakee Rivers
Outflow: Mississippi River
Length: 273 miles

James, U.S.
Source: confluence of the Jackson and Cowpasture Rivers
Outflow: Chesapeake Bay, Atlantic Ocean
Length: 340 miles

Kansas, U.S.
Source: confluence of the Republican and Smoky Hill Rivers
Outflow: Missouri River
Length: 170 miles

Klamath, U.S.
Source: Upper Klamath Lake, Oregon
Outflow: Pacific Ocean
Length: 250 miles

Koksoak, Canada
Source: confluence of the Larch and Caniapiskau
    Rivers
Outflow: Ungava Bay, Hudson Strait
Length: 90 miles

Kootenay, U.S., Canada (also known as **Kootenai**)
Source: southeastern British Columbia
Outflow: Columbia River
Length: 448 miles

Liard, Canada
Source: Yukon Territory
Outflow: Mackenzie River
Length: 570 miles

Little Bighorn, U.S.
Source: Bighorn Mountains
Outflow: Bighorn River
Length: 90 miles

Mackenzie, Canada
Source: Great Slave Lake
Outflow: Mackenzie Bay
Length: 1,060 miles

Merrimack, U.S.
Source: confluence of the Winnipesaukee and
    Pemigewasset Rivers
Outflow: Atlantic Ocean
Length: 110 miles

Milk, U.S., Canada
Source: northwestern Montana
Outflow: Missouri River
Length: 625 miles

Minnesota, U.S.
Source: Big Stone Lake
Outflow: Mississippi River
Length: 332 miles

Mississippi, U.S.
Source: Lake Itasca, Minnesota
Outflow: Gulf of Mexico
Length: 2,348 miles

Missouri, U.S.
Source: confluence of the Jefferson, Madison, and
    Gallatin Rivers in western Montana
Outflow: Mississippi River
Length: 2,466 miles

Mohawk, U.S.
Source: near Rome, New York
Outflow: Hudson River
Length: 140 miles

Neches, U.S.
Source: Sandy Hills, Texas
Outflow: Sabine Lake
Length: 416 miles

Nelson, Canada
Source: Lake Winnipeg
Outflow: Hudson Bay
Length: 410 miles

Neuse, U.S.
Source: confluence of the Flat and Eno Rivers in
    North Carolina
Outflow: Atlantic Ocean
Length: 275 miles

Nueces, U.S.
Source: Edwards Plateau, Texas
Outflow: Gulf of Mexico
Length: 315 miles

Ohio, U.S.
Source: confluence of the Allegheny and
    Monongahela Rivers in Pennsylvania
Outflow: Mississippi River
Length: 981 miles

Osage, U.S.
Source: confluence of the Marais des Cygnes and
    Little Osage Rivers in Kansas
Outflow: Missouri River
Length: 500 miles

Ottawa, Canada
Source: Hudson Bay and St. Lawrence drainage
area
Outflow: St. Lawrence River
Length: 696 miles

Ouachita, U.S.
Source: Ouachita Mountains, Arkansas
Outflow: Red River
Length: 605 miles

Peace, Canada
Source: Stikine Mountains
Outflow: Slave River
Length: 1,054 miles

Pearl, U.S.
Source: Red Hills, Mississippi
Outflow: Gulf of Mexico
Length: 485 miles

Pecos, U.S.
Source: Sangre de Cristo Mountains, New Mexico
Outflow: Rio Grande
Length: 926 miles

Penobscot, U.S.
Source: western Maine
Outflow: Penobscot Bay, Atlantic Ocean
Length: 350 miles

Platte, U.S.
Source: confluence of the North and South Platte
Rivers
Outflow: Missouri River
Length: 310 miles

Potomac, U.S.
Source: Meadow Mountain, West Virginia
Outflow: Chesapeake Bay, Atlantic Ocean
Length: 290 miles

Powder, U.S.
Source: Bighorn Mountains, Wyoming
Outflow: Yellowstone River
Length: 486 miles

Rappahannock, U.S.
Source: Manassas Gap, Blue Ridge Mountains
Outflow: Chesapeake Bay, Atlantic Ocean
Length: 185 miles

Red, U.S.
Source: Texas panhandle
Outflow: Mississippi River
Length: 1,270 miles

Red River of the North, U.S., Canada
Source: confluence of the Bois de Sioux and Otter
Tail Rivers in Minnesota
Outflow: Lake Winnipeg
Length: 545 miles

Republican, U.S.
Source: confluence of the North Fork and Arikaree
Rivers in Nebraska
Outflow: Kansas River
Length: 422 miles

Rio Grande, U.S., Mexico
Source: San Juan Mountains
Outflow: Gulf of Mexico
Length: 1,800 miles

Roanoke, U.S.
Source: Blue Ridge Mountains, Virginia
Outflow: Atlantic Ocean
Length: 410 miles

Rock, U.S.
Source: eastern Wisconsin
Outflow: Mississippi River
Length: 285 miles

Sabine, U.S.
Source: northeastern Texas
Outflow: Sabine Lake
Length: 578 miles

Sacramento, U.S.
Source: Klamath Mountains, California
Outflow: San Francisco Bay, Pacific Ocean
Length: 380 miles

Saguenay, Canada
Source: Lake St. John, Quebec
Outflow: St. Lawrence River
Length: 110 miles

Saint Francis, U.S.
Source: St. François Mountains, Missouri
Outflow: Mississippi River
Length: 475 miles

Saint John, U.S., Canada
Source: Somerset County, Maine
Outflow: Bay of Fundy
Length: 400 miles

Saint Johns, U.S.
Source: central Florida
Outflow: Atlantic Ocean
Length: 285 miles

Saint Lawrence, U.S., Canada
Source: Lake Ontario
Outflow: Gulf of Saint Lawrence, Atlantic Ocean
Length: 745 miles

Salt, U.S.
Source: confluence of the Black and White Rivers
    in Arizona
Outflow: Gila River
Length: 200 miles

Sangamon, U.S.
Source: central Illinois
Outflow: Illinois River
Length: 250 miles

San Joaquin, U.S.
Source: Sierra Nevada
Outflow: Sacramento River
Length: 350 miles

San Juan, U.S.
Source: San Juan Mountains, Colorado
Outflow: Colorado River
Length: 400 miles

Santee, U.S.
Source: confluence of the Congaree and Wateree
    Rivers in South Carolina
Outflow: Atlantic Ocean
Length: 143 miles

Santiago, Rio Grande de, Mexico
Source: Lake Chapala
Outflow: Pacific Ocean
Length: 275 miles

Saskatchewan, Canada
Source: confluence of the North Saskatchewan and
    South Saskatchewan Rivers
Outflow: Lake Winnipeg
Length: 340 miles

Savannah, U.S.
Source: confluence of the Tugaloo and Seneca
    Rivers in South Carolina
Outflow: Atlantic Ocean
Length: 314 miles

Severn, Canada
Source: Sandy Lake, Ontario
Outflow: Hudson Bay
Length: 610 miles

Shenandoah, U.S.
Source: confluence of the North Fork and South
    Fork near Front Royal, Virginia
Outflow: Potomac River
Length: 200 miles

Skeena, Canada
Source: Skeena Mountains, British Columbia
Outflow: Pacific Ocean
Length: 360 miles

Snake, U.S.
Source: Yellowstone National Park, Wyoming
Outflow: Columbia River
Length: 1,038 miles

Stikine, Canada, U.S.
Source: Stikine Mountains, British Columbia
Outflow: Pacific Ocean
Length: 335 miles

Susquehanna, U.S.
Source: Otsego Lake, New York
Outflow: Chesapeake Bay, Atlantic Ocean
Length: 444 miles

Suwannee, U.S.
Source: Okefenokee Swamp, Georgia
Outflow: Gulf of Mexico
Length: 250 miles

Tanana, U.S.
Source: Yukon, Alaska
Outflow: Yukon River
Length: 600 miles

Tennessee, U.S.
Source: confluence of the Holston and French
   Broad Rivers
Outflow: Ohio River
Length: 652 miles

Thelon, Canada
Source: near the Great Slave Lake
Outflow: Chesterfield Inlet, Hudson Bay
Length: 550 miles

Tombigbee, U.S.
Source: northeastern Mississippi
Outflow: Alabama River
Length: 409 miles

Trinity, Texas
Source: confluence of the West and Clear Forks in
   northeastern Texas
Outflow: Galveston Bay, Gulf of Mexico
Length: 510 miles

Usumacinta, Guatemala, Mexico
Source: Sierra de los Altos, Guatemala
Outflow: Gulf of Mexico
Length: 270 miles

Wabash, U.S.
Source: Grand Lake, Ohio
Outflow: Ohio River
Length: 475 miles

White, U.S.
Source: northwestern Nebraska
Outflow: Missouri River
Length: 507 miles

Willamette, U.S.
Source: Cascade Range, Oregon
Outflow: Columbia River
Length: 190 miles

Wisconsin, U.S.
Source: northern Wisconsin
Outflow: Mississippi River
Length: 430 miles

Yellowstone, U.S.
Source: Absaroka Range, Wyoming
Outflow: Missouri River
Length: 671 miles

Yukon, U.S.
Source: confluence of the Lewes and Pelly Rivers
Outflow: Bering Sea
Length: 1,979 miles

OCEANIA

Cooper's Creek, Queensland, Australia (formerly
   known as the **Barcoo**)
Source: confluence of the Barcoo and Thompson
   Rivers
Outflow: Lake Eyre
Length: 880 miles

Darling, eastern Australia
Source: western slopes of the Great Dividing
   Range
Outflow: Murray River
Length: 1,704 miles

Diamantina, Queensland, Australia
Source: Selwyn Range of Queensland
Outflow: Warburton River
Length: 560 miles

Fitzroy, Western Australia, Australia
Source: Kimberly Plateau
Outflow: King Sound, Indian Ocean
Length: 350 miles

Fly, Papua New Guinea
Source: New Guinea Highlands
Outflow: Gulf of Papua
Length: 700 miles

Hunter, New South Wales, Australia
Source: Liverpool Range
Outflow: Pacific Ocean
Length: 290 miles

Lachlan, New South Wales, Australia
Source: Cullarin Range of the Great Dividing
Range
Outflow: Murrumbidgee River
Length: 920 miles

Murray, New South Wales, Australia
Source: Snowy Mountains
Outflow: Encounter Bay, Indian Ocean
Length: 1,609 miles

Murrumbidgee, New South Wales, Australia
Source: Snowy Mountains
Outflow: Murray River
Length: 1,050 miles

Ord, Western Australia, Australia
Source: King Leopold Range
Outflow: Timor Sea
Length: 300 miles

Snowy, Victoria, Australia
Source: Mount Kosciusko, Snowy Mountains
Outflow: Bass Strait
Length: 270 miles

South America

Amazon, Peru, Brazil
Source: Peruvian Andes
Outflow: Atlantic Ocean
Length: 3,900 miles

Araguaia, Brazil (also known as **Araguaya**)
Source: Mato Grosso plateau
Outflow: Tocantins River
Length: 1,100 miles

Caquetá–Japurá, Colombia (**Caquetá**), Brazil
(**Japurá**)
Source: Colombian Andes
Outflow: Amazon River
Length: 1,500 miles

Cauca, Colombia
Source: Andes
Outflow: Magdalena River
Length: 610 miles

Chubut, Argentina
Source: Andes
Outflow: Atlantic Ocean
Length: 430 miles

Colorado, Argentina
Source: confluence of the Grande and Barrancas
Rivers
Outflow: Atlantic Ocean
Length: 530 miles

Courantyne, Guyana
Source: Serra Acaraí
Outflow: Atlantic Ocean
Length: 450 miles

Essequibo, Guyana
Source: Serra Acaraí
Outflow: Atlantic Ocean
Length: 600 miles

Japurá–Caquetá: *see* **Caquetá–Japurá**

Juruá, Brazil
Source: Andes
Outflow: Amazon River
Length: 900 miles

Madeira, Boliva, Brazil
Source: confluence of the Beni and Mamoré Rivers
in Bolivia
Outflow: Amazon River
Length: 2,000 miles

Magdalena, Colombia
Source: Cordillera Central
Outflow: Caribbean Sea
Length: 1,000 miles

Mamoré, Bolivia
Source: confluence of the Chaparé and Ichilo
Rivers
Outflow: Madeira River
Length: 1,200 miles

Marath, Peru
Source: Peruvian Andes
Outflow: Amazon River
Length: 1,000 miles

Negro, Colombia, Brazil
Source: highlands of Colombia (as the **Guainía**)
Outflow: Amazon River
Length: 1,400 miles

Negro, Brazil, Uruguay
Source: southern Brazil
Outflow: Uruguay River
Length: 500 miles

Paraguay, Brazil, Paraguay, Argentina
Source: Serra dos Parecis, Brazil
Outflow: Paraná River
Length: 1,500 miles

Paraná, Brazil, Paraguay, Argentina
Source: confluence of the Paranaiba and the Rio
Grande
Outflow: Plate River
Length: 2450 miles

Pilcomayo, Bolivia
Source: Cordillera de los Frailes in the eastern
Andes
Outflow: Paraguay River
Length: 750 miles

Purus, Peru, Brazil
Source: Peruvian Andes
Outflow: Amazon River
Length: 1,995 miles

Putumayo, Colombia, Ecuador, Peru, Brazil
Source: Colombian Andes
Outflow: Amazon River
Length: 1,000 miles

Rimac, Peru
Source: Western Cordillera
Outflow: Pacific Ocean
Length: 80 miles

Rio Grande, Brazil
Source: Serra de Mantiqueira
Outflow: Paraná River
Length: 650 miles

São Francisco, Brazil
Source: Serra da Canastra
Outflow: Atlantic Ocean
Length: 1,800 miles

Tapajós, Brazil (also known as **Tapajóz**)
Source: Brazilian plateau
Outflow: Amazon River
Length: 1,200 miles

Tocantins, Brazil
Source: Brazilian plateau
Outflow: Atlantic Ocean at Rio do Pará
Length: 1,678 miles

Ucayali, Peru
Source: Peruvian Andes
Outflow: Amazon River
Length: 850 miles

Uruguay, Brazil, Argentina, Uruguay
Source: Serra do Mar, Brazil
Outflow: Plate River
Length: 1,000 miles

ROCK CLASSES

Magma Molten rock beneath the surface

Igneous Formed from a molten state (magma)
    Intrusive Formed beneath the earth's surface
    Extrusive Formed by volcanic flows and
    eruptions

Sedimentary Formed from sediment that is -
    compacted and hardened
    Clastic Formed from fragments of existing
    rocks
    Chemical Formed from dissolved minerals

Metamorphic Formed from igneous or sedi-
    mentary rock through pressure and
    increased temperature

SEAS

Aden, Gulf of
Location: western arm of Arabian Sea between
    southern coast of Arabian Peninsula
    and Horn of Africa
Length: 550 miles
Width: 300 miles

Adriatic Sea
Location: between coast of Italy and Balkan
    Peninsula
Length: 500 miles
Width: 60–140 miles

Aqaba, Gulf of
Location: northeastern arm of Red Sea between
    Sinai and Arabian Peninsulas
Length: 100 miles
Width: 12–17 miles

Arabian Sea
Location: northern part of Indian Ocean between
    Arabian Peninsula and India
Width: 1,500 miles
Depth: 16,500 feet

Azov, Sea of
Location: northern arm of Black Sea, European
    Russia
Area: 14,500 square miles
Depth: 3–52 feet

Bab el Mandeb
Location: between Arabian Peninsula and Africa,
    connects Red Sea and Gulf of Aden
Length: 20 miles
Width: 20 miles

Baffin Bay
Location: northern Atlantic Ocean between
    Greenland, several Canadian islands, and the
    Arctic Ocean
Length: 700 miles
Width: up to 400 miles

Baltic Sea
Location: northern Europe between Sweden,
    Poland, Latvia, Lithuania, Estonia, Russia,
    and Germany
Area: 160,000 square miles
Depth: 1,519 feet

Barents Sea
Location: north of Norway and Russia
Length: 800 miles
Width: 650 miles

Beaufort Sea
Location: arm of Arctic Ocean north of Canada
and   Alaska
Area: 170,000 square miles
Depth: 15,000 feet

Bengal, Bay of
Location: arm of Indian Ocean between India and
    Burma
Length: 1,300 miles
Width: 1,000 miles

Bering Sea
Location: part of northern Pacific Ocean between
  Russia, Alaska, and the Arctic Ocean
Area: 878,000 square miles
Depth: 13,422 feet

Biscay, Bay of
Location: part of Atlantic Ocean between France
  and Spain
Length: 400 miles
Width: 400 miles

Black Sea
Location: between Europe and Asia, bounded by
  Romania, Bulgaria, Turkey, and Russia
Area: 159,000 square miles
Depth: 7,360 feet

Botany Bay
Location: inlet of Tasman Sea, New South Wales,
  Australia
Width: 1 mile
Diameter: 5 miles

Bothnia, Gulf of
Location: northern arm of Baltic Sea between
  Sweden and Finland
Length: 400 miles
Width: 50–150 miles

California, Gulf of
Location: arm of Pacific Ocean between Mexico
  and Baja California
Length: 700 miles
Width: 30–150 miles

Caribbean Sea
Location: Atlantic Ocean, bounded by Central
  America, South America, and West Indies
Area: 750,000 square miles
Depth: 24,720 feet

Carpentaria, Gulf of
Location: arm of Arafura Sea, northern Australia
Length: 500 miles
Width: 400 miles

China Sea
Location: western Pacific, bordering China,
  bounded by Japan, Borneo, and Malay Penin-
  sula; portion north of Taiwan is the East
  China Sea; portion south of Taiwan is South
  China Sea
Area: 1,375,000 square miles
Depth: over 15,000 feet

Corinth, Gulf of
Location: arm of Ionian Sea between Peloponnesus
  and central Greece
Length: 80 miles
Width: 15 miles

Delaware Bay
Location: inlet of Atlantic Ocean between New
  Jersey and Delaware
Length: 50 miles
Width: 4–30 miles

English Channel
Location: between Great Britain and France
Width: 21–112 miles
Area: 30,000 square miles

Finland, Gulf of
Location: arm of Baltic Sea between Finland and
  Estonia
Length: 250 miles
Width: 12–80 miles

Fundy, Bay of
Location: inlet of Atlantic Ocean between New
  Brunswick, Nova Scotia, and Maine
Length: 171 miles
Width: 50 miles

Hudson Bay
Location: northeastern Canada
Length: 900 miles
Width: 600 miles

Inland Sea
Location: arm of Pacific Ocean, southern Japan;
  bounded by islands of Honshu, Kyushu, and
  Shikoku
Length: 240 miles
Width: 8–40 miles

Ionian Sea
Location: arm of Mediterranean Sea, bounded by
Italy, Greece, Albania, and Sicily
Depth: 12,000 feet

Kattegat
Location: strait south of Sweden connecting North
Sea and Baltic Sea
Length: 137 miles
Width: 37–100 miles

Massachusetts Bay
Location: inlet of Atlantic Ocean between Cape
Ann and Cape Cod
Length: 65 miles

Mediterranean Sea
Location: arm of Atlantic Ocean between Europe
and Africa
Area: 969,000 square miles
Depth: 16,896 feet

Mexico, Gulf of
Location: arm of Atlantic Ocean bounded by south
eastern United States and eastern Mexico
Area: 700,000 square miles
Depth: 12,480 feet

Naples, Bay of
Location: inlet of Tyrrhenian Sea, south central
Italy
Length: 20 miles
Width: 10 miles

Narragansett Bay
Location: inlet of Atlantic Ocean in Rhode Island
Length: 26 miles
Width: 3–12 miles

North Sea
Location: arm of Atlantic Ocean, bounded by
Great   Britain and the European conti-
nent
Area: 222,000 square miles
Depth: 2,165 feet

Okhotsk, Sea of
Location: northwestern arm of Pacific Ocean,
bounded by Kamchatka Peninsula and Kuril
Islands
Area: 590,000 square miles
Depth: 11,060 feet

Persian Gulf
Location: arm of Arabian Sea between Iran and
Arabian Peninsula
Area: 90,000 square miles
Depth: 300 feet

Red Sea
Location: between Arabian Peninsula and north
eastern Africa
Area: 170,000 square miles
Depth: 7,000 feet

Ross Sea
Location: inlet of Pacific Ocean, Antarctica
Area: 370,000 square miles

San Francisco Bay
Location: inlet of Pacific Ocean, western
California
Length: 50 miles
Width: 3–12 miles

Skagerrak
Location: inlet of North Sea between Norway and
Sweden
Length: 150 miles
Width: 75–90 miles

Viscount Melville Sound
Location: arm of Arctic Ocean north of Canada
Length: 250 miles
Width: 100 miles

Wash, The
Location: inlet of North Sea, eastern Great Britain
Length: 20 miles
Width: 15 miles

White Sea
Location: inlet of Barents Sea, northwestern Russia
Length: 365 miles
Area: 37,000 square miles

Yellow Sea
Location: arm of Pacific Ocean between China and
    Korean peninsula
Length: 400 miles
Width: 400 miles

ACTIVE VOLCANOES

AFRICA

Erta-Ale, Ethiopia
Fogo Caldera, Cape Verde Islands
Karthala, Comoros
Lake Nyos, Cameroon
Mount Cameroon, Cameroon
Nyamuragira, Congo
Ol Doinyo Lengai, Tanzania
Piton de la Rournaise, Reunion Island

ASIA

Akita Komaga-take, Japan
Akita-Yakeyama, Japan
Alaid, Russia
Asama, Japan
Aso, Japan
Awu, Indonesia
Azuma, Japan
Baitoushan, China-Korea
Bandai, Japan
Barren Island, India
Batur, Indonesia
Bezymianny, Russia
Bulusan, Philippines

Canlaon, Philippines
Chokai, Japan
Fuji, Japan
Galunggung, Indonesia
Gamalama, Indonesia
Gamkonora, Indonesia
Karangetang, Indonesia
Karymsky, Russia
Kelud, Indonesia
Kerinci, Indonesia
Kirishima, Japan
Klyuchevskoi, Russia
Krakatau, Indonesia
Lokon-Empung, Indonesia
Mayon, Philippines
Me-Akan, Japan
Merapi, Indonesia
Nasu, Japan
Niigata-Yakeyama, Japan
On-take, Japan
Oshima, Japan
Pinatubo, Indonesia
Raung, Indonesia
Sakura-jima, Japan
Sangeang Api, Indonesia
Sarychev Peak, Russia
Semeru, Indonesia
Sheveluch, Indonesia
Siamet, Indonesia
Soputan, Indonesia
Suwanose-jima, Russia
Taal, Philippines
Tiatia, Russia
Tolbachik, Russia
Unzen, Japan
Usu, Japan

EUROPE

Ararat, Turkey
Beerenberg, Norway
Etna, Italy
Grimsvotn, Iceland
Hekla, Iceland
Laki, Iceland
Krafla, Iceland
Santorini, Greece

Surtsey, Iceland
Stromboli, Italy
Vesuvius, Italy

NORTH AMERICA

Acatenango, Guatemala
Akutan, Alaska
Arenal, Costa Rica
Augustine, Alaska
Baker, Washington
Cerro Negro, Nicaragua
Citlaltepetl, Mexico
Cleveland, Alaska
Colima, Mexico
Concepción, Nicaragua
El Chichon, Mexico
Fuego, Guatemala
Gareloi, Alaska
Great Sitkin, Alaska
Iliamna, Alaska
Irazu, Costa Rica
Izalco, El Salvador
Katmai, Alaska
Kilauea, Hawaii
Kiska, Alaska
Korovin, Alaska
Lassen, California
Makushin, Alaska
Masaya, Nicaragua
Mauna Loa, Hawaii
Momotombo, Nicaragua
Mount Saint Helens, Washington
Okmok, Alaska
Pacaya, Guatemala
Pavlof, Alaska
Paricutin, Mexico
Pelee, Martinique
Póas, Costa Rica
Popocatepetl, Mexico
Rainier, Washington
Redoubt, Alaska
Rincón de la Vieja, Costa Rica
San Cristobal, Nicaragua
San Miguel, El Salvador
Santa Maria, Guatemala
Shasta, California

Shishaldin, Alaska
Seguam, Alaska
La Soufrière, Saint Vincent
Soufrière Hills, Montserrat
Tacana, Guatemala
Turrialba, Costa Rica
Veniaminof, Alaska
Wrangell, Alaska

OCEANIA

Ambrym, Vanuatu
Bagana, Papua New Guinea
Karkar, Papua New Guinea
Langila, Papua New Guinea
Lopevi, Vanuatu
Manam, Papua New Guinea
Ngauruhoe, New Zealand
Pagan, Mariana Islands
Rabaul Caldera, Papua New Guinea
Ruapehu, New Zealand
Ulawan, Papua New Guinea
White Island, New Zealand
Yasur, Vanuatu

SOUTH AMERICA

Cerro Hudson, Chile
Chimborazo, Galapagos Islands
Cotopaxi, Ecuador
Fernandina, Galapagos Islands
Galeras, Ecuador
Guagua Pichincha, Ecuador
Guallatiri, Chile
Irruputuncu, Chile
Láscar, Chile
Liaima, Chile
Llullaillaco, Chile
Misti, Peru
Purace, Colombia
Ruiz, Colombia
Sangay, Ecuador
Tupungatito, Chile
Villarrica, Chile

THE SKY

LAYERS OF THE ATMOSPHERE

Homosphere Defined by its chemical composition; the inner shell of the atmosphere, starting at Earth's surface and rising to 80 km.

Troposphere Defined by its temperature; the area from Earth's surface to 18 km.

Tropopause The upper limit of the troposphere.

Stratosphere Defined by its temperature; the area from 18 to 50 km.

Stratopause The upper limit of the stratosphere.

Ozonosphere (ozone layer) Defined by its function to filter ultraviolet radiation; its area corresponds with the stratosphere.

Mesosphere Defined by its temperature; the area from 50 km to 80 km.

Mesopause The upper limit of the mesosphere.

Heterosphere Defined by its chemical composition; the outer atmosphere, beginning at 80 km altitude and continuing to about 480 km, the top of Earth's atmosphere.

Thermosphere Defined by temperature; the "heat sphere" corresponds to the heterosphere, beginning at 80 km and going to 480 km.

Thermopause The upper limit of the thermosphere.

Ionosphere Defined by its function to filter solar radiation; it extends through the thermosphere and mesosphere.

Exosphere Above the atmosphere, composed of lightweight hydrogen and helium atoms as far as 32,000 km from earth.

CLOUD TYPES

Low-Level (up to 6,500 feet)
Stratus Featureless, misty, foglike, horizontal clouds
Stratocumulus Lumpy, globular clouds in irregular layers or patterns
Nimbostratus Stratus clouds, producing precipitation

Middle-Level (6,500–20,000 feet)
Altostratus Mid-level stratus clouds, producing a grey day
Altocumulus Piled-up, fluffy clouds arranged in groups or lines

High-Level (20,000–43,000 feet)
Cirrus "Mares'-tails"; light, wispy streaks or plumes
Cirrostratus High-level stratus clouds composed of ice crystals
Cirrocumulus "Mackerel sky"; small, white, puffy clouds in groups or lines

Vertically Developed (near surface to 43,000 feet)
Cumulus Flat-based, puffy clouds with swelling tops
Cumulonimbus Dark, heavy storm clouds with anvil-shaped tops

RECURRING COMETS

A list of periodic comets including a few major long-period comets. A long-period comet is a comet with an orbital period of a million years or more. A periodic comet is a comet with an interval of less than 200 years.

Comet	Period
D'Arrest	6.39 years
Biela	6.8 years (broke apart and never returned after 1852)
Borrelly	6.88 years
Brooks 2	6.89 years
Chiron	51 years
Daniel	7.06 years
Donati	2,000 years
Encke	3.3 years
Faye	7.34 years
Finlay	6.95 years
Giacobini-Zinner	6.5 years
Hale-Bopp	long
Halley	76 years
Holmes	7.09 years
Hyakutake	long
Kobayashi	24.53 years
Kohoutek	6.65 years
Kopff	6.45 years
Montani	21.80 years
Olbers	69.56 years
Pons-Brooks	70.92 years
Pons-Winnecke	6.38 years

Comet	Period
Schaumasse	8.22 years
Schwassmann-Wachmann 1	14.85 years
Shoemaker-Levy 9	broke up in 1992 and crashed into Jupiter in 1994
Spacewatch	5.57 years
Swift-Tuttle	135.01 years
Tempel 1	5.5 years
Tempel 2	5.48 years
Tempel-Tuttle	32.9 years
Tuttle	13.51 years
West	long
Wolf	8.25 years

THE CONSTELLATIONS

Andromeda The Woman Chained
Antila The Air Pump
Apus The Bird of Paradise
Aquarius The Water Carrier
Aquila The Eagle
Ara The Altar
Aries The Ram
Auriga The Charioteer
Boötes The Herdsman
Caelum The Sculptor's Chisel
Camelopardalis The Giraffe
Cancer The Crab
Canes Venatici The Hunting Dogs
Canis Major The Greater Dog
Canis Minor The Lesser Dog
Capricornus The Sea Goat
Carina The Keel
Cassiopeia The Queen of Ethiopia

Centaurus The Centaur
Cepheus The King of Ethiopia
Cetus The Whale (or Sea Monster)
Chamaeleon The Chameleon
Circinus The Compasses
Columba The Dove
Coma Berenices The Hair of Berenice
Corona Australis The Southern Crown
Corona Borealis The Northern Crown
Corvus The Crow
Crater The Cup
Crux The Cross
Cygnus The Swan
Delphinus The Dolphin (or Porpoise)
Dorado The Swordfish
Draco The Dragon
Equuleus The Foal
Eridanus The River Eridanus
Fornax The Furnace
Gemini The Twins
Grus The Crane
Hercules Hercules (The Hero)
Horologium The Pendulum Clock
Hydra The Water Snake
Hydrus The Lesser Water Snake
Indus The Indian
Lacerta The Lizard
Leo The Lion
Leo Minor The Lesser Lion
Lepus The Hare
Libra The Scales
Lupus The Wolf
Lynx The Lynx
Lyra The Lyre
Mensa The Table Mountain
Microscopium The Microscope
Monoceros The Unicorn
Musca The Fly
Norma The Carpenter's Square
Octans The Octant
Ophiuchus The Serpent Bearer
Orion Orion (The Hunter)
Pavo The Peacock
Pegasus Pegasus (The Winged Horse)
Perseus Perseus (The Hero)
Phoenix The Phoenix
Pictor The Painter's Easel
Pisces The Fishes

Piscis Austrinus The Southern Fish
Puppis The Stern
Pyxis The Compass
Reticulum The Net
Sagitta The Arrow
Sagittarius The Archer
Scorpius The Scorpion
Sculptor The Sculptor
Scutum The Shield
Serpens The Serpent
Sextans The Sextant
Taurus The Bull
Telescopium The Telescope
Triangulum The Triangle
Triangulum Australe The Southern Triangle
Tucan The Toucan
Ursa Major The Great Bear
Ursa Minor The Lesser Bear
Virgo The Virgin
Volans The Flying Fish
Vupecula The Fox

HURRICANES

A list of the costliest and most deadly hurricanes since 1954 (the year hurricanes were first given proper names).

Name	Location	Year
Carol	northeastern U.S.	1954
Hazel	Caribbean, Carolinas	1954
Connie	southeastern U.S.	1955
Diane	northeastern U.S.	1955
Audrey	Louisiana, Texas	1957
Flora	Haiti, Cuba	1963
Betsy	Florida, Gulf Coast	1965
Camille	Gulf Coast	1969

Name	Location	Year
Agnes	East Coast, U.S.	1972
Fifi	Honduras	1974
Eloise	Florida, Puerto Rico	1975
Frederick	Gulf Coast	1979
David	Florida, Carolinas	1979
Allen	Haiti, southeastern U.S.	1980
Alicia	Texas	1983
Joan	Caribbean	1988
Gilbert	Caribbean, Mexico	1988
Hugo	South Carolina	1989
Andrew	Florida	1992
Luis	Caribbean	1995
Marilyn	Virgin Islands, Caribbean	1995
Opal	Mexico, Guatemala, Florida	1995
Bertha	Caribbean, eastern U.S.	1996
Fran	North Carolina, Virginia, West Virginia	1996
Hortense	Caribbean	1996
Danny	southeastern U.S.	1997
Pauline	Mexico	1997
Georges	Caribbean, Gulf Coast	1998
Mitch	Central America (Honduras, Nicaragua)	1998
Floyd	Bahamas to New England	1999

PLANETS OF OUR SOLAR SYSTEM

Mercury
Diameter: 3,100 miles
Average distance from sun: 36 million miles
Orbital period: .24 years

Venus
Diameter: 7,518 miles
Average distance from sun: 67 million miles
Orbital period: .62 years

Earth
Diameter: 7,927 miles
Average distance from sun: 93 million miles
Orbital period: 1 year

Mars
Diameter: 4,219 miles
Average distance from sun: 142 million miles
Orbital period: 1.9 years

Jupiter
Diameter: 88,012 miles
Average distance from sun: 483 million miles
Orbital period: 12 years

Saturn
Diameter: 74,500 miles
Average distance from sun: 886 million miles
Orbital period: 29 years

Uranus
Diameter: 31,550 miles
Average distance from sun: 1,782 million miles
Orbital period: 84 years

Neptune
Diameter: 30,190 miles
Average distance from sun: 2,793 million miles
Orbital period: 165 years

Pluto
Diameter: 1,500 miles
Average distance from sun: 3,670 million miles
Orbital period: 248 years

SATELLITES (MOONS) AND RINGS

Satellites are listed with their average distance from the planet.

Earth
Moon: 384,000 km

Mars
Phobos: 9,400 km
Deimos: 23,500 km

Jupiter
Metis: 128,000 km
Adrastea: 129,000 km
Amalthea: 181,300 km
Thebe: 221,900 km
Io: 421,600 km
Europa: 670,900 km
Ganymede: 1,070,000 km
Callisto: 1,883,000 km
Leda: 11,094,000 km
Himalia: 11,480,000 km
Lysithea: 11,720,000 km
Elara: 11,737,000 km
Anake: 21,200,000 km
Carme: 22,600,000 km
Pasiphaë: 23,500,000 km
Sinope: 23,700,000 km

Saturn
Satellites
(Note: More unconfirmed satellites have been discovered by the Hubble Space Telescope.)
Pan: 133,600 km
Atlas: 137,700 km
Prometheus: 139,400 km
Pandora: 141,700 km
Janus: 151,400 km
Epimetheus: 151,400 km
Mimas: 185,500 km

Enceladus: 238,000 km
Tethys: 294,700 km
Telesto: 294,700 km
Calypso: 294,700 km
Dione: 377,400 km
Helene: 377,400 km
Rhea: 527,000 km
Titan: 1,221,900 km
Hyperion: 1,481,100 km
Iapetus: 3,561,300 km
Phoebe: 12,950,000 km

Rings
D Ring
C Ring
B Ring
Cassini Division
A Ring
F Ring
G Ring
E Ring

Uranus
Satellites
Cordelia: 49,000 km
Ophelia: 53,800 km
Bianca: 59,200 km
Cressida: 61,800 km
Desdemona: 62,700 km
Juliet: 64,600 km
Portia: 66,100 km
Rosalind: 69,900 km
Belinda: 75,300 km
Puck: 86,000 km
Miranda: 130,000 km
Ariel: 191,000 km
Umbriel: 266,000 km
Titania: 435,900 km
Oberon: 483,000 km

Rings
6 Ring
5 Ring
4 Ring
Alpha
Beta
Eta
Gamma

Delta
Lambda
Epsilon

Neptune
Satellites
Naiad: 48,000 km
Thalassa: 50,000 km
Despina: 52,500 km
Galatea: 62,000 km
Larissa: 73,600 km
Proteus: 117,600 km
Triton: 354,000 km
Nereid: 5,513,000 km

Rings
Galle
Leverrier
Lassell
Arago
Adams

Pluto
Charon: 19,700 km

NOTABLE STARS

Stars (Designation)

Achernar (α Eridani)
Acrux (α Crucis)
Adhara (ϵ Canis Majoris)
Aldebaran (α Tauri)
Alioth (ϵ Ursae Majoris)
Alkaid (η Ursae Majoris)
Alnair (α Gruis)
Alniam (ϵ Orionis)
Alnitak (ξ Orionis)
Altair (α Aquilae)
Antares (α Scorpii)
Arcturus (α Bootis)

Atria (α Trianguli Australis)
Avior (ϵ Carinae)
Bellatrix (γ Orionis)
Betelgeuse (α Orionis)
Canopus (α Carinae)
Capella (α Aurigae)
Castor (α Geminorum)
Deneb (α Cygni)
Denebola (β Leonis)
Diphda, Deneb Kaitos (β Ceti)
Dubhe (α Ursae Majoris)
El Nath (β Tauri)
Eltanin (γ Draconis)
Enif (ϵ Pegasi)
Fomalhaut (α Piscis Austrinis)
Gacrux (γ Crucis)
Hadar (β Centauri)
Hamal (α Arietis)
Kaus Australis (ϵ Sagittarii)
Kochab (β Ursa Minoris)
Menkent (η Centauri)
Miaplacidus (β Carinae)
Mimosa, Becrux (β Crucis)
Mirfak (α Persei)
Nunki (δ Sagittarii)
Peacock (α Pavonis)
Pollux (β Geminorum)
Procyon (α Minoris)
Rasalhague (α Ophiucchi)
Regulus (α Leonis)
Rigel (β Orionis)
Rigil Kentaurus (Toliman) (α Centauri)
Schedar (α Cassiopiae)
Shaula (λ Scorpii)
Sirius (α Canis Majoris)
Spica (α Virginis)
Vega (α Lyrae)
Wezen (δ Canis Majoris)

REAL AND IMAGINARY PLACES

BIBLICAL CITIES AND THEIR MODERN NAMES/ LOCATIONS

The Arabic words *Tell* and *Khirbet,* which mean "mound" and "ruin" respectively, are abbreviated as T. and Kh.

Abdon A city in Asher, now Kh. Abda

Acco A coastal city north of Mt. Carmel, now T. el-Fukkhar

Adamah A city in Naphtali, now possibly Qarn Hattin

Adullam A city in Shephelah, now T. esh-Sheikh Madhkur

Ai A city in the Saddle of Benjamin, now Kh. et-Tell

Aijalon A city now known as Yalo

Alemeth A city in Benjamin, now Kh. Almit

Almon A city in Moab, now Kiblathaim esh-Sherqiya

Anathoth A city in Benjamin, now Ras el-Kharruba

Anim A city now known as Kh. Ghuwein et-Tahta

Antioch A city in Syria, now Antakiya

Aphekah A city in Judah, now possibly Kh. el-Hadab

Ar A city on the south bank of the Arnon River, now el-Misna

Arad A city in Negev, now T. el-Milh

Aroer A city on the northern rim of the Arnon River gorge, now Kh. Arair

Arpad A city in northern Syria, now T. er-Refad

Ashdod A city on the southern coastal plain, now Isdud

Ashkelon A seaport on the southern coast, now T. Asqalan

Ashtaroth A city in Gilead, now T. Ashtarah

Azekah A city in Shephelah, now T. ez-Zakariya

Beeroth A city on the plateau northwest of Jerusalem, now possibly Nebi Samwil

Beer-Sheba A city in the Negev, now T. es-Saba

Beroea A city in Macedonia, now Verroia

Beth-Anath A city in Upper Galilee, now possibly Safed el-Battikh

Beth-Sh'an A city at the junction of the Jezreel and Jordan valleys, now T. el-Husn

Beth-Shemesh A city in the Sorek valley, now T. er-Rumeila

Bezer A city in northern Moab, now possibly Umm el-Amad

Bozrah A city in northern Edom, now Buseirah

Caesaria A port in Judea, now Qaisariya

Caesarea Philippi A city at the southwestern foot of Mt. Hermon, now Banias

Calah A city near the junction of the Tigris and Upper Zab Rivers in Mesopotamia, now Nimrud

Cana A city in Lower Galilee, now possibly Kh. Qana

Carchemish A city in northern Syria, now Jerablus

Caspin A city east of the Sea of Galilee, now Khisfin

Cherphirah A city on the plateau northeast of Jerusalem, now Kh. el-Kefira

Cinnereth A city on the northwestern shore of the Sea of Galilee, now Kh. el-Ureima

Cuth A city in Babylonia, now T. Ibrahim

Cyrene A city in northern Africa, now Cirene

Dan A city in the Huleh valley, now T. el-Qadi

Debir A city in southern Judah, now possibly T. Rabud

Dibon A city north of the Arnon River in Moab, now Dhiban

Dor A city south of Mt. Carmel, now Kh. el-Burj

Dortham A city in northern Samaria, now T. Duthan

Ecbatana The capital of Media, now Hamadan

Edrei A city in Bashan, now Dera

Eglon A city in northwestern Negev, now possibly Hesi

Ekron A city on the southern coastal plain, now Kh. el-Muqanna

Elealeh A city in Moab, now el-Al

Erech A city in southern Mesopotamia, now Warka

Eshtemoa A city in the hill country of Judah, now es-Samu

Gadara A city southeast of the Sea of Galilee, now Umm Qeis

Gath A city on the southern coastal plain, now possibly T. es-Safi

Gath-Rimmon A city on the central coastal plain, now possibly T. Jerisha

Gaza A city on the southern coastal plain, now el-Ghazza

Gerar A city in northern Negev, now T. Abu Hurreira

Gerasa A city in Gilead, now Jerash

Gezer A city in northern Shephelah, now T. Jazer

Gibbethon A city in northern Shephelah, now T. el-Melat

Gibeon A city northwest of Jerusalem, now el-Jib

Golan A city in Bashan, now Sahm el-Jaulan

Hamath A city on the Orontes River in Syria, now Hama

Haran A city in northwestern Mesopotamia, now Harran

Hazor A city north of the Sea of Galilee, now T. el-Qedeh

Hebron A city in the hill country of Judah, now el-Khalil

Hepher A city on the Plain of Sharon, now possibly T. el-Ifshar

Heshbon A city in northern Moab, now Hisban

Hippus A city east of the Sea of Galilee, now Qalaat el-Husn

Horoniam A city in southern Moab, now possibly el-Iraq

Ibleam A city south of the Great Plain, now Kh. Balama

Iconium A city in Galatia in central Asia Minor, now Konya

Jabesh A city in Gilead, now T. el-Maqlub

Jarmuth A city in Shephelah, now Kh. Yarmuk

Jattir A city in the southern hill country of Judah, now Kh. Attir

Jazer A city in Gilead, now Kh. es-Sar

Jericho A city in the lower Jordan valley, now T. es-Sultan

Jerusalem The capital city of Israel, in the eastern-central region of the West Bank

Jezreel A city north of Mt. Gilboa, now Zirin

Jogbehah A city in Ammon, now Kh. el-Jebeihat

Jokneam A city northwest of Megiddo, now T. Qeimun

Kadesh A city in Syria, now T. Nebi Mend

Kedemoth A city in eastern Moab, now possibly Qasr ez-Zaferan

Kedesh A city in Upper Galilee, now T. Kedesh

Keilah A city in Shephelah, now Kh. Qeila

Kir-Hareseth A city in western Moab, now el-Kerak

Lachish A city in Shephelah, now T. ed-Duweir

Laodicea A city in southwestern Asia Minor, now Eskihisar

Libnah A city in Shephelah, now possibly T. el-Beida

Lodebar A city northwest of Gilead, now Umm ed-Dabar

Madon A city in Galilee, now possibly T. el-Khirbeth

Mahanaim A city in Gilead, now possibly T. ed-Dhahab el-Garbi

Mareshah A city in Shephelah, now T. Sandahannah

Megiddo A city at the northern end of the Wadi-Ara, now T. el-Mutesellim

Mizpah A city north of Jerusalem, now T. en-Nasba

Moresheth A city in Shephelah, now possibly T. el-Judeida

Myndos A city in southwestern Asia Minor, now Gumushli

Nineveh A city in central Mesopotamia, now T. Nebi Yunus and T. Quyunjiq

Paphos A city on the western coast of Cypress, now Baffo

Pella A city southeast of Beth-shan, now Kh. Fahil

Penuel A city in Gilead, now Tulul edh-Dhahab

Perga A city in south-central Asia Minor, now Murtana

Pergamum A city in western Asia Minor, now Bergama

Persepolis A city in Persia, now Takht-i Jamshid

Petra A city southeast of the Dead Sea, now Rekem

Philadelphia A city in western Asia Minor, now Alashehir

Phillipi A city in Macedonia, now Filibedjik

Pibeseth A city on the Nile, now T. Basath

Rabbath A city in Ammon, now Amman

Ramoth-Gilead A city in northern Gilead, now T. Ramith

Raphia A city on the southern coastal plain, now T. Rafah

Raphon A city east of the sea of Galilee, now er-Rafeh

Riblah A city in Syria, now Ribla

Salecah A city in eastern Bashan, now Salkhad

Samaria A city in Samaria, now Sebestiya

Sela The capital of Edom, now possibly es-Sela

Sepphoris A city in western Lower Galilee, now Saffuriya

Shechem A city in central Samaria, now T. Balata

Shimron A city in Lower Galilee, now Kh. Sammuniya

Sidon A port city north of Tyre, now Saida

Smyrna A city in western Asia Minor, now Izmir

Susa A city in eastern Mesopotamia, now Shush

Sychar A city in Samaria, now Askar

Taamach A city on the southern edge of the Great Plain, now T. Tinnik

Tahpanhes A city in Lower Egypt, now T. Dafanna

Tamar A city south of the Dead Sea, now Ein Hub

Thessalonica A city in Macedonia, now Salonika

Thyatira A city in western Asia Minor, now Akhisar

Tiberias A city on the western shore of the Sea of Galilee, now Tabariya

Tiphsah A city on the Euphrates in Mesopotamia, now Dibse

Tirzah A city on the western end of the Wadi Farah, now T. el-Farah

Ur A city in lower Mesopotamia, now el-Muqeiyar

Yiron A city in Upper Galilee, now Yarum

Zaphon A city in the Jordan valley, now Kh. Buwaby

Zarethan A city in the Jordan valley, now T. es-Saidiya

Zemer A city in northwestern Syria, now Sumra

COUNTRIES OF THE WORLD AND THEIR CAPITAL CITIES

AFRICA

Algeria Algiers
Angola Luanda
Benin Porto-Novo (official); Cotonou (de facto)
Botswana Gaborone
Burkina Faso Ouagadougou
Burundi Bujumbura
Cameroon Yaoundé

Cape Verde Praia
Central African Republic Bangui
Chad N'Djamena
Comoros Moroni
Congo, Democratic Republic of (formerly **Zaire**) Kinshasa
Congo, Republic of the Brazzaville
Côte d'Ivoire Yamoussoukro (official); Abidjan (administrative)
Djibouti Djibouti
Egypt Cairo
Equatorial Guinea Malabo
Eritrea Asmara
Ethiopia Addis Ababa
Gabon Libreville
Gambia, The Banjul
Ghana Accra
Guinea Conakry
Guinea-Bissau Bissau
Kenya Nairobi
Lesotho Maseru
Liberia Monrovia
Libya Tripoli
Madagascar Antananarivo
Malawi Lilongwe
Mali Bamako
Mauritania Nouakchott
Mauritius Port Louis
Morocco Rabat
Mozambique Maputo
Namibia Windhoek
Niger Niamey
Nigeria Abuja
Rwanda Kigali
São Tomé and Principe São Tomé
Senegal Dakar
Seychelles Victoria
Sierra Leone Freetown
Somalia Mogadishu
South Africa Pretoria, Cape Town, and Bloemfontein
Sudan Khartoum
Swaziland Mbabane
Tanzania Dar es Salaam and Dodoma
Togo Lomé
Tunisia Tunis
Uganda Kampala

Zambia Lusaka
Zimbabwe Harare

ASIA

Afghanistan Kabul
Armenia Yerevan
Azerbaijan Baku
Bahrain al-Manama
Bangladesh Dhaka
Bhutan Thimpu
Brunei Bandar Seri Begawan
Cambodia Phnom Penh
China Beijing
Cyprus Lefkosia (Nicosia)
Georgia Tbilisi
India Delhi
Indonesia Jakarta
Iran Teheran
Iraq Baghdad
Israel Jerusalem
Japan Tokyo
Jordan Amman
Kazakhstan Astana (formerly Aqmola)
Korea, North Pyongyang
Korea, South Seoul
Kuwait Kuwait City
Kyrgyzstan Bishkek (formerly Frunze)
Laos Vientiane
Lebanon Beirut
Malaysia Kuala Lumpur
Maldives Malé
Mongolia Ulan Bator
Myanmar (Burma) Rangoon (Yangon)
Nepal Kathmandu
Oman Muscat
Pakistan Islamabad
Philippines, The Manila
Qatar Doha
Russia Moscow
Saudi Arabia Riyadh
Singapore Singapore
Sri Lanka Sri Jayawardenepura and Colombo
Syria Damascus
Taiwan Taipei
Tajikistan Dushanbe
Thailand Bangkok

Turkey Ankara
Turkmenistan Ashgabat
United Arab Emirates Abu Dhabi
Uzbekistan Tashkent
Vietnam Hanoi
Yemen Sanaá

EUROPE

Albania Tiranë
Andorra Andorra la Vella
Austria Vienna
Belarus Minsk
Belgium Brussels
Bosnia and Herzegovina Sarajevo
Bulgaria Sofia
Croatia Zagreb
Czech Republic Prague
Denmark Copenhagen
Estonia Tallinn
Finland Helsinki
France Paris
Germany Berlin
Greece Athens
Hungary Budapest
Iceland Reykjavik
Ireland Dublin
Italy Rome
Latvia Riga
Liechtenstein Vaduz
Lithuania Vilnius
Luxembourg Luxembourg
Macedonia Skopje
Malta Valletta
Moldova Chisinau
Monaco Monaco
Netherlands Amsterdam; The Hague
Norway Oslo
Poland Warsaw
Portugal Lisbon
Romania Bucharest
Russia Moscow
San Marino San Marino
Slovakia Bratislava
Slovenia Ljubljana
Spain Madrid
Sweden Stockholm

Switzerland Bern
Ukraine Kiev
United Kingdom London
Vatican City Vatican City
Yugoslavia Belgrade

NORTH AMERICA

Antigua and Barbuda St. Johns; Codrington
Bahamas Nassau
Belize Belmopan
Canada Ottawa
Costa Rica San José
Cuba Havana
Dominica Roseau
Dominican Republic Santo Domingo
El Salvador San Salvador
Grenada St. George's
Guatemala Guatemala City
Haiti Port-au-Prince
Honduras Tegucigalpa
Jamaica Kingston
Mexico Mexico City
Nicaragua Managua
Panama Panama City
Saint Kitts and Nevis Basseterre
Saint Lucia Castries
Saint Vincent and the Grenadines Kingstown
Trinidad and Tobago Port-of-Spain
United States of America Washington, D.C.

OCEANIA

Australia Canberra
Fiji Suva
Kiribati Tarawa
Marshall Islands Majuro
Micronesia Paliker
Nauru Yaren
New Zealand Wellington
Palau Koror
Papua New Guinea Port Moresby
Solomon Islands Honiara
Tonga Nuku'alofa
Tuvalu Funafuti
Vanuatu Port Vila
Western Samoa Apia

SOUTH AMERICA

Argentina Buenos Aires
Bolivia La Paz and Sucre
Brazil Brasilia
Chile Santiago
Colombia Bogotá
Ecuador Quito
Guyana Georgetown
Paraguay Asunción
Peru Lima
Suriname Paramaribo
Uruguay Montevideo
Venezuela Caracas

COUNTRIES THAT USED TO BE CALLED SOMETHING ELSE

Armenia A country of Asia Minor, east of Turkey, formerly the Armenian Soviet Socialist Republic.

Azerbaijan A country north of Iran, south of Russia, formerly the Azerbaijan Soviet Socialist Republic.

Belarus A country east of Poland, formerly the Belorussian Soviet Socialist Republic (or Belorussia, also Byelorussia).

Belize A country east of Guatemala in the Caribbean, formerly British Honduras.

Benin A country in western Africa, formerly Dahomey.

Botswana A country in south-central Africa, formerly Bechuanaland.

Cambodia A country in southeast Asia on the Gulf of Thailand, formerly Khmer Republic.

Central African Republic A country in central Africa, formerly Central African Empire.

Djibouti A country in eastern Africa, formerly Afars and Issas.

Egypt A country in northeast Africa on the Mediterranean Sea, formerly the United Arab Republic between the years 1958 and 1961.

Estonia A country in north-central Europe west of Russia, formerly the Estonian Soviet Socialist Republic.

Ethiopia A country in northeast Africa, formerly Abyssinia.

Germany This country was divided into the German Democratic Republic (East Germany) and the German Federal Republic (West Germany) at the end of World War II.

Greece A country in southeast Europe, including many Mediterranean islands, formerly Hellas.

Guyana A country off the Atlantic, formerly British Guiana.

Indonesia A country in southeast Asia in the Malay Archipelago, formerly the Netherlands East Indies, or Dutch East Indies.

Jordan A country in northwest Arabia, formerly Transjordan.

Kazakstan A country in west-central Asia, south of Russia, formerly Kazakh Soviet Socialist Republic.

Kyrgyzstan A country in west-central Asia, formerly Kirghiz Soviet Socialist Republic.

Latvia A country in north-central Europe on the Baltic Sea, formerly Latvian Soviet Socialist Republic.

Lesotho A country in southern Africa, formerly Basutoland.

Lithuania A country in north-central Europe on the Baltic Sea, formerly Lithuanian Soviet Socialist Republic.

Madagascar An island country in the Indian Ocean off the southeast coast of Africa, formerly Malagasy Republic.

Malawi A country in southeast Africa, east of Zambia, formerly Nyasaland.

Maldives An island country in the Indian Ocean, southwest of Sri Lanka, formerly Maldive Island.

Moldova A country in Europe bordering on Romania, formerly Moldavian Soviet Socialist Republic.

Mongolia A country in north-central Asia between Russia and China, formerly Outer Mongolia.

Mordovia A country in west-central Russia, formerly Mordovian Autonomous Soviet Socialist Republic.

Myanmar A country in southeast Asia on the Bay of Bengal, formerly Burma.

Namibia A country in southwest Africa on the Atlantic, formerly South-West Africa.

Nauru An island country in the Pacific, south of the equator and west of Kiribati, formerly Pleasant Island.

Oman A sultanate on the southeast Arabian Peninsula off the Gulf of Oman, formerly Muscat and Oman.

Rwanda A country in east-central Africa, formerly Ruanda.

Samoa formerly Western Samoa.

Sri Lanka An island country in the Indian Ocean off southeast India, formerly Ceylon.

Suriname A country on the Atlantic, formerly Dutch Guiana.

Taiwan An island country off the southeast coast of China in the South China Sea, formerly Formosa.

Tajikistan A country in south-central Asia, formerly Tadzhik Soviet Socialist Republic.

Thailand A country in southeast Asia on the Gulf of Thailand, formerly Siam.

Turkmenistan A country in west-central Asia east of the Caspian Sea, formerly Turkmen Soviet Socialist Republic.

Tuvalu An island country in the western Pacific Ocean off Fiji, formerly Ellice Islands.

Ukraine A country in eastern Europe bordering the Black Sea, formerly Ukrainian Soviet Socialist Republic.

United Arab Emirates A country in eastern Arabia, formerly Trucial Oman.

Uzbekistan A country in west-central Asia, formerly Uzbek Soviet Socialist Republic.

Vanuatu An island country in the southern Pacific Ocean east of northern Australia, formerly New Hebrides.

Zaire A country in central Africa on the equator, formerly the Congo Free State (1885–1908); Belgian Congo (1908–60); Congo (1960–71).

Zimbabwe A country in southern Africa, formerly Rhodesia.

IMAGINARY PLACES

Alali This village of gigantic women in the heart of the Great Thorn Forest is featured in Edgar Rice Burroughs's *Tarzan and the Ant Men*.

Amazonia Bordering Albania is this empire of women where men are slaves or eunuchs, from Sir John Mandeville's *Voiage de Sir John Maundevile*.

Ape Kingdom This treetop society located in Africa comes from Edgar Rice Burroughs's *Tarzan of the Apes*.

Atlantis This underwater continent originates from Plato's *Critias*.

Avalon This isle of magic women where King Arthur received Excalibur is featured in Sir Thomas Malory's *Le Morte D'Arthur*.

Batcave Americans got their first glimpse of this secret lair of Batman on the ABC television network in 1966.

Black Chapel This is one of the supposed resting places of the body of King Arthur from the anonymous *La Mort le Roi Artu*.

Brigadoon This Scottish village that reappears once every hundred years comes from the eponymously named musical by Alan Jay Lerner.

Brobdingnag Gulliver discovered this peninsula inhabited by giants in Jonathan Swift's *Gulliver's Travels*.

Calypso's Isle Ogygia is the other name for this western Mediterranean island where Odysseus encounters this nymph in *The Odyssey*.

Camelot King Arthur ruled this kingdom in southern Britain in Sir Thomas Malory's *Le Morte D'Arthur*.

Celestial City This city built of precious stones and streets of gold comes from John Bunyan's *The Pilgrim's Progress*.

Cyclops' Island Somewhere in the Mediterranean Odysseus found this land of gigantic one-eyed men.

Dagobah This swampy world is home to the Jedi master Yoda in the 1980 movie *The Empire Strikes Back.*

Dictionapolis City of Words is the other name of this place where letters can be bought to eat or create new words in Norton Juster's *The Phantom Tollbooth.*

The Doldrums This area in the Wisdom Kingdom inhabited by Lethargians comes from Norton Juster's *The Phantom Tollbooth.*

Dracula's Castle Somewhere in the Carpathian Mountains in eastern Hungary is the home of Count Dracula, as described by Bram Stoker in *Dracula.*

El Dorado A kingdom somewhere between Amazon and Peru where gold abounds, from the writings of Sir Walter Raleigh.

Emerald City Ozma rules this capital of Oz in L. Frank Baum's *The Wonderful Wizard of Oz.*

Erehwon This idyllic kingdom, probably located in central or northern Australia, was first glimpsed in Samuel Butler's 1872 *Erewhon.*

Fairyland In his *Phantastes*, George MacDonald describes this land where time is elongated and money is useless.

Forest Moon of Endor The verdant moon Han Solo and his band of rebels must land on to knock out the tractor beam that secures the Death Star in the 1983 movie *Return of the Jedi.*

Freedonia This small European country is ruled by Rufus T. Firefly (who looks remarkably like Groucho Marx) in Bert Kalmar's film *Duck Soup.*

Gilligan's Island A shipwrecked cast of incongruous characters—including the skipper; his first mate, Gilligan; a professor; a starlet; a girl-next-door; and a millionaire couple—made for a long-running television show set on an uncharted island.

Gondor Middle Earth's most important kingdom was ruled by Aragon at the conclusion of the War of the Rings in J. R. R. Tolkien's *The Return of the King.*

Gotham The city of Batman, filled with comic book villains like the Joker and the Penguin, was created by Bob Kane and Bill Finger for Detective Comics in 1940.

Hoth The ice planet Luke Skywalker and the other rebels must escape from in the 1980 movie *Return of the Jedi.*

Jabberwocky Wood Somewhere in England lies the home of a terrible creature who gives his name to the woods in Lewis Carroll's *Through the Looking-Glass.*

King Solomon's Mines This African diamond mine appears in Henry Rider Haggard's *King Solomon's Mines.*

Krypton The home planet of Superman from which he was sent away as a youth before the planet's destruction.

Laputa This floating island hovering over Balnibarbi can be found in Jonathan Swift's *Gulliver's Travels.*

Lilliput Lemuel Gulliver discovers this island inhabited by people less than six inches high in Jonathan Swift's *Gulliver's Travels.*

Looking-Glass Land This land of changing characteristics can be entered by climbing on the mantle in the deanery of Christ Church, Oxford, England, in Lewis Carroll's *Through the Looking-Glass.*

Island of the Lord of the Flies William Golding describes this coral island in the South China Sea in his book *The Lord of the Flies.*

Lotus-Eater's Island In Homer's *The Odyssey,* this isle in the Mediterranean has lotus blossoms that cause obliviousness if eaten.

Maple White Island This lost world, where many extinct animals still exist, resides in a high plateau in the jungle of Brazil in Sir Arthur Conan Doyle's *The Lost World.*

Metropolis Clark Kent (a.k.a. Superman) calls this city home, where he works as a reporter for the *Daily Planet.*

Metropolis Fritz Lang created this enormous and ultimately destructive city in his 1926 movie *Metropolis.*

Middle Earth This land of men, dwarves, elves,

hobbits, and wizards is detailed in J. R. R. Tolkien's *The Lord of the Rings*.

Narnia In *The Chronicles of Narnia*, C. S. Lewis describes this land created by Aslan, a lion, by singing.

Never-Never Land No girls (except for Wendy) are to be found on this island of Lost Boys, as detailed in Sir James Matthew Barrie's *Peter Pan*.

Ork The ABC television network discovered this home planet of Mork, where people grow young, on the show *Mork and Mindy* in 1978.

Outer Limits This land of science fiction and horror was first seen on the ABC television network in 1963.

Oz L. Frank Baum tells of an old, merry land (that is, in *The Wonderful Wizard of Oz*, a place dissimilar to Kansas) where sickness, money, and poverty do not exist.

Pepperland This is a place that can be accessed through the Sea of Holes, where overruning Blue Meanies are repulsed by the Beatles' music, in Lee Minoff's *Yellow Submarine*.

Planet of the Apes The movie of the same name introduced this planet ruled by apes to a large audience in 1968.

Ptolemais Creatures called Shadows, who foreshadow death, inhabit this Grecian city in Edgar Allen Poe's "Shadow: A Parable."

Rigmarole South of Oz is the location of this town where the inhabitants don't talk clearly, as told by L. Frank Baum in *The Emerald City of Oz*.

Rip Van Winkle's Village In the Catskill Mountains lies this village where ghosts play ninepins in Washington Irving's *Rip Van Winkle*.

Shangri-La This temperate valley in the mountains of Tibet, from James Hilton's *Lost Horizon*, is home to many world-weary travellers.

Shire This pleasant land in Middle Earth, inhabited by hobbits, can be found in J. R. R. Tolkien's *The Hobbit*.

Snark Island Lewis Carroll describes this dismal island inhabited by snarks, jubjubs, and a bandersnatch in his *The Hunting of the Snark*.

Snow Queen's Castle Nasty snowflakes and frozen boys live in this unhappy castle in a desolate area of Finland in Hans Christian Andersen's *Snedronningen*.

Tatooine The desert planet that is home to Luke Skywalker and Jabba the Hutt in George Lucas's *Star Wars* movies.

Toyland Enid Blyton created this magical land filled with nursery-rhyme characters and toys in *Noddy Goes to Toyland*.

Treasure Island Robert Louis Stevenson describes this island off the coast of Mexico, first charted by Captain Flint, in *Treasure Island*.

Twilight Zone This bizarre dimension was created by writer Rod Serling and debuted on the CBS television network in 1959.

Utopia Fifteen miles off the coast of South America lies this island where people live and work in a communal fashion in Sir Thomas More's *Utopia*.

Valhalla The great hall where Odin receives the souls of heroes who have fallen bravely in battle in Norse myths.

Vanity Fair John Bunyan tells of this town along the way to the Celestial City, where a fair is constantly being held to sell works of vanity, in *The Pilgrim's Progress*.

Wonderland Ruled by the King and Queen of Hearts, this kingdom is accessible through a rabbit hole in Lewis Carroll's *Alice's Adventures in Wonderland*.

Xanadu Kubla Khan ordered a pleasure dome constructed in this land, found in Samuel Taylor Coleridge's "Kubla Khan: A Vision in a Dream."

Zenda Surrounded by wooded hills, this country town in Ruritania can be found in Anthony Hope's *The Prisoner of Zenda*.

LOST CITIES OF THE BIBLE

Admah A city south of the Dead Sea. (Gen. 14:1–12)

Ai A Canaanite city where Abraham pitched his tent. (Gen. 12:8)

Aijalon An Amorite city in the highlands of Judah. (Josh. 10:12)

Ain A city on the boundary of Canaan. (Num. 13:11)

Alemeth A Levitical city in Benjamin. (1 Chron. 6:60)

Aman A city in Judah. (Josh. 15:26)

Amphipolis A city in Macedonia. (Acts 17:1)

Anem A Levitical city located in Issachar. (1 Chron. 6:73)

Apollonia A city in Macedonia. (Acts 17:1)

Arbatta A city mentioned in 1 Macc. 5:23.

Ashen A city in the Shephelah. (Josh. 19:7)

Ashnah A city in Judah. (Josh. 15:23)

Ashtoroth A city in Gilead. (Josh. 13:31)

Athach A city in Judah. (1 Sam. 30:30)

Athroth-Shophan A city in Gilead. (Num. 32:35)

Baal-Hermon A Hivite city on the border of Manasseh. (Judg. 3:3)

Beeroth A Hivite city northwest of Jerusalem. (Josh. 9:17)

Berothah A Syrian city in northern Israel. (Ezek. 47:16)

Berothai A city in Syria. (2 Sam. 8:8)

Bethulia A city in Samaria. (Jth. 4:6)

Bileam A Levitical city in Manasseh. (1 Chron. 6:70)

Bosor A city in Gilead. (1 Macc. 5:26)

Calah A city near the junction of the Tigris and Upper Zab Rivers in Mesopotamia. (Gen. 10:11)

Calneh A city in Mesopotamia. (Amos 6:2)

Chelous A city in southern Judah. (Jth. 1:9)

Chilmand A city in Mesopotamia. (Ezek. 27:23)

Debir A Canaanite royal city in southern Judah. (Josh. 11:21)

Dibon A Moab city north of the Arnon River. (Num. 21:30)

Dinhabah A city in Edom. (Gen. 36:32)

Ebez A city in Issachar. (Josh. 19:20)

Edrei A city in Upper Galilee. (Josh. 19:37)

Eltolad A city in the south of Judah. (Josh. 15:30)

Emek-Keziz A city in the vicinity of Jericho. (Josh. 18:21)

En-Hazor A city in Upper Galilee. (Josh. 19:37)

Ether A city somewhere in Judah. (Josh. 15:42)

Gomorrah A city in the valley of Siddim in the Dead Sea area. (Gen. 14:2)

Halah A city in Assyria. (2 Kings 17:6)

Hamonah A city mentioned in Ezekiel 39:16.

Hanes A city in Upper Egypt. (Isa. 30:4)

Kartah A Levitical city in Zebulun. (Josh. 21:34)

Kiriath-Huzoth A city in Moab. (Num. 22:39)

Lasharon A city mentioned in Joshua 12:18.

Nahor A city in Mesopotamia. (Gen. 24:10)

Pithom A city on the eastern Nile Delta. (Exod. 1:11)

Rehoboth A city in Assyria. (Gen. 10:11)

Resen An Assyrian city. (Gen. 10:12)

Sepharvaim A city in northern Syria. (2 Kings 17:24)

Sodom A city east of the southern Dead Sea. (Gen. 13:10)

Sur A coastal city mentioned in Judith. (Jth. 2:28)

Tabor A Levitical city near Mt. Tabor. (1 Chron. 6:77)

Tel-Assar A city probably conquered by Mesopotamia. (2 Kings 19:12)

Zeboiim A city in the southern Dead Sea area. (Gen. 14:2)

Zer A city in Lower Galilee. (Josh. 19:35)

THE SEVEN WONDERS OF THE ANCIENT WORLD

The Great Pyramid of Giza The only one of the Seven Wonders that still stands in almost complete and recognizable form, it is also the oldest; built by Khufu (a.k.a. Cheops) for the Fourth Dynasty, about 2500 BCE.

The Hanging Gardens of Babylon Though they have never been conclusively identified nor has their existence been proven, the gardens are thought to have been built on the rooftop of the royal palace of King Nebuchadnezzar.

The Statue of Zeus at Olympia The statue centrepiece of the temple and altar of Zeus, king of the Greek gods, drew pilgrims from all parts of the Greek world. One important element of the rituals practised there was the celebration of athletic contests.

The Temple of Artemis at Ephesus Believed to have been located in what is today Turkey, this temple was thought to have been destroyed by Ostrogoths in 262 CE. It combined both Greek and Near Eastern elements into a simple rectangular temple surrounded on all sides by a colonnade.

The Mausoleum at Halicarnassus This was the tomb monument of Maussollos, who ruled Caria from 377 to 353 BCE in what is today Bodrum, in southwest Turkey.

The Colossus of Rhodes This statue was situated on the island of Rhodes, off the southwest corner of what is today Turkey, at the junction of two ancient sea lanes.

The Pharos at Alexandria The great lighthouse of Alexandria, on the northwest coast of the Nile Delta, was the last structure of the Seven Wonders to be built. It took its name from the island in front of the harbour of Alexandria.

THINGS

ANIMAL

ANIMAL COLLECTIVE NOUNS

Bale of turtles
Band of gorillas
Bed of clams
Bed of oysters
Bevy of quail
Bevy of swans
Brace of ducks
Brood of chicks
Cast of hawks
Cete of badgers
Charm of finches
Cloud of gnats
Clowder of cats
Clutch of chicks
Clutter of cats
Congregation of plovers
Covey of partridge
Covey of quail
Crash of rhinoceros
Cry of hounds
Down of hares
Drift of swine
Drove of cattle
Drove of sheep
Exaltation of larks
Flight of birds
Gaggle of geese
Gam of whales
Gang of elks
Herd of elephants
Horde of gnats
Husk of hares
Kindle of kittens
Knot of toads
Labour of moles

Leap of leopards
Leash of greyhounds
Litter of pigs
Mob of kangaroos
Murder of crows
Muster of peacocks
Mute of hounds
Nest of pheasants
Nest of vipers
Pack of hounds
Pack of wolves
Paddling of ducks
Parliament of owls
Peep of chickens
Pod of seals
Pod of whales
Pride of lions
Rag of colts
Rafter of turkeys
School of fish
Shrewdness of apes
Siege of cranes
Siege of herons
Shoal of fish
Shoal of pilchards
Skein of geese
Skulk of foxes
Sloth of bears
Smack or smuck of jellyfish
Sounder of boars
Sounder of swine
Span of mules
Spring of teals
Team of ducks
Tribe of goats or trip of goats
Troop of kangaroos
Troop of monkeys
Volery of birds
Watch of nightingales
Wing of plovers
Yoke of oxen

BIRDS

Order	Family	Common name	General characteristics of order
Struthioniformes	Struthionidae	ostriches	Largest living bird, quick, flightless, and an herbivore
Rheiformes	Rheidae	rheas	Swift, flightless bird with short wings and tail feathers like an ostrich
Casuariiformes	Casuariidae Dromaiidae	cassowaries emus	Fast, large, flightless birds with hairlike feathers
Apterygiformes	Apterygidae	kiwis	Small flightless birds that are primarily nocturnal
Tinamiformes	Tinamidae	tinamous	Ground-nesting birds that can fly but usually do not
Sphenisciformes	Spheniscidae	penguins	Flightless, aquatic birds adapted to live in cold climates
Gaviformes	Gaviidae	divers or loons	Ground-nesting birds that dive into the water to feed on fish and insects
Podicipediformes	Podicipedidae	grebes	Water-nesting birds that dive to feed on fish and insects
Procellariiformes	Diomedeidae Procellariidae Hydrobatidae Pelecanoididae	albatrosses petrels, fulmars storm petrels diving petrels	Seabirds with long wings and partly webbed toes; secrete oil as a defence mechanism
Procellariiformes	Pelecanidae Sulidae Phaethontidae Phalacrocoracidae Fregatidae Anhingidae	pelicans gannets, boobies tropicbirds cormorants frigatebirds darters	Large order of diving birds found worldwide
Ciconiiformes	Ardeidae Scopidae Balaenicipitidae Ciconiidae Threskiornithidae Phoenicopteridae	herons, bitterns hammerheads whale-headed storks storks spoonbills, ibises flamingos	Wading birds that stand upright; often have webbed toes and specialized beaks

Order	Family	Common name	General characteristics of order
Anseriformes	Anatidae	ducks, geese, swans	Marsh-dwelling waders
	Anhimidae	screamers	that eat vegetation and nest on the ground
Falconiformes	Cathartidae	vultures (New World)	Large birds of prey, or
	Sagittariidae	secretary-bird	raptors, with hooked beaks
	Pandionidae	osprey	and talons
	Falconidae	falcons, caracaras	
	Accipitridae	kites, Old World vultures, harriers, hawks, eagles, and buzzards	
Galliformes	Megapodidae	megapodes	Gamebirds with short
	Cracidae	curassows	rounded wings poorly
	Tetraonidae	grouse	adapted for extended flight
	Phasianidae	pheasants, quail, and partridges	
	Numididae	guineafowl	
	Meleagrididae	turkeys	
Gruiformes	Mesitornithidae	mesites	Ground-feeding birds,
	Turnicidae	buttonquails, hemipodes	generally brown or grey, with long, rounded wings
	Perdionomidae	plains wanderer	
	Gruidae	cranes	
	Aramidae	limpkin	
	Psophiidae	trumpeters	
	Rallidae	rails	
	Heliornithidae	finfoots	
	Rhynochetidae	kagu	
	Eurypygidae	sunbitterns	
	Cariamidae	seriemas	
	Otididae	bustards	
Charadriiformes (Suborder Charadrii)	Jacanidae	jacanas or lily-trotters	Small to medium-sized
	Rostratulidae	painted snipe	seabirds and shorebirds,
	Haematopodidae	oystercatchers	generally with long
	Charadriidae	plovers, lapwings	narrow wings that act
	Scolopacidae	sandpipers	as paddles in the water
	Recurvirostridae	avocets, stilts	
	Phalaropodidae	phalaropes	
	Dromadidae	crab plovers	
	Burhinidae	stonecurlews or thick knees	
	Glareolidae	pratincoles or coursers	
	Thinocoridae	seed snipe	
	Chionididae	sheathbills	

Order	Family	Common name	General characteristics of order
(Suborder Lari)	Stercorariidae Laridae Sternidae Rynchopidae	skuas, jaegers gulls terns, noddies skimmers	
(Suborder Alcae)	Alcidae	auks	
Columbiformes	Pteroclididae Columbidae	sandgrouse pigeons, doves	Small to medium-sized with heavy, thick plumage
Psittaciformes	Psittacidae	parrots, lovebirds, and cockatoos	Distinguished by zygodactyl toes: two pointing forward and two backward, which enable them to climb and hold objects
Cuculiformes	Musophagidae Cuculidae Opisthocomidae	turacos cuckoos, anis, and roadrunners hoatzin	Diverse order of terrestial and arboreal birds
Strigiformes	Strididae Tytonidae	owls barn owls	Nocturnal raptors with binocular vision
Caprimulgiformes	Caprimulgidae Podargidae Aegothelidae Hyctibiidae Steatornithidae	nightjars or goatsuckers frogmouths owlet-nightjars potoos oilbird	Generally insectivorous, with hooked beaks, large eyes, and short legs with weak feet
Apodiformes	Apodidae Hemiprocnidae Trochilidae	swifts crested swifts hummingbirds	Insectivorous and migratory with strong flying skills
Coliiformes	Coliidae	mousebirds or collies	Very social herbivores that can become a nuisance to farmers
Trogoniformes	Trogonidae	trogons	Arboreal birds that often nest in termite mounds

Order	Family	Common name	General characteristics of order
Coraciiformes	Alcedinidae	kingfishers	Birds with three united
	Todidae	todies	anterior toes, making
	Momotidae	motmots	them well adapted to tree
	Meropidae	bee-eaters	climbing
	Leptosomatidae	cuckoo-roller	
	Coraciidae	rollers	
	Upupidae	hoopoe	
	Phoeniculidae	woodhoopoes	
	Bucerotidae	hornbills	
Piciformes	Galbulidae	jacmars	Arboreal birds that feed on
	Bucconidae	puffbirds	insects and plants
	Capitonidae	barbets	
	Indicatoridae	honeyguides	
	Ramphastidae	toucans	
	Picidae	woodpeckers, piculets, wrynecks	
Passeriformes (Suborder Eurylami)	Eurylaimidae	broadbills	Largest order,
	Menuridae	lyrebirds	encompassing over half of all birds; all members well adapted to perching and most feed off both plants and insects
(Suborder Menuare)	Atrichornithidae	scrub-birds	
(Suborder Tyranni)	Furnariidae	ovenbirds	
	Dendrocolaptidae	woodcreepers	
	Formicariidae	antbirds	
	Tyrannidae	tyrant flycatchers	
	Pittidae	pittas	
	Pipridae	manakins	
	Cotingidae	cotingas	
	Conopophagidae	gnateaters	
	Rhinocryptidae	tapaculos	
	Oxyruncidae	sharpbill	
	Phytotomidae	plantcutters	
	Xenicidae	New Zealand wrens	
	Philepittidae	sunbird astites	

Order	Family	Common name	General characteristics of order
(Suborder Oscines)	Hirundinidae	swallows, martins	
	Alaudidae	larks	
	Motacillidae	wagtails, pipits	
	Pycnonotidae	bulbuls	
	Lamidae	shrikes	
	Campephagidae	cuckoo-shrikes	
	Irenidae	leafbirds	
	Prionopidae	helmet shrikes	
	Vangidae	vanga shrikes	
	Bombycillidae	waxwings	
	Dulidae	palmchat	
	Cinclidae	dippers	
	Troglodytidae	wrens	
	Mimidae	mockingbirds	
	Muscicapidae subfamilies		
	Prunellidae	accentors	
	Turdinae	thrushers	
	Timaliinae	babblers	
	Sylviinae	Old World warblers	
	Muscicapinae	Old World flycatchers	
	Malurinae	fairy-wrens	
	Paradoxornithinae	parrotbills	
	Monarchinae	monarch flycatchers	
	Orthonychinae	logrunners	
	Acanthizinae	Australian warblers	
	Rhipidurinae	fantail flycatchers	
	Pachycephalinae	thickheads	
	Paridae	tits	
	Aegithalidae	long-tailed tits	
	Remizidae	penduline tits	
	Sittidae	nuthatches	
	Climacteridae	Australian treecreepers	
	Certhiidae	holarctic treecreepers	
	Rhabdornithidae	Philippine treecreepers	
	Zosteropidae	white-eyes	
	Dicaeidae	flowerpeckers	
	Pardalotidae	pardalotes or diamond eyes	
	Nectariniidae	sunbirds or spider hunters	
	Meliphagidae	honeyeaters	
	Ephthianuridae	Australian chats	

Order	Family	Common name	General characteristics of order
	Emberizidae subfamilies		
	Emberizinae	Old Word buntings, New World sparrows	
	Catamblyrhynchinae	plush-capped finch	
	Thraupinae	tanagers, honeycreepers	
	Cardinalinae	cardinal grosbeaks	
	Tersininae	swallow tanagers	
	Parulidae	wood warblers	
	Vireonidae	vireos, pepper shrikes	
	Icteridae	American blackbirds	
	Fringillidae subfamilies		
	Fringillinae	fringilline finches	
	Carduelinae	cardueline finches	
	Drepanidinae	Hawaiian honeycreepers	
	Estrildidae	waxbills	
	Ploceidae subfamilies		
	Ploceinae	true weavers	
	Viduinae	widow birds	
	Bubalornithinae	buffalo weavers	
	Passerinae	sparrow weavers and sparrows	
	Sturnidae	starlings	
	Oriolidae	orioles, figbirds	
	Dicruridae	drongos	
	Callaeidae	New Zealand wattlebirds	
	Grallinidae	magpie larks	
	Corcoracidae	Australian mudnesters	
	Artamidae	wood swallows	
	Cracticidae	bell magpies	
	Ptilonorhynchidae	bowerbirds	
	Paradisaeidae	birds of paradise	
	Corvidae	crows, magpies, and jays	

CAT BREEDS

Abyssian An ancient shorthaired breed with large ears and eyes and a long slender body.

American curl A breed distinguished by ears that curl gently backward.

American shorthair A breed developed from native American cats, the American shorthair comes in over eighty different colours and patterns.

American wirehair A shorthaired or longhaired breed, with the distinction that every hair is crimped and springy, including the whiskers.

Balinese Very similar to the Siamese, but with a semilong, rather than a short coat.

Bengal A breed created from a cross between the wild Asian leopard and the American shorthair, that often exhibits the wild traits of a feral cat.

Birman A breed supposedly from Burma, with a long, silky coat, a stocky body, and four distinctive white paws.

Bombay A glossy black shorthair with rounded, copper-coloured eyes, resembling a very small panther.

British shorthair A stocky, sturdy, shorthaired breed with a large round head set on a short thick neck, coming in many different colours and patterns and said to resemble a teddy bear.

Burmese An affectionate breed with short, silky hair, and large eyes. It comes in four recognized colours: sable, champagne, blue, and platinum.

Burmilla A cross between the Persian Chinchilla and the Burmese, the Burmilla has a short, usually silver coat, and green eyes.

Chartreux A very old shorthaired breed known for its woolly blue coat, bright orange eyes, and smiling expression.

Colourpoint shorthair Very similar to the Siamese, but comes in a wider variety of colours.

Cornish rex A breed with a soft, short velvety coat, and a body similar to a whippet dog, with a small, egg-shaped head.

Cymric A longhaired version of the Manx.

Devon rex A small, "pixie-ish" cat with large eyes and ears, with a short, soft curly coat similar to the Cornish rex.

Egyptian mau An Egyptian breed (*mau* means "cat" in Egyptian) with a spotted tabby pattern that comes in three colours: silver, bronze, and smoke.

Exotic A breed with the body and head type of the Persian, but with a short, plush coat.

Havana brown A chocolate-brown shorthaired breed with green eyes and brown whiskers.

Japanese bobtail A Japanese breed that comes in many different colours and patterns, distinguished by its short tail, which resembles a pom-pom or bunny tail.

Javanese A breed very similar to the Siamese, but with a long silky coat like the Balinese, and appearing in a wide range of colours like the Colourpoint shorthair.

Korat A small shorthaired breed from Thailand, with a blue-silver coat, heart-shaped head, and large, round, brilliant green eyes.

Maine coon The native American longhaired breed, large and shaggy and available in a wide variety of colours and patterns.

Manx A tailless breed that comes in both long- and shorthaired varieties and all colours and patterns.

Norwegian forest cat A large, sturdy Norwegian longhaired breed that comes in all colour varieties.

Ocicat A new American breed with a distinctive spotted coat, long body, short hair, and a doglike devotion to its owners.

Oriental longhair The semilonghaired variety of the Oriental shorthair.

Oriental shorthair A breed identical to the Siamese in every way except that its coat lacks all point markings (the darker colourations on the mask, ears, legs, and tail).

Persian A placid, gentle, fluffy longhaired breed with large eyes and a flat face that comes in seven different colour divisions.

Ragdoll A large, semilonghaired breed with Siamese-like markings, so named for its propensity to go entirely limp when picked up.

Russian blue A plush shorthaired breed with a silvery blue coat and vivid green eyes.

Scottish fold A medium-sized breed with distinctive folded ears, medium to long hair, and large rounded eyes. It comes in all patterns and colours.

Selkirk rex A curly-haired rex breed that differs from the others (Cornish and Devon) because it has a stocky body and comes in long- and shorthaired varieties.

Siamese A slender, shorthaired breed with large ears, blue eyes, and a pale body with coloured points (the mask, ears, legs, and tail).

Singapura A small shorthaired breed from Singapore, characterized by large eyes and a ticked (agouti) coat.

Snowshoe A cross between the Siamese and the American shorthair, this breed has a short, dense coat with points and white markings on the face, chest, and feet.

Somali A longhaired Abyssinian with a soft coat in a ticked tabby pattern, said to resemble a fox.

Sphynx A medium-sized breed distinguished by the fact that it is hairless, except for a light down that covers its face, ears, legs, tail, and paws.

Tiffany, or **Tiffanie** A cross between the Burmese and the Persian, with long silky hair and green eyes.

Tonkinese A cross between the Burmese and the Siamese, with a slender body, short hair in a unique pattern known as "mink," and aqua-coloured eyes.

Turkish angora A semilonghaired breed from Turkey that comes in a variety of colours and patterns.

Turkish van A white, semilonghaired breed from Turkey, with coloured markings on the tail and head.

DOG BREEDS

Afghan hound A large, longhaired dog with a silky topknot, Roman profile, and all-around aristocratic appearance.

Airedale terrier The largest of the terrier breeds, with small folded ears and a keen terrier expression.

Akita A large, aggressive Japanese breed with a distinctive curled tail and small, erect ears.

Alaskan malamute A strong and powerful Arctic sled dog with a thick double coat.

Australian cattle dog A sturdy, compact Australian dog bred to herd cattle.

Australian shepherd A medium-sized breed that comes in a variety of colours; known for being very active and athletic.

Australian terrier A small, working terrier bred in Australia from a variety of British terriers, with a harsh outer coat and silky topknot.

Basenji A small shorthaired hunting breed from Africa with a gazellelike appearance.

Basset hound A short-legged scent-hound with soulful eyes and long silky ears.

Beagle A small, shorthaired breed known for its playfulness and hunting ability.

Bearded collie A medium-sized dog with a long, flat coat, bred as a working dog.

Bedlington terrier Originally bred as a hunting dog, the Bedlington terrier has a lamblike appearance: a thick, woolly coat, gentle expression, and long, narrow head.

Belgian Malinois A large Belgian shepherd breed with a short, thick coat.

Belgian sheepdog Known in most parts of the world as the Groenendael, this large, longhaired working breed is always black.

Belgian Tervuren Identical to the Belgian sheepdog, with the difference that all shades of red, fawn, and grey with a black overlay are allowed.

Bernese mountain dog A large tricoloured breed with a medium-length, silky tail.

Bichon frise A small, white, fluffy breed with round, dark, expressive eyes.

Bloodhound A large shorthaired breed noted for its loose skin (which falls in folds around the head and neck) and finely tuned sense of smell.

Border collie The world's premier sheepdog, usually black and white, but other combinations are also acceptable.

Border terrier An active terrier breed with a distinctive otter-shaped head.

Borzoi Originally bred by the Russian aristocracy, this dog is tall and slender with a long, silky coat and distinctive Roman nose.

Boston terrier A native American breed, medium-sized, with a short coat and compact build.

Bouvier des Flandres A large, powerful herding breed with a coarse, rough coat.

Boxer A medium-sized working breed from Germany with a short coat and playful personality.

Briard A large, boisterous dog with distinct beard and eyebrows.

Brittany A compact, midsized dog that is quick and agile, with a wavy coat, usually white with yellow or liver patches.

Brussels griffon A lively toy dog with a moustachioed face and widely set eyes; can have either a rough or a smooth coat.

Bull terrier A short, strong breed with an egg-shaped head; bred for fighting.

Bulldog A medium-sized dog with short legs, large chest, and a massive head.

Cairn terrier A small, strong breed with a coarse coat that is usually black or tan.

Cavalier King Charles spaniel A toy spaniel known for being active and intelligent.

Chesapeake Bay retriever A strong, medium-sized dog with a long nose, and small ears that hang loosely; it is agile both on land and in the water.

Chihuahua A very small dog with a rounded head and large ears and eyes.

Chinese shar-pei A compact breed with a large nose, wrinkled brow, and small ears set wide apart on top of the head.

Chow chow An ancient breed from China, with a large body and head surrounded by a lionlike mane.

Clumber spaniel A breed with a long, low, sturdy body and a sedate disposition.

Cocker spaniel A sturdy dog with a luxuriant coat and distinctive chiselled head.

Collie (rough) Originally a sheepdog, this long-haired, medium-sized breed is now a common family pet.

Collie (smooth) Similar to the rough collie but with a short, rough coat.

Curly coated retriever A tall, strong dog with a coat that is a dense mass of tight curls of fur.

Dachshund (longhaired) Both a standard and a miniature breed, the longhaired dachshund has a thick, waterproof, well-feathered coat.

Dachshund (smooth) Both a standard and a miniature breed, the smooth dachshund has a sleek, odorless shorthaired coat that shines when polished.

Dachshund (wirehaired) Both a standard and a miniature breed, the wirehaired dachshund has a short, tight, rough outercoat and a softer undercoat, along with a bushy beard and eyebrows.

Dalmatian A shorthaired dog with a distinctively spotted coat, the Dalmatian is bred for speed and endurance.

Doberman pinscher A medium-sized breed with a square body, sleek glossy shorthaired coat, and a muscular build.

English cocker spaniel One of the smallest gundogs, this breed has a fine silky coat and very long ears.

English setter An elegant gundog with a feathered flat coat and a smooth gait.

English springer spaniel A medium-sized long-haired dog with a liver-and-white or black-and-white coat and a docked tail.

Flat-coated retriever A working hunting dog with a thick, flat-lying coat and a long distinctive head.

Fox terrier (smooth) Originally a British hunting dog, it is very lively and has a smooth, short coat.

Fox terrier (wire) A very active, midsized breed with long legs and rough coat.

German shepherd dog A long, deep-bodied dog with a noble head and a dense, harsh coat.

German shorthaired pointer A powerful hunting breed with a sleek short coat.

Golden retriever A gentle, patient hunting breed with a butterscotch coat and dark-rimmed eyes.

Gordon setter A large black-and-tan breed from Scotland.

Great Dane A giant, muscled, square-bodied breed developed in Germany to hunt wild boars.

Great Pyrenees A majestic, midsized dog with a great coat; known for being extremely coordinated and agile.

Greyhound A tall, lean, strong dog with a wide chest and long legs.

Irish setter An active breed, aristocratic in appearance, known as one of the premier hunting dogs.

Irish wolfhound A strong, massive dog with a gentle demeanour.

Italian greyhound Small, graceful, and pristine, this breed is shorter and more slender than the greyhound.

Jack Russell terrier A small, hardy dog that is very brave for its size, with a white coat covered by brown or black markings.

Japanese chin A toy dog with an oriental, aristocratic appearance.

Keeshond A small Dutch breed with a thick coat and an alert, pleasant expression.

Labrador retriever A medium-sized dog known for its docile nature and desire to be with humans.

Lhasa apso A very small, assertive dog that is very wary of strangers; it has a long, dense coat.

Maltese A toy dog with a long, silky white coat; it was popular with nobility in ancient Mediterranean cultures.

Mastiff A large dog, once bred for fighting; it is now known as a dignified, well-mannered pet.

Miniature pinscher A small, lively, proud dog that resembles a toy Doberman.

Newfoundland A large, strong breed known for its kind disposition and affinity for water.

Old English sheepdog A medium-sized dog with a profuse, thick coat and a stocky, compact body.

Papillon A very small breed named after the French word for "butterfly," partly because its ears resemble butterfly wings.

Pekingese A toy dog from China, known for its thick coat as well as its direct and independent personality.

Pointer A strong, energetic sporting breed, named for its ability to "point" to game.

Pomeranian A cocky toy dog with a two-layered coat consisting of a dense undercoat and a large, coarse outercoat.

Poodle (miniature) A midsized poodle with a distinct curly coat, generally between 10 and 15 inches tall; like other varieties of poodles, it is a retriever breed.

Poodle (standard) Similar to other poodles, but generally taller than 15 inches.

Poodle (toy) Similar to other poodles, but generally shorter than 10 inches.

Pug A toy breed with a dark, wrinkled face, large head, and pleasant disposition.

Rhodesian ridgeback A large shorthaired dog, originally bred to hunt lions; it is distinguished by the clearly defined ridge of hair that grows down its back.

Rottweiler A medium-large shorthaired dog, black with rust markings, known for its great strength and endurance.

Saint Bernard A large Swiss breed known for its huge head and gentle temperament; the Saint Bernard comes in longhaired and shorthaired varieties.

Saluki A large dog with a long, narrow head; it is one of the oldest known breeds of domesticated dogs.

Samoyed A large, white, fluffy Siberian breed with dark eyes and a smiling expression.

Schipperke A small, black, tailless dog with a foxlike face, it is a talented watchdog and vermin hunter.

Schnauzer (giant) Appears almost identical to a standard schnauzer—prolific facial hair, coarse coat, and vigorous personality—but is larger and more powerful.

Schnauzer (miniature) Smaller, but otherwise very similar in appearance to other schnauzer breeds.

Schnauzer (standard) The original schnauzer breed, it is a robust, medium-sized dog, bred to be strong.

Scottish terrier Better known as the "Scottie", this breed is small and short-legged with a harsh and wiry coat; it is usually black, but other colours are also acceptable.

Shetland sheepdog A small descendant of the Scottish border collie, this breed is known for its abundant mane and frill.

Shih tzu A sturdy toy dog from China with a long flowing coat and tail curved over its back.

Siberian husky A sled dog from northeastern Asia, this breed is known for its beautiful almond-shaped eyes, wolflike appearance, and strength and endurance.

Silky terrier A toy breed with an inquisitive nature and a long, silky coat.

Skye terrier A small longhaired terrier twice as long as it is high.

Staffordshire bull terrier A British smooth-coated breed, extremely strong and muscular.

Tibetan spaniel A small longhaired breed from Tibet with dark brown eyes.

Vizsla A medium-sized hunting dog with an aristocratic appearance, short coat, and lean build.

Welsh corgi (Cardigan) A small, long dog with a long, bushy tail, originally used for herding.

Welsh corgi (Pembroke) Not as long as the Cardigan variety, it also has smaller ears and little or no tail.

Weimaraner A medium-sized grey dog with a shorthaired coat and aristocratic features.

West Highland white terrier A small, hardy white terrier with a harsh double coat.

Whippet A shorthaired, medium-sized sighthound, known for its great speed.

Yorkshire terrier A longhaired toy terrier breed known for its silky blue-and-tan coat.

ENDANGERED SPECIES

Anteater, giant (South America) threatened by habitat destruction.

Armadillo, giant (South America) threatened by hunting and habitat destruction.

Ass, African wild (northeastern Africa) threatened by hunting and competition from introduced animals.

Aye-aye (Madagascar) threatened by hunting and habitat destruction.

Bison (Canada and U.S.) threatened by hunting.

Bobwhite, masked (quail) (Arizona and Mexico) threatened by habitat destruction.

Butterfly, mission blue (California) threatened by habitat destruction.

Caiman, broad-snouted (South America) threatened by hunting.

Cheetah (Africa to India) threatened by hunting and habitat destruction.

Chimpanzee (central Africa) threatened by hunting and habitat destruction.

Condor, California (western U.S.) threatened by hunting.

Cougar (eastern Canada and U.S.) threatened by hunting and habitat destruction.

Crane, Siberian white (Russia and Japan) threatened by hunting and habitat destruction.

Crane, whooping (North America) threatened by hunting and habitat destruction.

Crocodile, American (Florida, Mexico, Central and South America) threatened by hunting and habitat destruction.

Crocodile, Nile (Africa) threatened by hunting.

Curlew, Eskimo (Canada and Alaska) threatened by hunting.

Dolphin, Chinese river (Baiji) (China) threatened by accidents and habitat disruption (pollution).

Duck, Laysan (Hawaii) threatened by habitat destruction.

Dugong (coastal Australia) threatened by habitat destruction and hunting.

Elephant, Asian (south-central and Southeast Asia) threatened by habitat destruction (agricultural development).

Ferret, black-footed (originally in U.S., now only in captivity) threatened by destruction of prairie dog population.

Fox, northern swift (U.S. and Canada) threatened by hunting.

Gibbon (Southeast Asia) threatened by habitat destruction.

Gorilla (central and western Africa) threatened by poaching and habitat destruction.

Hawk, Hawaiian (Hawaii) threatened by hunting and habitat destruction.

Hyena, brown (South Africa) threatened by hunting.

Jaguar (Central and South America) threatened by hunting and habitat destruction.

Kakapo (New Zealand) threatened by habitat destruction and competition from introduced animals.

Kite, snail (Florida) threatened by habitat destruction and loss of food source (snails).

Komodo dragon (Indonesia) threatened by hunting.

Lemur (Madagascar) threatened by habitat destruction.

Leopard (Africa and Asia) threatened by habitat destruction, fur trade.

Leopard, snow (Asia) threatened by hunting for the fur trade.

Lion, Asiatic (India) threatened by hunting and habitat destruction.

Macaw, indigo (Brazil) threatened by hunting and habitat destruction.

Manatee, West Indian (Caribbean) threatened by accidents and habitat destruction.

Marmoset, golden lion (Brazil) threatened by habitat destruction.

Monkey, woolly spider (Brazil) threatened by hunting and habitat destruction.

Nene (Hawaiian goose) (Hawaii) threatened by habitat destruction and competition from introduced animals.

Olm (central Europe) threatened by hunting and pollution.

Orangutan (Borneo and Sumatra) threatened by habitat destruction.

Oryx (Arabian) (Saudia Arabia, Jordan, and Oman) threatened by hunting.

Otter, giant (Amazon basin) threatened by hunting and habitat destruction.

Panda, giant (China) threatened by restrictive habitat.

Panther, Florida (southern U.S.) threatened by habitat destruction.

Parrot, imperial (West Indies) threatened by habitat destruction and illegal capture.

Parrot, Puerto Rico (Puerto Rico) threatened by habitat destruction.

Prairie dog (western U.S.) threatened by habitat destruction and poisoning.

Pupfish, Devil's Hole (Nevada) threatened by habitat destruction.

Python, Indian (India, Sri Lanka) threatened by hunting and capture for the pet trade.

Rhinoceros, black (sub-Saharan Africa) threatened by hunting and habitat destruction.

Rhinoceros, white (central and eastern Africa) threatened by poaching.

Salamander, Texas blind (Texas) threatened by habitat destruction.

Seal, Mediterranean monk (Mediterranean Sea) threatened by pollution and hunting.

Stork, oriental white (eastern Asia and Russia) threatened by pollution and habitat destruction.

Thylacine (Tasmania) possibly brought to extinction by hunting.

Tiger (Asia) threatened by hunting and habitat destruction.

Tortoise (Ecuador) threatened by hunting and competition from other animals.

Trout, Arizona (Arizona) threatened by habitat destruction.

Turtle, Kemp's ridley sea (warm seas and oceans) threatened by hunting and egg collection.

Turtle, leatherback sea (warm seas and oceans) threatened by hunting.

Warbler, Kirtland's (U.S. and Bahamas) threatened by habitat destruction.

Whale, blue (oceans) threatened by hunting.

Whale, finback (oceans) threatened by commercial hunting.

Whale, grey (northern Pacific) threatened by hunting.

Whale, humpback (oceans) threatened by hunting.

Wolf, red (southern U.S.) threatened by hunting.

Woodpecker, ivory-billed (southern U.S. and Cuba) threatened by habitat destruction.

Zebra, Grevy's (eastern Africa) threatened by habitat destruction.

Zebra, mountain (southern Africa) threatened by hunting and habitat destruction.

EXTINCT SPECIES

The date of extinction has been provided where available.

AMPHIBIANS

Palestine painted frog
Vegas Valley painted frog

BIRDS

Arabian ostrich
Auckland Island merganser: 1905
Balck mamo: 1907
Barred-wing rail: 1890
Bonin wood pigeon: 1889
Bourbon crested starling: 1862
Broad-billed parrot: 1638
Carolina parakeet: 1914
Choiseul crested pigeon: 1904
Crested shelduck: 1943
Cuban red macaw: 1885
Delalande's coucal: 1930
Dodo: 1681
Dominican macaw: 1791
Dwarf emu
Elephant bird: 1649
Eskimo curlew: 1963 (some unconfirmed sightings post-1963)
Forest spotted owlet: 1872
Gadwall
Great auk: 1844
Greater koa finch: 1896
Green and yellow macaw: 1791
Guadalupe caracara: 1900
Guadalupe storm petrel: 1912
Guadalupe vlicker
Hawaii O-o: 1934
Heath hen: 1926
Himalayan mountain quail: 1868
Huia: 1907
Ivory-billed woodpecker: 1950 (some unconfirmed sightings post-1950)
Jamaican pauraqué: 1859

Jerdon's courser: 1900
Kioea: 1859
Kona finch: 1894
Kusaie starling: 1827
Labat's conure: 1722
Labrador duck: 1875
Lanai alauwahio: 1937
Laysan rail: 1944
Lesser koa finch: 1891
Lord Howe white eye: 1918
Mamo: 1898
Mascarene parrot: 1834
Molokai alauwahio
Molokai O-o: 1915
Mysterious starling: 1774
New Caledonian lorikeet: 1860
North Island laughing owl: 1890
Oahu akepa: 1900
Oahu O-o: 1837
Painted vulture
Passenger pigeon: 1914
Pink-headed duck: 1944
Réunion fody: 1776
Réunion solitaire: 1746
Rodriguez little owl: 1730
Rodriguez parrot: 1730
Rodriguez solitaire: 1791
Rodriguez ring-necked parakeet: 1875
Ryukyu kingfisher: 1887
Samoan rail: 1873
Spectacled cormorant: 1852
Tahiti rail: 1925
Tahiti sandpiper: 1777
Tana dove: 1774
Tasmanian emu
Ula-ai-hawane: 1892
Wake Island rail: 1945

DINOSAURS

Albertosaurus A flesh-eating dinosaur related to the tyrannosaurus, but smaller and faster moving. Late Cretaceous Period.

Allosaurus A gigantic flesh-eating dinosaur weighing as much as two tons. Late Jurassic Period.

Altispinax A flesh-eating dinosaur with a fan of large spines across its back. Early Cretaceous Period.

Anchisaurus A small prosauropod (lizard foot) dinosaur, probably a plant eater. Late Triassic/Early Jurassic Period.

Ankylosaurus The largest of the ankylosaurid (armoured) dinosaur family. Late Cretaceous Period.

Apatosaurus Once called the brontosaurus, one of the largest dinosaurs ever known, a member of the sauropod (four-legged plant eater) family. Late Jurassic Period.

Archaeopteryx A creature with the feathers of a bird, and the teeth, claws, and tail of the early reptiles. Late Jurassic Period.

Bactrosaurus A small member of the hadrosaurid (duckbilled) family; a plant eater. Middle Cretaceous Period.

Brachiosaurus One of the biggest dinosaurs, with a length of 75 feet and a height of 40 feet; a plant eater. Late Jurassic Period.

Camarasaurus Similar to the brachiosaurus, but smaller; a member of the plant-eating sauropod family. Late Jurassic Period.

Camptosaurus An earlier relative of the iguanodon family, with a long snout and large beak that enabled it to eat the lower leaves of trees. Late Jurassic/Early Cretaceous Period.

Centrosaurus A member of the plant-eating, short-frilled ceratopsian (horned dinosaurs) family, with a single horn and bumpy frill. Late Cretaceous Period.

Ceratosaurus A large, horned carnivore related to allosaurus. Late Jurassic Period.

Cetiosaurus One of the earliest plant-eating dinosaurs; an early relative of diplodocus, with a similar tail. Middle to Late Jurassic Period.

Coelophysis One of the earliest dinosaurs; a small, fast carnivore that ran on two legs. Late Triassic Period.

Compsognathus A small, fast-running carnivorous dinosaur about the size of a chicken. Late Jurassic Period.

Corythosaurus A member of the hadrosaurid (duckbilled) family. Late Cretaceous Period.

Deinonychus A very fast predator whose name means "terrible claw." Early Cretaceous Period.

Dicraeosaurus A large, slow plant eater, often weighed up to six tons. Late Jurassic Period.

Dilophosaurus One of the early carnivores, it was smaller and more delicate than later predators. Early Jurassic Period.

Diplodocus A very large, slow plant eater; one of the longest dinosaurs known. Late Jurassic Period.

Dromaeosaurus A dromaeosaurid (running lizard) that was about the same size as a human being. Late Cretaceous Period.

Dryosaurus A very quick, "bird-footed" herbivore believed to be able to avoid many predators. Middle to Late Jurassic Period.

Edmontosaurus A large duckbilled plant eater with inflatable pouches around each nostril that could have been used to make loud noises. Late Cretaceous Period.

Euoplocephalus An armoured dinosaur, nearly twenty feet long, that had a clubbed tail it could use to swing at attackers. Late Cretaceous Period.

Gallimimus A medium-sized dinosaur whose name means "fowl mimic" because it had mannerisms that resemble modern ostriches and turkeys. Late Cretaceous Period.

Hadrosaurus One of the earliest species to be discovered in North America, it had a duck bill and a bony crest on the top of its head. Late Cretaceous Period.

Herrerasaurus A very early predator, found in South America. Late Triassic Period.

Heterodontosaurus A small herbivore whose teeth were very similar to human teeth. Late Triassic/Early Jurassic Period.

Homalocephale A member of the "bone head" family of dinosaurs, this species had an unusually thick skull. Late Cretaceous Period.

Hylaeosaurus An early member of the plant-eating "node lizard" group of ankylosaurs with bony plates and protruding spines. Early Cretaceous Period.

Hypselosaurus A high-backed member of the sauropod family, with a steep, sloping head set on a short neck. Late Cretaceous Period.

Hypsilophodon One of the longest-surviving dinosaurs, a small, fast plant eater. Early Cretaceous Period.

Iguanodon A large, plant-eating dinosaur named "iguana tooth" because it had teeth like modern iguana lizards. Early Cretaceous Period.

Kentrosaurus A small plated dinosaur with spines on its back and an extra pair of spines above its rear legs. Late Jurassic Period.

Kritosaurus A member of the hadrosaur (duckbilled) family, this large plant eater had a flat broad head and a humped nose. Late Cretaceous Period.

Lambeosaurus One of the largest of the helmeted hadrosaurs (duckbills), with a large crest on the top of its head. Late Cretaceous Period.

Lesothosaurus A member of the ornithopod (bird-footed) family; this plant eater was small and very fast. Late Triassic/Early Jurassic Period.

Lufengosaurus A large, heavy member of the

plateosaurid (flat lizard) family, with a long, strong tail. Late Triassic/Early Jurassic Period.

Maiasaura A duckbilled dinosaur without a crest and a long, straight bottom jaw. Late Cretaceous Period.

Mamenchisaurus A member of the sauropod family, with the longest neck of any dinosaur yet discovered. Late Jurassic Period.

Massospondylus A medium-sized herbivore that had large hands which it could use to dig up roots and tear up small trees. Late Triassic/Early Jurassic Period.

Mauttaburasaurus A relatively large dinosaur found in Australia; it had a beaked nose, sharp teeth, and spiked thumbs. Mid-Late Cretaceous Period.

Megalosaurus A large, heavy predator that was the first dinosaur ever to be named; its name literally means "big lizard." Early Jurassic to Early Cretaceous Period.

Opisthocoelicaudia A species found in Mongolia, with a rigid spine that helped keep its long tail elevated off the ground. Late Cretaceous Period.

Ornitholestes One of the smallest carnivores, its name means "bird robber" because it primarily ate small birds. Late Jurassic Period.

Ouranosaurus A duck-billed member of the iguanodon family, with a sailed back and a flat head. Early Cretaceous Period.

Oviraptor A scavenger whose name means "egg thief," this species had a large, birdlike skull and long fingers. Late Cretaceous Period.

Pachycephalosaurus A very large member of the "bone-head" family with a thick, helmetlike cap on the top of its head. Late Cretaceous Period.

Panoplosaurus A stout herbivore covered by bony armour; its name means "fully armoured lizard." Late Cretaceous Period.

Parasaurolophus A large duck-billed dinosaur, with a six-foot-long crest that swept back from its head. Late Cretaceous Period.

Pinacosaurus A small member of the "fused lizard" group, with a heavily armoured back and a bone club at the end of its tail. Late Cretaceous Period.

Plateosaurus A member of the prosauropod family, the first large plant-eating dinosaurs, which lived long before the larger sauropods. Late Triassic Period.

Protoceratops A small dinosaur about six feet long; the earliest known member of the family of horned dinosaurs. Late Cretaceous Period.

Psittacosaurus A member of the "parrot lizard" family, and an early relative of the horned dinosaurs such as protoceratops. Early Cretaceous Period.

Saltasaurus The first known sauropod dinosaur with any kind of bony armour. Late Cretaceous Period.

Saltopus A tiny member of the coelurosaur (hollow tail) family; a fast runner about the size of a domestic cat. Late Triassic Period.

Saurolophus An advanced member of the hadrosaurs, or duck-billed dinosaurs, with an inflatable balloon of skin over the top of its skull. Late Cretaceous Period.

Saurornithoides A small carnivore with large eyes and a large brain. Late Cretaceous Period.

Scelidosaurus One of the early members of the armoured group of dinosaurs, with a typical set of bone plates and a low-slung head. Early Jurassic Period.

Shantungosaurus At 50 feet long, perhaps the biggest hadrosaur (duckbill) ever discovered. Late Cretaceous Period.

Spinosaurus A large meat-eating dinosaur with large skin-covered spines across its back. Late Cretaceous Period.

Staurikosaurus A small, early meat-eating dinosaur, about 7 feet long. Middle Triassic Period.

Stegosaurus The largest known plated dinosaur, a plant eater, with two pairs of sharp spikes on the end of its tail. Late Jurassic Period.

Struthiomimus A fast member of the coelurosaurs (hollow-tail lizards), with an ostrichlike appearance. Late Cretaceous Period.

Styracosaurus A horned dinosaur with a spiked head frill, related to triceratops but little more than half its size. Late Cretaceous Period.

Tarbosaurus A flesh-eating dinosaur almost identical to tyrannosaurus. Late Cretaceous Period.

Torosaurus One of the last members of the family of long-frilled horned dinosaurs. Late Cretaceous Period.

Triceratops A massive species with three horns and a bony frill that extended behind the head. Late Cretaceous Period.

Tsintaosaurus One of the last living dinosaurs, it had a duck bill and a bony crest that extended from its head like an antenna. Late Cretaceous Period.

Tuojiangosaurus A relative of the stegosaurus, it had bony plates extending from its back and a spiked tail. Early Cretaceous Period.

Tyrannosaurus A very large, fast predator with massive teeth, small arms, and huge legs; it could reach speeds of 20 mph. Late Cretaceous Period.

Velociraptor A fast, agile predator; its name means "swift plunderer." Late Cretaceous Period.

Vulcanodon One of the first sauropods, it was a large herbivore with stout legs and a long neck. Early Jurassic Period.

FISHES

Ash Meadows killfish
Big Spring spinedace
Blackfin cisco: 1960s
Deepwater cisco: 1960s
Grass Valley speckled dace
Harelip sucker: 1900
June sucker
Lake Titicaca orestias
New Zealand grayling
Pahranagat spinedace
Parras pupfish
Parras roundnose minnow
Shortnose sucker
Spring Valley sucker
Stumptooth minnow
Tecopa pupfish
Thicktail chub
Utah Lake sculpin

MAMMALS

Atlas bear: 1841
Aurochs: 1627
Bali tiger: 1952
Barbary lion: 1922
Barbuda muskrat: 1902
Broad-faced potoroo: 1908
Bubal hartebeest: 1923
Bulldog rat: 1908
Cape lion: 1865
Cape red hartebeest: 1938
Caribbean monk seal: 1962
Caucasian wisent: 1925
Christmas Island shrew: 1908
Cuban nesophont: before 1800
Eastern barred bandicoot: 1867
Eastern bison: 1832
Eastern elk: 1880
Eastern hare wallaby: 1890
Gilbert's potoroo: 1840
Great rabbit bandicoot: early 1900s
Haitian long-tongued bat: around 1600
Hispanolian nesophont: before 1800
Jamaican long-tailed bat: before 1898
Jamaican rice rat: 1877
Maclear's rat: 1908

Martinique muskrat: 1902
Merriam's elk: 1906
Mexican grizzly: 1962
Pig-footed bandicoot: 1880
Puerto Rican nesophont: before 1800
Quagga: 1882
Schomburgk's deer: 1932
Sea mink: 1860 or 1894
St. Lucia muskrat: 1881
St. Vincent rice rat: 1897
Steller's sea cow: 1768
Syrian onager: 1927
Tarpan: 1851
Toolache wallaby: 1938
Western barred bandicoot: 1906

REPTILES

Abington Island tortoise
Barrington Island tortoise
Cape Verde giant skink
Charles Island tortoise
Grand Islet ameiva
Jamaica tree snake
Jamaican giant galliwasp
Jamaican iguana
Marion's (Seychelles) tortoise
Martinique giant ameiva
Martinique lizard
Martinique racer snake
Mauritian domed tortoise
Mauritian giant skink
Mauritian high-fronted tortoise
Narborough Island tortoise
Navassa iguana
Navassa Island lizard
Ratas Island lizard
Réunion skink
Réunion tortoise
Rodriguez day gecko
Rodriguez greater tortoise
Rodriguez lesser tortoise
Rodriguez night gecko
Round Island boa
San Stephano lizard
St. Croix tree snake
St. Lucia racer snake

FISHES

SUPERCLASS AGNATHA jawless fishes

Lampreys eel-shaped fishes that feed on blood and breed in fresh water
Hagfishes cylindrical-shaped fishes that feed on dead or dying fishes

SUPERCLASS GNATHOSTOMATA hinged jaw fishes
CLASS CHONDRICHTHYES cartilaginous fishes:

SELACHII

Sharks predatory fishes with acute sense of smell
    Angel shark
    Atlantic sharpnose shark
    Basking shark
    Bignose shark
    Black dogfish
    Blacknose shark
    Blacktip shark
    Blacktipped reef shark
    Blainville's dogfish
    Blue shark
    Bonnethead shark
    Bramble shark
    Brown catshark
    Bull shark
    Caribbean reef shark
    Caribbean sharpnose
    Chain dogfish
    Cocktail shark
    Common hammerhead
    Cookie-cutter shark
    Cowsharks
    Deepwater catshark
    Devil fish shark
    Dusky shark
    False catshark
    Fierce shark
    Filetail catshark
    Finetooth shark
    Florida dogfish shark
    Frilled shark
    Galapagos shark
    Ganges River shark

Grey reef shark
Grey smoothhound shark
Great hammerhead
Great white shark
Green dogfish
Greenland shark
Gulper shark
Head shark
Horn shark
Japanese goblin shark
Kitefin shark
Lantern shark
Lemon shark
Leopard shark
Longnose
Mako shark
Mexican horn shark
Narrowtooth shark
Night shark
Nurse shark
Oceanic whitetip shark
Pacific sharpnose shark
Pacific sleeper
Pigmy shark
Porbeagle shark
Port Jackson horn shark
Portuguese shark
Prickly shark
Rafinesque
Reef shark
Sandbar shark
Sawshark
Scalloped hammerhead
Scoophead hammerhead
Sevengill shark
Sharpnose shark
Sicklefin smoothhound
Silky shark
Silvertip shark
Six-gilled shark
Smalleye hammerhead
Smalltail shark
Smooth dogfish
Smoothhound shark
Soupfin shark
Spinner shark
Stellate smoothhound
Thresher shark

Tiger shark
Tsuranagakobitozame
Whale shark
Whitetip reef shark
Zebra shark

BATOIDEI

Rays bottom-dwelling fish with long winglike fins
and tails that act as rudders
    Manta ray
    Stingray
Skates similar to rays, often bury themselves on
the sea floor and wait for prey
Chimeras deep-water fishes that are closely
related to sharks, have large eyes and often poisonous spikes

CLASS OSTEICHTHYES bony skeleton fishes:

DIPNOI

Lungfishes large, aggressive fishes; possess organs
that are similar to amphibian lungs

ACIPENSERIFORMES

Sturgeons fishes that gather food by brushing
whiskers over the sea floor; good source for caviar
    Lake sturgeon
    White sturgeon
Paddlefishes fishes that feed by straining plankton
through a long, paddlelike snout

POLYPTERIFORMES

Bichirs or reedfishes nocturnal fishes that live in
swamps and rivers; feed on insects and fish

ELOPIFORMES

Bonefishes bottom-feeders with mouths adapted
for crushing shellfish
Tarpons predators that need some air to breathe
    Ladyfishes

ANGUILLIFORMES

Eels fishes with long, cylindrical bodies, often predators
    Conger eel
    Moray eel
    Slime eel

CLUPEIFORMES

Herrings fishes that swim in vast schools; teeth are usually absent or underdeveloped
    Atlantic herring
    Pacific herring
Anchovies fishes that swim in vast schools; often have many rows of teeth

OSTEOGLOSSIFORMES

Bony tongues freshwater fishes with large mouths, ears divided into two portions—upper for balance and lower for hearing
Butterfly fishes freshwater fishes with large pectoral fins that can be used for brief periods of flight

SALMONIFORMES

Salmon marine and freshwater fishes; often travel upstream to spawn
    Atlantic salmon
    Grayling
    Lake trout
    Oceanic trout
    Pink salmon
    Rainbow trout
    River trout
    Smelt
    Whitefish
Pikes freshwater fishes found in North America with elongated bodies
    Mudminnow

OSTARIOPHYSI

Carps small- to medium-sized fishes found in fresh and brackish water
    Flying barb
    Goldfish
    Minnow
    Sucker
    Zebra fish
Catfish small to large freshwater fishes, generally nocturnal
    Chanel catfish
    Electric catfish
    Giant catfish
    Stinging catfish
    Talking catfish

CHARACIFORMES

Tetras small freshwater fishes with many teeth, generally found in Africa and South America
    Piranha

PARACANTHOPTERYGII

Toadfishes fishes found in both fresh and salt water in tropical climates; some are poisonous
Trout-perches freshwater North American fishes, found very deep or in areas of low light
    Mammoth Cave blindfish
    Pirate perch
Codfishes fishes found in salt and fresh water, in shallow and deep water, largest species can grow to over six feet long
    Atlantic cod
    Cusk
    Forkbeard
    Hake

ATHERINIFORMES

Flying fishes marine fishes that live near the surface; can jump out of the water to evade predators
    Flying halfbeaks
Needlefishes marine and freshwater fishes with long snouts with formidable jaws
Cyprinodonts small fishes often found living in hot springs

GASTEROSTEIFORMES

Sticklebacks small fishes with well-armed jaws, found in the northern hemisphere
Tube snout fishes found in the Pacific Ocean, with long bodies, long snouts, and armoured plates
Sea horses small fishes covered in bony rings rather than scales; move using a small dorsal fin

SCORPAENIFORMES

Scorpion fishes found on the bottom or around coral, many species possess poisonous barbs
  Rockfish
  Redfish
  Lionfish
  Gunards

PERCIFORMES

Perches freshwater fishes found primarily in quiet waters
Tunas large marine fishes known to swim across entire oceans to spawn
  Yellowtail
Marlins large gamefish found in warm marine waters around the world
  Black marlin

PLEURONCETIFORMES

Flatfishes saltwater, bottom-dwelling fishes usually found in relatively deep water
Flounders bottom-dwelling fishes found in fresh and salt water
Soles fishes with flat bodies known for the twisted shape of their mouths

TETRAODONTIFORMES

Boxfishes found around coral reefs; can blow jets of water out of mouths to expose burrowing animals for food
Puffer or blow fishes poisonous fishes found around coral reefs; can inflate their bodies like a balloon when threatened

HORSE BREEDS

Akhal Teke One of the world's oldest breeds, developed in Turkmenistan, a part of the former Soviet Union. It has a distinctive honey-gold coat and a long body and is known for its endurance and ability to withstand extremes of drought, heat, and cold.

Alter Real An intelligent warmblood riding breed from Portugal, with a short, arched neck, small, elegant head, and a high-strung temperament.

American Shetland A descendant of the British Shetland that today bears little resemblance to its ancestor; it has a high-stepping action similar to that of the Hackney.

Andalusian An ancient breed from Portugal and Spain. The classic horse of the caballeros and conquistadores.

Anglo-Arab A cross between the world's two finest breeds—the Arabian and the Thoroughbred—the Anglo-Arab is tough and intelligent and has been very successful in a range of competitive sports.

Appaloosa First bred by the Nez Perce Indians, this hardy, compact horse has pink skin and small, irregular spots in various patterns.

Arabian An ancient breed indigenous to the Arabian Peninsula. Arabians are small, light, and known for their endurance. They have concave faces, wide eyes, and long manes and tails.

Ardennais An ancient breed from the Ardennes region on the border between France and Belgium, the Ardennais is a massive, compact horse with a huge neck, broad back, and immensely muscular legs.

Ariège, Ariègeois A small (13 to 15 hands), dark breed from the Pyrenees Mountains.

Barb An ancient North African breed, very tough and enduring, usually grey and standing from 14 to 15 hands.

Bashkir A small (usually under 14.2) breed from the Bashkir region of the Ural Mountain district of the former Soviet Union. They are used for both riding and draught purposes, and are also valued for their curly horsehair coats, which tend to be hypo-allergenic for humans.

Bashkir curly An American breed with the same curly coat as the Bashkir.

Bavarian warmblood A breed developed from the ancient Rottaler horse, with chestnut colouring, a docile temper, and strong shoulders and legs.

Belgian warmblood A breed developed in Belgium by crossing a Belgian farm horse with a Gelderlander, and later adding Thoroughbred blood, resulting in a powerful, calm, always solid-coloured horse.

Boulonnais A draught horse originating in France, the breed is large and heavy (16 to 17 hands) yet elegantly proportioned and graceful. It is also known for its strength and speed.

Brabant (Belgian heavy draught) A hugely muscular work breed from Belgium (15 to 17 hands), known for its strength and good temper.

Breton A sturdy French workhorse from Brittany, with thick, muscular legs, broad face, bright eyes, and a lively, good nature.

Brumby The name given to the wild horses that roam the Australian outback, descendants of the first horses ever imported to the country.

Budonny, Budyonny, Budenny A popular breed created in Russia for competitive sports, the Budonny is known for its fine proportions and steady temperament.

Camargue A wild French breed with a white coat, the sturdy Camargue usually stands at about 14 hands.

Caspian A miniature horse (10 to 12 hands) from the Caspian Sea area, with a slim body and fine head like an Arabian.

Chincoteague An indigenous American breed that lives in isolation on the Virginia islands of Chincoteague and Assateague.

Cleveland Bay A breed that originated in northeast England, the horses are bay-coloured with black points and are typically 16.2 hands tall, with a large head and a strong constitution.

Clydesdale A Scottish breed that originated in the mid-18th century, the large (around 16 to 17 hands) and muscular Clydesdale is known for its active moves, attractive markings (white feathers and face on bay, brown, or black bodies), and large, wide feet.

Connemara pony The only pony native to Ireland, this breed is well formed and graceful, skilled at jumping and also strong as a riding or harness pony.

Criollo An Argentinian breed standing at around 14 to 15 hands, the Criollo is remarkably tough, with great powers of endurance.

Dales pony A British pony with a long mane and tail, used for riding and particularly trekking because it is strong and hardy.

Dartmoor pony A British breed, popular with children (usually 12.1 hands), sturdy and rugged, with a small head and a full mane and tail.

Døle Gudbrandsdal A Norwegian breed similar to the Fell and Dales ponies from Britain, standing at about 15 hands, with the build of a draught horse (but not the huge size) and an active trot.

Døle trotter A cross between the English Thoroughbred and the Gudbrandsdal, resulting in an excellent trotter, lighter than the Gudbrandsdal, with great endurance.

Don A Russian breed famous for its use by the Cossacks, the rather substantial (15 to 16 hands) Don is known for its endurance and value as a workhorse.

Dutch warmblood A modern breed first bred in the

Netherlands in the 1960s from the Gelderlander and the Groningen, resulting in an athletic, docile horse.

Exmoor pony An English pony breed characterized by its wide "toad" eyes. It is usually around 12 hands tall, with a thick tail, short, strong legs, and good stamina.

Falabella horse A tiny (no more than 7 or 8 hands tall) horse originating in Argentina. Good-tempered and friendly, it makes a wonderful pet and is used for driving, since it is usually too small for riding.

Fell pony A British pony, no more than 14 hands in height, used for riding and driving.

Fjord A breed that originated in western Norway and was originally used by the Vikings. The Fjord is strong and stocky, stands at 13 to 14.2 hands, and is used for work and riding.

Frederiksborg An increasingly rare Danish breed, usually chestnut-coloured and standing at about 16 hands.

Freiberger A small (about 15 hands) mountain breed from Switzerland, good-natured, sturdy, and agile.

French trotter A French breed created in Normandy for the purpose of harness racing. The Trotter is a strong and robust horse with great stamina.

Friesian A relatively small (15 hands) Dutch breed, always black in colour and used mainly as a carriage horse.

Galiceno A small horse (12 to 13.2 hands) originally from Galicia in northwestern Spain. Tough, courageous, and versatile, Galicenos come in most colours and are used for riding, ranch work, and competition.

Gelderland, Gelderlander A Dutch warmblood breed mostly used as a carriage horse, usually chestnut-coloured with white markings on the face and legs.

Gidran A Hungarian half-breed (a cross between any warmblood parent and an Arabian or Thor-

oughbred) created with an Arabian, the Gidran is almost always chestnut-coloured, usually 16 hands, and is mostly used in competitive sport.

Gotland pony A breed that originated in the Gotland Islands of Sweden. Coloured dun, black, brown, or chestnut, and standing about 12 hands tall, it is excellent at jumping and trotting and is often used as a children's mount.

Groningen A Dutch breed with a long back and short but strong legs, known for its calmness and willingness to work.

Hackney One of the world's most impressive driving breeds, known for its high spirits, grace, and extraordinary high-stepping action. The Hackney pony (under 14 hands) and the Hackney horse (over 14 hands) are dark-coloured with high tails and smallish, convex heads.

Haflinger pony A mountain breed from the Tirol of western Austria, usually chestnut-coloured with a light mane and tail.

Hanoverian A German warmblood with Thoroughbred ancestry. An exceptional dressage and show-jumping horse.

Highland A large British pony (13 to 14 hands), strong and steady, once used as a workhorse, but now mainly for riding.

Hinny A cross between a male horse and a donkey mare, with a body shaped like a donkey and a coat that is usually grey.

Holsteiner, Holstein The oldest German breed, powerful and bold, and among the world's best show jumpers.

Icelandic horse A small (around 13 hands) horse that originated in Iceland and is kept purebred by regulations barring other breeds from entering the country. The Icelandic exhibits two unusual gaits (the "tolt" and the "pace") and is strong, friendly, and inexpensive to keep.

Irish draught A strong and athletic breed once

popular as a workhorse, now mainly used as breed stock and for riding, hunting, and jumping.

Jutland A muscular, sturdy breed from the Jutland region of Denmark, standing at 15.2 to 16.2 hands, with good endurance, agility, and willingness to work.

Kabardin A mountain breed from the northern Caucasus, the Kabardin is calm, hardy, and sturdy, and is thus ideally suited for traversing mountain trails.

Karabair A very tough Asian mountain breed, similar in looks to the Arabian.

Knabstrup, Knabstruper A spotted horse from Denmark, standing at about 15.2 to 15.3 hands.

Konick A pony breed from Poland, standing at 13 hands, with good strength and stamina.

Lippizan, Lippizaner An exceptionally high-quality breed known for its grace and elegance. It is usually white, but can be of any colour.

Lusitano An athletic breed from Portugal, used as a mount in Portuguese bullfighting.

Maremmano, Maremmana A sturdy working breed from Tuscany.

Missouri fox-trotter Developed in the Ozark Mountains of Missouri, this breed is known and selected for its ambling gait, the fox-trot (a gait ideal for rough trail riding).

Morgan An American breed produced from the offspring of a single stallion foaled in Massachusetts in 1789. It is around 14 to 15 hands, with a medium-sized head, very deep body, and possesses versatility and endurance.

Mule A cross between a male donkey and a female horse. The mule is stronger than the horse, tough, brave, and resilient, and very popular as a work animal.

Murakozi A heavyweight farm horse from Hungary, with a powerful body, calm temperament, and large, gentle eyes.

Mustang The original wild horse of the western United States, thought to trace back to the horses of Spanish explorers, but now well-crossed with other breeds. Often the horse of choice for cowboys, this small horse (about 14 hands) is known for being hardy and brave but sometimes unpredictable.

New Forest pony A breed that originated in the New Forest area of Hampshire, England, and comes in two types: lighter, under 13.2 hands; and heavier, between 13.2 and 14.2 hands. It is smart and gentle, with a narrow body and strong legs.

Nonius A Hungarian breed divided into a larger and a smaller type, both good all-round horses, late to mature.

Noriker A light draught horse that originated in Austria, with a sturdy compact body and standing about 16 hands tall.

North Swedish A robust, hardworking breed closely related to the Døle Gudbrandsdal, with a cheerful nature, long life span, and full mane and tail.

Oldenburg, Oldenburger The tallest (16.2 to 17.2 hands) and heaviest of the German warmbloods, the Oldenburg is strong and even-tempered with short legs and good hooves.

Orlov trotter A breed developed by Count Orlov of Russia in the 18th century, now primarily used to add quality to other breeds because of its strength and stamina.

Palomino A colour breed describing horses with a golden coat and blond mane, with white marks allowed only on the face and below the knee, and dark or hazel eyes.

Paso fino A Puerto Rican breed with a four-beat gait, the Paso Fino is famous for its smooth ride and gentle nature.

Percheron A French heavy draught horse, docile and elegant, with a broad body and short, sturdy legs.

Peruvian paso, Peruvian stepping horse A Peruvian breed with a unique smooth gait known as the *paso*. The horses come in all colours and are also known for their endurance.

Pinto, Paint A colour breed, the pinto is either white with brown or bay patches, or black with white patches.

Pony of the Americas A cross between the Appaloosa and the Shetland, which produced a minature (11.2 to 13 hands) version of the Appaloosa.

Quarter horse Bred in Virginia in the 17th century, this athletic horse has a compact body and muscular hindquarters, which make it an excellent racer and cow horse.

Riding pony A blend of Arabian, Thoroughbred, and British pony, resulting in a high-quality, well-proportioned breed with the size (around 14 hands) and head of a pony.

Russian trotter A cross between the Orlov trotter and the Standardbred.

Saddlebred A very attractive show horse, this American breed is known for its slender arched neck, long legs, a refined head shape, and a full mane and tail.

Salerno An Italian warmblood, the Salerno was once used as a cavalry horse and is now used successfully in sporting competition.

Schleswig A close relative of the Jutland, this north German breed is usually chestnut-coloured, but sometimes grey or bay.

Selle Français A modern French breed developed by crossing Thoroughbreds with sturdy native horses, the Selle Français is calm and intelligent and is used for all kinds of riding.

Shagya A tough and hardy Hungarian breed with Arabian origins, usually white and standing 15 hands high.

Shetland pony The smallest of the British breeds (9.2 to 10.2 hands), originating in the Shetland Islands off the north coast of Scotland. It is powerful, gentle, and well-proportioned, with a thick, shaggy mane and tail.

Shire The largest of the English heavy horse breeds (over 17 hands), weighing over a ton, with enormous strength and attractive features, including heavy, silky feathering on the lower legs.

Single-footing A light breed developed by trailriders for its ability to perform a near evenly timed four-beat gait of intermediate speed, from 5 to 20 miles per hour. All sizes and colours are acceptable.

Sorraia A tough Iberian pony, usually dun-coloured, with a dark stripe.

Standardbred The world's premier harness racer, both as a trotter and a pacer, the breed is descended from the Thoroughbred and is similar but less refined in appearance.

Suffolk, Suffolk punch A large, strong breed from England, standing at about 16 hands, with a muscled, sturdy body and short legs.

Swedish warmblood A breed originally developed by the Swedish cavalry. It is handsome, athletic, versatile, and exceptionally fine at dressage.

Tennessee walking horse, Plantation walking horse, Turn Row Developed in Tennessee in the mid-19th century, this large-boned breed is known for its three paces: the flat-foot walk, a smooth four-beat gait going 4 to 7 miles per hour; the unique running walk, which covers up to 10 miles per hour; and the canter.

Tersk, Tersky A good-natured Russian breed, 14 to 15 hands, usually grey, with good endurance.

Thoroughbred The world's fastest horse, originating in England around 1700. The breed is elegant and intelligent but high-strung.

Trakehner A European warmblood of East

Prussian origin, and an excellent all-round horse with a forehead and neck similar to that of the Thoroughbred.

Vladimir heavy draught A well-built Russian breed, usually bay-coloured, 15 to 16 hands, which matures quickly into a good-natured, enormously strong workhorse.

Welsh cob A courageous, muscular breed excellent for riding and driving because of its versatility and endurance.

Welsh mountain pony A strong, small (12.2 hands), intelligent breed, closely resembling the Arabian.

Welsh pony A descendant and larger version of the Welsh mountain pony (13.2 hands), this breed is also strong, highly intelligent, and excellent for riding.

Westfalen, **Westphalian** A German warmblood, always a solid colour and on average 16.1 hands tall, this breed is similar in physique to the Hanoverian but usually heavier and thicker-set.

Wielkopolski A Polish breed, useful for riding, with a good temperament, strong body, and muscular legs.

HUMAN BONES

Skull

occipital	1
parietal (1 pair)	2
sphenoid	1
ethmoid	1
inferior nasal conchae (1 pair)	2
frontal (1 pair, fused)	2
nasal (1 pair)	2
lacrimal (1 pair)	2
temporal (1 pair)	2
maxilla (1 pair)	2
zygomatic (1 pair)	2
vomer	1
palatine (1 pair)	2
mandible (1 pair, fused)	2
total	*24*

Ears

malleus	2
incus	2
stapes	2
total	*6*

Vertebrae

cervical	7
thoracic	12
lumbar	5
sacral (5 fused to form the sacrum)	1
coccyx (3–5 fused)	1
total	*26*

Vertebral ribs

true ribs (7 pairs)	14
false ribs (5 pairs; 2 are floating)	10
total	*24*

Sternum

manubrium	1
sternebrae	1
xiphisternum	1
total	*3*

Throat | **1**
| *total* | *1* |

Pectoral girdle

clavicle (1 pair)	2
scapula (including coracoid—1 pair)	2
total	*4*

Upper extremity (each arm and hand)

humerus	1
radius	1
ulna	1
carpus (the wrist)	
scaphoid	1
lunate	1
triquetral	1
pisiform	1
trapezium	1
trapezoid	1
capitate	1
hamate	1
metacarpals	5
phalanges (fingers)	
first digit (thumb)	2
second digit	3
third digit	3
fourth digit	3
fifth digit	3
total	*30*

Pelvic girdle

illium, ischium, and pubis (combined)—1 pair of hip bones, innominate	2
total	*2*

Lower extremity (each leg and foot)

femur	1
tibia	1
fibula	1
tarsus (the ankle)	
talus	1
calcaneus	1
navicular	1
cuneiform, medial	1
cuneiform, intermediate	1
cuneiform, lateral	1
cuboid	1
metatarsals	5
phalanges (toes)	
first digit (big toe)	2
second digit	3
third digit	3
fourth digit	3
fifth digit	3
total	*29*

GRAND TOTAL:

Skull	**24**
Ears	**6**
Vertebrae	**26**
Vertebral ribs	**24**
Sternum	**3**
Throat	**1**
Pectoral girdle	**4**
Upper extremity (arms and hands, 2 x 30)	**60**
Pelvic girdle	**2**
Lower extremity (legs and feet, 2 x 29)	**58**
HUMAN BONES:	*206*

HUMAN BRAIN

CEREBRUM

Largest part of the human brain, divided into right and left hemispheres, which are in turn divided into the frontal, parietal, temporal, occipital, and insular lobes.

CORPUS CALLOSUM

The nerve fibres that connect the two hemispheres of the cerebrum.

CEREBELLUM

The part of the brain essential to all motor activity, located in the hind part of the cranium, underneath the cerebral hemispheres.

BRAIN STEM

Thalamus Two masses of grey tissue in the middle of the brain, responsible for all sensory input to the brain (except for the sense of smell).

Hypothalamus Located below the thalamus; responsible for such activities as eating, drinking, sleep, and sex.

Midbrain Composed of the cerebral peduncles, corpora quadrigemina, and a central canal.

Pons Lies in front of the cerebellum, between the medulla and midbrain, made up principally of nerve fibres.

Medulla oblongata An enlargement of the spinal cord, located between the spinal cord and pons.

HUMAN MUSCLES

Abductor digiti minimi foot
Abductor digiti minimi hand
Abductor hallucis foot
Abductor pollicis brevis hand
Abductor pollicis longus arm
Adductor brevis pelvis
Adductor hallucis foot
Adductor longus pelvis
Adductor magnus leg
Adductor pollicis hand
Anconeus arm
Articularis genu leg
Aryepiglotticus throat
Auricularis head (ear)
Biceps brachii arm
Biceps femoris leg
Brachialis arm
Brachioradialis arm
Buccinator head (cheek)
Bulbospongiosus groin
Constrictor pharyngis inferior throat
Constrictor pharyngis medius throat
Constrictor pharyngis superior throat
Coracobrachialis arm
Corrugator supercilii head
Cremaster abdomen/groin
Cricothyroideus throat
Deltoid shoulder
Depressor anguli oris head (mouth)
Diaphragm torso
Extensor carpi radialis brevis arm
Extensor carpi radialis longus arm
Extensor carpi ulnaris arm
Extensor digiti minimi hand
Extensor digitorum hand
Extensor digitorum brevis foot
Extensor digitorum longus foot
Extensor hallucis brevis foot
Extensor hallucis longus leg, foot
Extensor indicis arm, hand
Extensor pollicis brevis arm, hand
Extensor pollicis longus arm, hand

External oblique abdominis stomach
Flexor carpi radialis arm
Flexor carpi ulnaris arm
Flexor digiti minimi brevis foot
Flexor digiti minimi brevis hand
Flexor digitorum brevis foot
Flexor digitorum longus foot
Flexor digitorum profundus arm
Flexor digitorum superficialis arm
Flexor hallucis brevis foot
Flexor hallucis longus foot
Flexor pollicis brevis hand
Flexor pollicis longus arm, hand
Frontalis forehead
Gastrocnemius leg
Genioglossus head (mouth)
Geniohyoid head (mouth)
Gluteus maximus buttocks
Gluteus medius buttocks
Gluteus minimus buttocks
Gracilis leg
Hyoglossus head (mouth)
Iliacus hip
Inferior oblique head (eye)
Inferior rectus head (eye)
Infraspinatus back
Intercostales chest
Internal oblique abdomen
Interossei dorsal of hand
Interossei dorsal of foot
Interossei palmar of hand
Interossei plantar of foot
Ishiocavernosus groin
Lateral cricoarytenoid throat
Lateral pterygoid head (mouth)
Lateral rectus head (eye)
Latissimus dorsi back
Levator anguli oris head (mouth)
Levator palpebrae superioris head (eye)
Levator scapulae neck, shoulder
Longus capitis spine
Longus colli spine
Lumbricals of foot
Lumbricals of hand
Masseter head (jaw)
Medial pterygoid head (jaw)
Medial rectus head (eye)
Mentalis head (mouth)
Mylohyoid head, neck

Nasalis head (nose)
Oblique arytenoid throat
Obliquus capitis inferior head, neck
Obliquus capitis superior head, neck
Obturator externus hip
Obturator internus (A) hip
Obturator internus (B) hip
Omohyoid neck, shoulder
Opponens digiti minimi hand
Opponens pollicis hand
Orbicularis oculi head (eyes)
Orbicularis oris head (eyes)
Palatopharyngeus head, throat
Palmaris brevis hand
Palmaris longus arm, hand
Pectineus hip
Pectoralis major chest
Pectoralis minor chest
Peroneus brevis leg
Peroneus longus leg
Peroneus tertius leg
Piriformis (A) hip
Piriformis (B) pelvis
Plantaris leg
Platysma neck
Popliteus knee
Posterior cricoarytenoid head, throat
Procerus head
Pronator quadratus arm
Pronator teres arm
Psoas major back, hip, leg
Psoas minor back, hip
Pyramidalis rectum
Quadratus femoris hip
Quadratus lumborum rib cage (12th rib)
Quadratus plantae foot
Quadriceps thigh
Rectus abdominis stomach
Rectus capitus anterior head, neck
Rectus capitus lateralis head, neck
Rectus capitus posterior major head, neck
Rectus capitus posterior minor head, neck
Rectus femoris leg
Rhomboid major shoulder, back
Rhomboid minor shoulder, back
Risorius head (mouth)
Salpingopharyngeus head, neck
Sartorius leg
Scalenus anterior neck

Scalenus medius neck
Scalenus minimus neck
Scalenus posterior neck
Semimembranosus leg
Semitendinosus leg
Serratus anterior chest
Serratus posterior inferior back
Serratus posterior superior back
Soleus leg
Sphincter ani buttocks
Sphincter urethrae pelvis
Splenius capitis neck
Splenius cervicis neck
Stapedius head (ear)
Sternocleidomastoid neck
Sternohyoid neck
Sternothyroid neck
Styloglossus head (mouth)
Stylohyoid neck
Stylopharyngeus neck
Subclavius shoulder
Subcostalis chest
Subscapularis shoulder
Superior oblique head (eye)
Superior rectus head (eye)
Supinator arm
Supraspinatus shoulder
Temporalis head (jaw)
Tensor fasciae latae hip, leg
Tensor tympani head (ear)
Teres major back
Teres minor back
Thyro-arytenoid and vocalis neck
Thyrohyoid neck
Tibialis anterior leg
Tibialis posterior leg, foot
Transversus abdominis stomach
Transversus perinei groin
Transversus thoracis spine
Trapezius back
Triceps arm
Vastus intermedius leg
Vastus lateralis leg
Vastus medialis leg
Zygomaticus major head (mouth)
Zygomaticus minor head (mouth)

HUMAN ORGANS

ALIMENTARY (DIGESTIVE) SYSTEM

Appendix No known function.
Oesophagus A muscular tube that passes food from the mouth to the stomach.
Gall bladder Helps the liver secrete digestive juices into the duodenum.
Large intestine (colon) Where body fluids are reabsorbed.
Liver Secretes digestive juices into the duodenum.
Mouth Breaks down food.
Rectum Excretes waste matter.
Small intestine (duodenum, jejunum, ileum) Controls the digestion and absorption of nutrients.
Stomach Begins the process of digestion.

CIRCULATORY AND RESPIRATORY SYSTEMS

Heart The muscular pump that moves blood through the body.
Lungs The process of respiration replaces oxygen content in the blood.

ENDOCRINE SYSTEM

Pituitary gland Produces hormones that control the other endocrine glands.
Thyroid gland Produces a hormone that controls the metabolic rate.
Parathyroid glands Control calcium levels in the body.
Pancreas Secretes insulin, regulating glucose levels in the body.
Adrenal glands Produce adrenalin and cortisone.
Ovaries Produce female sex hormones and release ovum.
Testes Produce sperm and the sex hormone testosterone.

Nervous System

Brain Relays and receives electrical impulses through the senses, nerves, and spinal cord.
Skin The outer covering of the body, controls heat loss.

Urinary System

Kidneys Purify the blood and produce urine.
Ureter Carries urine from the kidneys to the bladder.
Bladder Stores urine before it is excreted.
Urethra The canal through which urine and semen are excreted from the bladder.

INSECTS

Order	Common name	Description
Blattaria	cockroaches	Low body, long legs, some have wings; found worldwide
Coleoptera	beetles, weevils	Large eyes, hard outer skeleton, two pairs of wings
Collembola	springtails	Blind, wingless insects
Dermapetera	earwigs	Scavengers and predators with large pincers
Diplura	diplurans	Blind, small, thin insects that usually live in the ground
Diptera	true flies	Insects with two sets of wings, sucking mouthparts; known to carry disease
Embioptera	webspinners	Slender insects with short legs that live in masses of silk on trees, in garbage, or in the ground
Ephemeroptera	mayflies	Some species are herbivores and others are carnivores; females can live up to two years, while males live up to three days
Hemiptera	true bugs	Insects with large compound eyes and sucking mouthparts; most are terrestrial
Homoptera	cicadas, hoppers, aphids, scale insects	Herbivores adapted to suck plant sap
Hymenoptera	ants, bees, wasps	Plant pollinators with four membranous wings and mouthparts adapted for chewing and sucking
Isoptera	termites or white ants	Cellulose-eating, social insects with a caste system

Order	Common name	Description
Lepidoptera	butterflies, moths, skippers	Metamorphize from caterpillars; have two pairs of wings covered by dustlike scales
Mantodea	mantids, mantises	Predatory insects with mobile heads and large eyes
Mecoptera	scorpion flies	Live in moist forest areas; live on nectar or other insects
Neuroptera	alderflies, dobsonflies, lacewings, snakeflies	Biting insects with two pairs of wings
Odonata	dragonflies, damselflies	Carnivorous insects with aquatic larvae
Orthoptera	grasshoppers, locusts, and crickets	Hind limbs usually used for jumping; front limbs often rub together to produce sounds
Phasmida (Phasmoptera)	stick and leaf insects	Arboreal, nocturnal insects with camouflaged bodies
Phthiraptera	sucking, biting, book, and barklice	Parasites of birds or mammals
Protura	proturans	Wingless, white, blind; found under bark, stones, or rotting vegetation
Siphonaptera	fleas	Wingless parasites that feed mainly on mammals, but also some birds
Strepsiptera	stylopids	Parasites of other insects
Thysanoptera	thrips	Fringed wings; live in tropics
Thysanura	bristletails, silverfish	Wingless insects that feed on fungi, lichens, algae, pollen, or decaying vegetable matter
Trichoptera	caddisflies	Mothlike insects with hair-covered wings
Zorapetra	zorapterans	Tiny, slender, termitelike insects

MAMMALS

Order	Family name	Common name/examples	General characteristics of order
Monotremes	Ornithorhynchidae	platypus	Lay eggs
	Tachyglossidae	echidna	
Marsupialia	Burraymyidae	feathertail gliders	Have pouches
	Caenolestidae	rat opossums	
	Dasyuridae	native cats	
	Didelphidae	opossums	
	Myrmecobiidae	numbats	
	Notoryctidae	marsupial moles	
	Peramelidae	bandicoots	
	Phalageridae	phalangers, cuscuses	
	Thylacomydiae	burrowing bandicoots	
	Vombatidae	wombats	
Insectivora	Chrysochloridae	golden moles	Often nocturnal with
	Erinaceidae	hedgehogs	underdeveloped
	Macroscelididae	elephant shrews	vision
	Potamogalidae	otter shrews	
	Solenodontidae	solendon, almiqui	
	Soricidae	shrews	
	Talpidae	moles	
	Tenrecidae	tenrecs	
	Tupaiidae	tree shrews	
Chiroptera	Desmodontidae	vampire bats	Bats
	Emballonuridae	sheath tailed bats	
	Furipteridae	smoky bats	
	Hipposideridae	Old World leaf-nosed bats	
	Megadermatidae	false vampires	
	Molossidae	free-tailed bats	
	Mormoopidae	insectivorous bats	
	Mystacinidae	New Zealand short-tailed bats	
	Myzopodidae	Old World sucker-footed bats	
	Natalidae	funnel-eared bats	
	Noctilionidae	bulldog bats	
	Nycteridae	slit-faced or hollow-faced bats	
	Phyllostomatidae	American leaf-nosed bats	
	Pteropodidae	Old World fruit bats, flying foxes	
	Rhinolophidae	horseshoe bats	
	Rhinopomatidae	mouse-tailed bats	
	Thyropteridae	disk-wing bats	
	Vespertilionidae	common bats	

Order	Family name	Common name/examples	General characteristics of order
Rodentia	Abrocomidae	aborcomes	Gnawing animals
	Anomaluridae	scaly-tailed squirrels	with large incisors
	Aplodontidae	mountain beavers	that grow
	Bathyergidae	blesmols	throughout the
	Capromyidae	hutias, coypus	animal's life
	Castoridae	beavers	
	Caviidae	cavies, guinea pigs	
	Chinchillidae	chinchillas and viscachas	
	Cricetidae	field and deer mice, muskrats	
	Ctenodactylidae	gundis	
	Ctenomyidae	tuco-tucos	
	Dasyproctidae	pacas, agoutis	
	Dinomyidae	pacarana or Branick's paca	
	Dipodidae	jerboas	
	Echimyidae	spiny and rock rats	
	Erethizontidae	New World porcupines	
	Geomyidae	pocket gophers	
	Gliridae	dormice	
	Heteromyidae	mice, kangaroo rats	
	Hydrochoeridae	capybaras	
	Hystricidae	Old World porcupines	
	Muridae	Old World rats and mice	
	Octodontidae	octodonts, degus	
	Pedetidae	cape jumping hare, springhaas	
	Petromuridae	rock or desert rat	
	Rhizomyidae	bamboo and African mole rats	
	Sciuridae	squirrels, chimpmunks, marmots	
	Seleveniidae	jumping dormouse	
	Spalacidae	mole rats	
	Thryonomyidae	cane rats	
	Zapodidae	jumping and birch rats	
Edentata	Bradypodidae	tree sloths	Long, sticky tongue
	Dasypodidae	armadillos	
	Myrmecophagidae	anteaters	
Hyracoidea	Procaviidae	African rock hyrax	Gland on back
Lagomorpha	Leporidae	hares and rabbits	Herbivorous with
	Ochotonidae	pikas	well-developed incisors
Carnivora	Canidae	dogs, foxes, wolves, and jackals	Meat-eaters with high levels of
	Felidae	cats	intelligence, strong
	Hyaenidae	hyenas	sense of smell

Order	Family name	Common name/examples	General characteristics of order
	Mustelidae	weasels, otters, skunks, badgers	
	Procyonidae	raccoons, coatis, lesser pandas	
	Ursidae	bears, giant pandas	
	Viverridae	civets, mongooses, genet	
Cetacea	Balaenidae	Greenland right whales Biscayan right whales pigmy right whales	All members are aquatic and breathe through blowholes
	Balaenopteridae	rorquals, humpbacks, blue whales, fin whales, sei whales, Bryde's whale, little piked whale	
	Delphinidae sensu strictu	killer whales, Irawadi dolphin, pilot whale, Risso's dolphin, bottlenose dolphin, common dolphin, white-sided dolphin, rough-toothed dolphin, right whale dolphins, slender blackfish	
	Eschrichtiidae	grey whale	
	Hyperoodontidae	beaked whales	
	Monodontidae	beluga and narwhals	
	Phocoenidae	porpoises	
	Physeteridae	sperm whales, pigmy sperm whales	
	Platanistidae	river dolphins, Susu or Gangetic dolphins, Boutu or Amazonian dolphins, La Plata dolphins, Chinese river or white flag dolphins	
	Stenidae	long-snouted dolphins	
Proboscidea	Elephantidae	African, Asian elephants	Elephants
Pholidata	Manidae	pangolins	Scaly anteaters
Pinnipedia	Odobenidae	walrus	Primarily marine mammals with flippers for hind limbs
	Otariidae	eared seal, sea lion	
	Phocidae	earless seal	
Sirenia	Dugongidae	dugong	Totally aquatic with torpedo-shaped bodies
	Trichechidae	manatees	
Perissodactyla	Equidae	horses, asses, zebras and donkeys	Odd-toed hoofed mammals
	Tapirdae	tapirs	

| | Rhinocerotidae | rhinoceroses | |

Order	Family name	Common name/examples	General characteristics of order
Tubulidentata	Orycteropodidae	aardvarks	Aardvarks
Artiodactyla	Antilocapridae	pronghorn	Even-toed hoofed mammals
	Bovidae	cattle, goats, sheep, antelopes, gazelles	
	Camelidae	camels, llamas	
	Cervidae	deer	
	Giraffidae	giraffe, okapi	
	Hippopotamidae	hippopotamuses	
	Suidae	pigs	
	Tayassuidae	peccaries	
	Tragulidae	chevrotans	
Primates	Callitrichidae	tamarins, marmosets	Omnivorous, large-brained with five-digit hands and feet
	Cebidae	New World monkeys	
	Cercopithecidae	Old World monkeys	
	Cheirogaleidae	dwarf and mouse lemurs	
	Daubentoniidae	aye aye	
	Galagidae	galagos	
	Hominidae	man	
	Hylobatidae	gibbons, siamang	
	Indriidae	indrii, sifaka, avali	
	Lemuridae	lemurs	
	Lorisidae	lorises, pottos, hushbabies	
	Pongidae	gorilla, chimpanzee, orangutan	
	Tarsiidae	tarsiers	
	Tupaiidae	tree shrews	

CLASSIFICATION OF LIVING ORGANISMS

OBLIGATORY TAXONOMY

Kingdom
Phylum/Division
Class
Order
Family
Genus
Species

ANIMAL TAXONOMY

Kingdom
Subkingdom
Phylum
Subphylum
Superclass
Class
Subclass
Infraclass
Cohort
Superorder
Order
Suborder
Superfamily
Family
Subfamily
Tribe
Genus
Subgenus
Species
Subspecies

REPTILES

Order	Family name	Common name/ examples	General characteristics of order
Chelonia	Dermatemydidae	American river turtle	Aquatic and terrestrial
	Chelydridae	alligator and snapping reptiles turtles	
	Kinosternidae	mud and musk turtles	
	Emydidae	common turtle	
	Cheloniidae	sea turtles	
	Dermochelyidae	leatherback turtles	
	Carettochelyidae	New Guinea plateless turtle	
	Trionychidae	softshell turtles	
	Pelomediusidae	side-necked turtles	
	Chelyidae	snake-necked turtles	
Rhyncho-cephalia	Sphenodontidae	tuataras	Primitive, nocturnal animals, found in New Zealand

Order	Family name	Common name/ examples	General characteristics of order
Squamata (suborder sauria)	Gekkonidae	geckos	Order that contains
	Pygopodidae	flap-footed lizards	three suborders,
	Dibamidae	burrowers	including lizards,
	Iguanidae	iguanas	snakes, and worm
	Agamidae	agamid lizard	lizards; lizards are
	Chameloeontidae	Old World chameleons	herbivores and
	Scincidae	skinks	carnivores that
	Cordylidae	girdle-tailed lizards	have a skull made
	Lacertidae	Old World terrestrial lizards	of several
	Teiidae	whiptail lizards	mobile parts
	Anguidae	glass and alligator lizards	
	Anniellidae	California legless lizards	
	Helodermatidae	gila monster and bearded lizards	
	Varanidae	monitor lizards	
	Lanthanotidae	earless monitor lizard	
	Xantusiidae	night lizards	
(suborder serpentes)	Thyphlopidae	blind and worm snakes	Snakes have no
	Letotyphlopidae	slender blind snakes	limbs, lidless eyes,
	Xenopeltidae	sunbeam snakes	and are unable to
	Uropeltidae	shieldtail snakes	chew their food
	Boidae	pythons, boas, woodsnakes	
	Acrochordidae	wart snakes	
	Colubridae	terrestrial, aboreal, and aquatic snakes	
	Viperidae	vipers, rattlesnakes, and moccasins	
	Elapidae	cobras and coral snakes	
	Hydrophiidae	sea snakes	
(suborder Amphisbaenia)	Amphisbaenidae	worm lizards	Lizards without limbs
Crocodilia	Alligaridae	alligators, caiman	Carnivores with
	Crocodilidae	true crocodile	heavy, armoured
	Gavialidae	gavial or gharial	bodies and webbed toes

VEGETABLE

GARDEN FLOWERS

ANNUALS

Common name(s)	Latin name	Colours
Baby blue-eyes	*Nemophila menziesii*	blue
Baby's breath	*Gypsophila elegans*	white, pink
Black-eyed Susan	*Rudbeckia hirta*	yellow (purple-brown centre)
Blood flower, swallow wort, Indian root	*Asclepias curassavica*	orange-red
Blue daisy, blue marguerite, kingfisher daisy	*Felicia amelloides*	blue (yellow centre)
Blue lace flower	*Trachymene coerulea*	blue, lavender
Burning bush	*Kochia scoparia trichophylla*	greenish white
California poppy	*Eschscholzia californica*	yellow, red, white, orange
Candytuft	*Iberis umbellata*	pink, red, lilac, violet
Chrysanthemum	*Chrysanthemum* spp.	white, yellow, red, orange, purple
Cloud grass	*Agrostis nebulosa*	white
Common flax	*Linum usitatissimum*	blue, white
Corn cockle	*Agrostemma githago*	pinkish purple
Cosmos	*Cosmos binnatus*	white, pink, red (yellow centre)
Creeping zinnia	*Sanvitalia procumbens*	yellow (purple centre)
Dahlia	*Dahlia* spp.	yellow, red, pink, purple, white, orange, bicoloured
Dwarf morning glory, bindweed	*Convolvulus* spp.	blue, red, pink, purple, white
English daisy, daisy	*Bellis perennis*	white, pink, red (yellow centre)
Evening primrose	*Oenothera* spp.	yellow, white, rose
Flossflower, parlour maple	*Ageratum houstonianum*	white, blue, pink
Flowering maple, Indian mallow	*Abutilon hybridum*	red, pink, purple, yellow
Flowering tobacco	*Nicotiana alata*	pink, white, red, purple, green
Forget-me-not	*Myosotis sylvatica*	blue, pink, white
Foxglove	*Digitalis purpurea*	white, pink, yellow, purple
Garden balsam, rose balsam	*Impatiens balsamina*	pink, red, yellow, purple, white
Geranium	*Pelargonium* spp.	white, pink, red
Heliotrope, cherry pie	*Heliotropium arborescens*	blue, purple, white
Hollyhock	*Alcea rosea*	red, pink, yellow, white
Larkspur	*Consolida* spp.	blue, pink, purple, white

Common name(s)	Latin name	Colours
Marigold	*Tagetes* spp.	yellow, cream, orange, maroon
Mask flower	*Alonsoa warscewiczii*	red
Mignonette	*Reseda odorata*	greenish yellow, brownish red
Morning glory	*Ipomoea purpurea*	purple, pink, blue
Nasturtium	*Tropaeolum majus*	yellow, orange
Pansy	*Viola wittrockiana*	purple, white, blue, red, yellow
Patient Lucy, busy Lizzie, patience plant, sultana	*Impatiens walleriana*	red, pink, orange, purple, white
Petunia	*Petunia* spp.	white, pink, red, purple, blue, yellow
Phlox, annual phlox, drummond phlox	*Phlox drummondii*	white, red, lilac, purple
Poppy	*Papaver* spp.	orange, yellow, white, pink, red, purple
Pot marigold, ruddles, Scotch marigold, common marigold	*Calendula officinalis*	white, yellow, orange
Primrose	*Primula* spp.	yellow, white, red, blue, pink, purple
Sand verbena, beachs and verbena	*Abronia umbellata*	pink
Snapdragon	*Antirrhinum majus*	red, white, yellow, orange, pink
Sunflower	*Helianthus annuus*	yellow, orange, chestnut, maroon
Sweet basil	*Ocimum basilicum*	white, purplish
Sweet pea	*Lathyrus odoratus*	purple, pink, red
Trumpet flower, horn of plenty, downy thorn apple	*Datura metel*	white, yellow, purple, red, pink
Twinspur	*Diascia barberae*	pink
Wax begonia, bedding begonia	*Begonia semperflorens*	pink, white, red
Woodruff	*Asperula orientalis/Gallium odoratum*	blue
Zinnia	*Zinnia* spp.	white, yellow, red, orange

PERENNIALS

Common name(s)	Latin name	Colours
Adonis	*Adonis vernalis*	yellow
Ageratum	*Eupatorium coelestinum*	blue
Alkanet	*Anchusa azurea*	blue
Aster	*Aster* spp.	pink, blue, purple
Baby's breath	*Gypsophila paniculata*	white, pink
Balloon flower	*Platycodon grandiflorus*	blue, pink, white
Bee balm	*Monarda didyma*	pink, red, purple, white
Bellflower	*Campanula* spp.	white, blue
Blue daisy	*Felicia amelloides*	blue (yellow centre)
Candytuft	*Iberis sempervirens*	white
Chinese lantern	*Physalis alkekengi*	white
Christmas rose	*Hellborus niger*	white
Chrysanthemum	*Chrysanthemum morifolium*	white, yellow, bronze, purple, red

Common name(s)	Latin name	Colours
Columbine	*Aquilegia* spp.	yellow, red, pink, blue, white
Coneflower	*Rudbeckia* spp. v Echinacea	yellow
Coreopsis	*Coreopsis* spp.	yellow
Cornflower	*Centaurea montana*	blue, yellow
Day lilies	*Hemerocallis* spp.	yellow, orange, pink, red
Delphinium	*Delphinium* spp.	white, blue, yellow, pink, lavender
Dianthus (Pinks)	*Dianthus* spp.	pink, white, red
English daisy, daisy	*Bellis perennis*	pink, white, red
Epimedium	*Epimedium* spp.	rose, yellow, violet, white
Feverfew	*Tanacetum parthenium*	cream
Flax	*Linum* spp.	blue, yellow
Gentian	*Gentiana* spp.	blue, violet, white, yellow
Geranium	*Geranium* spp.	pink, red, purple
Globeflower	*Trollius europaeus*	yellow, orange
Golden marguerite, yellow chamomile, Dyer's chamomile	*Anthemis tinctoria*	yellow
Iceland poppy	*Papaver nudicaule*	white, pink, red, yellow, orange
Iris	*Iris* spp.	white, yellow, orange, red, pink, rose, lavender, purple, blue
Jacob's ladder	*Polemonium caeruleum*	blue
Jupiter's beard, red valerian, fox's brush	*Centranthus ruber*	rose, white
Lavender	*Lavandula angustifolia*	blue, lavender
Lavender cotton	*Santolina chamaecyparissus*	yellow
Meadow rue	*Thalictrum* spp.	yellow, white, lavender
Monkshood	*Aconitum* spp.	blue, yellow, white
Mullein	*Verbascum* spp.	yellow, white, pink, violet
Oriental poppy	*Papaver orientale*	red, white, pink, orange, lavender
Penstemon	*Penstemon* spp.	blue, purple, red, rose
Peony	*Paeonia* spp.	white, red, pink, yellow
Perennial sunflower	*Helianthus multiflorus*	yellow, orange
Phlox	*Phlox* spp.	white, pink, red, lavender, purple
Primrose	*Primula* spp.	white, pink, blue, red, gold
Sage	*Salvia* spp.	blue, blue-violet
Shasta daisy	*Chrysanthemum maximum*	white (yellow centre)
Speedwell, bird's eye	*Veronica* spp.	blue, white, pink
Spurge	*Euphorbia* spp.	yellow
Stoke's aster	*Stokesia laevis*	light blue, white
Sundrops, evening primrose, suncups	*Oenothera* spp.	yellow
Yarrow	*Achillea* spp.	white, red, yellow

HERBS

Acacia *(Acacia senegal)* a.k.a. Cape gum, Egyptian thorn, gum-arabic, Sudan gum-arabic. The gum of a small tree or shrub, used medicinally and as a thickener.

Adder's tongue *(Erythronium americanum)* a.k.a. dog-tooth violet, erythronium, lamb's tongue, rattlesnake violet, snake leaf, trout lily, yellow adder's tongue, yellow snakeleaf, yellow snowdrop. A plant from the lily family, used to cause vomiting.

Agrimony *(Agrimonia eupatoria)* a.k.a. cocklebur, stickwort. Used as a herbal remedy for diarrhoea.

Alexanders *(Smyrnium olusatrum)* a.k.a. black lovage. A herb whose flavour has been compared to both celery and parsley.

Alfalfa *(Medicago sativa)* a.k.a. buffalo herb, Lucerne, purple medic. Alfalfa leaves are often used in herbal teas and in herbal remedies.

Alliaria *(Alliaria petiolata)* a.k.a. donkey's foot, garlic mustard, Jack-by-the-hedge, onion nettle, sauce alone. Nettlelike leaves that have a strong garlic smell when crushed.

Aloe *(Aloe perryi; Aloe barbadensis; Aloe ferox)* a.k.a. Bombay aloe, Socotrine aloe, Turkey aloe, Zanzibar aloe, Barbados aloe, Curaçao aloe, medicinal aloe, unguentine cactus, Cape aloe. Extracts of aloe have a very bitter flavour; can be used as a medicinal herb. Some species are poisonous.

Alpine strawberry *(Fragaria vesca)* a.k.a. wild strawberry, earth mulberry. Alpine strawberry leaves are often used in herbal teas and in herbal remedies.

Althaea *(Althaea officinalis)* a.k.a. marsh mallow, marshmallow. Used as a herbal remedy for its anti-inflammatory properties.

Amaranth *(Amaranthus* spp.) a.k.a. love-lies-bleeding, red cocks-comb. Used in herbal remedies for its astringent properties.

Angelica *(Angelica archangelica)* a.k.a. archangel, archangelica, European angelica, wild parsnip, wild angelica, garden angelica. A member of the parsley family, with a very strong and acrid flavour. Can be used as a herbal remedy. *(Angelica atropurpurea)* a.k.a. Alexanders, American angelica, bellyache root, great angelica, masterwort, purple angelica. Has a less strong flavour than *A. archangelica.*

Angostura *(Galipea trifoliata)* a.k.a. cusparia bark. Small amounts of the powdered bark are used for diarrhoea, but larger quantities can cause vomiting.

Anise *(Pimpinella anisum)* a.k.a. aniseed, sweet cumin. Anise seeds are used whole or powdered; the leaves have a liquorice flavour and can be used in salads.

Anise hyssop *(Agastache foeniculum)* Used by the Plains Indians to make a tea.

Areca nut *(Areca catechu)* a.k.a. betel nut. A herb with highly astringent properties.

Arnica *(Arnica montana* and *cordifolia)* a.k.a. leopard's bane, mountain daisy, mountain tobacco, wolf's bane. Extracts from the flowers are sweet, and slightly bitter, somewhat like camomile. A herbal remedy for bruises, sprains, and strains.

Arrach *(Chenopodium olidum)* a.k.a. goosefoot, stinking arrach. Acts as a sedative and used for irritability and nervousness.

Arrowroot *(Maranta arundinacea)* The powdered root is used as a thickener, and can be made into a soothing drink for infants and convalescents.

Arugula *(Eruca sativa)* a.k.a. rocket, roquette, ruchetta, rugola. The young leaves have a warm, peppery flavour.

Asarabacca *(Asarum europaeum)* a.k.a. asarum, European snakeroot, hazelwort, wild nard. The root is used as an emetic, but can be dangerous in large doses.

Ash *(Fraxinus excelsior)* a.k.a. European ash. Used to make a tea that is diuretic and mildly laxative.

Avens *(Geum urbanum)* a.k.a. bennet, colewort, herb bennet, wood avens. The roots smell like cloves and are said to have stimulating properties. The young leaves can be used in salads.

Balm *(Melissa officinalis)* a.k.a. balm mint, bee balm, blue balm, cure-all, dropsy plant, garden balm, lemon balm, melissa, sweet balm. Lemon-scented leaves used fresh as a flavouring or dried in herbal teas.

Balmony *(Chelone glabra)* a.k.a. snakehead, turtlehead, turtlebloom. The leaves are used as an internal remedy to purge and cleanse.

Barberry *(Berberis vulgaris)* The bark and berries are used as a herbal remedy for a number of conditions including diarrhoea.

Basil *(Ocimum basilicum)* a.k.a. sweet basil, monk's basil, Saint Josephwort. The leaves are used fresh or dried—fresh leaves have a taste similar to cloves, but when dried have a more minty taste. Varieties include lemon-scented basil *(Ocimum basilicum,* var. *citriodora),* bush or dwarf basil *(Ocimum sanctum),* Indian holy basil *(Ocimum sanctum),* wild basil *(Clinopodium vulgare),* prairie or wild hyssop *(Pycnanthemum virginicum).*

Basil thyme *(Acinos arvensis)* A herb that combines the flavours of basil and thyme. Another variety is alpine basil thyme *(Acinos alpinus).*

Basswood *(Tilia americana)* a.k.a. American linden tree, lime tree, whitewood. The flowers are used to make a soothing tea.

Bayberry *(Myrica cerifera)* a.k.a. candleberry, wax myrtle. The leaves, bark, and roots have stimulant and astringent properties.

Bay leaf *(Laurus nobilis)* a.k.a. Grecian laurel, Indian bay, laurel, Roman bay, sweet bay, sweet laurel. Leaves are usually dried and used in soups, roasts, and stews. Another variety is red or sweet bay *(Persea borbonia),* not listed by the FDA and hence not recommended.

Bearberry *(Arctostaphylos uva-ursi)* The leaves can be smoked or used in a tea as a herbal remedy.

Bed straw *(Gallium aparine)* a.k.a. catchweed, cleavers, cleaverwort, clivers, goose grass, grip grass. Used as an internal and external herbal remedy.

Belladonna *(Atropa belladonna)* a.k.a. black cherry, deadly nightshade, dwale, poison black cherry. Used as a herbal remedy for inflammatory conditions, sleeplessness. Can be highly poisonous if dosage is not controlled.

Benzoin *(Styrax benzoin* and other spp.) Used both externally as an adhesive tincture and internally as an expectorant.

Bergamot *(Monarda didyma* or *fistulosa;* also *Monarda punctata)* a.k.a. bee balm, blue balm, high balm, low balm, mountain balm, mountain mint, wild bergamot, horse mint. Members of the mint family, whose flowers and leaves are used, fresh or dried, to make teas, or are added to salads, vegetable dishes, stews, poultry, and meats.

Betony *(Stachys officinalis)* a.k.a. woundwort. A medicinal herb with soft downy leaves that can be applied to cuts and abrasions.

Bistort *(Polygonum bistorta)* The root is used as a herbal remedy, but can be hazardous.

Bittersweet *(Solanum dulcamara)* a.k.a. nightshade, felonwood, felonwort, scarlet berry, violet bloom, woody nightshade. Although the twigs have been used in herbal remedies, all parts of this plant are considered poisonous, particularly the berries.

Blackberry *(Rubus villosus)* a.k.a. bramble. The bark, root, and leaves are used in herbal remedies as a tonic and an astringent.

Black alder *(Rhamnus frangula)* a.k.a. alder buckthorn. Used as a laxative but can be dangerous in large amounts or if used fresh as opposed to aged.

Black catechu *(Acacia catechu)* a.k.a. cutch. Herbal remedy used for its astringent properties.

Black cohosh *(Cimicifuga racemosa)* a.k.a. black snakeroot, rattleroot, squawroot. The roots are used medicinally for a variety of conditions. Large amounts can be poisonous.

Black currant *(Ribes nigrum)* A tea made from the leaves is thought to be useful for sore throats.

Black haw *(Viburnum prunifolium)* a.k.a. stagbush. The root is used as a herbal remedy for uterine disorders.

Black willow *(Salix negra)* Contains salicin, now produced synthetically as the active ingredient in aspirin. Used as a herbal remedy for fevers, arthritis, skin conditions.

Bog myrtle *(Myrica gale)* a.k.a. sweet gale. The leaves can be dried to make tea, or used fresh as a seasoning.

Boldo *(Peumus boldus)* The leaves of this Chilean evergreen tree smell like lemon balm and coriander.

Borage *(Borago officinalis)* a.k.a. bee plant, bee-bread, burridge, cool-tankard, talewort. Used fresh or dried; tastes vaguely like cucumber. Also used as a herbal remedy for its diuretic and laxative properties.

Box leaves *(Buxus sempervirens)* a.k.a. boxwood. Has been used in herbal remedies for its purgative effects; however, it should be considered a toxic plant.

Bouquet garni The name for a mixture of herbs (parsley, thyme, bay leaf) that are tied together and used as a seasoning in soups or stews.

Bryony *(Bryonia alba; Bryonia dioica)* a.k.a. (respectively) tetterberry, white bryony, wild bryony, wild hops, wild vine, wild white vine; devil's turnip, red bryony. Used in herbal remedies for the flu, among other ailments; the berries are highly poisonous.

Buchu *(Agathosma betulina)* a.k.a. bookoo. The dried leaf is a weak diuretic and urinary antiseptic and is used as a remedy for kidney disorders.

Buckthorn *(Rhamnus cathartica)* The berries are pressed to make a laxative tonic that can be extremely dangerous in large doses.

Burdock *(Arctium lappa* or *Arctium minus)* a.k.a. beggar's-buttons, burr seed, clotbur, cockle buttons, cocklebur, cuckold, edible burdock, lappa, or common burdock. The roots are edible and cultivated in Japan as a vegetable. The roots and seeds are also used in herbal remedies.

Burnet *(Sanguisorba officinalis* or *Poterium sanguisorba)* a.k.a. burnet bloodwort, great burnet, Italian burnet, Italian pimpernel, or garden burnet, pimpinella, pimpinelle, salad burnet. Similar to borage with its cucumber-like flavour, burnet is used fresh or dried as a seasoning.

Calamint *(Satureja glabella)* Used in herbal tea, or occasionally in salad or cooking, calamint has a spicy flavour a little like peppermint.

Calamus *(Acorus calamus)* a.k.a. flagroot, grass myrtle, myrtle flag, sweet calamus, sweet flag, sweet grass, sweet myrtle, sweet rush. All parts of this plant are sweet and aromatic and can be used as flavouring, particularly for liqueurs. Excessive amounts of the root oil can cause drowsiness.

Camomile *(Chamaemelum nobile* or *Chamomilla recutita)* a.k.a. chamomile, English camomile, garden camomile, ground apple, lawn camomile, little apple, manzanilla, may-then, Roman camomile, Scotch camomile, true camomile, Whig plant, or German camomile, Hungarian camomile, sweet false camomile, wild camomile. The dried, strongly scented flowers and leaves are used to make herbal teas. As a remedy, thought to be soothing and calming.

Cascara *(Rhamnus purshiana)* a.k.a. bearberry, bearwood, cascara sagrada, California buckthorn, chittam bark, sacred bark. The bark is used for its laxative properties.

Castor oil plant *(Ricinus communis)* a.k.a. palma Cristi. The oil from this plant is well known for its laxative effects.

Catechu *(Uncaria gambier)* Used for its astringent properties to treat diarrhoea and sore throats. Dangerous if overused.

Catnip *(Nepeta cataria)* a.k.a. catmint, catnep, catrup, catswort, field balm. A member of the mint family used in teas. Cats are supposed to be highly attracted to it.

Cat thyme *(Teucrium marum)* Not related to other thymes. Cats are attracted to it, and it is used in herbal remedies.

Celandine *(Chelidonium majus)* a.k.a. great celandine. A plant with very caustic juices sometimes used as a herbal remedy despite the fact that it can be dangerously toxic.

Celery leaves *(Apium graveolens)* The leaves can be used fresh or dried as a seasoning, particularly in soups or stews.

Centuary *(Centaurium erythraea)* a.k.a. minor centuary. Extracts from the flowers are very bitter and have been used in herbal remedies.

Cherry laurel *(Prunus laurocerasus)* The leaves have been used in herbal remedies but they contain large quantities of cyanide-related compounds and are extremely poisonous.

Chervil *(Anthriscus cerefolium)* a.k.a. cicely, French parsley, garden chervil. A parsleylike plant with a taste reminiscent of tarragon or anise. Used fresh or dried.

Chickweed *(Stellaria media)* Used as a herbal remedy for constipation; can also be used as a salad green.

Chicory *(Cichorium intybus)* a.k.a. barbe-de-capuchin, Belgian endive, blue-sailors, coffeeweed, succory, witloof. The root can be dried and used as a coffee substitute. The leaves can be used as a salad green.

Chives *(Allium schoenoprasum)* a.k.a. cive, schnittlauch. The light green stems have a delicate onion flavour.

Clary sage *(Salvia sclarea)* a.k.a. clary, muscatel sage. A member of the sage or salvia family, the leaves are strongly aromatic and can be used either fresh or dried as a seasoning.

Clover *(Trifolium spp.)* a.k.a. red clover. The dried blossoms are used in herbal remedies.

Coltsfoot *(Tussilago farfara)* a.k.a. ass's foot, British tobacco, bullsfoot, butterbur, coughwort, flower velure, foal's-foot, hallfoot, horsefoot, horsehoof. Coltsfoot and sweet coltsfoot *(Petasites, various species)* are used in old remedies for sore throats and coughs; the fresh leaves are sometimes eaten as a vegetable.

Comfrey *(Symphytum officinale)* a.k.a. blackwort, boneset, bruisewort, consormol, gum plant, healing herb, knitback, knitbone, salsify, slippery root, wallwort. A relative of borage; the dried leaves are used in teas, the fresh leaves are used in salads. Also used to heal wounds and fractures. Varieties include prickly comfrey *(Symphytum asperum)* and Russian comfrey *(Symphytum uplandicum)*.

Coriander *(Coriandrum sativum)* a.k.a. Chinese parsley, cilantro, yuen sai. The leaves have a fresh taste like soap or orange peel.

Costmary *(Saussurea costus)* a.k.a. alecost, Bible leaf, mint geranium, sweet Mary, tansy. A spicy, slightly bitter herb, once used to flavour beer.

Couch grass *(Agropyrum repens)* a.k.a. cutch, dog grass, durfa grass, durfee grass, quack grass, quick grass, quitch grass, scutch, twitch grass, witchgrass. A herb with a diuretic effect.

Cowslip *(Primula veris)* a.k.a. butter rose, English cowslip, keyflower, palsywort, primrose. The flowers are used to make wine and tea and are also put in salads.

Cranesbill *(Geranium maculatum)* a.k.a. wild geranium. An astringent, used to control bleeding or diarrhoea.

Cubeb *(Piper cubeba)* a.k.a. Java pepper, tailed pepper. Used as a diuretic and urinary antiseptic and sometimes as an expectorant, but is toxic in large doses.

Culver's root *(Veronicastrum virginicum)* a.k.a. blackroot, bowman's root, leptandra, tall speedwell, tall veronica. Has strong emetic and cathartic properties and can be extremely dangerous if used incorrectly.

Curry leaf *(Murraya koinigii)* The leaves of this tree, fresh or dried, are a curry ingredient, usually chopped and fried in oil.

Damiana *(Turnera diffusa)* The dried leaves are said to have aphrodisiac, diuretic, and stimulant properties.

Dandelion *(Taraxacum officinale)* a.k.a. blowball, cankerwort, fairy clock, lion's tooth, pee-in-the-bed, priest's crown, puffball, swine snout, white endive, wild endive. The leaves can be used as vegetable greens, the flowers can be used to make wine, and the leaves have a diuretic effect.

Dill *(Anethum graveolens)* a.k.a. dill weed, anet. Both the leaves (fresh or dried) and the seeds are used. The leaves are pungent and aromatic; the seeds are more bitter, like caraway, and are used most famously to flavour pickles.

Dittany, common *(Cunila origanoides)* a.k.a. American dittany. Closely related to the genus *Origanum,* and the leaves smell something like wild marjoram. Used as a substitute for oregano and as a herbal remedy.

Dittany of Crete *(Origanum dictamnus)* a.k.a. Spanish hops, true dittany. A member of the oregano family, used in cooking in Spain, Italy, Greece, Mexico, and Latin American countries.

Dogbane *(Apocynum androsaemifolium)* a.k.a. bitter root. Used in herbal remedies, but toxic in large doses.

Dogwood *(Cornus florida)* The bark is used as a herbal remedy for fevers.

Echinacea *(Echinacea, various species)* a.k.a.

black sampson, purple coneflower. A herb said to have antiseptic qualities destroying bacteria and cleansing the blood. Used by the Plains Indians to treat a wide variety of ailments.

Elder *(Sambucus canadensis; Sambucus nigra)* a.k.a. American elder, black elder, rob elder, sweet elder, black-berried European elder, boor tree, bore tree, bounty, elfhorn, ellanwood, European elder, German elder. The flowers are used as a herbal remedy; the berries can be made into jams, pies, and wine.

Elecampane *(Inula helenium)* a.k.a. alant, elfdock, elfwort, horse-elder, horsehead, horseheal, inula, scabwort, yellow starwort, wild sunflower. Used as a herbal remedy or as a flavouring.

Endive *(Chichorium endivia)* Leaves are used as a salad green. A close relation to chicory.

Epazote *(Chenopodium ambrosiodes* or *Chenopodium botrys)* a.k.a. American wormseed, goosefoot, Jesuits' tea, Mexican tea, Spanish tea, wormseed or feather geranium, Jerusalem oak. Widely used as a green herb in Mexican cooking and as a herbal tea in Europe. Supposedly has anti-gas properties.

Ephedra *(Ephedra spp.)* a.k.a. Brigham Young weed, desert herb, desert tea, joint fir, Mormon tea, squaw tea, Teamster's tea. Used as a herbal tea with diuretic properties. The Asian species *(Ephedra sinica)* is known as ma huang, and contains concentrated amounts of ephedrine, a nervous system stimulant. The North American variety contains only trace amounts.

Eucalyptus *(Eucalyptus globulus)* a.k.a. blue gum tree. The oil is used in salves and ointments and is also taken internally, but large doses can be very dangerous.

European ash *(Fraximus excelsior)* a.k.a. bird's tongue. The leaves and shoots can be used in salads or boiled to make a tea that is mildly laxative.

Evening primrose *(Oenothera biennis)* a.k.a. fever plant, field primrose, German rampion, king's cureall, night willow-herb, primrose, scabish, scurvish, tree primrose. The shoots can be eaten in salads, and the roots can be eaten as a vegetable. It is used in numerous herbal remedies.

Eyebright *(Euphrasia officinalis)* a.k.a. euphrasy, red eyebright. A meadow plant used to treat colds and allergies.

Fairy-wand *(Chamaelirium luteum)* a.k.a. devil's bit. Used as a herbal remedy for infertility in women and impotence in men.

Fennel *(Foeniculum vulgare)* a.k.a. wild fennel, Roman fennel, Florence fennel. The seeds, dried root, stems, and leaves (which taste like anise) are all used—the seeds to make Italian sausage, the stems are eaten as a vegetable, and the leaves are used as a seasoning, both raw and cooked. Fennel tea can be used as a herbal remedy to ease digestion.

Feverfew *(Chrysanthemum parthenium)* a.k.a. febrifuge plant, pellitory. The dried flowers are used in herbal remedies.

Feverweed *(Aureolaria pedicularia)* a.k.a. American foxglove, bushy gerardia, false foxglove, fern-leaved false foxglove, lousewort. Used in herbal remedies for its diaphoretic and sedative properties.

Figwort *(Scrophularia* spp.) a.k.a. heal-all, kernel-wort, knotty-rooted figwort, scrofula plant. The name refers to about 200 species. Used as a herbal remedy for skin conditions, primarily scrofula.

Fines herbes A French mixture of fresh herbs including parsley, chives, tarragon, and chervil. In the Mediterranean region, basil, fennel, oregano, sage, and saffron are added.

Flax *(Linum usitatissimum)* a.k.a. flax seed, linseed. The seeds and oil have been used in herbal remedies but can cause fatal overdoses.

Foxglove *(Digitalis,* various species) a.k.a. dead men's bells, digitalis, fairy fingers, fairy gloves, folk's-glove, ladies' glove, purple foxglove. This herb's active ingredient is digitalis, which is used

to treat heart disease, but it should never be used as a home remedy since improper use can be fatal.

Garlic *(Allium sativum)* A perennial bulb that is divided into cloves and used fresh or dried in garlic powder.

Gelsemium *(Gelsemium sempervirens)* a.k.a. yellow jasmine, woodbine. A powerful sedative that is poisonous and can cause respiratory failure.

Gentian *(Gentiana lutea)* a.k.a. bitter root, yellow gentian. Used as a herbal remedy and for flavouring vermouth.

Geranium *(Pelargonium)* The leaves of certain varieties are used for flavouring: *(Pelargonium fragrans)* nutmeg-scented, *(crispum)* lemon-scented, *(citrosum)* orange-scented, *(odoratissimum)* apple-scented, and *(tomentosum)* peppermint-scented.

Ginseng *(Panax ginseng; Panax quinquefolia)* a.k.a. Asiatic ginseng, Chinese ginseng, Eastern Asian ginseng, Korean ginseng, San Qi ginseng, wonder of the world, American ginseng, five-fingers, five-leafed ginseng, North American ginseng, redberry. An aromatic root with a sweet liquorice-like taste. Used as a seasoning and as a herbal remedy.

Goat's rue *(Galega officinalis)* Used in herbal remedies.

Goldenseal *(Hydrastis canadensis)* a.k.a. eye balm, eye root, ground raspberry, Indian plant, Indian turmeric, jaundice root, orangeroot, turmeric root, yellow puccoon, yellowroot. Extracts of the rhizomes (the stem just below the surface) and the roots are used in herbal medicines.

Good-King-Henry *(Chenopodium bonus-henricus)* a.k.a. fat hen, mercury. A very bitter herb that is used more as a cooked green than as a seasoning.

Goose tansy *(Potentilla anserina)* Used as a herbal remedy for diarrhoea.

Ground ivy *(Glechoma hederacea)* a.k.a. alehoof, cat's-foot, cat's-paw, creeping Charlie, field balm, gill tea, gill-over-the-ground, gillrun, hay maids, hedge maids, runaway robin, turnhoof. The dried blossoms and leaves can be made into a medicinal tea used to treat coughs and colds.

Hawthorn (*Crataegus*, various species) a.k.a. cockspur, cockspur thorn, English hawthorn, may bush, may tree, mayblossom, quick-set thorn, red haw, thorn apple, summer haw, Washington thorn, white thorn, yellow-fruited thorn. The flowers are used to make a herbal tea with sedative powers.

Heather (*Calluna vulgaris*) a.k.a. ling, Scotch heather. The common heather found in Scotland and Europe whose shoots are used as an ingredient in herbal remedies.

Hedge hyssop (*Gratiola officinalis*) Used as a herbal remedy, but has potent cardiac effects and should be regarded as dangerous.

Hedge mustard (*Sisymbrium officinale*) Used dried as a herbal remedy.

Hemp agrimony (*Eupatorium cannabinum*) a.k.a. sweet-smelling trefoil, water maudlin. Used in many herbal remedies externally and internally. In large doses it is both laxative and emetic.

Henna (*Lawsonia inermis*) a.k.a. alcanna, Egyptian privet, Jamaica mignonette, mignonette tree, reseda. Has astringent properties; often used in herbal remedies.

Herb Robert (*Geranium robertianum*) A small plant used as a herbal remedy, it has red stems, red leaves, and reddish-purple flowers.

Honeysuckle (*Lonicera* spp.) Refers to more than 150 species, used in herbal remedies, particularly for the skin.

Hops (*Humulus lupulus*) a.k.a. bine, European hop, lupulin. Used as a flavouring for beer, but also as a sleep aid, in tea, or stuffed in pillows.

Horehound (*Marrubium vulgare*) a.k.a. hoarhound, hoarehound, white horehound. A member of the mint family, used as a flavouring for candy and as a herbal remedy for coughs and colds.

Horseradish (*Armoracia rusticana*) The root is pungent and spicy and used fresh as a condiment.

Horsetail (*Equisetum hyemale*) a.k.a. bottle brush, scouring rush. A herb related to ferns, and commonly used in herbal remedies, although improper doses can cause poisoning.

Houseleek (*Sempervivum tectorum*) The fresh leaves are placed directly on various skin conditions.

Hyssop (*Hyssopus officinalis*) The flowers and the leaves, both fresh or dried, are used in cooking and in herbal remedies. They have a pungent, minty, bitter flavour.

Imperatoria (*Peucedanum osthruthium*) a.k.a. masterwort. A perennial plant whose roots are used in herbal remedies.

Iris (*Iris versicolor, Iris* spp.) a.k.a. blue flag. A cathartic and emetic, iris can be dangerous if used incorrectly, causing liver and kidney damage and skin rashes.

Ironweed (*Vernonia* spp.) Refers to between 500 and 1,000 species, all known as ironweed, and used in herbal remedies.

Jamaican dogwood (*Piscidia piscipula*) a.k.a. fish fuddle, fish-poison tree, West Indian dogwood. Used in some herbal remedies as a sedative and pain killer.

Joe Pye weed (*Eupatorium purpureum*) A herb with diuretic properties, used by some Native American tribes as an aphrodisiac.

Kidney vetch (*Anthyllis vulneraria*) a.k.a. ladies' fingers, lamb's toes, staunchwort, woundwort. The flowers are used as an ingredient in herbal remedies.

Knotweed (*Polygonum aviculare*) Used as a herbal remedy for kidney and bladder stones, but can cause diarrhoea and vomiting in large doses.

Lady's-mantle (*Alchemilla vulgaris; Alchemilla arvensis; Alchemilla microcarpa*) a.k.a. bear's foot, lion's foot, field lady's mantle, parsley piert. Extracts of the leaves and roots are very astringent and have been used to control external bleeding.

Lady's smock (*Cardamine pratensis*) a.k.a. bitter cress, cardamine, cuckooflower, mayflower, meadow cress. A common meadow plant that is similar to watercress and can also be used as a salad plant.

Lamb's-ears (*Stachys byzantina*) a.k.a. woolly betony. The leaves are used to make a mild tea. Fresh leaves have a mild, aromatic taste; dried leaves have an apple flavour.

Lamb's quarters (*Chenopodium album*) a.k.a. pigweed, white goosefoot. The leaves are sometimes eaten as greens.

Larkspur (*Consolida regalis*) a.k.a. knight's spur, lark's claw, lark's heel. Has been used as a herbal remedy but should be treated as a toxic plant.

Lavender (*Lavandula angustifolia; Lavandula stoechas*) a.k.a. (respectively) English lavender, true lavender; French lavender, Spanish lavender. The leaves and flower spikes are primarily used as fragrance, but can be used medicinally as an antispasmodic. Lavender is part of the mint family.

Lemon verbena (*Aloysia triphylla*) a.k.a. herb Louisa, lemon-scented verbena, verbena oil. The leaves have a strong lemon scent and can be used fresh as a seasoning or dried in a tea.

Lemongrass (*Cymbopogon* spp.) Refers to several different varieties, all containing citric oils that give them a lemony flavour. The stalks are used as a seasoning, ground, dried, or fresh.

Liquorice (*Glycyrrhiza glabra*) The ground or sliced root is used in candies and drinks.

Lily of the valley (*Convallaria majalis*) a.k.a. May lily. Has similar effects to digitalis and should be considered a dangerous plant.

Linden flowers (*Tilia* spp.) Used mostly in herbal teas.

Lion's-ear (*Leonotis leonurus*) Used as a herbal remedy and as an ornamental border.

Lobelia (*Lobelia inflata*) a.k.a. bladderpod, emetic herb, emetic weed, gagroot, Indian tobacco, vomitwort, wild tobacco. Used as a herbal remedy for a variety of conditions, but contains toxic alkaloids and should be considered very dangerous.

Loosestrife (*Lythrum salicaria*) a.k.a. long purples, milk willow-herb, purple loosestrife, purple willow-herb, rainbow weed, soldiers, spiked loosestrife, spiked willow-herb, willow sage. A plant with astringent properties, sometimes used in herbal remedies for diarrhoea.

Lovage (*Levisticum officinale*) a.k.a. European lovage, garden lovage, Italian lovage, lavose, love parsley, sea parsley, wild parsley. A large celery-like plant. The leaves (fresh or dried), stems, and seeds are all used.

Lungwort (*Pulmonaria officinalis*) Used in herbal remedies and as a flavouring for vermouth.

Lycopodium (*Lycopodium clavatum*) a.k.a. foxtail, lycopod, vegetable sulphur, wolf claw. A poisonous plant, except for its spores, which are used as a herbal remedy both internally and externally.

Madder (*Rubia tinctorum*) Used in a number of herbal remedies for diarrhoea and urinary tract problems among other conditions.

Mallow (*Malva sylvestris; Malva rotundifolia*) a.k.a. cheese flower, cheese plant, cheeses, country mallow, high mallow, blue mallow, dwarf mallow, low mallow. An ingredient in a number of internal and external herbal remedies.

Marigold (*Calendula officinalis*) a.k.a. calendula, holigold, Mary bud, poet's marigold, pot marigold. The petals are used fresh or dried as a seasoning or food dye. Used in herbal remedies for cuts and burns.

Marjoram and oregano (*Origanum* spp.) a.k.a. common marjoram, knotted marjoram, pot marjoram, sweet marjoram, wild marjoram. So closely related that they are not classified separately; marjoram has a more delicate flavour than oregano, which is actually a wild variety of marjoram with a stronger, peppery flavour. The leaves of both are used fresh and dried as a seasoning.

Marsh mallow (*Althea officinalis*) a.k.a. althea. Extracts of the roots and flowers are used in beverage and liqueur flavourings.

Maté (*Ilex paraguayensis*) a.k.a. Paraguayan holly, Paraguayan tea, yerba maté, Saint Bartholomew's tea. The dried leaves of this holly plant with a high caffeine content are made into tea that is both diuretic and purgative.

Meadowsweet (*Filipendula* spp.) The flowers can be used as a flavouring or dried in a tea used to treat rheumatism and kidney problems.

Mexican giant hyssop (*Agastache mexicana*) Used by the Plains Indians to make a herbal tea to treat coughs and other respiratory problems.

Milk thistle (*Silybum marianum*) a.k.a. holy thistle, Marythistle, Saint Mary's thistle. Used in herbal remedies.

Milkweed (*Asclepias* spp.) Used as a herbal remedy for bronchitis and rheumatism, but many of the species are known to be poisonous and large amounts can cause vomiting and catharsis.

Milkwort (*Polygala vulgaris; Polygala senega*) A herbal remedy that is supposed to increase milk supply in nursing mothers, but can cause vomiting and purging in large amounts.

Mint (*Mentha* spp.) Varieties include peppermint (*Mentha piperita*), spearmint (*Mentha spicata*), applemint (*Mentha suaveolens*), round-leaved mint (*Mentha rotundifolia*). The leaves are used fresh or dried as a seasoning.

Mistletoe (*Phoradendron serotinum* or *Viscum album*) a.k.a. American mistletoe, birdlime, golden bough or all-heal, European mistletoe. Although the leaves of both have been used in herbal remedies, they can dangerously increase blood pressure. The berries are poisonous.

Monkshood (*Aconitum napellus*) a.k.a. aconite, bear's-foot, friar's-cap, helmet flower, mousebane, soldier's cap, Turk's cap, wolfsbane. Used in herbal remedies, but can be poisonous in large doses.

Mountain ash (*Sorbus aucuparia*) a.k.a. Rowan tree. The edible berries contain sorbitol, which is used as a sweetener and also as a diuretic and cathartic.

Mouse ear (*Hieracium pilosella*) a.k.a. felon herb, hawkweed, mouse bloodwort, pilosella. Used in herbal remedies for its astringent and diuretic properties.

Mugwort (*Artemisia vulgaris*) a.k.a. felon herb. Used in herbal remedies.

Mullein (*Verbascum thapsus*) Used in many old herbal remedies.

Myrtle (*Myrtus communis*) a.k.a. dwarf myrtle, German myrtle. Extracts from the leaves are used to flavour alcoholic beverages; the leaves are thought to be healing when applied to wounds.

Nasturtium (*Tropaeolum majus*) a.k.a. garden nasturtium, Indian cress, tall nasturtium, capucine. The fresh leaves and flowers have a peppery flavour and can be used in salads; the dried leaves can be used as a seasoning.

Nettle (*Urtica dioica*) a.k.a. stinging nettle. The leaves produce hives if touched when fresh, but once they are cooked or dried are safe to use as a cooked green or as a seasoning with a slightly salty flavour.

Oregon grape (*Mahonia aquifolium*) a.k.a. blue barberry, California barberry, holly barberry, holly mahonia, mountain grape, rocky mountain grape, trailing mahonia, wild Oregon grape. The roots have diuretic and laxative properties and are used in herbal remedies.

Orris *(Iris germanica,* var. *florentina)* a.k.a. Florentina, Florentine iris. The root has a liquorice-like flavour, and is used as a flavouring and in cough drops and lozenges.

Parsley *(Petroselinum crispum,* var. *crispum)* a.k.a. garden parsley, rock parsley; *(Petroselinum crispum,* var. *neapolitanum)* a.k.a. flat-leaf parsley, Italian parsley. The leaves are used fresh or dried as a seasoning.

Partridgeberry *(Mitchella repens)* a.k.a. squaw vine. Used as a herbal remedy for insomnia, and to ease childbirth.

Passionflower *(Passiflora,* various species) Extracts of the flower have sedative qualities, and the leaves are used in herbal teas.

Pasque flower *(Anemone patens)* a.k.a. Easter flower, meadow anemone, prairie anemone, pulsatilla, wild crocus, wind flower. Used as a herbal remedy for colds; can be highly poisonous.

Pennyroyal *(Mentha pulegium; Hedoma pulegioides)* a.k.a. European pennyroyal, lurk-in-the-ditch, American pennyroyal, mock pennyroyal, mosquito grass, pudding grass, squaw balm, squaw mint, stinking balm, tickweed. Used as a herbal medicine and for making teas.

Perilla *(Perilla frutescens)* a.k.a. shiso, shiso zuku. The Japanese use all parts of the plant for cooking but substances in the leaves are thought to cause pulmonary disease.

Peyote *(Lophophora williamsii)* a.k.a. mescal buttons, Pellote. Used in herbal remedies, also a hallucinogenic drug that can cause changes in the cardiac rhythm.

Pilewort *(Ranunculus ficaria)* a.k.a. lesser celandine, small celandine. Has been used as a remedy for haemorrhoids but should be treated as a toxic plant.

Pimpernel *(Pimpinella major; Pimpinella saxifrage)* a.k.a. false pimpernel, greater pimpernel, burnet saxifrage, small pimpernel. Used in a number of herbal remedies for a number of conditions.

Pinkroot *(Spigelia marilandica)* a.k.a. Carolina pink, India pink, worm grass. The root has been used as a herbal remedy but large doses can be fatal.

Pipsissewa *(Chimaphila* spp.) A herb with diuretic properties.

Pitcher plant *(Sarracenia purpurea)* a.k.a. flytrap, saddleplant, watercup. A carnivorous plant whose powdered root is used in herbal remedies.

Plantain *(Plantago major)* a.k.a. way bread. The leaves are used in herbal remedies.

Pleurisy root *(Asclepias tuberosa)* a.k.a. butterfly weed. A toxic plant, used as a herbal cure-all by some Native American tribes.

Psyllium *(Plantago psyllium)* The seeds of the plantain, which serve as a mild laxative when wet.

Purslane *(Portulaca oleracea)* a.k.a. Continental parsley, kitchen-garden purslane, pusley. The leaves can be used fresh or cooked as a seasoning.

Pussytoes *(Antennaria dioica)* a.k.a. catsfoot. Used in herbal remedies.

Pyrethrum *(Chrysanthemum cinerariifolium)* The dried flower heads are used to make the insecticide pyrethrum.

Queen's delight *(Stillingia sylvatica)* a.k.a. queen's root, silver leaf, yaw root. Has laxative and diuretic properties.

Rampion *(Campanula rapunculus)* The leaves and roots of the young plants are eaten raw in salads.

Red maple *(Acer rubrum)* a.k.a. swamp maple. Extracts of the bark have been used as Native American remedies.

Red root *(Ceanothus americanus)* a.k.a. Jersey tea, New Jersey tea root. A tea made from the root-bark is used as a herbal remedy.

Restharrow *(Ononis spinosa)* a.k.a. cammock,

petty whin, stayplough. Used in herbal remedies, and long ago as a salad plant.

Rhatany *(Krameria triandra)* a.k.a. Peruvian rhatany. The roots are used in flavouring and as an internal and external herbal remedy for diarrhoea, haemorrhages, and fissures.

Rhubarb *(Rheum officinale)* a.k.a. Chinese rhubarb. A larger variety of ordinary garden rhubarb *(Rheum rhabarbarum)* whose roots are used in herbal remedies for their cathartic and astringent properties.

Rose *(Rosa* spp.) The leaves, petals, roots, and seed pods have all been used to make teas or herbal remedies.

Rosella *(Hibiscus sabdariffa)* a.k.a. flor de Jamaica, Guinea sorrel, Indian sorrel, Jamaica sorrel, roselle. A species of hibiscus whose sepals are used to make drinks and preserves.

Rosemary *(Rosmarinus officinalis)* a.k.a. old man. An evergreen shrub with spiky, needlelike leaves used as a seasoning and also as a herbal remedy.

Rue *(Ruta graveolens, montana, bracteosa,* and *calpensis)* a.k.a. garden rue, German rue, herb-of-grace, herb-of-repentance. The bitter leaves can be used fresh or dried as a seasoning; also used as a herbal remedy, but large quantities can induce internal bleeding or an allergic reaction.

Sage *(Salvia officinalis)* a.k.a. Dalmatia sage, garden sage, salvia. Greyish-green leaves are dried or used fresh as a seasoning. It is also used as a herbal remedy for snakebites, among other maladies.

Saint John's wort *(Hypericum perforatum; Hypericum calycinum)* a.k.a. (respectively) amber, goatweed, Johnswort, Klamath weed, Tipton weed, Aaron's beard, creeping Saint John's wort, gold flower, rose-of-Sharon. Used as a herbal remedy for injuries to nerves, or to body parts rich with nerves. Also used as an antidepressant.

Samphire *(Crithmum maritimum)* The leaves are pickled, or eaten fresh in salads, or cooked as a vegetable.

Santolina *(Santolina chamaecyparissus)* a.k.a. lavender cotton. A herbal remedy for stomach aches; the dried leaves and flowers can be used as moth repellent.

Sarsaparilla *(Smilax,* various species) The dried roots yield an extract with a bitter liquorice taste; they are also used as a herbal remedy because they contain parillin, a substance that lowers the heart rate, and also have astringent properties.

Sassafras *(Sassafras variifolium)* a.k.a. ague tree, cinnamon wood, saxifrax. The root bark provides sassafras oil, which is used as a flavouring; the dried root bark is used as a herbal remedy; the dried leaves are used to make the Creole seasoning filé.

Saw palmetto *(Serenoa repens)* The berries, fresh or dried, are used in herbal remedies.

Scotch broom *(Cytisus scoparius)* Used as a cathartic, diuretic, and emetic. Can be dangerous in large doses.

Senna *(Cassia acutifolia)* The pods of the cassia tree, used as a herbal remedy for their strong purgative effect.

Shallot *(Allium cepa,* var. *aggregatum)* A plant with a mild taste of garlic. Both the mature red bulb and the immature green stem are used.

Shepherd's-purse *(Capsella bursa-pastoris)* a.k.a. cocowort, mother's heart, pepper and salt, pick-pocket, Saint James's weed, shepherd's-bag, shepherd's-heart, shepherd's-pouch, toywort, witch's pouches. A member of the mustard family used in herbal remedies.

Shungiku *(Chrysanthemum coronarium)* a.k.a. cooking chrysanthemum, garland chrysanthemum. A species of *Chrysanthemum* grown in the Orient, where the young leaves are used fresh in salads or cooked as a seasoning.

Skullcap *(Scutellaria lateriflora)* a.k.a. maddogweed, madweed. This bitter herb is used as a remedy for nervous conditions and as an ingredient in commercial herbal teas.

Slippery elm *(Ulbus rubra)* a.k.a. moose elm, red elm. The dried inner bark is used in many herbal remedies.

Snakeroot *(Aristolochia serpentaria)* a.k.a. serpentaria, Virginia snakeroot. Used as a herbal remedy, but should be considered toxic because an alkaloid found in the roots can cause respiratory paralysis.

Soapbark *(Quillaja saponaria)* a.k.a. Panama bark, quillaia. A solution made from the powdered bark is used as an internal and external herbal remedy.

Soapwort *(Saponaria officinalis)* a.k.a. bouncing bet. The juice of the plant will form a lather when water is added and is used as a remedy for skin conditions. The root extracts have a laxative effect that can be dangerous in large quantities.

Sorrel *(Rumex spp.)* The various species of sorrel have sour tasting leaves and bitter roots. French sorrel is used in particular as a seasoning.

Southernwood *(Artemisia abrotanum)* a.k.a. lad's love, old man. A strong-smelling herb used in France as a moth and flea repellent.

Spicebush *(Lindera benzoin)* The twigs and bark can be used as a seasoning; the leaves, berries, and oil from the seeds are used in herbal remedies.

Stargrass *(Aletris farinosa)* Used as a herbal remedy but is dangerous in large doses and can cause vomiting and diarrhoea.

Stonecrop *(Sedum reflexum)* There are many varieties within the species, some of which are used as salad plants or as flavouring.

Strawberry leaves *(Fragaria spp.)* Used as an ingredient in herbal teas.

Sumac *(Rhus glabra)* a.k.a. dwarf sumac, mountain sumac, scarlet sumac, smooth sumac, vinegar tree. The bark, leaves, and fruit are used in Native Amer

ican herbal remedies. Should not be confused with other species of sumac that are very poisonous.

Summer savory *(Satureja hortensis)* a.k.a. bean herb, savory. The leaves are used fresh or dried as a seasoning. They have a strong, slightly peppery taste, similar to thyme. *See also* winter savory.

Sundew *(Drosera rotundifolia)* A carnivorous plant used as a herbal remedy.

Sweet cicely *(Myrrhis odorata)* a.k.a. anise chervil, European sweet chervil, European sweet cicely, Spanish chervil, sweet chervil. Fernlike leaves have a sugary taste; the seeds taste of anise or liquorice; the roots can be boiled and eaten in salads.

Sweet clover *(Melilotus officinalis)* a.k.a. garden balm, hay flowers, king's clover, lotus, melilot, melist, sweet trefoil, Swiss melilot, trefoil, yellow melilot, yellow sweet clover. The leaves, stems, and flowers have a sweet fragrance, especially when dried. Can be used in stews and marinades.

Sweet goldenrod *(Solidago odora)* a.k.a. Blue Mountain tea. The leaves have an aniselike odour, and are used to make Blue Mountain tea, a substitute for tea made from genuine tea leaves.

Sweet marigold *(Tagetes lucida)* a.k.a. anise-scented marigold, Mexican tarragon, winter tarragon. Smells like tarragon and has a strong anise flavour.

Sweet woodruff *(Galium odoratum)* a.k.a. mugwort, quinsywort, sweet grass, woodruff. A perennial herb used to infuse alcoholic beverages. Said to be a mild anaesthetic.

Tansy *(Tanacetum vulgare)* a.k.a. bitter buttons, golden-buttons, hindheal, parsley fern. The bitter leaves are chopped fresh and added sparingly as a seasoning. Can be poisonous if consumed in large doses.

Tarragon *(Artemisia dracunculus)* a.k.a. estragon, French tarragon, Russian tarragon. Has a flavour between anise and bay leaf. Used fresh or dried as a seasoning.

Thoroughwort *(Eupatorium perfoliatum)* a.k.a. boneset, Indian sage. Used in many medicinal remedies, particularly to reduce fever.

Thyme *(Thymus vulgaris)* a.k.a. common thyme, garden thyme. The leaves are used fresh or dried as a seasoning and as a herbal remedy for muscle cramps, nervous disorders, and headaches. There are over 300 varieties, including lemon thyme *(Thymus x citriodorus)* and caraway thyme *(Thymus herba-barona)*.

Toadflax *(Linaria vulgaris)* a.k.a. butter and eggs. Extracts have been used in herbal remedies, but it can cause liver and kidney damage if taken internally.

Tormentil *(Potentilla erecta)* Used as a herbal remedy for diarrhoea.

Trillium *(Trillium pendulum)* a.k.a. bethroot, lamb's quarter. Used as an internal and external herbal remedy for a variety of conditions.

Valerian *(Valeriana officinalis)* a.k.a. all-heal, cat's valerian, English valerian, garden heliotrope, garden valerian, German valerian, great wild valerian, Saint George's herb, setwall, Vandal root, Vermont valerian, wild valerian. A herbal remedy for nervousness and anxiety.

Veronica *(Veronica beccabunga)* a.k.a. beccabunga, European brooklime, mouth-smart, neckweed, speedwell, water pimpernel, water purslane. Used in various herbal remedies, also as a salad green.

Vervain *(Verbena officinalis)* a.k.a. enchanter's plant, European vervain, herb of the cross, Juno's tears, pigeon's grass, pigeonweed, simpler's joy. Used to make medicinal teas; thought to be a very effective love potion.

Vetiver *(Vetiveria zizanioides)* a.k.a. khas-khas, khus-khus. Use in the United States is restricted to alcoholic beverage flavourings.

Violet *(Viola odorata)* a.k.a. sweet violet. The flowers are edible and can be candied and used as decorations.

Viper's bugloss *(Echium vulgare)* a.k.a. blue-devil, blueweed. Similar to borage, although not as strong, and can be used in similar ways. The flowers are edible and can be used as decorations or to make a blue dye.

Watercress *(Nasturtium officinale)* The leaves and stems have a peppery flavour.

White birch *(Betula pendula)* a.k.a. birch, European birch, European white birch. Extracts of the leaves, bark, and sap of this tree are used in a variety of herbal remedies.

White deadnettle *(Lamium album)* a.k.a. dead nettle, dumb nettle, snowflake, stingless nettle, white archangel. Can be used in soups, eaten as a vegetable, or used as a herbal remedy.

White pine *(Pinus strobus)* Has been used as an ingredient in herbal cough remedies.

Wild indigo *(Baptisia tinctoria)* Used as a herbal remedy, usually externally. Dangerous in large doses.

Wild rosemary *(Ledum palustre)* a.k.a. crystal tea, marsh cistus, marsh tea, moth herb, narrow-leaved Labrador tea, swamp tea. Has a similar aroma to rosemary. A tea made from its dried leaves is used as a herbal remedy.

Wild sarsaparilla *(Aralia nudicaulis)* The root of the plant is used as a herbal remedy, and also as a liquorice-like flavouring.

Wild yam *(Dioscorea villosa)* a.k.a. China root, colic root, devil's bones, rheumatism root, yuma. Used as a herbal remedy for colic and PMS symptoms.

Wintergreen *(Gaultheria procumbens)* The oil from this creeping evergreen shrub is used as a seasoning; it also contains methyl salicylate, which is used medicinally in salves and liniments.

Winter savory *(Satureja montana)* Similar to summer savory, but a perennial, rather than an annual, and with an inferior flavour.

Witch hazel *(Hamamelis virginiana)* Extracts from the bark and leaves have astringent properties and are used for the treatment of numerous skin irritations.

Wormwood *(Artemisia absinthium)* a.k.a. absinthe. Used medicinally and to make apéritifs and herb wines.

Yarrow *(Achillea millefolium)* a.k.a. herb carpenter, iva, milfoil, musk yarrow, noble yarrow, nosebleed, sanguinary, soldier's woundwort, thousandleaf, thousand-seal. Used as a herbal remedy to stop bleeding because of its astringent properties.

Yellow jessamine *(Gelsemium sempervirens)* a.k.a. Carolina jasmine, Carolina jessamine, evening trumpet flower, gelsemin, gelsemine, wild jessamine, woodbine, yellow jasmine. Used in herbal remedies for flu, fatigue; however, if used incorrectly it is a poisonous plant that can cause respiratory failure.

Yerba buena *(Satureja douglasii)* A very strong wild mint closely related to savory.

Yerba santa *(Eriodictyon californicum)* a.k.a. bear's weed. Used as a flavouring and in herbal remedies.

POISONOUS PLANTS

Common name	Latin name
Aconite	*Aconitum* spp.
Angel's trumpet	*Datura* spp.
Autumn crocus	*Colchicum autumnale*
Azalea	*Rhododendron* spp.
Baneberry	*Actaea* spp.
Belladonna	*Atropa belladonna*
Bittersweet	*Celastrus scandens*
Black cherry	*Prunus serotina*
Black locust	*Robinia pseudoacacia*
Black nightshade	*Solanum nigrum*
Bleeding heart	*Dicentra* spp.
Bloodroot	*Sanquinaria canadensis*
Bouncing bet	*Saponaria officinalis*
Bracken fern	*Pteridium aquilinium*
Broad bean	*Vicia faba*
Buckwheat	*Fagoypyrum esculentum*
Buttercup	*Ranunculus* spp.
Caladium	*Caladium* spp.
Cardinal flower	*Lobelia* spp.
Castor bean	*Ricinus communis*
Celandine	*Chelidonium majus*
Christmas rose	*Helleborus niger*
Corn cockle	*Agrostemma githago*
Crowfoot	*Ranunculus* spp.
Daffodil	*Narcissus* spp.
Daphne	*Daphne* spp.
Deadly nightshade	*Atropa belladonna*
Death angel mushroom	*Amanita virosa/Amanita bisporigera*
Death camass	*Zigadenus* spp.
Delphinium	*Delphinium* spp.
Devil's trumpet	*Datura metel*
Dock	*Rumex* spp.
Dogbane	*Apocynum cannabinum*
Downy thornapple	*Datura metel*
Drooping leucothoe	*Leucothos fontanesiana*
Dumbcane	*Dieffenbachia* spp.
Dutchman's breeches	*Dicentra* spp.
Elderberry	*Sambucus canadensis*
Elephant ear	*Alocasia* spp.
Everlasting pea	*Lathyrus* spp.

Common name	Latin name	Common name	Latin name
False hellebore	*Veratrum viride*	Red sage	*Lantana camara*
Flax	*Linum usitatissimum*	Rhubarb	*Rheum rhaponticum*
Foxglove	*Digitalis purpurea*	Rosary pea	*Abrus precatorius*
Golden chain tree	*Laburnum anagyroides*	Senecio	*Senecio* spp.
Groundsel	*Senecio* spp.	Singletary pea	*Lathyrus* spp.
Henbane	*Hyoscyanmus niger*	Snow-on-the-mountain	*Euphorbia marginata*
Horse chestnut	*Aesculus hippocastanum*	Spurge	*Euphorbia maculata*
Horse nettle	*Solanum carlinense*	Squirrel corn	*Dicentra* spp.
Hyacinth	*Hyacinthus orientalis*	Star-of-Bethlehem	*Ornithogalum umbellatum*
Indian tobacco	*Lobelia* spp.	Stinging nettle	*Urtica dioica*
Iris	*Iris* spp.	Sweet pea	*Lathyrus* spp.
Jack-in-the-pulpit	*Arisaema* spp.	Tobacco	*Nicotiana* spp.
Jessamine	*Gelsemium sempervirens*	Tung oil tree	*Aleurites fordii*
Jimsonweed	*Datura stramonium*	Water hemlock	*Cicuta maculata*
Johnson grass	*Sorghumhalepense*	White snakeroot	*Eupatorium rugosum*
Lantana	*Lantana camara*	Wild cherry	*Prunus serotina*
Larkspur	*Delphinium* spp.	Wisteria	*Wisteria* spp.
Lily-of-the-valley	*Convallaria majalis*	Yew	*Taxus cuspidata*
Locoweed	*Astragalus* and *Oxytropis* spp.		
Lupine	*Lupinus* spp.		
Mandrake	*Podophyllum peltatum*		
Marijuana	*Cannabis sativa*		
Marsh marigold	*Caltha palustris*		
Mayapple	*Podophyllum peltatum*		
Milkweed	*Asclepias* spp.		
Mistletoe	*Phoradendron leucarpum*		
Monkshood	*Aconitum* spp.		
Morning glory	*Ipomoea tricolour*		
Mountain fetter-bush	*Pieris floribunda*		
Narcissus	*Narcissuss* spp.		
Nightshade	*Solanum americanum*		
Oak	*Quercus* spp.		
Oleander	*Nerium oleander*		
Opium poppy	*Papaver somniferum*		
Pin cherry	*Prunus pensylvanica*		
Philodendron	*Philodendron* spp.		
Poinsettia	*Euphorbia pulcherrima*		
Poison hemlock	*Conium maculatum*		
Poison ivy	*Toxicodendron radicans*		
Poison oak	*Toxicodendron pubescens*		
Poison sumac	*Toxicodendron vernix*		
Pokeweed	*Phytolacca americana*		
Poppies	*Papaver* spp.		
Potato	*Solanum tuberosum*		
Prickly poppy	*Argemone mexicana*		

SHRUBS

Common name	Latin name	Colours
Abelia	*Abelia*	pink, white, purple
Abutilon	*Abutilon*	white, pink, orange, yellow, red
Acacia, mimosa	*Acacia*	yellow
Andromeda	*Pieris*	red, pink, white
Azalea	*Rhododendron*	pink, red, purple, white, yellow
Barberry	*Berberis*	yellow
Bayberry	*Myrica*	white
Bearberry	*Arctostaphylos*	pink
Blue hibiscus	*Alyogyne*	lilac
Bog rosemary	*Andromeda*	pink
Bottle brush	*Callistemon*	red
Bougainvillea	*Bougainvillea*	pink, red
Bramble	*Rubus*	white, pink
Breath of heaven	*Coleonema*	white, pink
Broom	*Cytisus*	yellow
Broom	*Genista*	yellow
Burning bush	*Euonymous*	purple
Butterfly bush	*Buddleia*	purple, white, mauve, pink, blue
Californian lilac	*Ceanothus*	blue, pink
Camellia	*Camellia*	white, pink, red
Carissa	*Carissa*	white
Carpentaria	*Carpentaria*	white
Christmas box, Sweet box	*Sarcococca*	white
Clematis	*Clematis*	blue, mauve, purple, pink, red
Clerodendrum	*Clerodendrum*	pink, white, blue
Clethra	*Clethra*	white, pink
Convulvus	*Convulvus*	pink, white, blue
Cornel	*Cornus*	white, pink
Cotoneaster	*Cotoneaster*	white, pink
Cotton lavender	*Santolina*	yellow
Daphne	*Daphne*	pink, white, yellow
Escallonia	*Escallonia*	white, pink, red
Euonymus	*Euonymus*	white, purple
Fatsia	*Fatsia*	white
Fir	*Abies*	not flowering
Forsythia	*Forsythia*	yellow
Fothergilla	*Fothergilla*	white
Fuschia	*Fuschia*	red, pink, mauve, purple, white
Gardenia	*Gardenia*	white, yellow, pink
Gaultheria	*Gaultheria*	white, pink
Gorse	*Ulex*	yellow

Common name	Latin name	Colours
Grevillia	*Grevillea*	red, cream, yellow
Hazel, hazelnut	*Corylus*	yellow
Heather	*Erica*	white, pink, purple, red
Heather, Scotch heather	*Calluna*	white, purple, mauve, pink
Hemlock	*Tsuga*	not flowering
Holly	*Ilex*	white, red
Honeysuckle	*Lonicera*	pink, cream, yellow, red
Hydrangea	*Hydrangea*	blue, white, pink, purple
Japanese snowbell	*Styrax*	light green
Japonica	*Chaenomeles*	red, pink, white
Jasmine	*Jasminum*	yellow, white
Juneberry	*Amelanchier*	white
Juniper	*Juniperus*	not flowering
Kalmia	*Kalmia*	pink
Lavender	*Lavandula*	blue, purple
Leucothoe	*Leucothoe*	white
Lilac	*Syringa*	purple, white, lavender, pink
Magnolia	*Magnolia*	white, pink
Mexican orange	*Choisya*	white
Mock orange	*Philadelphus*	white, cream
Oleander	*Nerium*	white, pink, red, pale yellow
Ornamental cherry	*Punus*	pink, white
Osmanthus	*Osmanthus*	white
Periwinkle	*Vinca*	white, blue, purple
Pine	*Pinus*	not flowering
Powderpuff	*Calliandra*	red, pink
Privet	*Ligustrum*	white
Rhododendron	*Rhododendron*	red, purple, pink, white
Rock rose	*Cistus*	red, white, pink
Rose	*Rosa*	red, white, yellow, pink
Rose of Sharon, shrub althea	*Hibiscus*	white, pink, blue, red, purple
Rosemary	*Rosmarius*	violet blue
Saint John's wort	*Hypericum*	yellow
Sand myrtle	*Leiophyllum*	pink, white
Shrubby plumbago	*Ceratostigma*	blue
Smokebush	*Cotinus*	pink
Strawberry tree	*Arbutus*	white
Sumac	*Rhus*	greenish white
Sweet shrub	*Calycanthus*	red
Sweetspire	*Itea*	green-white
Tassel bush	*Garrya*	white
Tea tree	*Leptospermum*	white, pink, red
Veronica	*Hebe*	white, blue, mauve, purple, red
Viburnum	*Viburnum*	white, pink

Common name	Latin name	Colours
Virginia sweetspire	*Itea*	white
Weigela	*Weigela*	pink, red, white, yellow
White forsythia	*Abeliophyllum*	white
Wintersweet	*Chimonanthus*	yellow
Wisteria	*Wisteria*	purple, blue
Witch hazel	*Hamamelis*	yellow, orange
Yew	*Taxus*	not flowering
Zenobia	*Zenobia*	pulverulenta

TREES

Common name	Latin name	Varieties
Alder	*Alnus*	Black, European, Italian, White, Red
Arborvitae	*Thuja*	American
Ash	*Fraxinus*	Green, Red, White
Aspen	*Populus*	Bigtooth
Bay	*Laurus*	
Beech	*Fagus*	American, European, Weeping
Birch	*Betula*	Canoe, Cherry, Paper, Red, River, Silver, Sweet
Buckeye	*Aesculus*	Ohio, Yellow
Butternut	*Juglans*	*cinerea*
California laurel	*Umbellularia*	*californica*
Catalpa	*Catalpa*	Common, Hardy
Cedar	*Cedrus*	Deodar
Cherry	*Prunus*	Bird, Black, Choke, Sargent, Weeping, Yoshino
Chestnut	*Castanea*	
Chinaberry	*Melia*	*azedarach*
Common pawpaw	*Asimina*	*triloba*
Cottonwood	*Populus*	
Crab apple	*Malus*	*baccata, lemoinei,* Japanese, Profusion
Crapemyrtle	*Lagerstroemia*	*indica*
Cypress	*Taxodium*	Bald
Dogwood	*Cornus*	Flowering, Red Flowering
Elm	*Ulmus*	Chinese, English, American, Slippery
False acacia	*Robinia*	*pseudacacia*
Fir	*Abies*	Balsam, White, Nikko, Korean
Giant sequoia	*Sequoiadendron*	*giganteum*
Ginkgo	*Ginkgo*	*biloba*

Common name	Latin name	Varieties
Golden rain	*Laburnum*	Common, Scotch
Gum	*Eucalyptus*	Red flowering
Hackberry	*Celtis*	Common
Halesia	*Halesia*	Silver bell tree
Hawthorn	*Crataegus*	*crusgalli*
Hazel	*Corylus*	*aurea*, Corkscrew, *purpurea*
Hemlock	*Tsuga*	Canada, Western
Hickory	*Carya*	Shagbark, Shellbark, Bitternut
Holly	*Ilex*	American
Honey locust	*Gleditsia*	*triacanthos*
Hornbeam	*Carpinus*	Common
Horse chestnut	*Aesculus*	Red, Ohio Buckeye
Indian bean	*Catalpa*	Indian bean, aurea
Jacaranda	*Jacaranda*	*mimosifolia*
Judas	*Cercis*	Judas, White Judas, Redbud
Juniper	*Juniperus*	Rocky Mountain Juniper, Red Cedar, Western Red Cedar
Larch	*Larix*	European, Golden, Alpine, Black, Western
Lawson cypress	*Chamaecyparis*	*lawsonia*
Lime, Linden	*Tilia*	Common, American, Little Leaf, Large Leaved
Locust	*Robinia*	Clammy, Bristly, Black
Magnolia	*Magnolia*	*virginiana, grandiflora, acuminata*
Mango	*Mangifera indica*	Mango
Maple	*Acer*	Norway, Red, Paperback, Sycamore, Sugar
Mountain ash	*Sorbus*	European, Heath, Rowan, Joseph Rock
Mulberry	*Morus*	White
Oak	*Quercus*	Red, Willow, Shingle, Valley, Pin, Live
Olive	*Olea*	*europaea*
Palm	*Palmae*	Coconut, Royal, Cabbage, Sugar, Date, Cohune
Paulownia	*Paulownia*	*tomentosa*
Peach	*Prunus*	*persica*
Pear	*Pyrus*	Bradford, Common
Persimmon	*Diospyros*	*virginiana*
Pine	*Pinus*	Austrian, Loblolly, Monterey, Norway, Red, Scotch, Sugar, Long-leaf, White, Lacebark, Japanese Red, Limber
Plane, Sycamore	*Platanus*	
Plum	*Prunus*	
Poplar	*Populus*	Balsam, Carolina, Grey, White
Redwood	*Sequoia*	California
Sassafras	*Sassafras*	*albidum*
Serviceberry	*Amelanchier*	*laevis*
Sourwood	*Oxydendrum*	*arboreum*
Spruce	*Picea*	Colorado, Norway, White
Sweet gum	*Liquidambar*	*styraciflua*
Tree of Heaven	*Ailanthus*	*altissima*

Common name	Latin name	Varieties
Tulip	*Liriodendron*	*tulipfera*
Tupelo	*Nyssa*	*sylvatica*
Walnut	*Juglans*	Black, California
Willow	*Salix*	Golden, Weeping, Black
Yellow wood	*Cladrastis*	American
Yew	*Taxus baccata*	Common, Irish
Zelkova	*Zelkova*	Japanese

WILDFLOWERS

Common name	Latin name	Colours
Alaska goldthread	*Coptis trifolia*	white
Anemone	*Anemone* spp.	white
Aster	*Aster* spp.	white, purple
Baby blue-eyes	*Nemophila menziesi*	blue
Baneberry	*Actaea* spp.	white
Bee balm	*Mondara didyma*	red
Bellflower	*Campanula* spp.	white, blue, purple
Bellwort	*Uvularia perfoliata*	pale yellow
Black-eyed Susan	*Rudbeckia hirta*	yellow
Bloodroot	*Sanguinaria canadensis*	white
Blue beadlily	*Clintonia borealis*	yellow-green
Blue cohosh	*Caulophyllum thalictroides*	green, yellow
Blue-eyed crass	*Sisyrinchium angustifolium*	blue
Bluet	*Houstonia caerulea*	white
Boneset	*Eupatorium per-foliatum*	white
Bowman's root	*Gillenia trifoliata*	white, pink
Bunchberry	*Cornus canadensis*	greenish white
Camass	*Camassia* spp.	white, blue, cream
Cardinal flower	*Lobelia Cardinalis*	red
Checkerberry	*Gaultheria procumbens*	white
Closed gentian	*Gentiana andrewsii*	violet blue

Common name	Latin name	Colours
Columbine	*Aquilegia* spp.	yellow, blue, red
Coreopsis	*Coreopsis* spp.	pink, yellow, white
Cow parsnip	*Heracleum lanatum*	white
Crested iris	*Iris cristata*	violet
Dragonroot	*Arisaema dracontium*	white-green
Dutchman's breeches	*Dicentra cucullaria*	white, yellow
Early saxifrage	*Saxifraga virginiensis*	white
Evening primrose	*Oenothera* spp.	yellow
Fairy bells	*Disporum* spp.	green-white
Fawn lily	*Eruthronium* spp.	white, yellow, violet, pink
Fringed gentian	*Gentiana cinita*	blue
Gay-feather	*Liatris* spp.	purple
Ginseng	*Panax quinquefolius*	green-white
Goat's beard	*Aruncus dioicus*	yellow-white
Goldenrod	*Solidago* spp.	yellow
Goldenseal	*Hydrastis canadensis*	greenish-white
Goldfields	*Baeria chrysostoma hirsutula*	yellow
Great lobelia	*Lobelia syphilitica*	blue
Green dragon	*Arisaema dracontium*	white-green
Hepatacia	*Hepatacia* spp.	white, purple
Herb Robert	*Geranium Robertianum*	magenta
Indian cucumber root	*Medeola virginica*	greenish-yellow
Indian paint brush	*Castilleja* spp.	red, yellow-green, white
Indian turnip	*Arisaema tripyllum*	purple-brown and green
Jack-in-the-pulpit	*Arisaema tripyllum*	purple-brown and green
Joe Pye weed	*Eupatorium purpureum*	pink, red
Lady's slipper	*Cypripedium* spp.	pink, yellow, purple, brown
Larkspur	*Delphinium* spp.	blue, red, white, yellow
Lily	*Lilium* spp.	yellow, orange, red, white, purple
Mandrake	*Podophyllum peltatum*	white
Marsh marigold	*Caltha palustris*	yellow
May apple	*Podophyllum peltatum*	white
Mayflower	*Epigaea repens*	white, pink
Meadow rue	*Thalictrum* spp.	green, white, purple
Meadow-beauty	*Rhexia virginica*	pink
Milkweed	*Asclepias* spp.	pink, white
Monkey flower	*Mimulus* spp.	orange, buff, salmon, purple
Moth mullein	*Verbascum blattaria*	yellow, white
Oswego tea	*Mondara didyma*	red
Painted cup	*Castilleja* spp.	red, yellow-green, white
Penstemon	*Penstemon* spp.	red, yellow, white, blue, pink
Phlox	*Phlox* spp.	purple, lilac, violet, pink
Pitcher plant	*Sarracenia* spp.	red, yellow
Prickly pear	*Opuntia* spp.	yellow
Prickly poppy	*Argemone* spp.	white, yellow

Common name	Latin name	Colours
Purple coneflower	*Echinacea purpurea*	magenta
Rattlesnake plantain	*Goodyera* spp.	white, cream, green
Rose mallow	*Hibiscus palustris*	pink, white
Roundleaf sundew	*Drosera rotundifolia*	white
Rue anemone	*Anemonella thalictroides*	white
Sand verbena	*Abronia umbellata*	pink
Shooting star	*Dodecatheon* spp.	pink, purple, red, white
Sneezeweed	*Helenium* spp.	yellow
Solomon's seal	*Polygonatum* spp.	pale green
Speckled beadlily	*Clintonia umbellulata*	white
Spiderwort	*Tradescantia virginiana*	purple-blue
Squirrel corn	*Dicentra canadensis*	white, pink
Star grass	*Aeletris farinosa*	white
Star grass	*Hypoxis hirsuta*	yellow
Sundrop	*Oenothera fruticosa*	yellow
Sunshine	*Baeria chrysostoma hirsutula*	yellow
Thin-leaved sunflower	*Helianthus decapetalus*	yellow
Thoroughwort	*Eupatorium perfoliatum*	white
Trailing arbutus	*Epigaea repens*	white, pink
Trillium	*Trillium* spp.	maroon, white, green
Turkeybeard	*Xerophyllum* spp.	white
Turtlehead	*Chelone* spp.	pink, white
Twinleaf	*Jeffersonia diphylla*	green, yellow
Twisted stalk	*Streptopus roseus*	pink-purple
Violet	*Viola* spp.	purple, white, blue
Virginia spring beauty	*Claytonia Virginica*	pink, white
Virginia strawberry	*Fragaria virginiana*	white
Water lily	*Nympaea odorata*	white, pale pink
Wild bergamot	*Mondara fistulosa*	purple
Wild ginger	*Asarum* spp.	brown-purple
Wild indigo	*Baptisia tinctoria*	yellow
Wood betony	*Pedicularis canadensis*	yellow
Wood-sorrel	*Oxalis* spp.	white, pink, yellow
Yellow clintonia	*Clintonia borealis*	yellow-green
Yellow false indigo	*Baptisia tinctoria*	yellow

MINERAL

COLOURS

Abalone
Abbey brown
Absinthe
Acorn
Admiral
Adobe
Aegean
African violet
Agapanthus
Airy
Alabaster
Aladdin green
Alaskan blue
Allspice
Alluring blue
Almond
Almost aqua
Alpine
Alps blue
Aluminium
Amaranth
Amber
Amethyst frost
Amethystine
Anchovy
Anemones
Angelica
Angora
Antiquarian grey
Antique ivory
Antique linen
Antler
Apple blossom
Apple cider
Applesauce
Apricot
Apricot pink

April glow
Aqua mint
Aquamarine
Aquarium
Arabian night
Arboles
Arbor
Arctic
Arizona white
Armour grey
Army green
Arrowroot
Artichoke
Ash
Ashes of roses
Asparagus
Astral
Atlantic
Atmosphere
Atomic tangerine
Aubergine
Auburn
Audubon buff
Autumn bronze
Avocado
Azalea
Aztec rouge
Aztec yellow
Azure
Baby's breath
Bachelor button
Bahama
Baked clay
Bamboo
Banana
Banker's grey
Barely
Barnacle
Battleship
Bayberry
Beanstalk

Beech
Beeswax
Begonia
Belgian grey
Bering sea
Bermuda
Berries
Beryl
Bibb lettuce
Bing cherry
Birch bark
Bishop brown
Black
Black walnut
Blackberry cream
Blazing sun
Bleached oak
Bleached wood
Blizzard blue
Blond wisp
Blue
Blue chip
Blue diamond
Blue dolphin
Blue grass
Blue green
Blue jeans
Blue slate
Blue violet
Blueberry
Bohemian green
Bone china
Boston cream
Boulder
Bourbon
Boysenberry cream
Bramble tan
Brandy Alexander
Brick red
Brie
Bright sun
British blue
Broccoli
Bronze
Brook
Brown
Brown bread
Brown ochre

Brown sugar
Brussels sprouts
Buckwheat
Buff
Burgundy
Burnished brass
Burnt green earth
Burnt orange
Burnt sienna
Burnt umber
Burnt yellow ochre
Butter cream
Buttermilk
Cabernet
Cactus
Cactus flower
Cadet blue
Café au lait
Calico
California poppy
Cambridge
Cameo
Camouflage
Canal blue
Canary
Candy apple
Cantaloupe
Canton jade
Canvas
Canyon coral
Cape Cod blue
Capitol blue
Caramel corn
Carbon
Caribou
Carmine
Carnation pink
Carrot
Cashew
Cassel earth
Cattails
Cauliflower
Cayenne
Cedar beige
Celadon
Celery green
Celery seed
Celestial blue

Cement
Ceramic green
Cerise
Cerulean
Cerulean blue
Ceylon ivory
Chablis
Chalk
Chamois
Champagne
Chapel grey
Charcoal
Chardonnay
Chartreuse
Chateau rose
Cherry
Cherry red
Chestnut
Chilli pepper
Chimney sweep
Chinese gold
Chinese white
Chive
Chocolate mousse
Chopstick
Christmas green
Chrome green
Chutney
Chrysanthemum
Cider
Cinnabar green
Cinnabar red
Cinnamon
Citron
Clam shell
Clay pot
Clear lemon
Cloud pink
Clover
Cobalt blue
Cobalt violet
Cobblestone
Coffee bean
Cognac
Cold grey
Colonial white
Colony green
Confederate

Copper
Coral reef
Cordovan
Cork
Cornflower
Cornsilk
Cottage white
Cotton
Cracked wheat
Cracker Jack
Cranberry ice
Cream puff
Creamy apricot
Creme de menthe
Cremnitz white
Crocodile
Crystal
Cucumber slice
Cumulus
Currant
Currency
Custard
Cyan
Cypress
Daiquiri
Daisy
Dandelion
Dapple grey
Dark blue
Dark brown
Dark green
Deep lagoon
Deep river
Deepblack
Delft blue
Della Robbia blue
Denim
Derby brown
Desert beige
Desert bloom
Dolphin
Dried moss
Driftwood
Duckling
Dune
Dust storm
Dusty rose
Earthenware

Egg nog
Egret
Electric blue
Electric lime
Ember glow
Emerald green
Emerald sea
Endive
English red
English saddle
Espresso
Eucalyptus
Faded rose
Fireglow
Flesh colour
Flesh ochre
Foam
Foam green
Foggy day
Forest
Forest green
Forsythia
French blue
Friar's brown
Fuchsia
Gentle lavender
Georgia peach
Geranium
Ginger ale
Ginger snap
Gold
Gold ochre
Gold yellow
Goldenrod
Granny Smith apple
Grape jelly
Grape mist
Grapeade
Grapefruit
Graphite
Grassy knoll
Grey
Grey flannel
Grey hint
Grey kitten
Green
Green shoot
Green umber

Green yellow
Grenadine
Guacamole
Gunmetal
Hazelnut
Hearts of palm
Heather tint
Heliotrope
Hemp
Henna
Hepatica
Highland grey
Honey
Honeycomb
Hooker's green
Hot chocolate
Hot magenta
Hyacinth
Hydrangea
Ice
Iced apricot
Igloo
Imperial white
India ink
India spice
Indian red
Indian yellow
Indigo
International green
Iris
Iron gate
Iron oxide black
Ivory
Ivory black
Jack o' lantern
Jade
Jalapeño
Jungle green
Juniper
Just blush
Jute
Kashmir petal
Kelp
Khaki
King's blue
Koala bear
Kumquat
Lacy Fern

Lamp black
Lapis
Laser lemon
Lava
Lavender
Leaf green
Leaves
Lemon drop
Lemon ice
Lemon peel
Lemon yellow
Leprechaun
Lichen
Light birch bark
Light blue
Light brown
Light green
Lilac
Lilac spray
Lily of the valley
Lily pad
Lime sherbet
Lime soda
Limeade
Linden green
Log cabin
London sky
Macaroni and cheese
Magenta
Magic mint
Magnolia
Mahogany
Maize
Malachite
Marble white
Margarita
Marigold
Marina
Marmalade
Maroon
Marshmallow
Mauve
Mauvelous
May green
Mayan brick
Mayonnaise
Melon
Middy blue

Midnight blue
Military blue
Mimosa
Mincemeat
Ming vase
Mint
Monaco blue
Monterey pine
Moss
Mountain fog
Mountain lake
Mousegrey
Mud pie
Mulberry
Mushroom
Mushroom white
Mustard seed
Naples yellow
Navajo white
Navy
Navy blue
Nectarine
Neon carrot
Normandy rose
Northern blue
Nouveau pink
Nude
Nutmeg
Oatmeal
Ocean
Okra
Old lace
Old rose
Olive
Olive green
Olympic gold
Opaque white
Orange
Orange chiffon
Orangeade
Orchid
Orchid bouquet
Oriental ivory
Original cinnamon
Otter
Outrageous orange
Overcast
Oyster white

Pacific blue
Pale mint
Paris blue
Pastelrose
Paté
Payne's grey
Pea pod
Peach
Peach blossom
Peacock
Peanut butter
Pearl grey
Pearl pink
Pearl white
Pebble pink
Pecan
Peppermint
Perfect peach
Periwinkle
Permanent green
Persian blue
Persimmon
Petal pink
Pewter
Phantom grey
Pilgrim blue
Piña colada
Pine cone
Pine green
Pine needle
Pineapple
Pink
Pink arbutus
Pink dogwood
Pink hibiscus
Pioneer red
Pistachio
Plum
Plum wine
Plymouth red
Polar bear
Polynesian sun
Pond
Popcorn
Poppy
Potato skin
Pozzuola earth
Pralines 'n' cream

Primary blue
Primary red
Primary yellow
Prussian blue
Puce
Pueblo
Pumpernickel
Pumpkin patch
Purple aster
Purple mountain's majesty
Purple pizzazz
Putting green
Putty
Radical red
Raffia
Raspberry
Raw sienna
Raw umber
Razzle dazzle rose
Razzmatazz
Red
Red clay
Red earth
Red orange
Red river
Red violet
Reflex white
Regatta blue
Regency blue
Rich butterscotch
Ripple green
Rising sun
Riviera sand
Roasted chestnut
Robin's egg blue
Rocky road
Roman ochre
Root beer
Rose quartz
Rosewood
Royal blue
Royal purple
Ruby
Rust
Safari
Saffron
Sagebrush
Sahara

Sailcloth
Salad green
Salmon
Salmon pink
Salsa
Sand dollar
Sand dune
Sand tan
Sandalwood
Sangria
Sap green
Sapphire
Screamin' green
Sea green
Sepia
Scotch tan
Sea coral
Sea foam
Sealskin
Sentry grey
Shale
Shamrock
Sheer peach
Shell
Shell white
Sherry
Shocking pink
Shrimp
Shutter green
Signal red
Silver
Silver cloud
Silver fox
Silver wing
Silvergate
Sky blue
Slate
Slate green
Smoke signal
Smoked salmon
Smokestone
Snow lilac
Snow shadow
Snowy peach
Soft white
Sorrel
Southern mint
Spanish olive

Spanish tile
Sparkling grape
Spearmint
Spice tan
Spiced peach
Spinach
Split pea
Sponge cake
Spring leaf
Spring green
Squash
St. Louis blue
Stone
Strawberry
Stucco
Sugar cookie
Sugar plum
Sugar 'n' spice
Sumatra green
Sunflower
Sunglow
Sunlight
Sunset
Suntan
Sutter's gold
Swan grey
Sweet basil
Sweet butter
Sweet pea
Swiftsure blue
Swiss mocha
Tabasco
Tampico sand
Tan
Tangelo
Tangerine
Tapestry rose
Tarragon
Taupe tone
Tea biscuit
Teakwood
Teal blue
Terra cotta
Thistle
Tickle me pink
Tile red
Timber wolf
Tin

Titanium white
Titian
Toasted almond
Toffee crunch
Tomato bisque
Topaz
Touch of spring
Traditional green
Train smoke
Tree bark
Tropical rain forest
Tropical sun
Tumbleweed
Turquoise
Turquoise blue
Turquoise green
Turtledove
Twig
Ultramarine
Ultramarine violet
Unmellow yellow
Van Dyck brown
Vanilla cream
Verdant
Verde
Verona green
Vibrant green
Villa tan
Vine black
Violet (purple)
Violet red
Viridian
Vivid tangerine
Vivid yellow
Warm white
Watercress
Waterfall
Wedgwood green
Whale
Wheat fields
White
White sand
White shadow
White shoulders
White white
Wicker
Wild strawberry
Wild watermelon

Wildflower
Willow
Windsor tan
Wintergreen
Wisteria
Yellow
Yellow bird
Yellow green
Yellow ochre
Yellow orange
Zinc green
Zinc white
Zinnia

ELEMENTS

Ac Actinium
Ag Silver
Al Aluminium
Am Americium
Ar Argon
As Arsenic
At Astatine
Au Gold
B Boron
Ba Barium
Be Beryllium
Bi Bismuth
Bk Berkelium
Br Bromine
C Carbon
Ca Calcium
Cd Cadmium
Ce Cerium
Cf Californium
Cl Chlorine
Cm Curium
Co Cobalt
Cr Chromium
Cs Cesium
Cu Copper

Dy Dysprosium
Er Erbium
Es Einsteinium
Eu Europium
F Fluorine
Fe Iron
Fm Fermium
Fr Francium
Ga Gallium
Gd Gadolinium
Ge Germanium
H Hydrogen
He Helium
Hf Hafnium
Hg Mercury
Ho Holmium
I Iodine
In Indium
Ir Iridium
K Potassium
Kr Krypton
La Lanthanum
Li Lithium
Lu Lutetium
Lw Lawrencium
Md Mendelevium
Mg Magnesium
Mn Manganese
Mo Molybdenum
N Nitrogen
Na Sodium
Nb Nobelium
Nd Neodymium
Ne Neon
Ni Nickel
Np Neptunium
O Oxygen
Os Osmium
P Phosphorus
Pa Protactinium
Pb Lead
Pd Palladium
Pm Prometheum
Po Polonium
Pr Praseodymium
Pt Platinum
Pu Plutonium
Ra Radium

Rb Rubidium
Re Rhenium
Rh Rhodium
Rn Radon
Ru Ruthenium
S Sulphur
Sb Antimony
Sc Scandium
Se Selenium
Si Silicon
Sm Samarium
Sn Tin
Sr Strontium
Ta Tantulum
Tb Terbium
Tc Technetium
Te Tellurium
Th Thorium
Ti Titanium
Tl Thalium
Tm Thulium
U Uranium
V Vanadium
W Tungsten
X Xenon
Y Yttrium
Yb Ytterbium
Zn Zinc
Zr Zirconium

GEMS

A list of naturally occurring stones that are considered precious or semiprecious because of their appearance, rarity, and hardness.

Amber
Benitotite
Beryl aquamarine, emerald, morganite
Chrysoberyl
Corundum ruby and sapphire
Diamond

Garnet garnet, demantoid, rhodolite, spessarite
Jade jadeite and nephrite
Jet
Opal
Spinel
Spodumene
Topaz
Tourmaline schorl, dravite, uvite, elbaite
Turquoise
Zircon

SILICATE MINERALS

Nesosilicates kyanite

Sorosilicates epidote

Cyclosilicates tourmaline

Inosilicates diopside

Phyllosilicates muscovite

Tectosilicates orthoclase

MINERAL CLASSIFICATION

NONSILICATE MINERALS

Native elements gold, silver, copper, platinum, iron, sulphur, graphite, diamond

Sulphides and sulpharsenides pyrrhotite, cinnabar, pyrite, molybdenite, galena

Sulphosalts pyragyrite, tetrahedrite, enargite

Oxides cuprite, corundum, hematite

Hydroxides goethite, romanechite, diaspore, manganite

Halides halite, fluorite, galena, sylvite

Carbonates calcite, dolomite

Nitrates nitratite

Borates borate, colemanite

Sulphates barite, gypsum, anhydrite

Phosphates, arsenates, vanadates apatite, turquoise, brazilinite, apatite

SUBATOMIC PARTICLES

A list of the smallest units of matter, often referred to as elementary particles because it was once believed they could not be divided. For each Lepton and Quark there is a corresponding antimatter with an equal mass and opposite charge.

Leptons
    electron
    electron neutrino
    muon
    muon neutrino
    tau
    tau neutrino

Quarks
Hadrons
    baryon
    proton
    neutron
    meson
    pion

MANMADE

ACTIVE RELIGIONS

Amish A strict Mennonite branch of Swiss Anabaptists that is found mostly in the northern United States.

Anabaptist The term *Anabaptist* applies to a broad group of religious sects who believe in adult baptism.

Anglican Anglicanism grows from the Church of England, believing that the final source of doctrine necessary for salvation is the Bible.

Armenian A church based in Armenia that accepts the dogmas of the first three ecumenical councils.

Baptist Baptists believe in the authority of the Bible, the right of private interpretation, and the baptism of adults only.

Brethren Nicknamed "Dunkers" because of their belief of adult immersion during baptism.

Buddhism This religious system, founded in India in the 5th century BCE, teaches the existence of suffering and the way of release from suffering.

Christian Science Founded by Mary Baker Eddy, Christian Scientists believe that healing, physical and otherwise, is divinely natural.

Church of Jesus Christ of Latter-day Saints, The The Mormons, as they are often called, were founded by Joseph Smith in 1830 and claim continuous divine revelation through their priesthood.

Confucianism This system of political, societal, and religious thought is based on the teachings of Confucius and his successors.

Conservative Judaism The largest branch of the main grouping of Judaism in the U.S. Conservative Judaism believes that Judaism must remain true to tradition.

Coptic This native Monophysite church of Egypt is a Christian religion whose head resides in Cairo.

Episcopal Episcopalians believe that all doctrine and church practice must answer to the three criteria of a trilateral authoritative structure—Scripture, tradition, and reason.

Ethiopic This indigenous church in Ethiopia is a Christian faith following the Coptic Church with some Jewish influences.

Falacha Judaism An Ethiopian sect that bases its beliefs on the Bible and some apocryphal writings.

Friends, Society of a.k.a. the Quakers, who believe that the divine light of Christ is in all people.

Greek Orthodox Similar to the Eastern Orthodox Church, the Greek Orthodox is the state church of Greece.

Hinduism Hinduism encompasses a variety of beliefs and practices that make up the major religious traditions of the Indian subcontinent.

Islam A monotheistic religion that follows the word of God through the prophet Muhammad.

Jacobite The Monophysite church of Syria is in agreement with the Coptic Church regarding faith and sacraments.

Jainism Found among Hindus, Jainism is a system of radical asceticism.

Jehovah's Witnesses This denomination stresses biblical literalism and aggressive evangelism.

Judaism The legal and ethical norms, rituals, and beliefs that comprise the religion of the Jewish people.

Kimbanguism The Church of Jesus Christ on Earth by the Prophet Simon Kimbangu is a fast-growing church founded in Africa in the 1920s by Kimbangu.

Lutheran Lutheranism is based upon the writings of Martin Luther, with an emphasis on scriptural authority.

Maronite This community of Syrians living primarily in Lebanon entered into a union with the Catholic Church in Rome in the 12th century.

Mennonite Menno Simons started this church in Holland in the 16th century. It now includes several Protestant bodies.

Methodist A Methodist is a member of any of the religious bodies that have grown out of the evangelical movement begun by John Wesley in the 18th century.

Moravian This Protestant denomination places an emphasis on ecumenical vision and traces its origin to John Hus.

Omoto This religious movement began in late 19th-century Japan, based on oracles received through Deguchi Nao.

Orthodox Judaism This contemporary interpretation of Judaism believes Jewish Law to be central in Jewish life and that the people of Israel exist to keep and serve the Torah, and not vice versa.

Pentecostal The Pentecostal movement began under the leadership of C. F. Parham in Topeka, Kansas.

Presbyterian This church is governed by elders, including ministers, who are equal in rank.

Protestant This form of Christianity does not accept the authority of the pope.

Reform Judaism Reform Judaism differs from the other branches of Judaism in that it stresses an internally pluralistic approach to theology and practice.

Roman Catholic Roman Catholics acknowledge Rome as the head of the universal church, and the pope as the Supreme Pontiff.

Russian Orthodox This Christian church accepts its head to be in Russia, not Rome.

Seventh-Day Adventist Believing the end of the world is near, this Christian church follows the writings of Ellen White, and accepts the Bible as its source of authority.

Shaker This small community believes in separation from the world and its temptations because sex is the source of most sin.

Shintoism Literally meaning "way of the gods," Shintoism has evolved from an ancient Japanese religion.

Sikhism This hybrid of Islamic and Hindu beliefs advocates the search for the eternal truths.

Taoism Taoism is a following of "the way" (Tao), and emphasis is placed upon striving for immortality.

Unification Founded by the Reverend Sun-Myung Moon, this church believes that sex was the original sin, as well as other revelations Moon is believed to have had.

United Church of Christ This is a combination of Congregational Christian churches with Evangelical and Reformed.

Vaisnavism Vaisnavism is a religious sect in India that has one of Vishnu's incarnations as its deity.

Zoroastrian This ancient Persian religion is based upon the dual principles of Ormuzd, the god of light and good, and Ahriman, the god of darkness and evil.

FAMOUS BATTLES

Actium (31 BC) Naval battle in the Roman civil war in which Octavian defeated Mark Antony and Cleopatra to become the ruler of the Roman world.

Aegospotami (405 BC) The final battle of the Peloponnesian War: a naval victory for Sparta over Athens.

Agincourt (1415) The English army, under Henry V, defeated the French in this battle during the Hundred Years' War.

Antietam (17 Sept 1862) The bloodiest battle of the American Civil War.

Arnhem (17–26 Sept 1944) Airborne operation by the Allies, in WWII, to secure a bridgehead over the Rhine which ended in retreat by the Allies.

Austerlitz (2 Dec 1805) One of Napoleon's greatest victories, over a combined Austrian/Russian force, which resulted in the collapse of the coalition against France.

Boyne (1 July 1690) The final battle of the War of English Succession in which William III defeated the exiled James II, thereby confirming a Protestant monarch.

Britain (10 July–31 Oct 1940) The battle between German and British air forces over Britain which Hitler intended as a preliminary to his invasion of Britain but which he abandoned on 10 Oct in favour of his invasion of Russia.

Bulge (or the Ardennes offensive) In WWII, Hitler's thwarted attempt to break through the US line in the Ardennes. The German offensive began on 16 Dec 1944 and was stopped by the Allies by 16 Jan 1945.

Cambrai Two battles between British and German forces in WWI. On 20–27 Nov 1917, the first battle in which tanks were used in large numbers, the British made gains which were resisted by a German counterattack, so that by 27 Nov the British were back to where they had started. The British regained Cambrai in the second battle 26 Aug–5 Oct 1918.

Clontarf (23 April 1014) The Irish, led by Brian Boru, defeated a Norse invasion in this Good Friday battle.

Culloden (16 April 1746) Final defeat of the Jacobite rebels, under Prince Charles Edward, the "Young Pretender", by the English at Culloden Moor about 7 miles east of Inverness.

D-Day (6 June 1944) The greatest amphibious assault in history when over 4,500 English and American ships crossed the English Channel.

Dien Bien Phu The fall of Dien Bien Phu (1 May 1954), the French chosen location of the final attacks in the Indochina War, resulted in the end of French control of Indochina.

First of June (1794) The first great naval engagement of the French Revolutionary Wars, fought between the French and the British in the Atlantic Ocean about 430 miles west of the Breton island of Ouessant.

Gettysburg (1–3 July 1863) One of the decisive battles of the American Civil War in which the Confederates, under General Robert E. Lee, were forced to retreat by Union forces.

Goose Green (28 May 1982) British victory over Argentine forces in the Falklands War.

Guadalcanal (Aug 1942–Feb 1943) In WWII, the first large-scale Allied victory over the Japanese.

Gujarat (21 Feb 1849) The massacre of 50,000 Sikhs under Shir Singh by the British in the Second Sikh War which annihilated the Sikh army.

Hastings (14 Oct 1066) Ended in the defeat of Harold II of England by William, duke of Normandy (the Conqueror) and established Norman rule over England.

Hattin (4 July 1187) This battle took place in northern Palestine and marked the defeat and annihilation of the Christian Crusader armies of Guy de Lusignan, king of Jerusalem, by Muslim forces of Saladin.

Issus (333 BC) Victory of Alexander the Great and the Macedonians over the Persians.

Kulikovo (1380) Military engagement in which the Russians defeated the forces of the Golden Horde, the Mongols.

Kursk (July 1943) Greatest tank battle in history in which the Russians defeated the Germans, to create the turning point in the Eastern Front campaign of WWII.

Lepanto (7 Oct 1571) The last major naval engagement to be fought by galleys, this battle, fought in the Adriatic, resulted in a victory for the Holy League over the Turks.

Lexington (19 April 1775) The first battle in the American War of Independence.

Little Bighorn (25 June 1876) General George Custer divided his forces against Crazy Horse and he and his entire column were killed.

Marengo (14 June 1800) One of Napoleon Bonaparte's greatest victories, his defeat of the Austrians at Marengo, a village in northern Italy, led to the Austrians ceding northern Italy to France.

Marne Two unsuccessful German offensives in northern France during WWI. In the second battle (15 July–4 Aug 1918) British, US and French troops, under French general Henri Pétain, defeated the German offensive.

Midway (June 1942) Decisive naval victory of Japan by the US in WWII over this island which lies northwest of the Hawaiian islands.

Passchendaele (July–Nov 1917) In WWI, at Ypres, a long and bitter battle between the Germans and the Allied forces, which achieved only a tiny advance and was of no strategic significance and in which the Allied forces alone suffered 300,000 casualties.

Rorke's Drift (22 Jan 1879) Resulted in a British victory during the Zulu War, at a farm about 105 miles north of Durban.

Shiloh (6–7 April 1862) A Confederate defeat during the American Civil War, at Shiloh Church, Tennessee.

Somme (July–Nov 1916) A major Allied offensive of WWI, at Beaumont-Hamel-Chaulnes, on the river Somme in northern France, which resulted in severe losses on both sides.

Stalingrad In WWII, the siege of Stalingrad lasted from Aug 1942–Jan 1943 when the German 6th Army surrendered, with the loss of 1.5 million men.

Tet Offensive (Jan 1968) Considered to be a watershed of the Vietnam War, this guerrilla operation by the North Vietnamese Army and Vietcong against the US and South Vietnamese forces was a tactical defeat but a political victory for the Vietcong.

Towton (1461) The largest and bloodiest battle of the Wars of the Roses, this battle, fought on Palm Sunday, near the village of Towton about 10 miles southwest of York, secured the English throne for Edward IV against his Lancastrian opponents.

Trafalgar (1805) A naval engagement of the Napoleonic Wars, which established British naval supremacy for more than 100 years. Lord Nelson led the British fleet.

Waterloo (18 June 1815) In this final battle of the Napoleonic Wars, Bonaparte's forces were defeated by those of the Duke of Wellington near this Belgian village about 10 miles south of Brussels.

NAMES OF WARS

Persian Wars (499–48 BC) Greek states v. Persia
Peloponnesian Wars (431–04 BC) Athens v.
 Sparta
Corinthian War (395–337 BC)
Punic Wars (First 264–241 BC; Second
 218–01 BC; Third 149–146 BC) Romans v.
 Carthaginians
The Crusades (First 1095–99; Second 1147–49;
 Third 1189–92; Fourth 1203; Fifth 1216–29;
 Sixth 1249; Seventh 1270–72)
English Civil War (Barons' War) 1265
Flemish Wars (first 1302; second 1382)
 Flanders v. France
Hundred Years War (1337–1453)
Hussite War (1420–34) Bohemian civil war
Ottoman Wars (1456)
Wars of the Roses (1455-85)
Burgundian Wars (1476)
War of the Holy League (1512)
Italian Wars (French v. Swiss) 1515
Spanish Conquest (of Mexico) 1519-21
Counts' War 1533 (Danish civil war)
French Religious Wars (1562–98)
Seven Years' War of the North (1563-70)
Cyprus War (Holy League v. Turks) 1571
Thirty Years' War (1618–48)
Candian War (1644)
War of Devolution (1665)
War of the Grand Alliance (1690)
War of the English Succession (1690) King
 William III v. the exiled James II)
Great Northern War (1700–21) Russia, Poland
 and Denmark v. Sweden
War of the Spanish Succession (1701–14)
Farukhsiyar Rebellion (Indian civil war) 1713
War of the Quadruple Alliance (1718) England,
 Netherlands, France, German Empire v. Spain)
War of the Polish Succession (1733–38)
War of Jenkins' Ear (1739) England v. Spain
War of the Austrian Succession (1740–48)
Jacobite Rebellion (1745–46)
Carnatic War (England v. France, in India) 1751
Seven Years' War (1756–63)
American War of Independence (1775–83)
French Revolutionary Wars (1792–1802)

Polish Rising (1794–95)
Irish Rebellion (1798)
Napoleonic Wars (1803–15)
Peninsular War (1808–14)
Opium War (1839–42)
Maori War (1843–48)
Kaffir War (1846–47)
Italian Rising (1849)
Crimean War (1854–56)
Mexican Uprising (1855–60)
Arrow War (1856–60)
Persian War (1856–57)
Indian Mutiny (1857–58)
American Civil War (1861–65)
Ashanti War (1863–64)
Satsuma Rebellion (1877) Japanese civil war
Zulu War (1879)
Boer Wars (1880–81, 1899–1902)
Egyptian Revolt (1881)
Boxer Rebellion (1900)
Balkan Wars (1912–13)
World War I (The Great War)
World War II
Chinese Civil War (1946–49)
French Indo-China War (1946–54)
Korean War (1950–53)
Vietnam War (1954–75)
Six Day War (1967) second Arab-Israeli war
Yom Kippur War (1973) (third Arab-Israeli war)
Iran-Iraq War (1980–88)
Falklands War (1982)
Gulf War (Operation Desert Storm) 1991

ARCHITECTURAL STYLES

Greek 600–100 BCE
Roman 100 BCE–370 CE
Byzantine 330–1450
Romanesque 850–1250
Gothic 1140–1560
Tudor 1485–1600
Baroque 1585–1770
Jacobean 1603–25
Colonial 1614–1776
Neoclassical 1760–1820
Federal 1790–1820
Industrial Age 1800–1915
Art Nouveau 1880–1920
Bauhaus 1919–37
Art Deco 1920–40
Modernism 1920–50
Brutalism 1950s
High Tech 1970s
Postmodern 1970s
Deconstructivism
Structuralism
Formalism

ART STYLES AND PERIODS

Paleolithic 40,000–8000 BCE
Neolithic 10,000–2300 BCE
Ancient Near Eastern 7000–331 BCE
Bronze Age 2300–1000 BCE
Ancient Egyptian 3100 BCE–400 CE
Ancient Aegean 3000–1100 BCE
Greek 1000–320 BCE
Hellenistic 320–30 BCE
Etruscan 700–509 BCE
Roman 500 BCE–400 CE
Early Christian 100–1100
Byzantine 527–1453
Islamic 633–1600

Romanesque 1050–1200
Gothic 1140–1300
Renaissance 1300–1545
Mannerism 1520–1600
Baroque 1600–1720
Rococo 1720–80
Neoclassical 1780–1850
Romanticism 1780–1850
Barbizon School 1830–50
Realism 1830–80
Pre-Raphaelite 1848–56
Art Nouveau 1890–1915
Impressionism 1874–86
Arts and Crafts 1876–1916
Pointillism 1880–1915
Modernism 1880–1939
Post-Impressionism 1880–1910
Fauvism 1905–07
Expressionism 1905–25
Cubism 1907–23
Futurism 1909–19
Dada 1915–23
Bauhaus 1919–33
Art Deco 1920–40
Surrealism 1924–60
Abstract Expressionism 1940–60
Pop Art 1957
Minimalism 1958–70
Conceptualism 1960s
Op Art 1960s
Postmodernism 1970s
Neo-Expressionism 1980s
Neo-Conceptualism 1980s

FAMOUS SHIPS AND BOATS

Achille Lauro This liner is famous for being hijacked by four Palestinians on October 7, 1985.

HMS Adventure Captain James Cook took this bark to explore New Zealand, Tahiti, and the South Seas in the 1770s.

Amistad Seized by slaves in 1839 under the command of a slave named Cinque, this topsail schooner set sail for the United States.

Andrea Doria The *Stockholm* rammed this liner in 1956. It sank, killing 43.

Argo The mythical Jason and the Argonauts sailed this vessel in the Bronze Age.

Ark, Noah's God instructed the biblical Noah to build this boat of gopher wood.

HMS Beagle In 1833 a botany student named Charles Darwin sailed to the Galapagos Islands in this bark.

Bismarck One of the largest battleships commissioned by the Germans in World War II. It was launched and sunk in May 1941.

Bonhomme Richard John Paul Jones's frigate was able to beat the British 44-gun *Serapis* in a famous American Revolution sea battle.

HMS Bounty Fletcher Christian led a mutiny against Captain Bligh on the deck of this ship in 1787 near Tahiti.

Brendan This sailing curragh was used for a 1976 re-creation of St. Brendan's journey from Ireland to North America somewhere around 500–1000 CE.

Calypso This research vessel was originally a mine-sweeper before Jacques Cousteau bought it in 1948.

Carpathia First on the scene after the *Titanic* disaster in 1912, this liner rescued 706 passengers.

USS Constitution "Old Ironsides" acquired its nickname during its service in the War of 1812.

Cutty Sark This was one of the last clipper ships, built in 1869 for the China tea trade.

HMS Discovery Captain Cook led an expedition to Hawaii, where he was killed in 1779. The *Discovery* was part of his fleet.

Edmund Fitzgerald In 1975, this ore barge sank on the Great Lakes leaving no survivors.

Essex The crew of this ship was eventually forced into cannibalism after the ship was rammed and sunk by a whale in 1820.

Exxon Valdez This tanker lost over 260,000 barrels of oil when it ran aground in Prince William Sound in Alaska.

Flying Cloud In 1851, this clipper set a record of 89 days for the fastest time from New York to San Francisco.

Gaspee American colonists seized and burned this British schooner that ran aground in 1772, an incident remembered as the Gaspee Affair.

USS Intrepid Before becoming a museum on a New York City wharf, this aircraft carrier survived five kamikaze attacks in the Pacific during World War II.

Kon-Tiki This re-creation of a South American vessel was sailed by Thor Heyerdahl in 1937 to a South Pacific island in 93 days.

RMS Lusitania In 1915, this U.S. liner was sunk by a German submarine.

USS Maine "Remember the Maine" was the battle cry leading the United States into war with Spain after this ship was blown up in Cuba in 1898.

Mary Celeste This brigantine was found abandoned and adrift in 1872.

Mayflower The Pilgrims ventured from Plymouth, England, in this galleon in 1620.

USS *Missouri* The Japanese surrendered to the United States on this battleship at the conclusion of World War II.

USS *Monitor* This iron-sided wooden vessel, built by the Union navy in 1862, participated in the first battle between ironclads on May 9, 1862.

USS *Nautilus* The first nuclear-powered submarine was also the first sailing vessel to cross the North Pole.

Nina This three-masted *caravela redonda* was one of Christopher Columbus's ships that ventured to the New World.

Pinta See Nina.

PT 109 Commanded by Lieutenant John F. Kennedy, this patrol boat was cut in half in Pacific waters in 1943.

Queen Elizabeth 2 This liner, launched in 1967, is one of the last big liners in operation.

Ra II In 1970, this papyrus and rope raft was sailed from Morocco to Barbados in 57 days.

Rainbow Warrior This research vessel of the environmentalist group Greenpeace was eventually scuttled after being bombed in New Zealand in July 1985.

Santa Maria This was the third ship in Columbus's flotilla that first discovered the New World.

RMS *Titanic* In 1912, this "unsinkable" liner struck an iceberg and sank on its maiden voyage.

Turtle Commissioned by George Washington, this early submarine was unsuccessful in deploying a bomb to the hull of a British ship.

CSS *Virginia* Originally known as the *Merrimack*, this ironclad was constructed by the Confederacy in 1862.

TYPES OF BOATS AND SHIPS

Aircraft carrier A major warship capable of handling aircraft, with landing decks; some carriers are large enough to operate 100 aircraft.

Antiaircraft cruiser A small cruiser fitted with high-angle antiaircraft batteries.

Ark A large flat-bottomed vessel used for carriage of produce down major rivers.

Balsa A raft or float used in South America, consisting of two cylinders of a buoyant wood, or inflated skins, with a platform between them.

Barge A large flat-bottomed coastal trading vessel with a large topsail, effective in shallow water.

Bark A sailing vessel with three sails, weighing anywhere between 3,000 and 5,000 tons, used for grain and nitrate transport. It is square-rigged on fore and mainmasts, and fore-and-aft-rigged on the mizzen.

Barquentine Similar to a bark, but square-rigged on foremast only.

Bateau Similar to a canoe, a double-ended, flat-bottomed boat that measures anywhere from forty to forty-five feet in length, used primarily on rivers and lakes.

Battle cruiser These fast and powerful ships serve as advance scouts for battle fleets.

Battleship A ship in the line of battle, with guns, armour, and machinery.

Bean-cod A small single-masted Portuguese vessel with a sharp and high curved bow, used for inshore and estuary fishing.

Blockship An obsolete vessel stripped and filled with cement and towed out to block a port entrance for war purposes.

Brigantine A two-masted vessel with a square-rigged foremast.

Bumboat A small boat used for carrying vegetables, fruit, and provisions to larger boats lying in harbour.

Camship A merchant ship fitted with a catapult with which to launch fighter aircraft.

Canoe These dugout Native American crafts that measured about 15 feet in length bear a distinct French influence.

Capital ship A term used to denote the most important warship in the national fleet.

Cartel A ship used in wartime to negotiate with the enemy.

Cat boat A very shallow, wide sailboat, great for coastal cruising.

Catamaran A sailboat with two symmetrical hulls connected by an above-water deck, used primarily for racing purposes.

Clipper A very fast sailing ship popular in the 19th century.

Coble A short, flat-bottomed boat used in salmon fishing and netting in mouths of rivers and estuaries.

Collier A ship fitted for carriage of up to 25 tons of coal.

Container ship A cargo vessel designed specifically for cargo prepacked in containers.

Cruiser A sail- and engine-powered yacht adapted for long-distance cruising.

Cutter Used primarily by law enforcement for seizing illegal goods, these fast ships measure between 20 and 28 feet in length.

Dahabeeyah A large sailing vessel with high lateen sails, usually seen on the Nile.

Destroyer A light, fast warship weighing over 5,000 tons and armed with guided missiles.

Dinghy A small open boat with decking but no cabin.

Dolphin A 17-foot dinghy with spinnaker and trapeze sails.

Dory A small, flat-bottomed boat that can be fitted with an outboard motor.

Dreadnought battleship A ship combining high speed, adequate protection, and a main armament comprised of large guns of uniform size.

Dredger A self-propelled vessel used to deepen harbours or clear river entrances by removing earth from the harbour bottom.

Ferry A vessel designed for transport of persons and goods from one place to another.

Freighter A large container ship.

Frigate A smaller warship used in all navies.

Gondola A light, much-ornamented pleasure boat with a high-rising and curving stem, propelled by one person with a single oar standing in the stern.

Gunboat A small, lightly armed vessel used mostly for war and policing purposes, particularly in rivers and along shallow coasts.

Hobie craft This single-handle catamaran is capable of speeds up to 20 mph.

Hovercraft A vehicle that rides on a cushion of air under pressure between the craft and the surface over which it is travelling.

Icebreaker A vessel designed with a reinforced bow and extremely powerful engines to force a way through pack ice in extreme latitudes.

Junk A flat-bottomed, high-sterned sailing vessel native to Far Eastern seas, with square bows and two or three sails.

Ketch A sailing vessel with two masts, used as a trading vessel.

Laser A light, single-handed racing dinghy.

Launch A small steam- or powerboat used to bring passengers to larger boats.

Life raft Any raft used for saving lives in a shipwreck, nowadays usually rubber and inflatable.

Lifeboat A boat designed for saving lives at sea. Attached to larger ships, it is fully stocked with food, water, and medical supplies.

Minesweeper A vessel designed to sweep and explode mines laid at sea.

Monkey A small coastal trading vessel, single-masted with a square sail.

Mosquito craft A generic name for all fast minor warships driven by internal combustion engines.

Motorboat A generic term for a small boat outfitted with a motor, outboard or otherwise.

Paddlesteamer—a.k.a. paddleboat A steam vessel in which propulsion is by a pair of paddle-wheels mounted amidship, or a single paddlewheel at the stern, driven by reciprocating engines.

Periagua A large dugout canoe fitted for sailing.

Pirogue A seagoing canoe formed out of the trunks of two trees hollowed out and fastened together.

Pontoon A float-bottomed boat used as a ferry or fitted with cranes and tackle.

Raft A floating framework of spars, planks, or timber used to carry goods from shore to ship.

Rig A boat with a short lower mast on which is hoisted a yard.

Schooner A sailboat set with Bermuda sails and no topsails. The name derives from the Scottish *scoon*—to skip over water like a flat stone.

Scow A large flat-bottomed boat, used for carrying freight.

Scull A highly efficient lightweight racing motorboat.

Sepulchral ships A term given to ships used in connection with burial rights.

Shallop A skiff rowed by one or two people.

Sharpie A type of flat-bottomed oyster dredger, usually between 30 and 60 feet in length.

Skiff A ship's working boat, used for small errands, usually rowed.

Skipjack A work boat with a jib-headed mainsail.

Sloop The modern sloop has a jib-headed mainsail and is distinguished from the cutter in having the mast farther forward and only a single headsail.

Submarine A vessel designed to operate below the surface of the sea.

Sunfish A single-handed sailboat, perfect for beginners.

Surfboat A large, open craft propelled by oar, used on the beaches of Africa and India for landing passengers when there is no deep-water port.

Tanker A ship designed for liquid cargo, especially oil in bulk at sea.

Tramp A cargo-carrying merchant vessel.

Transport A ship employed in the transport of troops or persons to and from overseas, either for wartime operations or as relief garrisons serving abroad in peacetime.

Trawler A fishing vessel designed to operate a large net in the form of a bat, for the catching of fish on the sea bottom.

Trimaran A sailboat with three symmetrical hulls.

Whaleboat A straight-keeled, sharp-ended boat built for speed.

Widgeon This smallest practical family sailboat needs only a two-person crew.

Windjammer A generic term for a square-rigged sailing ship.

Yacht A private pleasure boat.

Yawl This short, wide boat is rigged with one or two masts and measures 18 to 24 feet in length.

BOOKS OF THE BIBLE

THE OLD TESTAMENT

Genesis This first book of the Bible deals with the creation of the world, human beings, and specifically the Hebrew people.

Exodus Titled after the Greek word for "departure," this book deals with the oppression in Egypt, Moses in the desert, and the special covenant between God and the Israelites.

Leviticus This book contains the sacrificial and ritual laws for Israelites.

Numbers The name of this book comes from the account of two censuses taken of the Hebrew people. It also traces the progress of the Israelites from Sinai to the edge of the Promised Land.

Deuteronomy Meaning "second law," Deuteronomy presents Moses' testament on the eve of his death.

Joshua Named after the successor of Moses, this book presents God's fidelity by His giving of the Promised Land to the people of Israel and their descendants.

Judges The title refers to twelve military heroes of Israel. The book displays how Israel is subjugated by other nations when it is unfaithful to God.

Ruth This book is named after the Moabite woman who became an Israelite through marriage, and God's subsequent beneficence for piety, even for an outsider.

1 Samuel The title refers to Samuel, who led to the enthronement of David. This begins what are known as the Historical Books of the Old Testament.

2 Samuel The Second Book of Samuel is important because it promises a lasting dynasty to David.

1 Kings The First Book of Kings displays a succession of kings who when faithful to God are aided, but are punished when not.

2 Kings This second book continues through the fourth century BCE, ending in the Babylonian exile and the destruction of Jerusalem.

1 Chronicles The First Book of Chronicles is a record of the period of exile for the Israelite people from the reign of Saul to their return from exile.

2 Chronicles This second book was originally one book with 1 Chronicles.

Ezra This book is named after the legalist who gives the Israelite people spiritual unity after the Babylonian exile.

Nehemiah Nehemiah is an Israelite who rebuilds the walls of Jerusalem and institutes necessary administrative reforms.

Tobit The title of this book refers to an Israelite living in Ninevah who has his sight and wealth restored through the help of the angel Raphael.

Judith Judith is a pious woman who helps to save Jerusalem by killing an opposing general, Holofernes, after a period of fasting and prayer.

Esther This book is named after the Jewish heroine who is able to avert a pogrom against her people planned by the powerful vizier Haman the Agagite.

1 Maccabees written in 100 BCE, the name Maccabees refers to the son of a priest named Judas who leads a revolt against the Seleucid kings.

2 Maccabees Although most likely not written by the same writer as 1 Maccabees, this book gives a theological interpretation of the events in the previous book.

Job This begins what are known as the Wisdom

Books, finishing with Sirach. This poem is named after its protagonist, who loses all he has, questions, and finally accepts God's will.

Psalms A collection of hymns to God, generally either of praise, thanksgiving, or lament. Some of the psalms have been attributed to King David.

Proverbs A collection of didactic poetry to teach wisdom, of which all stems from the principle that "the fear of the Lord is the beginning of knowledge." Some of the writings have been attributed to King Solomon.

Ecclesiastes This book proposes that all things "under the sun" are works of vanity, and that true wisdom comes solely from the worship of God whose reign never ceases.

The Song of Solomon This parable of seemingly perfect human love is an allegory in which the Lord is the Lover, and His people are the object of His love.

Wisdom Written in about 100 BCE by a member of the Jewish community in Egypt, this book reflects upon God's role in Israel's past in the current time of Jewish persecution.

Sirach Written between 200 and 175 BCE by a Jerusalem sage named Jesus (son of Sirach), this book contains maxims on numerous different topics intended for the author's fellow Jews. This concludes the Wisdom Books.

Isaiah This begins what are known as the Prophetic Books. This anthology of poems was written chiefly by the great prophet Isaiah and his disciples during the second half of the eighth century, a period of great troubles for the nation of Israel.

Jeremiah This book tells of the prophet Jeremiah in the midst of a great ruler, King Josiah; an unfaithful one, Zedekiah; false prophets; and the overrunning of Jerusalem.

Lamentations Written in the sixth century BCE, Lamentations deals with the destruction of the

temple after the fall of Jerusalem, as well as the strength of God's love.

Baruch Written partly by the secretary of the prophet Jeremiah, this book includes a warning against idolatry, a hymn in praise of wisdom, and a prayer of penitence, among other topics.

Ezekiel This prophet bears the distinction of being the first to receive the call to prophecy outside the Holy Land. He tells the people of the imminent fall of Jerusalem and of its eventual redeemed glory.

Daniel This book draws its name from an exiled Jew in Babylon named Daniel, who along with his three friends resists temptation and remains faithful to God.

Hosea In this book the prophet Hosea bemoans the infidelities of his harlot wife as does God for Israel.

Joel During a great scourge of locusts, the prophet encourages Israel to repent and turn back to God.

Amos The prophet Amos condemns Israel for its idolatry.

Obadiah This shortest book in the Old Testament contains one of its strongest prophecies: the fall of Edom and the eventual rise of Israel.

Jonah In this book the prophet Jonah condemns Nineveh, whereupon the city immediately repents and is spared by God, much to Jonah's surprise and consternation.

Micah Decries the sins of Israel and speaks of the glory of a restored Zion.

Nahum Happily prophesies the destruction of the city of Ninevah.

Habakkuk The prophet conducts a dialogue with God in the time of Jerusalem's subjugation at the hands of the Babylonians.

Zephaniah The prophet predicts a day of destruction for Israel, its judgment, and the eventual mercy of the Lord for the restored Zion.

Haggai This prophet encourages a lethargic Israel after its exile in Babylon so that it will rebuild the temple.

Zechariah Zechariah is also a prophet encouraging a dispirited Israel to rebuild the temple after the exile.

Malachi This book makes a stern rebuke to the religious community of Israel, circa 455 BCE.

THE NEW TESTAMENT

Matthew The first of the Gospels was probably written after Jerusalem had fallen to the Romans in 70 CE. Authorship is uncertain.

Mark This shortest of the Gospels was probably also the first to be written, most likely before 70 CE.

Luke This Gospel was probably written around 80–90 CE, because of its reliance on Mark's Gospel and other first-generation source material.

John John's Gospel is a mixture of theology and history intended to emphasize Jesus' divinity. Probably written between 90 and 100 CE.

Acts of the Apostles Acts is considered the second of Luke's books. Here he traces the church's development from the Resurrection to Paul's imprisonment.

Romans In this first of the letters, or Epistles, Paul writes to the small Christian community in Rome from Greece, around 56 CE.

1 Corinthians Paul exhorts the Christian community he founded in Corinth on his second missionary journey around the year 51 CE.

2 Corinthians In this Epistle, Paul deals with several crises that have arisen in the young Christian community in Corinth.

Galatians Paul exhorts this community of recent converts from paganism to avoid following some of the precepts of Mosaic law instead of Christ.

Ephesians Most likely this letter was written by Paul while in a Roman jail around 62 CE to the community in the city of Ephesus in Asia Minor.

Philippians Paul admonishes this Christian community in Greece to avoid the more burdensome rules of Mosaic law.

Colossians In this letter, Paul advises the Colossians to shun false doctrines. This is another Epistle written from prison.

1 Thessalonians Paul sends his greetings to those in Thessalonica, giving several specific exhortations and sending his encouragement.

2 Thessalonians This continues in the same manner as Paul's previous letter to the young Christian community in Greece, as well as encouraging it in time of persecution.

1 Timothy Paul addresses the Ephesian community, writing on a number of topics—from aid to widows to liturgical celebrations.

2 Timothy In a more personal letter than the previous one, the ageing Paul tells Timothy to groom a successor, as Paul has done with Timothy.

Titus Paul addresses Titus on how to develop and strengthen the growing Christian community on the Mediterranean island of Crete.

Philemon Paul pleads the case of the slave Onesimus, a Christian, to his master so that he may be welcomed back because he is a "brother, beloved."

Hebrews The author, possibly Paul, buttresses the faith of this community of Jewish Christians, which has been weakened not by persecution, but by spiritual weariness within its own ranks.

James This letter, probably written by a relative of Jesus, emphasizes moral responsibility to "the twelve tribes in the dispersion."

1 Peter Peter encourages the Gentile community in Asia Minor to remain strong in its faith despite the persecutions it is suffering.

2 Peter Generally agreed among scholars to have a different author from 1 Peter, this letter exhorts its unnamed audience to beware false teachers and to lead a virtuous life.

1 John The style and terminology suggests that this author is the John of the Gospel. Here he emphasizes doctrinal teaching to combat false ideas.

2 John Most likely written from Ephesus by a disciple of an apostle, this letter preaches mutual love, the new commandment, the Antichrist, and "truth" Christology, among other things.

3 John This letter from John is the only one addressed to an individual, Gauis. Here the author writes about the missionary work of the early church.

Jude The Jude of the title is probably a relative of Jesus and not the apostle. This letter, addressed to a general Christian audience, warns against false teachers.

Revelation The last book of the Bible, portraying the Apocalypse, is dense with symbolism difficult for the modern reader to understand, but quite popular in the style of apocalyptic literature between 200 BCE and 200 CE.

CAR MANUFACTURERS, WORLDWIDE

Alfa Romeo Begun by the Societa Italiana Automobili Darracq in 1906 to produce low-cost cars. The factory was soon sold to a group of car enthusiasts who called themselves Anonima Lombarda Fabbrica Automobili who eventually sold it to Nicola Romeo, a native of Naples.

Aston Martin Partners Robert Bamford and Lionel Martin joined with Singer Motorcars to produce the first Aston Martin race car in 1919 in Great Britain.

Audi The roots of Audi began in 1899 when August Horch founded August Horch & Cie in Cologne. He produced his first shock-free two-cylinder engine the next year, incorporating ideas he tried to realize when working with former employer Carl Benz.

Bentley Walter Bentley, a British engineer, joined with F. T. Burgess and Harry Varley to build a sporting motorcar in 1919.

BMW (Bayerische Motoren Werke) The Rapp Motor Company was founded as an aircraft-engine factory in Munich in 1916. It was not until a year later that the company was renamed BMW. Throughout the years, BMW has supplied racing enthusiasts not only with car engines but motor cycle and speedboat engines as well.

Chrysler Walter P. Chrysler founded the Chrysler Corporation, whose first car bearing the Chrysler name, the Chrysler Six, was introduced in 1924.

Citroën Andre Citroën founded his car company, the Andre Citroën Motor Co., in France after six years in the gear-making industry.

Daihatsu Daihatsu began life as Hatsudoki Seizo Co. Ltd. in 1907 as a manufacturer of internal combustion engines. It began producing three-wheeled vehicles in 1930 and changed its name to Daihatsu Motor Co. Ltd. 21 years later.

Ferrari In 1929 Enzo Ferrari founded Scuderia Ferrari in Modena with the purpose of helping motorcar racers. It wasn't until after World War II (when the factory was bombed) and a move to Maranello that the company changed its name to Ferrari, designing the 125 Sport, a 12-cylinder 1500 cc car for racing.

Fiat The first Fiat factory opened in 1900, manufacturing thirty models of their three-and-a-half-horsepower two-seater, notable in that it did not feature a reverse gear.

Ford Ford Motor Company began on June 16, 1903, when Henry Ford and associates filed incorporation papers at Michigan's state capitol. This second-largest car and truck producer in the world started out in a converted Detroit wagon factory staffed with ten people.

GM General Motors has been one of the largest American and worldwide automobile manufacturers since its inception at the beginning of the 20th century. Some of its motor vehicle lines include Chevrolet, Geo, Pontiac, Oldsmobile, Buick, Cadillac, GMC, and Saturn.

Honda Honda's history begins with Soichiro Honda, who began rebuilding vehicles after the Tokyo earthquake of 1923. He finally began manufacturing his own cars in the early 1960s.

Hyundai Hyundai Motor Co. was established in 1967, but it was not until 1974 that their subcompact car, the Pony, Korea's first independently designed and manufactured model, was unveiled at the 55th Torino International Motor Fair, and it was not exported for sale until two years after that.

Isuzu Isuzu started manufacturing Japan's first cars in 1916, introducing the first 5.3 litre air-cooled diesel engine in 1936 and the first diesel-powered truck in the Japanese market the same year.

Jaguar Jaguar began with creator William Lyons and the SS Cars Ltd. Co. in Britain in the late 1920s, renaming it Jaguar Car Ltd. after World War II.

Kia Founded in 1944 as a bicycle parts maker in Seoul, South Korea, Kia Motors Corp. produces passenger cars, vans, and cargo trucks.

Lamborghini The year 1963 marks the inception of the Lamborghini when the company introduced its first model, the 350 GTV. Its creator, Ferruccio Lamborghini, turned from agricultural machinery to luxury sports cars, inspired by the success of his neighbour, Enzo Ferrari.

Lancia Vincenzo Lancia founded this company in 1906, producing its first model, the 1007 Apha, soon after.

Land Rover This granddaddy of the modern four-wheel-drive sport utility vehicle was the British answer to the U.S. Jeep after World War II.

M.G. ("Morris Garage") This British two-seater sports car actually descends from a rather larger 1923 vehicle known as the Bullnose Morris.

Maserati Brothers Carlo, Bindo, Alfieri, Ettore, and Ernesto Maserati formed their own car company in 1926 after years of involvement in auto racing.

Mazda Toyo Cork Kogyo founded Mazda in Hiroshima, Japan, in 1920. By 1931, Mazda had begun to produce three-wheeled trucks, by 1960, a two-door passenger car, and it eventually entered the U.S. market some 40 years later.

Mercedes-Benz Mercedes-Benz began when the first Benz car was granted a patent in 1886 for its four-stroke engine. Originally called Daimler-Benz, the name Mercedes comes from an agent for Daimler who wanted to sell a new model with his daughter's name.

Mitsubishi Mitsubishi Motors began over 80 years ago when its assembly line produced its first Mitsubishi Model A.

Morgan Motor Company H. F. S. Morgan turned from motorcycle manufacturing to cars, producing his first three-wheeled, one-seater in 1909 in Worcestershire, England.

Nissan The origins of Nissan go back to 1914, when Masujiro Hashimoto's Kwaishinisha Co. produced a car they called the "Dat," a name based on the initials of Hashimoto's three co-investors. The "sun" was added later to create the Datsun.

Opel The sons of bicycle manufacturer Adam Opel began producing their own vehicles in 1892, starting with the Opel-Lutzmann.

Panoz Auto Development Company Panoz was established in 1988 when Daniel Panoz purchased the rights to an Irish chassis designed by Frank Costin. The first automobile produced was the Panoz AIV Roadster in 1992.

Peugeot Automobiles Peugeot was born in 1889. Today, PSA Peugeot Citroen is spread out over five continents, and the company remains one of Europe's three major car manufacturers.

Porsche Ferdinand Porsche and his son Ferry unveiled the very first Porsche, the Type 356, in 1948.

Rolls-Royce Charles Rolls was looking to be associated with the finest motorcars available and found it in Frederick Royce's 1904 automobile. In 1906 Rolls-Royce was formed.

Saab Saab manufactured its first prototype in 1945, but it wasn't until 1949 that the company produced the first Saab series of cars.

Skoda Skoda Automobilova A.S. began manufacturing cars in 1898, but this Czech company almost didn't survive the fall of communism. A massive infusion of capital saved this car manufacturer, and now it is the largest industrial export from the Czech Republic.

Ssang Yong The inception of Ssang Yong Motor Company dates back to 1954 when the Korean Ha-Dong-Hwan Assembly Shop started the assembly of its first car. Its PyongTaek plant now produces 220,000 vehicles annually.

Subaru In 1953, five Japanese companies merged to form Fuji Heavy Industries Ltd., adopting the name Subaru, meaning "unite." Today, Fuji Heavy Industries is a global transportation conglomerate.

Suzuki Michio Suzuki turned from his Suzuki Loom Manufacturing Company to automobiles after the Japanese government encouraged domestic car manufacturing before World War II.

Toyota Sakichi Toyoda's textile company, Toyoda Automatic Loom, turned to car manufacturing when son Kiichiro began experimenting with a two-cylinder engine in the early 1930s. It changed its name to Toyota with a "t" when it entered the U.S. market.

Triumph Triumph Cycle Co. Ltd. transformed into Triumph Motor Company in 1930 with the creation of their six-cylinder engine.

Vauxhall Boats, not automobiles, were the first products from Vauxhall Iron Works in London, England. They turned to motorcars in 1903.

Volkswagen The inception of the original Volks wagen ("people's car") began in 1931 with the sketches of a vehicle called Project 21 that was to be an air-cooled, three-cylinder engine. It was Adolf Hitler, though, who ordered that an inexpensive car be made for the masses, and thus the Volkswagen was born.

Volvo This Swedish car manufacturer produced its first car in 1927 and introduced models into the United States in 1956.

CLASSIC CARS

Ferrari 250GTO Arguably the greatest Ferrari ever made, only 39 were built.
Mercedes-Benz 300SL Originally known as the W194, the 300SL was built for racing.
AC Cobra Created by Carroll Shelby.
Alfa Spider The durable classic.
Volkswagen Beetle Designed by Ferdinand Porsche before WWII, the Beetle has recently been redesigned and relaunched.
Jaguar E-Type Created a sensation when it was launched at the 1961 Geneva Motor Show.
Lotus Elan Years ahead of its time when it was launched in 1962.
Volkswagen Golf GTI This combination of sportscar performance with practicality started a whole new automotive fashion.
Austin Healey 100 & 3000 The British car that was a great hit in America.
Jaguar Mark II.
MGB Originally thought of as a cheap Aston Martin.
Mini The brainchild of Alec Issigonis.
Ford Mustang.
Rolls-Royce Silver Shadow The last word in car luxury
Triumph TR4/TR5/TR6 The TR4 was launched in 1962 and designed by Giovanni Michelotti. By the launch of the TR6 in 1968, the TR range was beginning to feel outdated.

SPORTS CARS

Caterham Seven
Mazda MX-5
MGF
Alfa Spider & GTV
Morgan
TVR Griffith
Porsche 911
Chevrolet Corvette
Honda NSX
Chrysler Viper
Aston Martin DB7
Ferrari F355
Jaguar XJ220
McLaren F1

CIGARS

Adante (Dominican Republic)
Aguila (Dominican Republic)
Alhambra (Philippines)
Aliados (Honduras)
Andujar (Dominican Republic)
Antelo (U.S.)
Antonio & Cleopatra (Puerto Rico)
Antonio y Cleopatra (U.S.)
Arango Statesman (Honduras)
Aromas De San Andreas (Mexico)
Arturo Fuente (Dominican Republic)
Ashton (Dominican Republic)
Astral (Honduras)
Avo (Dominican Republic)
Baccarat (Honduras)
Bauza (Dominican Republic)
Belinda (Honduras)
Beverly Hills (Honduras)
Blue Ribbon (Honduras)
Bohemia (Dominican Republic)
Boliver (Dominican Republic)
Boliver (Cuba)
Butera Royal Vintage (Dominican Republic)
Caballeros (Dominican Republic)
Calixo Lopex (Philippines)
Camacho (Honduras)
Canaria d'Oro (Dominican Republic)
Caribbean Round (U.S.)
Carrington (Dominican Republic)
Casa Blanca (Dominican Republic)
Casa de Nicaragua (Nicaragua)
Casa Martin (Dominican Republic)
Centennial V (Honduras)
Cervantes (Honduras)
Chavelo (U.S.)
Chevere (Jamaica)
Cibao (Dominican Republic)
Cohiba (Dominican Republic)
Cohiba (Cuba)
Condal (Canary Islands)
Cortesia (Honduras)
Credo (Dominican Republic)
Cruz Real (Mexico)
Cubanas (Dominican Republic)
Cubita (Dominican Republic)

Cuesta Rey (Dominican Republic)
Davidoff (Dominican Republic)
Davidoff (Cuba)
Diana Silvius (Dominican Republic)
Diplomaticos (Cuba)
Don Asa (Honduras)
Don Diego (Dominican Republic)
Don Juan (Nicaragua)
Don Leo (Dominican Republic)
Don Lino (Honduras)
Don Mateo (Honduras)
Don Ramos (Honduras)
Don Tomas (Honduras)
Dunhill (Dominican Republic)
Dunhill (Canary Islands)
Dutch Masters (U.S.)
Dutch Treats (U.S.)
Eden (U.S.)
El Beso (Mexico)
El Potosi (Honduras)
El Producto (U.S.)
El Rey Del Mundo (Honduras)
El Rico Habana (U.S.)
Evelio (Honduras)
Excalibur (Honduras)
F.D. Grave (U.S.)
Farnham Drive (U.S.)
Fonseca (Dominican Republic)
Garcia y Vega (U.S.)
Gioconda (U.S.)
Gispert (Cuba)
Griffans (Dominican Republic)
H. Upmann (Dominican Republic)
Harrows (Philippines)
Hauptmann's (U.S.)
Hav-A-Tampa (U.S.)
Henry Clay (Dominican Republic)
Henry Wintermans (Holland)
Hidalgo (Panama)
Hinds Brothers (Honduras)
Hinds Brothers (Nicaragua)
Holts (Honduras)
House of Windsor (U.S.)
Hoya Selecta (U.S.)
Hoyo de Monterrey (Cuba)
Hoyo de Monterrey (Honduras)
J.R. Famous (U.S.)
J.R. Ultimate (Honduras)
Jamaica Bay (Jamaica)

Jamaican Gold (Jamaica)
Jamaican Kings (Jamaica)
Jamaican Supreme (Jamaica)
Jose Benito (Dominican Republic)
Jose Marti (Dominican Republic)
Joya de Nicaragua (Nicaragua)
Juan Clemente (Dominican Republic)
Juan Lopez (Cuba)
King Edward (U.S.)
Kingstown (Mexico)
Knockando (Dominican Republic)
La Carona (Dominican Republic)
La Emincia Tampa (U.S.)
La Finca (Nicaragua)
La Flor De Cano (Cuba)
La Flor De Dominicana (Dominican Republic)
La Fontana (Honduras)
La Gloria Cubana (U.S.)
La Gloria Cubana (Cuba)
La Invicta (Honduras)
La Isla (U.S.)
La Plata (U.S.)
La Primadora (Honduras)
La Regenta (Canary Islands)
Las Cabrillas (Honduras)
Las Vegas Cigar Co. (U.S.)
Leon Jimenes (Dominican Republic)
Licenciados (Dominican Republic)
Lord Beaconfield (U.S.)
Lord Clinton (U.S.)
Macanudo (Dominican Republic)
Maria Mancini (Honduras)
Matacon (Mexico)
Mocha Supreme (Honduras)
Montecristo (Dominican Republic)
Montecristo (Cuba)
Montecruz (Dominican Republic)
Montesino (Dominican Republic)
Montezuma (Dominican Republic)
Muriel (U.S.)
Nestor 747 (Honduras)
Onyx (Dominican Republic)
Optimo (U.S.)
Padron (Honduras)
Partagas (Cuba)
Paul Garmirian Gourmet (Dominican Republic)
Phillies (U.S.)
Pleiades (Dominican Republic)
Por Larranaga (Dominican Republic)

Primo Del Rey (Dominican Republic)
Punch (Cuba)
Punch (Honduras)
Quorum (Dominican Republic)
Ramon Allones (Dominican Republic)
Ramon Allones (Cuba)
Riata (Honduras)
Robert Burns (U.S.)
Roi-Tan (U.S.)
Romeo y Julieta (Dominican Republic)
Romeo y Julieta (Cuba)
Royal Dominicana (Dominican Republic)
Royal Jamaica (Dominican Republic)
Saint Luis Rey (Cuba)
San Cristobal (Dominican Republic)
Sancho Panza (Cuba)
Santa Clara (Mexico)
Santa Cruz (Jamaica)
Santa Damiana (Dominican Republic)
Savinelli Extra Ltd. Reserve (Dominican Republic)
Schimmelpennick (Holland)
Shakespeare (Dominican Republic)
Sosa (Dominican Republic)
Special Caribbeans (Dominican Republic)
Special Coronas (Dominican Republic)
Suerdieck (Brazil)
Swisher Sweets (U.S.)
Tampa Cub (U.S.)
Tampa Nugget (U.S.)
Tampa Sweet (U.S.)
Te Amo (Mexico)
Temple Hall (Jamaica)
Tena y Vega (Costa Rica)
Tiparillo and Tijuana (U.S.)
Topper (U.S.)
Topstone (U.S.)
Torcedor (Nicaragua)
Tresado (Dominican Republic)
Trinidad (Cuba)
Upmann (Cuba)
Veracruz (Mexico)
Villa de Cuba (U.S.)
Villazon Deluxe (U.S.)
Vueltabajo (Dominican Republic)
White Owl (U.S.)
Whitehall (Jamaica)
William Penn (U.S.)
Zino (Honduras)

COMMERCIAL AIRLINES

AB Airlines
Above It All
ABX Air
Aces
Action Airlines
Adria Airlines
Adventure Airlines
Aer Lingus
Aero Asia
Aero Continente-Peru
Aero Costa Rica
Aero Peru
Aerochago
Aeroejecutivo
Aeroflot
Aerolineas Argentinas/Austral
AeroLloyd
Aeromar
Aeromexico
Aeromiles
Aerosweet
Air Afrique
Air Alma
Air Antillean
Air Aruba
Air Atlanta
Air Atlantic Airlines
Air Aurora
Air BC
Air Caledonia
Air Canada
Air Caribbean
Air China
Air Cruise America
Air Europa
Air Fiji
Air Foyle
Air France
Air Greece
Air Guadeloupe
Air India
Air Inter-French Airlines
Air Jamaica

Air Jet
Air Labrador
Air Lanka
Air Macau
Air Madagascar
Air Malta
Air Mandalay
Air Mauritius
Air Metro
Air Midwest
Air Namibia
Air Nauru
Air Negril
Air Nevada
Air New Zealand
Air Niugini
Air North
Air Nova
Air One Compagnia Aerea
Air Ontario
Air Pacific
Air Panama
Air Paraguay
Air Partner Group
Air Sedona
Air Seychelles
Air South
Air Sunshine
Air Tech Ltd.
Air Trails
Air UK
Air Ukraine
Air Vantage
Air Vanuatu
Air Vegas
Air Virginia
Air Wisconsin
Air Zaire
Air Zimbabwe
AirCal
Airianka
AirTran Airlines
Airways, Inc.
Alaska Airlines
Alitalia
All Nippon Airways
Alliance Airlines
ALM Antillean Airlines
Aloha Airlines

America West Airlines
American Airlines
American Eagle
Amerijet International
Ansett Airlines
AOM Airlines
APG: Air Partner Group
ArcticAir
Arkia Israeli Airlines
Armenian Airlines
Aserca Air
Asiana Airlines
Aspen Mountain Air
Astral
Atkin Air
Atlantic Coast Airlines
Atlas Air
Austin Express
Austrian Airlines
Avensa/Servivensa Airlines
Avianca Colombian Airlines
Aviateca Guatemala
Avioimpex
Bahamas Air
Balaire/CTA
Balkin Bulgarian Airlines
Baltic International Airlines
Bangkok Airways
BAS Airlines
Bearskin Airlines
Bemidji Airlines
Big Island Air
Big Sky Airlines
Bouraq
Braathens
Branson Airlines
Brazilian Airlines
British Airways
British Midland
British West Indian Airlines
Buffalo Airways
BWIA Airways
Calm Air
Canadian Airlines
Cape Air Nantucket Airlines
Carnival Airlines
Carson Air
Castle Air
Cathay Pacific

Cayman Airways
Chart Air San Juan
Chautauqua Airlines
Chelan Airways
Chicago Express Airlines
China Airlines
China Eastern Airlines
China Northwestern Airlines
China Southern Airlines
City Bird
Colgan Air
COMAIR
Conquest Airlines
Continental Airlines
Continental Micronesia
COPA Airlines
Coratia Airlines
Cork Aviation
Corporate Airlines
Corsair
Croatia Airlines
Cubana
Cyprus Airways
Cyprus Turkish Airlines
Czech Airlines
Delta Airlines
Deutsche BA
DHL Airways
Direct Air
Dragon Air
Eagle Canyon Airlines
East-West Airlines
Eastwind Airlines the Bee Line
EasyJet
Ecuatoriana
Egyptair
El Al
Emery Worldwide Airlines
Emirates
Ethiopian Air
Euram
EuroWings
Eva Air
Evergreen International Airlines
Faucett Peru Airlines
Fine Airlines
Finnair
First American Airlines
Flight West Airlines

Flying Enterprises
Freedom Air International
Frontier Airlines
Funjet Express
Garuda Indonesia
GB Airways
Ghana Airways
Grand Aire Express
Grand Canyon Airlines
Great Lakes Aviation
Greenlandair
Greyhound Air
Grupo Air Europa
Gulf Air
Gulfstream International Airlines
Hainan Airlines Company Ltd.
Haines Airways
Hang Khong
Harbour Air
Hawaiian Airlines
Hemus
Horizon Air
Iberia Airlines
Icelandair
Indian Airlines
Intercontinental de Aviacion
InterIsland Airways
Iran Air
Island Air
Island Airlines Nantucket
Islandflug
Japanlines
JAT
Jersey European Airways
Jet Airways
Kenmore Aire
Kenya Airways
Kitty Hawk Air Cargo
KIWI International Airlines
KLM
Korean Air
Kuwait Airways
L.A.B. Flying Service, Inc.
Ladeco Chilean Airlines
Laker Airways
LanChile Airlines
Lasca
Lauda Airlines
Liat Ltd.

Lloyd Aereo Boliviano
Lone Star Airlines
LOT Polish Airlines
LTU International Airways
Lufthansa
Luxair
Lynx Air
Maersk Air
Mahalo Air
Makung Airlines
Malaysia Airlines
Malev Hungarian Airlines
Malmo Aviation
Mandarin Airlines
Manx Airlines
Mark Air
Martinair Holland
MaxAir
Maya Airways
MEA Middle Eastern Airlines
Merpati
Mesa Air Group
Mesaba Airlines
Mexicana
MIAT Mongolian Airlines
Midway Airlines
Miles Above
Mount Cook Airlines
Mountain Air Express
Myrtle Beach Jet Express
Nantucket Airlines
Natair
Nations Air
Necon Air
Nepal Airways
New England Airlines
Nica Airlines
Nordeste Linhas Aereas
Nordic East Airways
Northwest Airlines
NWT Air Canada
Olympic Airways
Orca Air
Orient-Avia
Pacific Coastal Airlines
Pacific Island Aviation
Pacific Southwest Airlines
Pakistan Airlines
Pan American Airlines

Pananal Linhas Aereas
Paradise Island Airlines
Pelangi Air
Penair
Peninsula Airways
Philippines Airlines
Polonia Airlines
Polynesian Airlines
Qatar Airways
Qantas
Reeve Aleutian Airways
Reno Air
Rio-Sul
Rover Airways International
Royal Air Maroc
Royal Express Travel
Royal Jordanian Airlines
Royal Nepal Airlines
Royal Swai National Airlines
Royal Tonga
Royal Wings Airways
Ryan International Airways
Sabena
Saeta
Sandpiper Air Charter Service
Saro Airlines
SAS
SATA Air Acores
Saudi Arabian Airlines
Scenic Airlines
Sempati Airways
Shangdong Airlines
Shanghai Airlines
Sichuan Airlines
SilkAir
Siroe's Flyveselskap ASA
Singapore Airlines
Skyways
SkyWest Airlines
Solomon Airlines
South Africa Airlink
South African Airways
South Central Air
Southern Airtransport
Southwest Airlines
Spanair
Spirit Airlines
Starship Airlines
Sun Air

Sun Coast Airlines, Inc.
Sun Country Airlines
Sun Jet
Sunflower Airlines
Surinam Airways
Swissair
TACA Airlines
Taesa Airlines
Tamair
Tan Sasha Honduras
Tap Air Portugal
Tarom Romanian Air Transport
Thai Airways
Tower Air
Transbrasil Airlines
Transwede Airlines
Trans States Airlines
Travelai S.A.
Tropic Air
Turkish Airlines
Turks and Caicos Airway
TW Express
TWA
Tyrolian Airways
Uganda Airlines
Ukraine Airlines
U-Land Airways
United Airlines
United Parcel Service
US Airways
USA Jet
Uzbekistan Airways
Vanguard Airlines
Varig Airlines
VASP Brazilian Airlines
Viasa International Airways
Virgin Atlantic Airways
Virgin Express
Westair Commuter Airlines
Western Pacific Airlines
WestJet Airlines
Wiggins Airways
Wings West Airlines
World Airways
Yemen Airways
Yugoslav Airways
YTA Freniva
Zambia Airways
Zimbabwe Express Airlines

DANCES

Aattetur A Norwegian dance in 3/4 time for four couples in a ring.

Abhia This ceremonial mourning dance from southern Sudan is done by tribal women around a mango tree.

Abraxas A serpentine ritual dance of the Greek Gnostics.

Afwi A French Guinea dance done by men to initiate children into the tribe.

Ahidous Done by Berbers in Morocco with men and women in increasing and decreasing circles.

Alegrias This solo dance is done by Andalusian women in 3/4 or 6/8 time.

Alemander Also known as Allemande or Allemandler, this folk dance in 2/4 time is performed in Germany and Switzerland.

Aparina A Tahitian dance for 60 men and women sitting in four rows.

Arch dances There are numerous variations of this worldwide dance; it can be performed under swords, tools of the trade, plain staves, etc.

Aurresku This ceremonial dance is performed in a plaza by young Basque men and women.

Baboraschka Performed in the Czech Republic, this Bohemian national dance is in 2/4 time.

Baguettes, Danse des This dance from Brittany is done in 4/4 time.

Bandltantz This Austrian dance is performed at a wedding ceremony in which ribbons are plaited around a pole.

Blaize This dance around a fire is done in England to mark the two solstices.

Bolero Done in 3/4 time, this Spanish dance is performed by a couple with castanets.

Bruicheath This Scottish battle dance is done by two men with knife and shield to the music of the bagpipes.

Calata An Italian town dance done in triple time.

Cana This Spanish "couple dance" of Moorish origin is done in Andalusia.

Can-can A whole family of dances, the most famous being the vulgar type done in Paris for U.S. sightseers.

Charleston A popular dance in U.S. ballrooms in the 1920s.

Conga This 2/4 march is named after a large Cuban drum and is done in a street procession during Carnival.

Cordon, Baile del This Catalonian ribbon dance is done around a pole.

Dagger dance A man's solo dance done in Georgia to the sounds of an accordion or balalaika.

Dervish dance Usually done in religious communities in Turkey and Arabia, it is intended to induce a state of ecstasy.

Doulukka A dance of sacrifice to Sudanese river gods.

Epilenios This Greek "Dance of the Winepress" mimes the creation of wine.

Ezpata dantza A sword dance with the famous Basque high kicks.

Fan dance This Japanese dance uses two fans to suggest different objects through movement.

Fandango A Spanish dance for two people done in a lively 3/4 or 6/8 time.

Fox-trot This congregational shuffle is used in modern ballrooms in a 4/4 two-step.

Gallegada A Spanish couple dance done in bright costumes and castanets.

Gato, El Called "The Cat" in Argentina, this is a rapid 3/4-time dance done by couples who at times recite verses of poetry to each other.

Godalet dantza A lively 2/4-time dance done around a half-filled glass in the Pyrenees.

Guabina In Colombia this 2/4-time dance in a quick tempo is accomplished by couples with a kerchief held between them.

Highland fling This Scottish dance is done by four or eight men standing on one leg while moving the other backward and forward.

Hora A 6/8-time dance done in large circles, often at weddings in Rumania.

Hula This is a general term for a Hawaiian performance that includes dancing, gestures, and chanting.

Jibiri, Le This round dance of High Brittany is done in circles in a lively 2/4 time.

Jig An Irish couples dance done with hands on hips with legs crossing every other step.

Jitterbug A modern American dance done to syncopated jazz rhythm in nightclubs.

Jota In quick 3/4 or 3/8 time, this Spanish dance is done by couples facing each other.

Kalamajka A Czech dance done in 2/4 time by couples with their hands on hips and not touching.

Kalamantianos Performed in a circle in 7/8 time, this national dance of Greece is led by a person in the centre of the circle.

Kyndeldans This Norwegian couples dance is usually performed at weddings.

Landler Done in triple time, this Austrian alpine dance is done by couples.

Lechwallen This Swedish ring dance is performed to the music of a fiddler.

Leventikos This Greek dance is done by either two men or two women, the participants never touching.

Limbo From Trinidad comes this solo male dance done under a bar.

Listones, Danze de los This maypole dance done in Mexico is usually performed by men.

Llamddaunsio A Welsh quick jig.

Loure Done in 6/4 time, this slow country dance originated in France.

Lundu This Brazilian song-dance is done in 2/4 time.

Magilluk Accompanied by drums, women from the Celebes Islands are known to have performed this trance dance.

Maileken A German wedding dance.

Mambo This ritual dance of voodoo originates in Haiti.

Marinera This lively dance done in 3/4 time is done in Peru to the waving of handkerchiefs.

Maypole dance This rural dance is done in England to celebrate the First of Spring festival.

Mohobelo This vigorous dance is done by South African men to the sound of clapping.

Montoneros, Danza de los A harvest dance performed in Mexican churchyards.

Morna Residents of the Cape Verde Islands are known to do this dance of the islands to the tune of guitars.

Nazun In India, this Hindu-Moslem festival dance is performed by men.

Nussler In Switzerland, masked dancers perform this dance at pre-Lent festivals.

Odori This broad classification of dances is performed by geisha girls in Japan during religious festivals.

Ohorodnik This Ukrainian wedding dance is performed by 12 dancers.

Okina A Japanese ritual dance symbolizing long life.

Otuhaka In Tonga, this dance is done by oiled and scented dancers who remain seated and perform elaborate hand gestures.

Paoa This solo woman's dance is done in Tahiti.

Pasillo This "short-step" Latin American dance is done in 3/8 or 3/4 time.

Pelele, Lou A lively dance done at French weddings.

Pericote This courting dance from northern Spain is done in 2/4 time.

Piler-lan In France, this couple's dance is done in 4/4 time.

Polka This dance, originally from Poland and Czechoslovakia and done in 2/4 time, is now performed in 3/4 time.

Polo This Andalusian gypsy dance from Spain is usually done in 3/8 time.

Punto Done in 6/8 time, this dance for engaged couples originates from Panama.

Raigoe This Japanese ritual dance is done for the initiation of young unmarried men.

Rachenitza This Bulgarian dance is usually done in 7/16 time.

Renningen A dance for Swiss couples in 4/4 time.

Ridée This French round dance is done in either 2/4 or 4/4 time.

Rueda This Castilian round dance from Spain is done in 2/4 time.

Rumba From Cuba comes this dance to the beat of a syncopated African rhythm in 2/4 time.

Samba This Brazilian dance is done in 2/4 time in a melody in a major key.

Sanjuanito A chief dance in Ecuador, the San-juanito is done in a minor key in 2/4 time.

Sarba This Romanian dance is done by young men whose speed increases as the dance progresses.

Satacek Performed by couples, this circle dance is done in 3/4 and 2/4 time.

Siebensprung A German dance in 2/4 time for couples.

Sjalaskuttan This Finlandian "Seal's Jump" is done in 3/8 time by couples.

Strathspey This is a simplified version of the Scottish Highland dance done in 4/4 time.

Tamborito Popular during Carnival, this Pana-manian dance is done in a lively 2/4 time.

Tarantella This courting dance of southern Italy is done in 3/8 time.

Tirana Derived from the fandango, this Spanish dance is done to the accompaniment of a guitar in 6/8 time.

Traipse This slow dance from the West Indies is done during fiesta time to a calypso tune.

Trata This chain dance is done by girls in Greece on Easter Tuesday.

Treilles, danse des This French "Garland Dance" is done in a lively 6/8 time by dancers holding garlands over their heads.

Trescone Done in a quick 6/8 time at harvest time, this Italian dance is performed by four couples.

Tsamikos In Greece, this chain dance by men and women is performed in 3/8 time.

Ula-no-weo This standing hula is done in Hawaii in a fast tempo.

Vava vadmol A Swedish dance where lines of women and men "weave" between each other, showing the movement of the weaver's shuttle.

Vingaker danseu This Swedish courting dance is performed by two girls and one man.

Weggis dance This round dance from Switzerland is for couples.

Yumari In Mexico, this ritual dance of the Tarahumara Indians is performed in the Chihuahua mountains.

Zamacueca In Chile, this song-dance of Spanish origin is done in 6/8 time.

Zevensprong, De Meaning "seven jumps," this amusement dance from the Netherlands and Belgium is done in a circle to 4/4-time music.

FADS

Barbie doll 1959

Beanie babies 1990s

Bell bottoms were hailed by *Esquire* in 1966 as a vital addition to any modern guy's wardrobe

Big Brother 2000

Bikini 1946

Brassiere 1913

Bungee jumping 1980s

Campaign ribbons 1990s

Chippendales 1979

Crayons 1902

Day-Glo 1933 (as fad in 1960s)

Designer jeans
  Jordache 1977
  Gloria Vanderbilt 1979
  Calvin Klein 1980

Digital watch 1980s

Elevator shoes 1953

Fantasy Football 1990s

Feng Shui late 1990s

Filofaxes 1990s

Frisbee 1960s

Happy face (on stickers, buttons, T-shirts, patches, posters) 1960s

Hawaiian shirts first invented in 1930s (rayon), and still popular today

Hula Hoop 1958

Jogging 1968

Lava lamps 1964

Lego 1955

Legwarmers early 1980s

Miniskirt 1965

Mr. Potato Head 1952

Muzak 1922

Pet rocks 1970s

Pokémon 2000

Polyester invented in 1953. Double-knit polyester invented in 1974

Pong, the first computer game, was invented in 1972

Ronco! and **Popeil** products (Veg-O-Matic, Mr. Microphone, Miracle Broom, Pocket Fisherman, etc.) 1969

Rubik's Cube 1979

Scooters 2001

Scrabble 1948

Shell Suits mid-1980s

Singing Fish 2001

Star Wars 1977

Tamagotchi Japanese computer baby or pet 1997

Teddy bear 1902

Text messaging 2001

Trainers

Tupperware 1945

TV dinners 1954

Waterbed 1969

MILITARY BATTLESHIPS AND OTHER SHIPS

The British had a certain flair for naming their battleships and battlecruisers. The United States, however, did not. While the Royal Navy mined mythology and history for stirring appellations for its warships, the United States merely looked to the states of the Union. Here are some examples of the Royal Navy names:

Dreadnought (1906)
Bellerophon (1907)
Collingwood (1907)
Indomitable (1907)
Inflexible (1907)
Invincible (1907; sunk 1916)
Superb (1907)
Temeraire (1907)
St. Vincent (1908)
Indefatigable (1909; sunk 1916)
Neptune (1909)
Vanguard (1909; sunk 1917)
Colossus (1910)
Hercules (1910)
Lion (1910)
Orion (1910)
Australia (1911)
Centurion (1911)
Conqueror (1911)
King George (1911)
Monarch (1911)
New Zealand (1911)
Princess Royal (1911)
Thunderer (1911)
Ajax (1912)
Audacious (1912)
Iron Duke (1912)
Marlborough (1912)
Queen Mary (1912; sunk 1916)
Agincourt (1913)
Benbow (1913)

Canada (1913)
Emperor of India (1913)
Erin (1913)
Queen Elizabeth (1913)
Tiger (1913)
Warspite (1913)
Barham (1914; sunk 1941)
Royal Oak (1914)
Valiant (1914)
Malaya (1915)
Resolution (1915)
Revenge (1915)
Royal Sovereign (1915)
Courageous (1916)
Furious (1916)
Glorious (1916)
Ramillies (1916)
Renown (1916)
Repulse (1916; sunk 1941)
Hood (1918)
Nelson (1925)
Rodney (1925)
King George V (1939)
Prince of Wales (1939; sunk 1941)
Anson (1940)
Duke of York (1940)
Howe (1940)
Vanguard (1944)

The era of the great battleships was relatively short—from around the turn of the century to World War II—after which the aircraft carrier became the most powerful ship on the oceans. The U.S. aircraft carrier names are not much better than those of its battleships, although there are a few interesting ones.

Midway Class
 Midway

Forrestal Class
 Forrestal
 Saratoga

Kitty Hawk Class
 Kitty Hawk
 Constellation
 America

John F. Kennedy Class
  John F. Kennedy

Enterprise Class
  Enterprise

Nimitz Class
  Nimitz
  Dwight D. Eisenhower
  Carl Vinson
  Theodore Roosevelt
  Abraham Lincoln
  George Washington
  John C. Stennis
  United States

But when it came to submarines, the U.S. began to get a little more creative:

Lafayette Class
  Alexander Hamilton
  Woodrow Wilson

James Madison Class
  James Madison
  Tecumseh
  Daniel Boone
  John C. Calhoun
  Ulysses S. Grant
  Von Steuben
  Casimir Pulaski
  Stonewall Jackson

Benjamin Franklin Class
  Benjamin Franklin
  Simon Bolivar
  Kamehameha
  George Bancroft
  Lewis and Clark
  James K. Polk
  George C. Marshall
  Henry L. Stimson
  George Washington Carver
  Francis Scott Key
  Mariano G. Vallejo
  Will Rogers

Permit Class
  Flasher

Greenling
Gato
Haddock

Sturgeon Class
  Sturgeon
  Whale
  Tautog
  Grayling
  Pogy
  Aspro
  Sunfish
  Pargo
  Puffer
  Ray
  Sand Lance
  Lapon
  Gurnard
  Hammerhead
  Guitarro
  Hawkbill
  Bergall
  Spadefish
  Seahorse
  Finback
  Pintado
  Flying Fish
  Trepang
  Bluefish
  Drum
  Acherfish
  Silversides
  William H. Bates
  Batfish
  Tunny
  Parche
  Cavalia
  L. Mendel Rivers
  Richard B. Russell

The remaining submarines are named after U.S. cities.

MILITARY AIRCRAFT

U.S. Attack Helicopters

Some U.S. attack helicopters are named after Native American tribes:

UH-1D/N *Iroquois*
OH-58 *Combat Scout*
RA H-66 *Comanche*
CH-47 *Chinook*
CH46 *Sea Knight*
AH-64 *Apache*
UH-60 *Black Hawk*
CH-53 *Sea Stallion*
S-61 *Seaking*
SH-60 *Seahawk*

U.S. Jet Fighter Planes

Jet fighter planes are given a letter and number designation, and most are also given a name appropriate for the mission they are designed to perform.

A-10 *Thunderbolt* Antiarmour/close support
F-111 Attack plane
A-6 *Intruder* 2-seat, carrier-based
EA-6B *Prowler* Electronic warfare
E-2 *Hawkeye* Carrier-borne aircraft
F-14A *Tomcat* Ship-borne interceptor
F-14B/D *Tomcat* Fighter-bomber
GD EF-111 *Raven* Electronic warfare
C-5 *Galaxy* Heavy-lift transport
C-130 *Hercules* Transport
C-141 *StarLifter* Transport
F-16A/B *Fighting Falcon* Fighter-bomber
F-104 *Starfighter* Fighter-bomber
F-117 *Nighthawk* Stealth attack
P-3 *Orion* Transport
S-3 *Viking* Antisubmarine
U-2R Reconnaissance
F-22 (not yet named) Advanced tactical fighter
A-4 *Skyhawk* Attack training
KC-10 *Extender* Tanker/transport

C-17 *Globemaster* Long-range transport
F-4 *Phantom* Multirole fighter
F-15A/C *Eagle* Air-superiority fighter
F-15E *Strike Eagle* Strike fighter-bomber
F/A-18 *Hornet* Fighter-bomber
AV-8B *Harrier* Close support
B-2 *Spirit* Stealth bomber
F-5 *Freedom Fighter* Tactical fighter
F-5E *Tiger* Tactical fighter
B-1B *Lancer* Strategic heavy bomber

American armed services personnel have always nicknamed enemy aircraft. Below are the official letter-number designations followed by the American nicknames of the aircraft.

Russian Helicopters

Mi-8 "Hip"
Mi-24 "Hind"
Mi-28 "Havoc"

Russian Jets

MiG-21 "Fishbed" Tactical fighter
MiG-23 "Flogger" Tactical fighter
MiG "Foxbat" Reconnaissance
MiG-29 "Fulcrum" Multirole fighter
MiG-31 "Foxhound" Long-range interceptor

Su-17-17 "Fitter" Fighter-bomber
Su-24 "Fencer" All-weather fighter
Su-25 "Frogfoot" Support
Su-27 "Flanker" Air-superiority fighter

Tu-16 "Badger" Multirole bomber
Tu-22 "Blinder" Missile carrier
Tu-22M "Backfire" Bomber-striker
Tu-95 "Bear" Multirole strategy
Tu-160 "Blackjack" Strategic bomber

Chinese Fighters

Nanchang A/Q-5 "Fantan"
Shenyang J-8 "Finback"

BRITISH MILITARY AIRCRAFT

RAF AIRCRAFT

OFFENSIVE

Harrier GR7/T10
Jaguar GR1B/GR3/T2A
Tornado GR1/GR1B/GR4

DEFENSIVE

Sentry AEW1
Hawk T1A
Tornado F3

RECONNAISANCE AND MARITIME PATROL

Canberra PR9/T4
Nimrod MR2
Nimrod R1
Tornado GR1A/GR4A

TANKER AND TRANSPORT

Hercules C1/C3/C4/C5
Tristar
VC10 C1K/K3/K4

TRANSPORT

Bae 125 CC3
Bae 146 CC2
Squirrel HCC1

HELICOPTERS

Chinook HC2

Puma HC1
Merlin HC3
Sea King HAR3
Wessex HC2

TRAINING AIRCRAFT

Bulldog T1
Dominie T1
Firefly
Hawk T1
Jetstream T1
Tucano T1
Tutor
Griffin HT1
Squirrel HT1

FUTURE

C-17A Globemaster III
Eurofighter
Joint Strike Fighter

MUSICAL INSTRUMENTS BY CATEGORY

Idiophones Sound is produced by a vibration of the instrument itself (castanets, cymbal, bell).

Membranophones Sound is produced by a vibrating skin or membrane (tambourine, drum).

Chordophones Sound is produced by a vibrating string (violin, harp).

Keyboard instruments Sound produced by striking a key on a board (piano, organ).

Aerophones Sound is produced by the vibration of a column of air (trumpet, flute, harmonica).

Electronic instruments Sound produced or manipulated by an electronic device (synthesizers).

IDIOPHONES

Bells Made from bronze or other metals, bells are struck by either an internal or external clapper. Can be mechanically operated.

Cabasa A South American rattle. It is cylindrical and strung with steel beads on the outside.

Castanets Typically used by flamenco dancers, they are palm-sized shells attached by rope and clapped together to mark a rhythm.

Chimes Metal blocks struck with a beater.

Claves Round wooden sticks knocked together to create a rhythm.

Cymbals Dish-shaped metal discs clashed together or struck with a stick.

Glockenspiel Similar to a xylophone, though often handheld.

Gong A metal disc suspended from its rim and struck by a beater on the central "boss."

Guiro A hollow gourd with deep scratches, against which forklike tines are rubbed to produce a soft rasping sound.

Handbells Small handheld bells.

Hi-hat A pair of cymbals operated by a pedal mechanism.

Jew's harp or **Jaw harp** A small metal-framed instrument with a narrow metal tongue which is plucked while the frame is held in the player's mouth.

Maracas South American rattles traditionally made of hollow gourds partially filled with seeds.

Marimba An African form of the xylophone.

Rattle A handheld wooden instrument with one or more tongues that snap against a cog when it is spun to produce a loud clatter.

Sansa or **thumb piano** Metal tongues attached to a resonating box, which are plucked with the thumbs. South American.

Schleffele A Swiss version of castanets.

Slotted drum An African instrument made from a hollowed tree trunk. It is played by beating with large sticks.

Temple blocks or **mu-yus** Semihollow Chinese blocks struck with a beater.

Triangle A steel bar, triangular-shaped and struck with a steel beater.

Tubular bells Suspended metal tubes struck with a beater.

Vibraphone Similar to the xylophone, but with metal bars and an electrical mechanism to create a vibrato effect.

Xylophone Wooden bars attached to a frame. The bars are arranged by pitch and struck with sticks or hammers. Gourds or other resonating boxes are sometimes attached under the bars.

MEMBRANOPHONES

Bass drum A large drum which lies on its side, played by a felt-covered beater attached to a foot pedal. Often part of a drum set.

Bayan and Tabla Two North Indian single-skinned drums used together.

Bongos Small single-headed drums played with the hands.

Darabukka An Arabic drum, single-headed and cup- or goblet-shaped.

Floor tom A large tom-tom with a deep note. Part of a drum set.

Kalengo The Nigerian "talking" drum, similar to the Japanese otsuzumi.

Kettledrum or **Timpanum** A kettle-shaped resonating chamber covered by a skin and tunable by a pedal mechanism.

Mridanga A South Indian drum with two membranes, both of which are struck.

Nungu A Siberian frame drum beaten with a skin-covered stick.

Odaiko A large Japanese drum played with large mallets and a lot of effort.

Otsuzumi An hourglass-shaped, double-headed Japanese drum with cords joining the wide ends, which when squeezed change the drum's pitch.

Rattle drum A small handheld Asian drum, with strings attached to the sides, each having a bead or knot that strikes the drum as the handle is rotated.

Snare drum A double-headed drum with a wire snare on the underside which vibrates when the drum is beaten. Often part of a drum set.

Steel drum A shaped oil drum lid from the West Indies, struck with a beater. The surface is divided into several areas, each of which has a different pitch.

Tabor An old European handheld drum beaten single-handed with a stick.

Tambourine A shallow wooden hoop with a membrane stretched over it and pairs of small metal plates set into the rim. Shaken or struck.

Tom-toms Small high-pitched drums often used in the rock or jazz drum set.

CHORDOPHONES

Autoharp Similar to the zither but with chord bars which hold down all the strings of the chord to be played. Played by strumming.

Balalaika A Russian three-stringed lute.

Bandura A Ukrainian lute/zither combination.

Banjo An American folk instrument with a round body and a long neck, having five to nine strings.

Beganna An Ethiopian lyre.

Biwa A Japanese short-necked, four-stringed lute.

Bouzuki A Greek lute.

Cello The baritone of the violin family, played upright with a bow.

Celtic harp An Irish harp with a curved pillar.

Charango A South American lute, traditionally made with an armadillo carapace for the body.

Chyn or Qin An ancient Chinese seven-stringed zither still used today.

Cittern A 16th-century English instrument similar to a lute.

Double bass The deepest member of the violin family, played upright with a bow or plucked for rhythmic effect in jazz and folk music.

Dulcimer or **Hammer dulcimer** A flat, shallow sound box over which ten or more groups of strings are stretched. Played by striking the strings with small hammers.

Fiddle A bowed stringed instrument similar to the violin, used predominantly for folk music and dancing.

Guitar A long-necked, figure-eight-shaped, fretted, six-stringed instrument with a soundhole in the top third of the body.

Harp A triangular wooden frame consisting of an upright pillar, a top part called a neck, and a joining soundboard. The soundboard and the neck are strung with as many as forty-six strings, which are plucked.

Kit A tiny European violin from the 17th and 18th centuries.

Kithara An ancient Greek lyrelike instrument.

Koto A Japanese thirteen-stringed zither.

Lute Descended from the Arabic al'ud, the European lute has a half-pear-shaped body, a wide, flat neck, and a pegbox bent backwards from the top of the neck. The lute is fretted and the strings are finger-plucked.

Lyre A soundbox with two arm extensions connected by a crossbar, from which strings run back to the body, sometimes over a bridge. Plucked.

Mandolin An Italian lute.

Psaltery Similar to the dulcimer, but the strings are plucked. Part of the zither family.

Qanun An Arabic psaltery.

Rajao A 19th-century Portuguese lute.

Rebec A European bowed stringed instrument, a forerunner of the modern violin.

Sarangi An Indian fiddle.

Shamisen A long-necked, three-stringed Japanese lute, plucked with a large ivory or bone plectrum.

Sitar A northern Indian multistringed fretted lute. Intrinsic to Indian music.

Spanish guitar *See* Guitar.

Tambura An Indian lute with four unfretted strings, each playing a single note.

Tanbur A Persian long-necked lute.

Ud An Arabic precursor of the lute.

Ukulele A Hawaiian/Portuguese-derived, four-stringed, half-sized guitar.

Vihuela A small guitar from Spain with six pairs of strings.

Vina An Indian instrument with seven strings; four are melody strings, the rest being single-pitched drones. The strings are attached to a fretted bamboo stick attached to a number of gourd resonators.

Viol Resembling a violin, the viol has six strings and frets like a guitar and is played with a bow. Descended from the vihuela.

Viola Slightly larger than the violin, this is the alto of the family.

Violin The smallest and highest-pitched member of the violin family, all of which are four-stringed and fretless. Played with a bow.

Zither A flat, shallow soundbox, over which are stretched a number of melody strings over frets, and a dozen or more accompaniment strings. Played with both hands, the strings are usually plucked.

KEYBOARD INSTRUMENTS

Accordion A bellows connected to two boxlike boards, one with a keyboard to play treble notes, the other with buttons to play chords and bass. The boards contain reeds which sound as the air from the squeezed bellows blows past them.

Celeste Resembles a piano, with a series of tuned steel bars that are struck by hammers connected to a keyboard.

Clavichord A rectangular box with keys on one long side, which when played strike strings set parallel to the keyboard.

Concertina Similar to the accordion, but smaller and simpler.

Grand piano The strings in this large piano are horizontal.

Harpsichord Similar in shape to a grand piano, but the strings are plucked rather than struck when a key is pressed. Each key sounds as many as five strings.

Hurdy-gurdy/barrel organ A folk instrument in which a crank turns a wooden wheel, which rubs across a set of strings that are stopped at different pitches by a keyboard mechanism.

Organ A system of keyboards and foot pedals, together with a series of stops, which allow air from a bellows to pass through ranks of pipes to produce sound. The longer the pipe, the deeper its pitch.

Piano The keys cause hammers to strike strings inside the piano body. There are also at least two foot pedals that either sustain or dampen the sound produced.

Spinet A small harpsichord in which the single strings are set diagonally to the keyboard.

Upright piano A smaller piano with vertical strings.

Virginal A small harpsichord with single strings running parallel to the keyboard.

Aerophones

Alphorn A wooden tube five to thirteen feet long, used by European Alpine herdsmen as a signal.

Bagpipe Several reed pipes attached to a windbag. One is the blowpipe to get air into the bag; one is the melody, which has finger holes; and one is a continuous drone. The bagpipe is held under the arm while being played.

Bansor A Pakistani flute.

Bass clarinet Similar to a clarinet, but deeper-pitched and with an upturned metal bell.

Bassoon The bass of the oboe family, nearly nine feet long but double-backed on itself.

Bugle A conically bored, curved oval-shaped brass instrument without keys.

Clarinet A woodwind instrument with a single reed set on a mouthpiece at one end of a tube, with keys covering holes down its length.

Cor anglais A mellow member of the oboe family, with a bulb-shaped bell.

Cornet A small trumpet with three piston valves, a cup-shaped mouthpiece, and a conical bore which widens out towards the bell.

Didgeridoo An Aboriginal hollow wooden tube blown through one end.

Double bassoon The lowest member of the oboe family. Eighteen feet long, it is doubled back four times.

Euphonium A brass baritone similar to a tuba.

Fipple flute A flute blown from one end, in which a small plug—the fipple—allows only a narrow slit for air to pass through. A small hole with a sharp edge is made below the fipple, and this causes the air to vibrate as it passes down the body of the instrument.

Flageolet A small fipple flute.

Flugelhorn A brass instrument similar to a cornet.

Flute The modern flute is a wood or metal tube about two feet long, closed at one end with an opening in the wall near the closed end. There are holes along the length of the body which can be covered by keys or fingers. It is played sideways by blowing across the opening.

French horn A conically bored brass tube, coiled into a spiral, with a wide bell and a cone-shaped mouthpiece and three valves.

Harmonica/mouth organ A small, handheld metal box containing pairs of free reeds which vibrate as air is blown past them.

Kazoo A blown membranophone consisting of a small tube with a slitlike hole covered with a thin membrane which buzzes when the instrument is blown.

Natural trumpet A straight or curved metal tube, without holes or valves, with a flared bell.

Nose flute A flute played by nose instead of mouth.

Oboe A double-reed woodwind with a conical bore and a flared bell.

Ocarina An oval or globe-shaped body, with finger holes and a whistlelike mouthpiece.

Panpipes Cut reeds of different lengths, closed at one end. The player blows across the open end.

Piccolo A small flute with a high range.

Quena An Andean reed-pipe flute.

Recorder The commonest fipple flute, it has seven to nine finger holes in the front and one thumb hole in the back. Available in different sizes and pitches.

Saxophone A mouthpiece and single reed like a clarinet, attached to a conically bored metal body with a key arrangement like an oboe and an upturned bell. Available in different sizes and ranges.

Serpent A curved, snakelike, leather-covered

wooden tube with a conical bore, six finger holes, and a cup-shaped mouthpiece.

Shakuhachi A Japanese flute with four finger holes and one thumb hole.

Shanai An Indian oboe.

Shawm A Near Eastern and African precursor of the oboe.

Sheng A Chinese mouth organ with seventeen pipes, each with a reed, inserted into a wooden wind box.

Sho A Japanese version of the sheng.

Shofar An Ancient Hebrew animal horn.

Soprano saxophone The smallest and highest-pitched saxophone, with a straight body.

Sousaphone A large bass tuba with a very wide bell.

Trombone A brass tube with a cup-shaped mouthpiece and a flared bell. There is a brass sliding section which takes the place of valves.

Trumpet A coiled brass tube, which only widens near the bell, with three valves and a cup-shaped mouthpiece.

Tuba A coiled brass bass instrument, with a very wide conical bore and bell, with three to five valves and a cup-shaped mouthpiece. Available in various sizes and ranges.

Zummara A Bedouin double clarinet.

Zurna A Turkish oboe.

ELECTRONIC INSTRUMENTS

Instruments in which the sound is either changed by means of electronic devices such as amplifiers and loudspeakers, or actually produced by electronic devices. **Electric guitars** are the commonest amplified electronic instrument. **Synthesizers** make music electronically and can produce an orchestra of sound, and more, from a keyboard.

MOST FREQUENTLY PERFORMED OPERAS

Opera	Composer	Premiere
Aida	Giuseppe Verdi	Cairo; 1871
Amahl and the Night Visitors	Gian Carlo Menotti	1951
Amelia Goes to the Ball	Gian Carlo Menotti	1937
Andrea Chenier	Umberto Giordano	La Scala, Milan; 1896
Ariadne auf Naxos	Richard Strauss	Hoftheatre, Stuttgart; 1912
Atys	Jean Baptiste Lully	Paris; 1676
Ballad of Baby Doe, The	Douglas Moore	1956
Barber of Seville, The	Gioacchino Rossini	Teatro Argentina, Rome; 1816
Bartered Bride, The	Bedrich Smetana	National Theatre, Prague; 1866
Boris Godunov	Modest Mussorgsky	Maryinsky Theatre, St. Petersburg; 1874
Cardillac	Paul Hindemith	Staatsoper, Dresden; 1926
Carmen	Georges Bizet	Opéra-Comique, Paris; 1875
Castor et Pollux	Jean-Philippe Rameau	Paris Opéra; 1737
Cavalleria Rusticana	Pietro Mascagni	Teatro Costanzi, Rome; 1890
Child and the Spells, The	Maurice Ravel	Monte Carlo Opera; 1925
Cosi Fan Tutte	Wolfgang Amadeus Mozart	Burg Theatre, Vienna; 1790
Cradle Will Rock, The	Marc Blitzstein	1937
Crucible, The	Robert Ward	1961
Cunning Little Vixen, The	Leos Janacek	National Theatre, Brno, Moravia; 1924
Daughter of the Regiment, The	Gaetano Donizetti	Opéra-Comique, Paris; 1841
Der Freischutz	Carl Maria von Weber	Schauspielhaus, Berlin; 1821
Der junge Lord	Hans Werner Henze	Deutsche Oper, Berlin; 1965
Der Prinz von Homberg	Hans Werner Henze	Staatsoper, Hamburg; 1960
Der Rosenkavalier	Richard Strauss	Dresden Opera, Germany; 1911
Devils of Loudun, The	Krzysztof Penderecki	Staatsoper, Hamburg; 1969
Dialogues of the Carmelites	Francis Poulenc	La Scala, Milan; 1957
Dido and Aeneas	Henry Purcell	London; 1689

Opera	Composer	Premiere
Die Fledermaus	Johann Strauss the Younger	Theatre an der Wien, Vienna; 1874
Die Frau ohne Schatten	Richard Strauss	Staatsoper, Vienna; 1919
Die Meistersinger von Nurnburg	Richard Wagner	Royal Court Theatre, Munich; 1868
Die Soldaten	Bernd Alois Zimmermann	Cologne Opera House; 1965
Die tote Stadt	Erich Wolfgang Korngold	Hamburg & Cologne; 1920
Don Carlos	Giuseppe Verdi	Paris Opera; 1867
Don Giovanni	Wolfgang Amadeus Mozart	National Theatre, Prague; 1787
Don Pasquale	Gaetano Donizetti	Theatre des Italiens, Paris; 1843
Duke Bluebeard's Castle	Bela Bartok	Budapest Opera; 1918
Einstein on the Beach	Philip Glass	1976
Elektra	Richard Strauss	Dresden Opera; 1909
Elixir of Love, The	Gaetano Donizetti	Teatro della Canobbiana, Milan; 1832
Emperor Jones, The	Louis Greunberg	1933
Ernani	Giuseppe Verdi	Teatro la Fenice, Venice; 1844
Eugene Onegin	Pyotr Ilich Tchaikovsky	Moscow; 1879
Falstaff	Giuseppe Verdi	La Scala, Milan; 1893
Faust	Charles Gounod	Theatre-Lyrique, Paris; 1859
Fidelio	Ludwig van Beethoven	Theatre an der Wien, Vienna; 1805
Flying Dutchman, The	Richard Wagner	Dresden, Germany; 1843
Force of Destiny, The	Giuseppe Verdi	Bolshoi Theatre, St. Petersburg; 1862
Four Saints in Three Acts	Virgil Thomson	1934
Gianni Schicchi	Giacomo Puccini	The Metropolitan, New York; 1918
Girl of the Golden West, The	Giacomo Puccini	The Metropolitan, New York; 1910
Hansel und Gretel	Engelbert Humperdinck	Hoftheater, Weimar; 1893
Il Trovatore	Giuseppe Verdi	Teatro Apollo, Rome; 1853
Italian Girl in Algiers, The	Gioacchino Rossini	Teatro San Benedetto, Venice; 1813
Jenufa	Leos Janacek	National Theatre, Brno, Moravia; 1904
Jonny spielt auf	Ernst Krenek	Stadttheater Leipzig; 1927
Julius Caesar	George Frideric Handel	King's Theatre, London; 1724
King Priam	Michael Tippett	Covent Garden, London; 1962
King's Henchman, The	Deems Taylor	1927

Opera	Composer	Premiere
La Boheme	Giacomo Puccini	Teatro Regio, Turin; 1896
La Gioconda	Amilcare Ponchielli	La Scala, Milan; 1876
La Traviata	Giuseppe Verdi	Teatro la Fenice, Venice; 1853
Lady Macbeth of the Mtsensk District	Dmitri Shostakovich	Maly Opera, Leningrad; 1934
Lakme	Leo Delibes	Opéra-Comique, Paris; 1883
Le Coq d'Or	Nicolai Rimsky-Korsakov	Moscow; 1909
Les Huguenots	Giacomo Meyerbeer	Paris Opéra; 1836
Les Troyens	Hector Berlioz	Theatre Lyrique, Paris; 1863
Lohengrin	Richard Wagner	Weimar Opera, Germany; 1850
Louise	Gustave Charpentier	Opéra-Comique, Paris; 1900
Love for Three Oranges	Sergei Prokofiev	Auditorium, Chicago; 1921
Lucia di Lammermoor	Gaetano Donizetti	Teatro San Carlo, Naples; 1835
Lulu	Alban Berg	Zurich; 1937
Macbeth	Giuseppe Verdi	Teatro alla Pergola, Florence; 1847
Madame Butterfly	Giacomo Puccini	La Scala, Milan; 1904
Magic Flute, The	Wolfgang Amadeus Mozart	Theatre auf der Wieden, Vienna; 1791
Manon	Jules Massenet	Opéra-Comique, Paris; 1884
Manon Lescaut	Giacomo Puccini	Teatro Regio, Turin; 1893
Marriage of Figaro, The	Wolfgang Amadeus Mozart	Burg Theatre, Vienna; 1786
Martha	Friedrich von Flotow	Karntthnerthor Theatre, Vienna; 1847
Masked Ball, A	Giuseppe Verdi	Teatro Apollo, Rome; 1859
Mathis der Maler	Paul Hindemith	Stadt Theatre, Zurich; 1938
Mefistofele	Arrigo Boito	La Scala, Milan; 1868
Merry Mount	Howard Hanson	1934
Merry Widow, The	Franz Lehar	Theatre an der Wien, Vienna; 1905
Merry Wives of Windsor, The	Otto Nicolai	Berlin Hofoper; 1849
Midsummer Marriage, The	Michael Tippett	Covent Garden, London; 1955
Mignon	Ambroise Thomas	Opéra-Comique, Paris; 1866
Montezuma	Roger Sessions	1964
Moses und Aron	Arnold Schoenberg	Zurich; 1957
Nixon in China	John Adams	1987

Opera	Composer	Premiere
Norma	Vincenzo Bellini	La Scala, Milan; 1831
Orfeo	Claudio Monteverdi	Palazzo Ducale, Mantua; 1607
Orfeo ed Euridice	Christoph Willibald Gluck	Vienna; 1762
Otello	Giuseppe Verdi	La Scala, Milan; 1887
I Pagliacci	Ruggero Leoncavallo	Theatro del Verme; 1892
Pal Joey	Richard Rodgers and Lorenz Hart	1940
Parsifal	Richard Wagner	Bayreuth; 1882
Pelleas et Melisande	Claude Debussy	Opéra-Comique, Paris; 1902
Peter Grimes	Benjamin Britten	Sadler's Wells, London; 1945
Porgy and Bess	George Gershwin	1934
Postcard from Morocco	Dominick Argento	1971
Prince Igor	Alexander Borodin	Maryinsky Theatre, St. Petersburg; 1890
Queen of Spades, The	Pyotr Ilich Tchaikovsky	Maryinsky Theatre, St. Petersburg; 1890
Rake's Progress, The	Igor Stravinsky	Teatro la Fenice, Venice; 1951
Regina	Marc Blitzstein	1949
Riders to the Sea	Ralph Vaughan Williams	Royal College of Music, London; 1937
Rigoletto	Giuseppe Verdi	Teatro la Fenice, Venice; 1951
Ring of the Nibelung, The	Richard Wagner	
(Das Rheingold)		Munich Opera; 1869
(Die Walkure)		Munich Opera; 1870
(Siegfried)		Bayreuth; 1876
(Gotterdammerung)		Bayreuth; 1876
Rise and Fall of the City of Mahagonny, The	Kurt Weill	Neves Theatre, Leipzig; 1930
Romeo et Juliette	Charles Gounod	Theatre-Lyrique, Paris; 1867
Rusalka	Antonin Dvorak	National Theatre, Prague; 1901
Salome	Richard Strauss	Dresden Opera; 1905
Samson et Dalila	Camille Saint-Saens	Hoftheatre, Weimar; 1977
Savitri	Gustav Holst	Wellington Hall, London; 1916
Simon Boccanegra	Giuseppe Verdi	Teatro la Fenice, Venice; 1857

Opera	Composer	Premiere
Six Characters in Search of an Author	Hugo Weisgall	1957
Sleepwalker, The	Vincenzo Bellini	Teatro Carcano, Milan; 1831
Spanish Hour, The	Maurice Ravel	Opéra-Comique, Paris; 1911
Susannah	Carlisle Floyd	1955
Tales of Hoffmann, The	Jacques Offenbach	Opéra-Comique, Paris; 1881
Tannhauser	Richard Wagner	Dresden Opera; 1845
Taverner	Peter Maxwell Davies	Covent Garden, London; 1972
Tender Land, The	Aaron Copland	1954
Threepenny Opera, The	Kurt Weill	Theatre am Schiffbauerdamm, Berlin; 1928
Tosca	Giacomo Puccini	Teatro Costanzi, Rome; 1900
Transatlantic	George Antheil	1930
Tristan und Isolde	Richard Wagner	Munich Opera, Germany; 1865
Trouble in Tahiti	Leonard Bernstein	1952
Turandot	Giacomo Puccini	La Scala, Milan; 1926
Turn of the Screw, The	Benjamin Britten	Teatro la Fenice, Venice; 1954
Vanessa	Samuel Barber	1958
War and Peace	Sergei Prokofiev	Moscow; 1945
Werther	Jules Massenet	Hofoper, Vienna; 1892
Wozzeck	Alban Berg	Berlin Staatsoper, Germany; 1925

PHOBIAS

Phobias are compulsive acts of avoidance by a person of an object (organic or otherwise), situation, or action due to excessive and unrealistic fear. The suffix "phobia" (from the Greek *phobos,* meaning "fear") is used with a Latin, or more commonly Greek, word to denote a specific phobia.

This list is not comprehensive, for there could be as many phobias as there are objects or situations in the world, but it gives a sample of the most common as well as a few esoterica.

air, flying aerophobia
animals zoophobia
auroral lights auroraphobia
bacteria bacteriophobia, microphobia
beards pogonophobia
bees apiphobia, melissophobia
being alone monophobia, autophobia
being beaten rhabdophobia
being bound merinthophobia
being buried alive taphophobia
being cold frigophobia
being dirty automysophobia
being looked at scopophobia
being scratched amychophobia
being touched haphephobia
birds ornithophobia
black people negrophobia
blood haematophobia
blushing ereuthophobia, eyrythrophobia
books bibliophobia
cancer carcinophobia, cancerophobia
cats ailurophobia, gatophobia
certain names onomatophobia
cheerfulness cherophobia
chickens alektorophobia
childbirth tocophobia
children paediphobia
cholera cholerophobia
churches ecclesiaphobia
clouds nephophobia
cold cheimatophobia
colour chromatophobia
crossing a bridge gephyrophobia

crossing streets dromophobia
crowds demophobia, ochlophobia
crystals crystallophobia
dampness hygrophobia
darkness nyctophobia
dawn eosophobia
daylight phengophobia
death, corpse necrophobia, thanatophobia
deformity dysmorphophobia
demons demonophobia
depth bathophobia
dirt mysophobia
disease nosophobia, pathophobia
disorder ataxiophobia
dogs cynophobia
dolls pediophobia
draughts anemophobia
dreams oneirophobia
drink, alcohol potophobia
drinking dipsophobia
drugs pharmacophobia
duration chronophobia
dust amathophobia
eating phagophobia
electricity electrophobia
enclosed spaces claustrophobia
England Anglophobia
everything pantophobia
eyes ommatophobia
faeces coprophobia
failure kakorraphiaphobia
fall of manmade satellites keraunothnetophobia
fatigue kopophobia, ponophobia
fears phobophobia
feathers pteronophobia
fire pyrophobia
fish ichthyophobia
flashes selaphobia
flogging mastigophobia
flood antlophobia
flowers anthophobia
flutes aulophobia
fog homichlophobia
food sitophobia
France Francophobia
freedom eleutherophobia
fur doraphobia
germs spermophobia

ghosts phasmophobia
glass nelophobia
God theophobia
going to bed clinophobia
graves taphophobia
gravity barophobia
hair chaetophobia
heart conditions cardiophobia
heat thermophobia
heaven ouranophobia
heights acrophobia, altophobia
hell hadephobia, stygiophobia
heredity patroiophobia
high places hypsophobia
home domatophobia, oikophobia
home surroundings ecophobia
homosexuals homophobia
horses hippophobia
human beings anthropophobia
ice, frost cryophobia
ideas ideophobia
illness nosemaphobia
imperfection atelophobia
infection mysophobia
infinity apeirophobia
injections trypanophobia
insanity maniaphobia, lyssophobia
insects entomophobia
itching acarophobia, scabiophobia
jealousy zelophobia
justice dikephobia
knees genuphobia
lakes limnophobia
leaves phyllophobia
leprosy leprophobia
lice pediculophobia
lightning astraphobia
machinery mechanophobia
making false statements mythophobia
many things polyphobia
marriage gamophobia
meat carnophobia
men androphobia
metals metallophobia
meteors meteorophobia
mice musophobia
microbes bacilliphobia
mind psychophobia

mirrors eisoptrophobia
missiles ballistophobia
money chrometophobia
monsters, monstrosities teratophobia
motion kinesophobia, kinetophobia
music musicophobia
names nomatophobia
narrowness anginaphobia
needles belonophobia
neglect of duty paralipophobia
new things neophobia
night, darkness achluophobia
noise phonophobia
novelty cainophobia
nudity gymnophobia
number thirteen triskaidekaphobia, terdekaphobia
odours osmophobia
odours (body) osphresiophobia
one thing monophobia
open spaces agoraphobia
pain algophobia, odynophobia
parasites parasitophobia
passing high objects batophobia
physical love erotophobia
pins enetephobia
places topophobia
pleasure hedonophobia
points aichurophobia
poison toxiphobia
poverty peniaphobia
precipices cremnophobia
pregnancy maieusiophobia
punishment poinephobia
rain ombrophobia
reptiles batrachophobia
responsibility hypegiaphobia
ridicule katagelophobia
rivers potamophobia
robbers harpaxophobia
ruin atephobia
rust iophobia
sacred things heirophobia
Satan Satanophobia
school scholionophobia
sea thalassophobia
sea swell cymophobia
semen spermatophobia
sex genophobia

sexual intercourse coitophobia
shadows sciophobia
shock hormephobia
singing canophobia
sinning peccatophobia
sitting idle thaasophobia
skin dermatophobia
skin disease dermatosiophobia
sleep hypnophobia
slime blennophobia
smell olfactophobia
smothering, choking pnigerophobia
snakes ophidiophobia, ophiophobia
snow chionophobia
soiling rypophobia
solitude eremitophobia, eremophobia
sound akousticophobia
sourness acerophobia
speaking halophobia, phonophobia
speech lalophobia
speed tachophobia
spiders arachnophobia
standing stasophobia
standing upright stasiphobia
stars siderophobia
stealing kleptophobia
stillness eremophobia
stings cnidophobia
stooping kyphophobia
strangers, foreigners xenophobia
string linonophobia
strong light photophobia
sun heliophobia
surgical operations ergasiophobia
syphilis syphilophobia
taste geumatophobia
technology technophobia
teeth odontophobia
thinking phronemophobia
thunder brontophobia, keraunophobia
touch haptophobia
touching haphephobia, thixophobia
travel hodophobia
travelling by train siderodromophobia
trees dendrophobia
trembling tremophobia
tuberculosis phthisiophobia
vehicles amaxophobia

venereal disease cypridophobia
void kenophobia
vomiting emetophobia
walking basiphobia
wasps spheksophobia
water hydrophobia
weakness asthenophobia
wind ancraophobia
women gynophobia
words logophobia
work ergophobia
worms helminthophobia
wounds, injury traumatophobia
writing graphophobia
young girls parthenophobia

SATANIC, ANGELIC, AND WICCAN HIERARCHIES

SATANIC HIERARCHY

FIRST HIERARCHY
Lucifer chief demon
Beelzebub demon of pride
Leviathan demon of heresy
Asmodeus demon of gluttony
Balberith demon of violence, blasphemy
Astaroth demon of sloth
Verrine demon of impatience
Gressil demon of impurity
Sonneillon demon of hatred

SECOND HIERARCHY
Carreau demon of hardheartedness
Carnivean demon of obscenity
Oeillet demon of greed
Rosier demon of lust
Verrier demon of disobedience

THIRD HIERARCHY
Belias demon of arrogance
Olivier demon of cruelty
Iuvart prince of fallen angels

ANGELIC HIERARCHY

HIGHER ORDER
Cherubim angels of faith
Seraphim angels of wisdom
Ophanim angels of patience

LOWER ORDER
Power angels of mercy
Principalities angels of judgment
Dominion angels of peace
Thrones angels of goodness

ARCHANGELS
Uriel chief of angels
Raphael angel of the human spirit
Raguel avenging angel
Michael guardian angel
Sariel avenging angel
Gabriel angel of paradise
Remiel angel of souls

WICCAN HIERACHY

SPIRITUAL
Maiden
Mother
Crone

COVEN
Covan noninitiate, auditor
First Degree Witch initiate, learner
Second Degree Witch performs rituals
Third Degree Witch elder, qualified to start a coven
Priestess and Priest elected leaders of a coven
High Priestess and High Priest reelected leaders

FAMILIARS
Physical actual creatures in rapport with a witch
Astral spirit creatures taking the form of a physical creature
Elemental fundamental, or other, world spirits

WORLD CURRENCIES

Pound and pence and equivalents	Where to spend them
afghani, puls	Afghanistan
baht (or tical), satang	Thailand
balboa, centesimos	Panama
birr, cents	Ethiopia
bolivar, centimos	Venezuela
boliviano, centavos	Bolivia
cedi, pesewas	Ghana
colon, centavos	El Salvador
colon, centimos	Costa Rica
cordoba, centavos	Nicaragua
cruzeiro, centavos	Brazil
dalasi, bututs	Gambia
deutsche mark, pfennig	Germany
dinar, centimes	Algeria
dinar, dirhams	Libya
dinar, fils	Bahrain, Iraq, Jordan, Kuwait, Yemen
dinar, millimes	Tunisia
dinar, paras	Yugoslavia
dirham, centimes	Morocco
dirham, fils	United Arab Emirates
dobra, centimos	São Tomé and Principe
dollar, cents	Antigua and Barbuda, Dominica, Grenada, St. Kitts–Nevis, St. Lucia, St. Vincent, Grenadines, Australia, Bahamas, Barbados, Belize, Bermuda, Brunei, Canada, Fiji, Guyana, Jamaica, Liberia, New Zealand, Singapore, Trinidad and Tobago, United States, Zimbabwe
dong, xu	Vietnam
drachma, lepta	Greece
emalangeni, cents	Swaziland
escudo, centavos	Cape Verde, Portugal
forint, filler	Hungary
franc, centimes	Belgium, Benin, Burkina Faso, Burundi, Cameroon, Central Africa, Chad, Congo, Djibouti, Equatorial Guinea, France, Gabon, Guinea, Ivory Coast, Luxembourg, Madagascar, Mali, Niger, Rwanda, Senegal, Switzerland, Togo
gourde, centimes	Haiti
guarani, centimos	Paraguay
gulden (or guilder, florin), cents	Netherlands, Suriname
kina, toea	Papua New Guinea
kip, at	Laos
koruna, haleru	Czech Republic, Slovakia
krona, aurar (*sing*. eyrir)	Iceland

Pounds and pence and equivalents	Where to spend them
krona, ore	Sweden
krone, ore	Denmark, Norway
kwacha, ngwee	Zambia
kwacha, tambala	Malawi
kwanza, lwei	Angola
kyat, pyas	Myanmar
lat	Latvia
lek, qindarka	Albania
lempira, centavos	Honduras
leone, cents	Sierra Leone
leu, bani (*sing*. ban)	Romania
lev, stotinki	Bulgaria
lira, centesimi	Italy
lira (or pound), cents	Malta
lira, kurus	Turkey
loti, licente (*sing*. sente)	Lesotho
markka, pennia	Finland
metical, centavos	Mozambique
naira, kobo	Nigeria
ngultrum, chetrums	Bhutan
ouguiya, khoums	Mauritania
pa'anga, seniti	Tonga
pataca, avos	Macao
peseta, centimos	Spain
peso, centavos	Argentina, Chile, Colombia, Cuba, Dominican Republic, Guinea-Bissau, Mexico, Philippines
peso, centesimos	Uruguay
pound, cents	Cyprus
pound, piastres	Egypt, Lebanon, Sudan, Syria
pound, pence (*sing*. penny)	Ireland, United Kingdom
pula, thebe	Botswana
quetzal, centavos	Guatemala
rand, cents	South Africa
rial, baiza	Oman
rial, dinars	Iran
rial, fils	Yemen
riel, sen	Cambodia
ringgit, sen	Malaysia
riyal, dirhams	Qatar
riyal, halala	Saudi Arabia
ruble, kopecks	Russia
rufiyas, laari	Maldives
rupee, paise	India
rupee, cents	Mauritius, Seychelles, Sri Lanka
rupee, paisa	Nepal, Pakistan
rupiah, sen	Indonesia

Pounds and pence and equivalents	Where to spend them
schilling, groschen	Austria
shekel, agorot	Israel
shilling, cents	Kenya, Somalia, Tanzania, Uganda
sol, centavos	Peru
sucre, centavos	Ecuador
taka, paisa	Bangladesh
tala, sene	Western Samoa
tugrik, mongo	Mongolia
vatu	Vanuatu
won, chon	North Korea, South Korea
yen, sen	Japan
yuan, cents	Taiwan
yuan, fen	China
zaire, makuta (*sing.* likuta)	Zaire
zloty, groszy	Poland

WORLD LANGUAGES

Countries or regions	What to speak there
Afghanistan	Dari, Pushtu
Albania	Albanian, Greek
Algeria	Arabic, French, Berber
Andorra	Catalan, Spanish, French
Angola	Portuguese, Bantu
Antigua and Barbuda	English
Argentina	Spanish
Armenia	Armenian, Azerbaijani, Russian
Australia	English
Austria	German
Azerbaijan	Azerbaijani, Armenian, Russian
Bahamas	English, Creole
Bahrain	Arabic, Farsi, Urdu, English
Bangladesh	Bengali, Dhaka, English
Barbados	English
Belarus	Belorussian, Russian
Belgium	Flemish, French, German
Belize	English, Spanish, Maya, Garifuna
Benin	French, Fon, Yoruba
Bhutan	Dzongkha, Tibetan, Nepali

Countries or regions	What to speak there
Bolivia	Spanish, Aymara, Quechua
Bosnia and Herzegovina	Bosnian, Croatian, Serbian
Botswana	English, Setswana
Brazil	Portuguese
Brunei	Malay, English
Bulgaria	Bulgarian
Burkina Faso	French
Burundi	French, Rundi, Swahili
Cambodia	Khmer, French
Cameroon	English, French
Canada	English, French
Cape Verde	Portuguese, Crioulo
Central Africa	French, Sango, Arabic, Hunsa, Swahili
Chad	Arabic, French, Sara, Sango
Chile	Spanish
China	Chinese, Mandarin, Yue, Wu, Minbei, Minnan, Xiang, Gan, Hakka
Colombia	Spanish
Comoros	Malagasy, French, Shaafi
Congo	French, Lingala, Kikongo
Costa Rica	Spanish
Croatia	Croatian
Cuba	Spanish
Cyprus	Greek, Turkish
Czech Republic	Czech
Denmark	Danish
Djibouti	Arabic, French, Somali, Afar
Dominica	English
Dominican Republic	Spanish
Ecuador	Spanish, Quechua
Egypt	Arabic, English
El Salvador	Spanish, Nahua
Equatorial Guinea	Spanish, Fang
Eritrea	Arabic, English
Estonia	Estonian, Russian
Ethiopia	Amharic, Tigrinya, Orominga, Arabic
Fiji	Fijian, English, Hindustani
Finland	Finnish, Swedish
France	French
Gabon	French, Fang, Myene, Bateke, Bapounou, Bandjabi
Gambia	English, Mandinka, Wolof, Fula
Georgia	Georgian, Armenian, Russian
Germany	German
Ghana	English, Akan, Moshi-Dagomba, Ewe, Ga
Greece	Greek
Greenland	Greenlandic, Danish
Grenada	English

Countries or regions	What to speak there
Guatemala	Spanish
Guinea	French
Guinea-Bissau	Portuguese, Criolo
Guyana	English
Haiti	Creole, French
Honduras	Spanish
Hungary	Hungarian
Iceland	Icelandic
India	Assamese, Bengali, English, Gujarati, Hindi, Kashmiri, Malayalam, Marathi, Oriya, Punjabi, Sindhi, Tamil, Telugu, Urdu
Indonesia	Bahasa
Iran	Farsi, Turki, Kurdish, Arabic
Iraq	Arabic, Kurdish, Assyrian, Armenian
Ireland	Gaelic, English
Israel	Hebrew, Arabic
Italy	Italian
Ivory Coast	French, Dioula
Jamaica	English, Creole
Japan	Japanese
Jordan	Arabic
Kazakhstan	Kazakh, Russian
Kenya	Swahili, English
Kirgizia	Kirghiz, Russian, Uzbek
Kiribati	English, Gilbertese
Kuwait	Arabic
Kyrgyzstan	Kyrgyz, Russian
Laos	Lao, French
Latvia	Latvian, Russian
Lebanon	Arabic, French, Armenian
Lesotho	Sesotho, English, Zulu, Xhosa
Liberia	English, Niger-Congo
Libya	Arabic, Italian
Liechtenstein	German, Alemannic
Lithuania	Lithuanian, Russian
Luxembourg	Luxembourgish, French, German
Macedonia	Macedonian, Flauvine, Serbian
Madagascar	Malagasy, French
Malawi	Chichewa, Tombuka, English
Malaysia	Malay, English, Chinese, Tamil
Maldives	Divehi, English
Mali	French, Bambara
Marshall Islands	Marshallese, English, Japanese
Mauritania	Arabic, Hasaniya, Toucouleur, Fula, Sarakole
Mauritius	English, Creole, French, Hindi, Urdu, Hakka, Bojpoori
Mexico	Spanish
Micronesia	English, Trukese, Pohnpeian, Yapese, Kosraen

Countries or regions	What to speak there
Moldova	Moldovan, Romanian, Russian
Monaco	Monegasque, French
Mongolia	Khalkha, Turkic, Russian, Chinese
Morocco	Arabic, Berber
Mozambique	Portuguese
Myanmar	Burmese
Namibia	English, Afrikaans
Nauru	Nauruan, English
Nepal	Nepali
Netherlands	Dutch
New Zealand	English, Maori
Nicaragua	Spanish
Niger	French, Hausa, Djerma
Nigeria	Hausa, Yoruba, Ibo, Fulani
North Korea	Korean
Norway	Norwegian, Lapp, Finnish
Oman	Arabic, Baluchi, Urdu
Pakistan	Urdu, Punjabi, Sindhi, Pashtu, Baluchi
Panama	Spanish, English
Papua New Guinea	English, Tok Pisin
Paraguay	Spanish, Guarani
Peru	Spanish, Quechua
Philippines	Filipino, English
Poland	Polish
Portugal	Portuguese
Qatar	Arabic
Romania	Romanian
Russia	Russian, Tatar
Rwanda	Kinyarwarda, French, Kiswahili
St. Kitts and Nevis	English
St. Lucia	English
St. Vincent and the Grenadines	English
San Marino	Italian
São Tomé and Principe	Portuguese
Saudi Arabia	Arabic
Senegal	French, Wolof, Pulaar Diola, Mandingo
Seychelles	Creole, English, French
Sierra Leone	English, Mende, Temne, Krio
Singapore	Chinese, English, Malay, Tamil
Slovakia	Slovak
Slovenia	Slovene
Solomon Islands	Melanesian, English
Somalia	Somali, Arabic
South Africa	Afrikaans, English, Zulu, Xhosa, Sotho, Tswana
South Korea	Korean
Spain	Spanish, Catalan, Galician, Basque

Countries or regions	What to speak there
Sri Lanka	Sinhala, Tamil
Sudan	Arabic, Nubian, Ta Bedawie, Nilotic, Nilo-Hamitic, Sudanic
Suriname	Dutch, Sranan Tongo, Hindi, Javanese
Swaziland	Siswati, English
Sweden	Swedish, Lapp, Finnish
Switzerland	French, German, Italian, Romansch
Syria	Arabic, Kurdish, Armenian, Aramaic, Circassian
Taiwan	Chinese, Taiwanese, Hakka
Tajikistan	Tajik, Uzbek, Russian
Tanzania	Swahili, English
Thailand	Thai
Togo	French, Ewe, Mina, Dagomba, Kabye
Tonga	Tongan, English
Trinidad and Tobago	English
Tunisia	Arabic
Turkey	Turkish, Kurdish, Arabic
Turkmenistan	Turkmenian, Russian, Uzbek, Kazakh
Uganda	English, Swahili, Luganda, Bantu, Nilotic
Ukraine	Ukrainian, Russian
United Arab Emirates	Arabic, Hindi, Urdu, Farsi
United Kingdom	English, Welsh, Scots
United States	English
Uruguay	Spanish
Uzbekistan	Uzbek, Russian, Kazakh, Tadzhik, Tatar
Vanuatu	English, French, Bislama
Venezuela	Spanish
Vietnam	Vietnamese
Western Samoa	Samoan, English
Yemen	Arabic
Yugoslavia	Serbian
Zaire	French, Lingala, Swahili, Kingwana, Kikongo, Tshiluba
Zambia	English
Zimbabwe	English, Chi Shona, Si Ndebele

FOOD AND BEVERAGES

BEER STYLES

ALES

Top-fermented, higher alcohol beers that tend to have a fruity flavour and flowery aroma.

American brown ale Deep copper to brown ale with evident hop aroma and increased bitterness.

American pale ale Medium-bodied ale with a golden to light copper colour and high hop bitterness, flavour, and aroma (created with aromatic American-variety hops).

American wheat Golden to light amber-coloured, made with an ale yeast and brewed with 30 to 50 percent wheat.

Barley wine A dark ale with a full body, fruity character, and high alcohol content.

Belgian golden ale A strong ale, golden to straw-coloured.

Belgian strong ale Highly alcoholic ale, powerfully flavoured, often with the addition of dark candy sugars.

Belgian white (or **Wit**) Very pale, typically cloudy ale made with a high proportion of wheat, sometimes with the addition of spices or orange flavouring.

English bitter Ranges from golden to copper in colour with good hop character, mild carbonation, distinct bitterness, and malty sweetness. Strength ranges from ordinary to best to extra special.

English brown ale Reddish-brown ale with a medium body, a light roasted malty taste, and a higher alcohol content than English mild ale.

English mild ale A dark brown beer, sweet and fruity, with a low alcohol content.

English strong ale Fairly dark beer, sometimes with high alcohol content, and a well-rounded, malty taste.

Flanders brown/Oud bruin A red, copper, or brown Belgian ale with medium bitterness and a spicy-sour to sweet-sour flavour.

India pale ale High in hops and alcohol content, with a dry, fruity flavour and a golden to deep copper colour.

Pale ale A classic British beer with a strong, fruity taste and bouquet; "pale" refers to its clearness and brilliance, not to its amber to dark brown colour.

Porter Medium to dark brown in colour, a medium-bodied beer ranging in flavour from bitter to sweet and made with black or roasted malt.

Saison beer A Belgian pale ale with a golden to deep amber colour, typified by a fruity character.

Scottish ale A variant of English pale ale, but sweeter, maltier, and less hoppy.
    Scotch ale An extra-strong version of Scottish ale, closely related to English strong ale.
    Scottish export ale Sweet, caramel-like, and malty, stronger and hoppier than the heavy.
    Scottish heavy ale Moderately strong, with a smooth, sweet maltiness balanced with low hop bitterness.
    Scottish light ale The mildest form of this ale, with little bitterness and a light body.

STOUTS

Ale styles that are dark like porter, but made with highly roasted barley.

Classic Irish-style dry stout A bitter, medium-bodied beer with good head retention and a strong roasted character.

Foreign-style stout Medium- to full-bodied, with a dry-roasted bitterness and excellent head retention.

Imperial stout Dark copper to very black, with a rich malty fruity flavour and very high alcohol content.

Oatmeal stout The addition of oats to the mash results in a pleasant, full flavour and a medium- to full-bodied beer.

Sweet stout a.k.a. Cream or **Milk stout** Full-bodied, sweet, and lower in alcohol than other stouts.

Trappist abbey beers Strong, fruity ales brewed in Belgian monasteries in *dubbel* and *tripple* varieties (the terms refer to gravity or density).

LAGERS

Produced at colder fermentation temperatures than ales, which creates a mellower, distinctly carbonated product.

American dark lager A darker beer more typical of an American lager than a European dark lager, although some do contain dark and caramel malts.

American lager Very pale lager with a medium alcohol content; clean and crisp and heavily carbonated with a minimal taste profile and hop content.

American lager ale or **Cream ale** A mild, pale, light-bodied ale lacking in hop bouquet.

American-style light lager Must have at least 25 percent fewer calories than the "regular" version of that beer, according to Food and Drug Administration regulations.

American-style premium lager Similar to American lager, but more flavourful, with a deeper colour and medium body and sometimes higher alcohol content.

Bock Brewed only from malted barley, this beer style is strong and malty sweet with a high alcohol content.

    American bock Similar to American dark beer, sometimes paler in colour, with an alcohol content of about 5 percent.

    Doppelbock A very strong lager characterized by a predominant malty flavour with a full body and a deep amber to dark brown colour.

    Eisbock Extremely alcoholic, very dark bock that is brewed by freezing the beer and removing the resulting ice to concentrate the beer's flavour and increase its alcohol content.

    Helles bock Light-coloured bock with a malty character that comes through in its aroma and flavour.

    Traditional bock Strong beer brewed from malted barley with a high alcohol content and a colour ranging from deep copper to dark brown.

Dortmunder A pale lager with a fuller body, medium bitterness, and a characteristically flowery aroma.

Dry lager Straw-coloured lager that lacks sweetness and is similar to American lager.

Märzen/Oktoberfest Medium-bodied, amber to pale copper in colour, with a toasted malt flavour.

Muenchner helles Pale straw- to golden-coloured beer, similar to Munich dunkel but less hoppy and maltier.

Munich dunkel Dark brown beer made with roasted Munich dark malt, which results in a clean and crisp malty flavour.

Pilsner A pale golden lager with a clean, dry taste and medium alcohol content.

    Bohemian pilsner Similar to the German pilsner, but with more malty fullness and a darker colour.

    Classic pilsner A pale golden beer with a medium alcohol content and a rich, malty flavour.

    German pilsner Very light straw- or golden-coloured beer with a dry flavour and lower alcohol content.

Vienna An amber- or copper-coloured beer with a light to medium body and a malty aroma and sweetness.

COMBINATION STYLES

Beers produced using a mix of brewing traditions.

Altbier Refers to any beer made by the old brewing tradition (warm-fermented, cold-aged).

Berliner weisse The lightest of all the German wheat beers, highly carbonated, and often served with a dash of raspberry syrup or grenadine.

Biere de garde A rich French-style beer with light to medium body and a rich golden to reddish-brown colour.

Dunkelweizen Similar to weissbier but darker in colour.

Dusseldorf-style altbier An aromatic beer, copper to dark brown in colour, with a medium body and malty, bitter flavour.

Kölsch Warm-fermented (using either ale or lager yeasts) and aged at cold temperatures, this altbier is a pale golden colour and has a delicate, dry flavour.

Weizen/Weissbier Made with at least 50 percent malted wheat, this beer is highly carbonated, with a lower alcohol content, a medium to full body, and spicy/fruity overtones.

Weizenbock A German wheat beer that can be either pale or dark, with high alcohol content, and a malty, fruitlike sweetness.

SPECIALTY BEERS

Any ale, lager, or combination style brewed using unusual techniques and/or ingredients other than (or in addition to) malted barley.

Common beer American beer made using unusual fermenting styles.
  California common beer A darker version of cream ale with a medium body and a toasted

or caramel-like maltiness in aroma and flavour.
  Kentucky common beer A dark beer made from sour-mash ferment.
  Pennsylvania swankey A common beer flavoured with aniseed.

Fruit and vegetable beer Any beer in which the fruit or vegetable provides a significant element of flavour.

Herb and spice beer Any beer in which herbs or spices are added to create a distinct character and flavour.

Lambic Brewed only in Belgium, a family of wheat beers made without the addition of yeast, similar to the preparation of wine.
  Belgian-style lambic Dry and light-bodied beer that is low in carbonation and often cloudy or hazy.
  Belgian-style gueuze lambic A combination of aged and new lambic, resulting in a beer that tastes like Belgian-style lambic, but sweeter.
  Belgian-style fruit lambic a.k.a. Framboise, Kriek, Pêche, etc. Characterized by fruit flavours and aromas, with an intense colour that reflects the choice of fruit.

Smoked beer Created by drying the malt with wood smoke, which gives the beer a dark smoky colour and intense smoky flavour.
  Bamberg-style rauchbier A toasted malty-sweet dark lager with a smoky flavour and aroma.
  Classic-style smoked beer Any classic style of beer that is smoked, and reaches a balance between its character and its smoky properties.
  Other smoked beer Any beer to which smoke flavours have been added.

CONFECTIONERY

Brittle A hard candy made from cooking sugar or a sugar syrup until golden brown, adding nuts, and cooling into a hard sheet.

Butterscotch A butter-flavoured caramel cooked longer to become a hard candy.

Candied peel Thinly sliced peel, usually from oranges, grapefruit, or lemons, cooked tender, then cooked in a sugar syrup.

Candied violets Violet flowers coated with egg white and sugar, then dried.

Caramel A chewy cooked mixture of sugar, cream, corn syrup, butter, and flavouring.

Chewing gum A mixture of chicle or another gum substance, sugar, and flavouring made into flat bars or small pellets that are chewed but not swallowed.

Chocolate A smooth mixture of roasted ground cacao beans, sugar, and milk solids shaped into bars or used as coating for other confections.

Divinity A porous mixture of cooked sugar, water, and corn syrup beaten into egg whites.

Fondant The cooked mixture of sugar, water, corn syrup, and flavouring that provides the centres for chocolate creams.

Fruit leather Ground fruit and sugar rolled out into strips.

Fudge A thick cooked mixture of milk, sugar, corn syrup, butter, and flavouring.

Gumdrops Soft, chewy candy made with corn syrup and gum arabic.

Jawbreakers Hard candy shaped into balls.

Jellies, jelly beans Soft, chewy, translucent candies made with sugar, corn syrup, and pectin or natural gum substance.

Lemon drops Hard candy flavoured with lemon, shaped into disks.

Liquorice sticks Chewy, soft candy made with flour, molasses, corn syrup, and sugar, and flavoured with liquorice.

Lollipops Hard candy on a stick.

Malt balls Porous malt-flavoured candy, usually chocolate covered.

Marshmallow An uncooked mixture of gelatin, water, sugar, corn syrup, and flavouring that is beaten until thick.

Marzipan A mixture of almond paste, confectioners' sugar, and rosewater shaped into miniature fruits and vegetables and painted with food colouring.

Mints A cooked mixture of sugar, water, corn syrup, and oil of mint that is stretched into a rope, like taffy, then cut into small rounds.

Nougat A chewy candy made by adding a sugar syrup to stiffly beaten egg whites, then stirring in chopped nuts, usually almonds.

Penuche A fudgelike mixture flavoured with brown sugar and chopped walnuts.

Popcorn balls Popcorn mixed with molasses, corn syrup, butter, and vinegar and shaped into 3-inch balls.

Pralines A cooked mixture of sugar, brown sugar, corn syrup, milk, flavourings, and usually pecans shaped into patties.

Rum balls An uncooked candy made from cookie crumbs, confectioners' sugar, cocoa, corn syrup, and rum.

Taffy A mixture of sugar, water, corn syrup, butter, and flavouring that is cooked, cooled, then stretched into a thin rope.

Toffee A cooked mixture of sugar, corn syrup, cream, butter, and flavouring that is cut into squares when cooled.

Truffles A chocolate fudgelike candy flavoured with rum, brandy, or liqueur.

White chocolate A cream-coloured, smooth mixture of cocoa butter, sugar, milk solids, and vanilla shaped into bars or used as coating for other confections.

CHEESES

Abertam A hard cheese with a rather strong flavour made from sheep's milk in the region of Carlsbad, Bohemia.

Adelost (Ädelost) A Swedish blue-mould cheese made with cow's milk. Similar to Roquefort.

Aettekees (Brussels kaas, Brusselsekaas, Het-tekaas, Brussels cheese) *See* Brussels kaas.

Akkawi (Akawi) A Lebanese cheese made from cow's milk.

Alcobaca A sheep's milk mountain cheese from Portugal, sometimes containing some cow's milk.

Alentejo (Alamtejo, Serpa) A soft cheese made in the mountains of Alentejo, Portugal, mostly from sheep's milk, but sometimes with the addition of goat's milk. It is similar to Serra, but with a stronger taste and odour.

Allgäuer Limburger A type of Limburger cheese made in Allgäu, Germany.

Allgäuer rundkäse (Allgäuer Emmentaler, Allgäuer bergkäse) A type of Swiss cheese named for the district of Allgäu in the Alps in southern Germany. It is similar to Emmental, but without the large holes.

Alpkäse A smaller version of Emmental made in the Austrian Alps.

Altaiski (Altajsky syr) A hard cow's milk cheese from the Altai mountain chain in the Caucasus mountain range in central Asia.

Altenberger A traditional goat's milk cheese (sometimes made with cow's milk) with caraway seeds made in Germany, especially in Thüringen in central Germany, where it is known as Altenburger Ziegenkäse.

Ambert (Fourme d'Ambert, Fourme de Mont-brizon) A cylindrical Roquefort-type cheese made in central France from cow's milk.

Ambrosia (Svensk Tilseter) A mild, soft, cow's milk cheese resembling Tilsit from southern Sweden.

American The term for a variety of cow's milk cheeses made in America, including Cheddar and Monterey Jack. Can also refer to a processed cheese product.

Anari (Anari analati) A soft sheep's or goat's milk cheese from Cyprus, drained in braided straw baskets.

Añejo (Queso añejo) A traditional skimmed goat's milk cheese (sometimes made from cow's milk) from Mexico.

Anthotiros (Anthotyro) A soft cheese from Crete made with goat's or sheep's milk.

Appenzeller A cow's milk cheese made in the canton of Appenzell, Switzerland, and also in Bavaria and Baden. It is semihard, with little holes the size of peas, and is matured by soaking in cider or white wine and spices.

Appetitost A Danish cheese made from sour buttermilk.

Ardi-Gasna (Ossau-Iraty-Brebis, Arnéguy) A firm, supple sheep's milk cheese from the Basque country of northern Spain.

Armada A semihard cheese from the province of Léon, in Spain.

Armavir A sour-milk cheese made in the western Caucasus from sheep's milk.

Arnéguy *See* Ardi-Gasna.

Asadero (Oaxaca) A Mexican pasta filata cheese made from whole cow's milk.

Asco A Corsican shepherd's cheese made from sheep's milk or a mixture of sheep's and goat's milk.

Asiago A pasteurized cow's milk cheese from Italy, which comes in several varieties, described below.

Asiago d'Allevo (Asiago d'Allievo) Made from a combination of skimmed and whole milk, or from partially skimmed milk. When it has matured for more than a year it is used as a grating cheese.

Asiago di Taglio Unaged Asiago, which can be sliced and served as table cheese.

Asiago pressato A full-fat cheese made from

whole milk which can be consumed after one month of maturation.

Asin (Water cheese) A soft washed-curd cow's milk cheese with a mild flavour from northern Italy.

Aulus *See* Bethmale.

Aunis A very rare small triangular cheese from France.

Aura A blue, Roquefort-type cheese from Finland.

Azeitão (Azeitas) A small round sheep's milk cheese from Portugal that resembles an unripe Queijo de Serra.

Backsteiner A modified Limburger-Romadur–type cheese, made in northern Germany and deriving its name from its bricklike shape.

Bagnes A firm, pliant cow's milk cheese from Switzerland, used for making raclette, a melted cheese dish.

Bagozzo (Grana Bagozzo, Bresciano) An Italian cow's milk cheese similar to Parmesan, but made in smaller wheels.

Baguette Lyonnaise (Baguette) A variety of the French cheese Maroilles, shaped like a loaf of French bread.

Baker's cheese Similar to cottage cheese, but softer and with finer granules. Generally used commercially to make pastries and cheesecake.

Balcan (Balkanski Kâskaval, Balcanski Katschkawalj) A sheep's milk cheese made in the Balkan Mountains of Bulgaria.

Bandal A smoked cheese from India made from cow's or buffalo's milk. The cheese is smooth and aromatic, and is usually eaten fresh.

Banon A goat's or cow's milk cheese made in Banon in Haute-Provence, France. It is sometimes soaked in eau-de-vie during its ripening period.

Banon au poivre d'ane A variety of seasoned Banon.

Barberey (Fromage de Troyes) A soft cow's milk cheese from France, similar to Camembert.

Barrel An American Cheddar cheese that is sold in barrels and can weigh up to 660 pounds. It is also available in smaller sizes.

Battelmatt A small cow's milk cheese made in Switzerland, sometimes compared to Tilset.

Bauden *See* Koppen.

Beaufort (Beaufort de montagne, Haute-montagne Beaufort) A type of Gruyère with an excellent flavour and aroma. The variety sold in the winter (Beaufort d'hiver or Laitier) is said to be the best, as it is made from the summer's milk.

Beda An Egyptian cheese made using skimmed milk from either cows or buffalos.

Bel paese An Italian dessert cheese whose name means "beautiful country"; it is a soft cow's milk cheese made in a flat, round shape.

Bellay (Tête de moine, Monk's head) A soft, blue-veined cheese originally made by Swiss monks in the 15th century and still made exclusively in that locality. It is a smooth and creamy cheese usually served spread on slices of bread.

Bergkäse The German name for a group of Alpine cheeses, including Battelmatt and Gruyère.

Bergquara A Swedish version of Gouda.

Berkeley A yellow marbled cow's milk cheese made in Great Britain.

Bernade (Formagelle Bernade, Bernarde) An Italian cheese made from cow's milk to which 10% goat's milk and saffron are added.

Bethmale A hard, spicy French cheese, suitable for grating. It is called by various names, according to the village it comes from: Ercé, Oust, Oustet, Esbareich, Aulus, etc.

Beynaz peynir The most common sheep's milk cheese made in Turkey; it is ripened in layers of salt for up to six or seven months.

Bgug panir *See* Daralagjazsky.

Bierkäse (Weisslacker bierkäse, Weisslacker) A semihard cheese from Germany, similar to Limburger and excellent with beer.

Billinge A firm, white Swedish cow's milk cheese, similar to Herrgårdsost but milder.

Bitto A Swiss cheese with small holes, made from cow's or goat's milk or a combination of both.

Biza *See* Fajy.

Blarney An old Irish cow's milk cheese still made today. It has small round holes and a mild flavour, resembling the Danish cheese Samsø.

Bleu d'Auvergne A French bleu made from cow's milk in the regions that once formed the old province of Auvergne.

Bleu de Corse A Roquefort-type cheese from Corsica.

Bleu de Gex A French blue-veined cheese made from cow's milk. It is milder than other bleus, with a sweeter aroma and a touch of bitterness.

Bleu de Laqueuille A bleu cheese from central France, which originated in the 19th century when a farmer added bread mould to cheese curds.

Bleu de Septmoncel Very similar to Bleu de Gex.

Bleu de Thiézac A French blue cheese made in the Thiézac region. It has a different flavour from other bleus because it is salted when warm.

Bleu des Causses A Roquefort-like cheese made with cow's milk. Like Roquefort, it is also matured in special *caves*.

Blue cheese Cheese of the Roquefort type that is made in the United States and Canada using cow's or goat's milk rather than sheep's milk.

Boerenkaas A farm-made Gouda from Holland.

Bola A Portuguese cow's milk cheese similar to Edam.

Bondon (Bondart, Bondard, Bonde) A small, whole-milk French cheese of the Neufchâtel variety.

Bondost Mild, round Swedish cow's milk cheese, ideal for melting.

Bossons macéré (Bossons macérés) Small French goat's milk cheese ripened with alcohol, olive oil, and herbs to give it a strong, tangy flavour.

Boulette d'Avesnes A French cheese in the Maroilles family, with a crumbly consistency and a very sharp flavour.

Boulette de Cambrai A French cow's milk cheese flavoured with herbs and eaten fresh.

Boursin A soft French cream cheese with a light taste; often garlic and herbs are added or the cheese is coated with crushed pepper.

Box A German cow's milk cheese which comes in two forms: soft box, which is seasoned with caraway seeds, and semihard box, which resembles American brick.

Bra A hard, white, salty cow's milk cheese from Italy.

Brand A German hand cheese made with butter and beer.

Braudost (Braudostur) The Icelandic version of Edam.

Brick cheese An American semisoft cow's milk cheese with a pungent and sweet flavour, less sharp than Cheddar and less strong than Limburger.

Brie A soft, creamy, round cheese encased in a layer of white mould, this French cheese is usually made from cow's milk.

Brie de Coulommiers A close relative of Camembert, originating in the French town of Coulommiers. It is also similar to Brie de Meaux, but with a smaller diameter.

Brie de Meaux A variety of Brie with a very good reputation and a nutty flavour. It is 25 to 35 cm in diameter.

Brie de Melun Slightly smaller than Brie de Meaux and made in a similar manner, except that it is ripened longer and has a sharper flavour.

Brie de Montereau A round cheese whose diameter never exceeds 20 cm, this cheese has the strongest aroma of all the Brie varieties.

Brillat-Savarin A cow's milk cheese from Normandy which resembles Camembert.

Brin d'amour A soft Corsican goat's milk cheese, shaped like a square with rounded corners and flavoured with rosemary and savory.

Brinza (Bryndza, Brinzâ) The traditional cheese of sheep farmers in central Europe and the Near East, Brinza is also made in Israel. It is a mild, almost soft cheese often spread on sandwiches.

Brinzâ de Burduf (Burduf Brinza) Brinza that is matured in sheep- or goat-skin bags using salted whey.

Brinzâ in Coajâ de Brad (Cochuletz Brinza) Salted and kneaded Brinza that is packed in the bark of fir trees, giving it a special flavour.

Brioler A soft cheese named after its town of origin in the former East Prussia; it is similar to Limburger.

Brique du Forez (Cabriou, Cabrion, Chèvreton d'Ambert) A cheese from central France, so named for its bricklike shape. It is a goat's milk cheese often made with the addition of cow's milk.

Broccio (Brucciu, Bruccio) A Corsican cheese similar to ricotta, made with either goat's or sheep's milk.

Brussels kaas (Aettekees, Brusselsekaas, Hettekaas) A Belgian cheese made with cow's milk, Brussels kaas is soft, white, and extremely salty, with a thin, sticky rind.

Buost A lowfat Swedish cheese made from cow's milk.

Burgos A Spanish cheese made from cow's, goat's, or sheep's milk.

Burmeister A Wisconsin variety of brick cheese.

Butterkäse A German cheese that is soft and mild. It is sold in several different shapes, loaf, round, or sausage.

Caboc A soft Scottish cheese with a butterlike consistency and an oatmeal coating.

Cabrales A rustic Spanish blue cheese made from goat's, sheep's, cow's, or a mixture of milks.

Cabreiro A Portuguese mountain cheese made from goat's or sheep's milk and ripened in brine.

Cabrion See Brique du Forez.

Cabriou See Brique du Forez.

Cachat A sheep's milk cheese from Provence.

Caciocavallo An ancient variety of Italian cheese whose name means "horseback cheese," Caciocavallo is shaped in the form of a gourd and hung by

rope while it is maturing. Caciocavallo is the oldest existing pasta filata (plastic curd) cheese. Mozzarella and Provolone are similar cheeses.

Caciofiore (Cacio fiore) A soft, saffron-tinted Italian cheese made from sheep's or goat's milk.

Caerphilly A semisoft cow's milk cheese made in Wales, popular with Welsh miners.

Caithness A soft, mild, creamy Scottish cheese made from cow's milk.

Cajassous A French goat's milk cheese from the Périgord.

Calcagno A hard Sicilian grating cheese made from sheep's milk.

Cambridge (York) A fresh cow's milk cheese made in England.

Camembert A soft cow's milk cheese first made in France, Camembert has a creamy yellow interior with a rind of grey mould. It is similar to Brie but smaller and with a different characteristic flavour.

Camosun A semisoft, open-textured cheese resembling Gouda and Monterey Jack, Camosun was developed in Washington State in 1932 as a way to utilize surplus milk on farms.

Cancoillotte (Canquillote, Fromagère, Tempête) A skim-milk cheese made in eastern France by mixing fermented cheese with one or more of the following: butter, milk, white wine, salt water, or eggs.

Cantal A French cheese, possibly one of the world's oldest, that is made with cow's milk and well aged until it is hard and dry with a piquant flavour.

Caprino A soft white goat's milk cheese made in Italy.

Carré de l'est A square-shaped cheese with a white mould coating; it is made in France with cow's milk, and is similar to Camembert.

Casigiolu (Panedda, Pera di vacca) A plastic curd (kneaded) cheese made in Sardinia by the same method used to make Caciocavallo.

Castelmagno A Gorgonzola-like cheese from Italy.

Castelo branco A soft cheese from Portugal, similar to Cabrales.

Castillon A cow's milk cheese similar to Bethmale, made in the French Pyrenees.

Cebrero A Spanish cow's milk cheese.

Cendré de la Brie (Cendré de Brie) A lowfat French cow's milk cheese dusted with ashes. Similar to Coulommiers.

Chabichou A small, soft goat's milk cheese from Poitou, France.

Champoléon (Queyras) A French cow's milk cheese similar to Cancoillotte.

Chana A sour-milk cheese made from cow's milk in India.

Chantelle A version of Bel paese produced in the United States and Canada.

Chaource A soft white-mould cheese from France, resembling Camembert.

Cheddar A hard cheese, ranging in colour from nearly white to yellow, and made from cow's milk. The cheese originated in the village of Cheddar in Somersetshire, England, but varieties are now made in Africa, America, Australia, Austria, Belgium, Canada, Denmark, Holland, New Zealand, and elsewhere.

Cheedam A mild Australian cheese with characteristics of Cheddar and Edam.

Cheshire (Chester) A firm, crumbly cow's milk cheese made in Great Britain.

Chèvreton d'Ambert See Brique du Forez.

Chevrotin Goat's milk cheese from the French Alps.

Chiavari A sour-milk cheese made from cow's milk in Italy.

Christalinna A hard cow's milk cheese from the mountains of central Switzerland.

Christian IX A Danish cow's milk cheese seasoned with caraway or other spices and made in the shape of a large wheel.

Chubut A soft cheese from Argentina.

Citeaux A French monastery cheese made from cow's milk, reminiscent of Reblochon.

Colby A firm cheese that is similar to Cheddar but is softer and more rubbery. Colby is made in the United States and New Zealand.

Cold pack cheese (Potted cheese, Cold-pack cheese, Club cheese, Comminuted cheese) A soft, spreadable cheese created by grinding and mixing together (without heating) one or more cheese types (usually Cheddar and/or Colby, Gorgonzola, Roquefort, or Limburger), often with the addition of vinegar, salt, spices, herbs, wine, or port.

Colwick See Slipcote.

Commissiekass (Commissekaas, Commission cheese, Mimolette, Dutch mimolette) A variety of Edam cheese weighing about eight pounds and often coloured orange.

Comté A variety of Gruyère made with cow's milk; Comté is a pressed, dry cheese with a scattering of small, moist holes.

Cornhusker A bland, moist, cow's milk cheese made in America, similar to Cheddar and Colby.

Cotherstone A cow's milk cheese made in Yorkshire, England, similar to Stilton.

Cotronese A sheep's milk plastic curd cheese from Italy.

Cotswold A version of Double Gloucester made with chives or onions.

Cottage cheese A soft fresh cheese, served after it has been cut into cubes. Acid curd cottage cheese is made without rennet and has a smooth texture; it has largely been replaced by sweet curd cottage cheese, which is prepared with rennet and has a very mild smell and taste.

Coulommiers See Brie de Coulommiers.

Coyolito A semihard cheese from Central America, Coyolito is washed in coconut milk and has a slightly piquant or pungent flavour.

Cream cheese A soft, mild, rich, uncured cheese made of cream or a mixture of cream and milk. It is similar to the French Neufchâtel, but has a higher fat content.

Crème Chantilly A very white, soft, delicate Scandinavian cheese made from cow's milk.

Crème Château A Swedish factory-made cheese comparable to Crème Chantilly.

Creole A soft, rich, unripened cheese similar to cottage cheese, very popular in New Orleans.

Crescenza (Stracchino crescenza) A soft cow's milk cheese made in Italy. Crescenza is uncooked, mildly sweet, fast-ripening, and yellowish.

Crottin de Chavignol A hard dry goat's milk cheese from the French region of Berry.

Crowdie A Scottish version of cottage cheese, prepared by adding rennet to tepid milk, draining the curd that forms, and mixing with cream and salt.

Cuajada A soft creamy Venezuelan cheese made from goat's milk and traditionally wrapped in banana or maize leaves.

Cuartirolo A soft Argentinian cheese made from cow's milk, based on the Italian Quartirolo.

Dacca A pressed, smoked cheese made with cow's or buffalo's milk in southern India.

Damen (Gloire de montagnes) A fresh cow's milk cheese from Hungary.

Damietta *See* Domiati.

Danablu A Danish blue cheese made from cow's milk, with a very pronounced flavour and a soft, crumbly consistency.

Danbo A semihard cheese made in Denmark. Danbo is similar to Samsø except that it is square instead of round, and is sometimes flavoured with caraway seeds.

Daralagjazsky (Bgug panir, Daralag) An Armenian cheese that is made from cow's or sheep's milk and matured in a sheepskin bag or in a stone bottle, resulting in a soft, crumbly cheese that is seasoned with salt, garlic, and thyme after it has ripened.

Dauphin (Dauphine) A French cheese of the Maroilles family, with a strong odour and spicy flavour.

Delft A spiced cheese, similar to Leyden, made in the Netherlands from partly skimmed cow's milk.

Demi-Balcan (Demi-Balkan, Polubalkanski kâskaval) Smaller and softer than Balcan, made in the lowlands of the Balkan Mountains.

Derby (Derbyshire) A hard cheese made from cow's milk in Derbyshire, England. It is similar to Cheddar and Lancashire cheese, but with a crumblier consistency.

Dessertnyj (Desertny syr) A soft white cow's milk cheese from the Volga Basin in the former Soviet Union, Dessertnyj is sprinkled with *Penicillium candidum* during its ten-day ripening period, which creates a pale orange/pink rind.

Domiati (Damietta, Dumyat) A soft white cheese from Egypt made from buffalo's or cow's milk.

Dorset (Dorset blue, Dorset blue vinney, Dorset blue vinny, Blue vinny, Blue veiney) One of the hard, blue-veined cheeses made in England. Dorset is dry and crumbly with a sharp flavour and a round shape.

Double Gloucester *See* Gloucester.

Drabant A mild, semihard Swedish cheese made from cow's milk.

Dreux à feuille A flat, round cow's milk cheese made in France and wrapped in chestnut leaves.

Duberki An Israeli cheese made by forming Lebbene into little balls and preserving them in olive oil.

Duel A soft, small, square cow's milk cheese from Austria.

Dumyat *See* Domiati.

Dunlop A rich, white, pressed cheese made in Scotland. Dunlop is soft and mild and similar to Cheddar.

Echourgnac A mild, aromatic cow's milk cheese from France.

Edam A Dutch cheese similar to Gouda, but with a lower fat content, which makes it drier. It is a pressed semihard to hard cheese with a mild flavour and a round shape. Edam prepared for export is coloured red, and Edam made in the United States is usually covered with red paraffin or some other red coating.

Edelpilzkäse (Pilzkäse) A semihard blue cheese from the Bavarian Alps. Edelpilzkäse is a very pale yellow with a smooth consistency and a mild taste that grows sharper with ageing.

Elbo A Danish cheese in the Samsø family. Elbo is a mild, aromatic cheese made in a loaf shape with fewer holes than the traditional Samsø.

Emiliano A very hard cheese from Italy, similar to Parmesan.

Emmental (Swiss cheese, Emmentaler) The best-known of the Swiss cheeses. Emmental is made in enormous wheels that weigh between 160 and 230 pounds. It is a pressed, cow's milk hard cheese, with large holes and a mild, nutty flavour. It is made in many other countries besides Switzerland, including France, Denmark, Israel, Germany, Austria, Finland, Russia, and the United States.

Engadine A local mountain cheese made from cow's milk in Switzerland.

Epoisses (Fromage d'Epoisses, Époisse) A French soft cheese with a washed rind, strong smell, and tangy flavour. The variety Epoisses au Marc de Bourgogne (Epoisses confits au vin blanc, Epoisses confits au Marc) is rinsed in a variety of eau-de-vie called Marc de Bourgogne.

Ercé A regional version of Bethmale.

Ervy A soft cow's milk cheese similar to Camembert.

Esrom An ancient variety of Danish cow's milk cheese which was recently rediscovered and reintroduced by the Danish Cheese Institute. Esrom is a yellow paste with a thin washed rind and a very mild, sweet flavour.

Excelsior A mild, smooth cow's milk cheese from Normandy.

Fajy (Biza) An Iraqi sheep's milk cheese flavoured with garlic and onion.

Feta The most famous Greek cheese, feta is made from sheep's, goat's, or cow's milk. It is a soft, white, crumbly cheese with a piquant, salty flavour. Feta means "slice" in Greece, and refers to the preparation of the cheese, which is matured in slices.

Fiore Sardo (Pecorino Sardo) An Italian cheese made from sheep's milk in Sardinia. It is eaten when it is either soft and fresh, or hard and matured.

Fløtost Similar to Mysost except that it has a higher fat content.

Foggiano A sheep's milk plastic curd cheese from Italy.

Fontina A cow's milk cheese from Italy that is white to light brown in colour, with a faintly nutty flavour and aroma. It may have a few small holes, and its surface is sometimes oiled.

Formagelle A soft cheese made from sheep's or goat's milk in the mountains of northern Italy.

Formagelle Bernade *See* Bernade.

Formaggi di pasta filata Literally "cheese from plastic curd." The name refers to a group of Italian cheeses that are made by kneading and shaping the curd into forms and shapes.

Formaggini A variety of small, round goat's milk cheeses from Italy and Switzerland.

Fourme d'Ambert *See* Ambert.

Fribourg vacherin (Fribourg, Vacherin Fribourgeois) An ancient cheese from Switzerland made with cow's milk. Vacherin is smooth and strong, with a brownish-yellow rind.

Friesekaas A Dutch cow's milk cheese

Friese kanterkaas *See* Kanterkaas.

Friese nagelkaas *See* Nagelkaas.

Friesian clove A spiced cheese from Holland similar to Leyden.

Fromage de curé (Fromage Nantais) A small, strong-tasting French cow's milk cheese made in the shape of a square.

Fromage de Troyes *See* Barberey.

Fromage Nantais *See* Fromage de curé.

Früstückäse A small round Limburger variety made in Germany. It may be eaten fresh or only a little ripened.

Fynbo A round Danish cheese similar to Danbo and Samsø, with eyes that are somewhat smaller than those in the original Samsø.

Gaiskäsli A small circular cheese made from goat's milk in Germany and Switzerland.

Galotyri (Galotiri) A Greek sheep's milk cheese similar to Feta. It is ripened for several months in a goatskin before it is ready to eat.

Gammelost A traditional, strong-flavoured Norwegian cheese made from goat's or cow's milk. Gammelost is often ripened by wrapping it in gin-soaked straw, which keeps away insects and bacteria.

Gautrias A French cheese similar to Port du Salut.

Gavot A French cheese made from goat's, cow's, or sheep's milk.

Geheimrath (Geheimratskäse) A small yellow cheese very similar to Edam or Gouda, and made in Germany.

Géromé (Munster des Vosges) A soft French cheese very similar to Munster, but larger and thicker.

Getmesost A Swedish goat's milk cheese that is low in fat.

Getost A Swedish cheese very similar to Getmesost and the Norwegian Gjetost.

Gibne An Arabian cheese made with sheep's or goat's milk.

Gislev A hard Danish cheese made from cow's milk.

Gjetost A brownish, rectangular Norwegian cheese made with whey from goat's milk (*gjet* is "goat" in Norwegian).

Glarner Schabzieger *See* Sapsago.

Glarnerkäse *See* Sapsago.

Gloucester A very old variety of British cheese. Gloucester is a hard cheese made in two varieties: Single Gloucester, which is smaller and lighter in texture and colour, and Double Gloucester, which is almost twice as heavy and golden-coloured.

Glumse A German version of cottage cheese.

Gomser A Swiss cheese of the raclette variety, which means that it is eaten by melting the cut surface of the cheese and scraping (*racler* means "to scrape") it onto a plate.

Gorbea A smoked white cheese from the Spanish Basque country, similar to Idiazabal.

Gorgonzola The principal blue-green veined cheese of Italy. Gorgonzola is made with cow's milk, and is traditionally matured in caves.

Gorgonzola bianca *See* Panarone.

Gornyaltajski (Gornoaltajsky syr) A sheep's milk cheese from the Altai mountain region in the Caucasus. It can be smoked and then eaten as a grating cheese when very hard.

Gotaost (Götaost) An ancient variety of Swedish cow's or goat's milk cheese made in Gotland, an island in the Baltic Sea.

Gouda A Dutch cheese named after the town of its creation. Gouda is a round, semihard cheese made from cow's milk in a manner similar to that of making Edam. Gouda is now made all over the world.

Gournay A soft French cheese of the fresh Neufchâtel type. It is similar to cream cheese.

Gournay fleuri (Gournay) A Gournay ripened with a surface mould, making it resemble Camembert in looks and flavour.

Goya An Argentinian cheese similar to Asiago.

Grana Lodigiano *See* Lodigiano.

Grana Lombardo *See* Lombardo.

Grana Padano A hard granular cheese from the Padana Valley in Italy; it is similar to Parmesan.

Granular cheese (Stirred curd) An American cheese with a granular, soft consistency, similar to Colby.

Graviera A Greek dessert cheese which is the equivalent of Gruyère.

Greve (Grevé) A mild, wheel-shaped cheese from Sweden, similar to the Swiss Emmental.

Gruyère A Swiss cow's milk cheese often confused with Emmental; it is smaller, denser, and harder, with smaller holes.

Güssing An Austrian cheese very similar to brick, except that it is made with skim milk.

Halloum (Halloumi) A small, soft Middle Eastern sheep's milk cheese, often grilled on skewers.

Haloumy The Australian version of Halloum.

Handkäse (Hand cheese) A small sour-milk cheese from Germany, now made in many places (and called many different names) all over the world. The name refers to the fact that it was originally hand-moulded.

Hauskäse A German Limburger-type cheese.

Havarti One of the most famous Danish cheeses. Havarti is round- or loaf-shaped, with a tangy flavour and small irregular holes.

Herkimer A variety of Cheddar made in limited quantities in Herkimer County, New York. It is a white cheese with a sharp flavour and a dry, crumbly texture.

Herrgårdsost (Herrgårdost) A Swedish cow's milk cheese with the same mild nutty flavour of Emmental, but with smaller holes.

Herve (Hervé) A Limburger-type cheese made in Belgium, known for its incredibly strong (some would say unpleasant) aroma.

Hettekaas (Hette-kees) *See* Brussels kaas.

Hopfenkäse A German cow's milk cheese cured between layers of hops and seasoned with caraway.

Hushållsost A small, mild, traditional cheese from Sweden made from whole cow's milk.

Idiazabal A Basque cheese made from sheep's milk and smoked over beech and hawthorn wood.

Ilha (Queijo da Ilha) Literally, "island cheese," a Portuguese cheese made in the Azores Islands and exported to the mainland. Ilha is a piquant, sharp cheese with a crumbly texture and a dry rind.

Ilves A Finnish farmhouse cheese made with the addition of an egg to the fresh curds.

Incanestrato A Sicilian pasta filata cheese made with sheep's or cow's milk, and sometimes seasoned with pepper.

Islay A small, soft cheese from the Hebrides Islands in Scotland.

Jarlsberg A large, firm cow's milk cheese from Norway. Jarlsberg has irregular round holes and a mild, nutty flavour similar to Emmental.

Jochberg An Austrian cheese made from a combination of cow's and goat's milk.

Josephine A Silesian soft paste cheese.

Juhla The Finnish version of Cheddar.

Jupneh A small, flattish cheese made with either goat's or sheep's milk by the Bedouins.

Juustoleipä (Juustoleipa) A Finnish farmhouse cow's milk cheese that is grilled in front of a fire before it is matured.

Kajmak Literally, "cream" in Turkish. The sheep's milk cheese kajmak is also known as "Serbian butter." It is very popular in Slovenia, Croatia, and Serbia.

Kanterkaas (Friese kanterkaas) The natural (unseasoned) version of the Dutch cow's milk cheese Friesekaas.

Kareish (Kariesch) An Egyptian cheese made with sour milk and ripened in salt.

Karpatski (Karpatsky syr) One of the firm or hard cheeses made in the Ukraine. The name indicates the mountain region in which it is made.

Kartano The Finnish version of Gouda.

Kasar peynir A hard cheese made from cow's, goat's, or sheep's milk in Turkey.

Kashkaval (Kaskaval) A pasta filata cheese made in Romania, similar to the Caciocavallo of Italy.

Kasseri A young version of the Greek cheese Kefalotyri, which is made supple by immersion in hot water and shaped into small bars.

Katschkawalj A pasta filata, Caciocavallo-type cheese similar to Kashkaval, made from sheep's milk in Bulgaria.

Kefalotyri (Kefalotyi) A Greek sheep's or goat's milk cheese, similar to Feta. Its name comes from the *kefalo*, the Greek hat the cheese is shaped to resemble.

Kjarsgaard A hard skim-milk cheese made in Denmark from cow's milk.

Klosterkäse A German cow's milk cheese similar to Romadur.

Kopanisti A Greek blue cheese with a sharp, peppery flavour.

Koppen (Bauden) A sour-milk goat's cheese with a very strong odour, made in the Sudety Mountains between Bohemia and Silesia.

Kryddost A cylindrical cheese flavoured with cloves, with a sharp and spicy taste. Kryddost is a variety of the Swedish cheese Sveciaost, and has a very long ripening period (up to one year).

Kubanski (Kubansky syr) Very similar to Karpatski, but made in the Kuban Mountains.

Kugelkäse An Austrian soft cheese that is seasoned with paprika, rolled into balls, and dried for two or three months. Kugelkäse can keep for years.

Kühbacher A soft, ripened cheese made in upper Bavaria, Germany.

Kuminost The name for several types of spiced cheese from Scandinavia.

Labaneh A Jordanian cheese made from cow's milk to which a small quantity of powdered milk is added.

Labneh A popular Middle Eastern cheese made by draining sour milk which has attained a yogurtlike consistency.

Laguiole A hard French cheese that resembles Cantal but has a milder taste.

Lancashire A white cheese made in England. Lancashire is soft and moist, with a stronger flavour than either Cheddar or Cheshire.

Langres A soft, orange-coloured, strong-smelling cheese made from cow's milk in northeastern France.

Lapland A hard cheese made from reindeer milk in Lapland; it is similar to Swiss.

Lappernas renost (Lapland cheese) A very hard cheese made from reindeer milk by the Laplanders, who dunk it in coffee before enjoying.

Latviiski (Latvysky syr) A Latvian cow's milk cheese, hard and salty.

Lebbene A drained yogurt cheese from Israel that is found in other Middle Eastern countries under other names (*see* Labneh). When it is formed into little balls and preserved in olive oil, it is known as Duberki.

Lebenen A Bedouin cheese made from sour milk and kneaded into little balls, which are then preserved in olive oil.

Leder A German cheese made from skim (cow's) milk with buttermilk added.

Leicester A mild British cheese with a deep orange colour, similar to Cheddar, Derby, and Cheshire.

Leidenkaas (Leyden, Leiden) A Dutch cow's milk cheese flavoured with caraway seeds. Its orange-red rind is imprinted with the famous crossed-keys stamp of the city of Leyden.

Lescin A Russian sheep's milk cheese wrapped in leaves for curing.

Licki (Licki sir) A smoked cheese from the mountains of Croatia.

Liederkranz An American cheese similar to a very mild Limburger.

Limburger A semisoft, yellow cow's milk cheese with a strong flavour and aroma. Limburger was first made in Belgium, and is now made all over the world, particularly in Germany, Austria, and the United States.

Liptauer A soft Hungarian cheese made with sheep's milk, sometimes with the addition of cow's milk, and flavoured with paprika. Liptauer is similar to Brinza.

Lisieux A less fully ripened Livarot, with a milder taste.

Livarot A soft cow's milk cheese from France, similar to Camembert, with a strong flavour and aroma.

Lodigiano (Grana Lodigiano) A Parmesan-type cheese, similar to Lombardo, from the vicinity of Lodi, Italy. The cheese is sharp, fragrant, and sometimes slightly bitter.

Lombardo (Grana Lombardo) A Parmesan-type cheese, similar to Lodigiano, from the province of

Milan. It has a sharp and aromatic flavour and a granular texture.

Lour A soft cheese from Iraq made of whey and fresh milk.

Luneberg A cheese resembling both Limburger and Emmental, made in Austria from cow's milk coloured with saffron.

MahÓn (Queso de MahÓn) A semihard cow's milk cheese from the Balearic Islands of Spain. MahÓn has a yellow colour, unevenly distributed holes, and a mellow flavour. Sometimes a small amount of goat's milk is added.

Maile A sheep's milk cheese made in the Crimea.

Maile pener Maile with rennet added; it has a crumbly, open texture.

Mainauer A cheese similar to Münster, from the island of Mainau in the German part of Lake Constance.

Mainzerkäse (Mainzer hand, Mainzer handkäse, Mainzer) A sour-milk, small, round, soft cheese made in Germany.

Malakoff A soft, Neufchâtel-type cheese made in France.

Mammoth A variety of American Cheddar weighing at least 110 pounds; it is little brother to the immense Barrel cheese.

Manchego A Spanish cheese made from sheep's milk, with a firm, creamy white interior and a straw-yellow rind.

Manchego curado Manchego ripened for at least two months.

Manchego en aceite Manchego immersed in olive oil, which creates a grey to black rind.

Manchego viejo Manchego ripened for nine to twelve months in a damp cellar.

Manteca A piece of whey butter surrounded by a "bag" of mozzarella cheese.

Manur A Serbian cheese made from cow's or sheep's milk.

Maribo A Gouda-like cheese from Denmark, semi-hard, with a distinctive flavour and a wax coating.

Marienhofer A Limburger-type cheese made in Austria.

Maroilles A very strong-smelling cow's milk cheese from France. Maroilles is square, with a reddish rind and a pale, soft paste.

Mascarpone A very soft cream cheese from Italy, used primarily as a dessert cheese and in the preparation of certain dishes.

Mecklenburg skim A hard, skim (cow's) milk cheese made in Germany.

Meira An Iraqi sheep's milk cheese that is cut into strips and matured before being sold at market.

Mesitra A soft sheep's milk cheese made in the Crimea.

Mesost A light-brown, lowfat, firm Swedish cheese made from whey.

Mimolette The French version of Commissiekaas.

Minas frescal A soft cow's milk cheese made in the Brazilian state of Minas Gerais.

Minas prensado Similar to Minas frescal but pressed in moulds, with a resulting firmer consistency.

Mintzitra A soft Macedonian cheese made from sheep's milk.

Misch An Egyptian cheese that is matured in salted, spiced milk, resulting in a very strong, Roquefort-like flavour.

Mitzithra A Greek cheese similar to Ricotta, made from the whey that is a by-product of Feta cheese.

Molbo A variety of the Swedish Samsø, Molbo is a round cheese with a red rind. It has a distinct nutty aroma and a firmer consistency than the other Samsøs.

Moliterno A pasta filata cheese originally from Italy and now also made in Argentina.

Moncenisio A blue-mould, Gorgonzola-like cheese made in Italy.

Mondseer schachtelkäse (Mondseer) A soft Austrian cow's milk cheese similar to the German Münster. Mondseer has a sharp, acidic flavour close to that of a mild Limburger.

Monostorer A sheep's milk cheese from Transylvania.

Mont Cenis A hard blue-mould cheese made in France.

Mont d'Or *See* Vacherin Mont d'Or.

Montasio A large round Italian cheese. When it has matured for more than six months, it develops a sharp taste and is used as a grating cheese.

Montavoner A sour-milk, herb-flavoured cow's milk cheese from Austria.

Monterey Jack An American cheese similar to Cheddar or Colby, with a creamy texture and medium-sized holes.

Motal A brine-ripened cheese from the Caucasus.

Mozzarella A pasta filata cheese from Italy (but now manufactured in the United States and other countries as well). Mozzarella is moist and giving, with a delicate flavour. Originally made from buffalo's milk, it is now mostly made with cow's milk.

Mozzarella di bufala Mozzarella made from buffalo's milk.

Mozzarella di bufala affumicata Smoked mozzarella made from buffalo's milk.

Munster (Muenster) A soft French cheese with a strong odour, full-bodied flavour, and a thin orange-coloured rind.

Munster des Vosges *See* Géromé.

Münster The German version of Munster.

Mycella A creamy Danish blue cheese, similar to Gorgonzola.

Mysingur A soft brown cheese made from cow's milk whey in Iceland.

Mysost A brown, smooth, sweet cheese made in Norway (and other Scandinavian countries). Mysost is the equivalent of Gjetost, except that it is made with cow's milk whey.

Nagelkaas (Friese nagelkaas) A version of the Dutch Friesekaas, flavoured with cloves and sometimes caraway or cumin.

Neufchâtel A soft, mild cheese with a white rind, made in France from cow's milk.

Nieheimer (Nieheimer hopfenkäse) A sour-milk cheese named for the city of Nieheim in the province of Westphalia. Nieheimer is a dry cheese, traditionally packed with hops for curing.

Niolo A square and creamy goat's milk cheese from Corsica.

Niza A Portuguese mountain cheese (Queijo da serra) made from sheep's or goat's milk.

Nökkelost (Nokkelost, Nøkkelost, Nögelost) A semihard Norwegian cheese spiced with cloves. Nökkelost bears the stamp of the keys of the town of Leyden on its rind (*nökkel* is Norwegian for "keys").

Norbo A Norwegian semihard cheese that originated in Holland.

Oaxaca *See* Asadero.

Odalostur (Odalsost) The Icelandic version of Emmental.

Oka The Canadian version of Port du Salut, originally made in the Trappist monastery at Oka. It is a rubbery cheese with a mild aroma and soft, spicy flavour.

Olivet A soft, rather sharp cow's milk cheese from France.

Olivet blue A half-ripened Olivet with a bluish tint.

Olmützer quargel A Moravian sour-milk cheese similar to Handkäse and Quark and sometimes seasoned with caraway.

Olsztynski (Ser Olsztynski) A traditional Polish skimmed-milk cheese, matured in a barrel of brine.

Orduna (Prensado de Orduna) A Basque cheese similar to Idiazabal.

Orkney A small, soft Scottish cheese with a natural rind and a strong odour.

Oschtjepka (Oschtjepek) A smoked plastic curd sheep's milk cheese from the mountains of Slovakia.

Ossau-Iraty-Brebis *See* Ardi-Gasna.

Ossetin A sheep's or cow's milk cheese from the Caucasus, matured in brine.

Oustet A variety of Bethmale, named after the French region in which it is made.

Ovari The Hungarian version of Tilset.

Ovcji sir A salt-cured sheep's milk cheese from the Slovenian Alps.

Paglia A cow's milk cheese from Switzerland, similar to Gorgonzola.

Pago Sheep's milk cheese made on the island of Pag, off the west coast of Yugoslavia.

Panarone (Pannarone, Gorgonzola bianca) A rapidly matured Gorgonzola that does not form blue marbling.

Parenica A Slovakian sheep's milk cheese similar to Caciocavallo and Oschtjepka.

Parmesan (Parmigiano Reggiano) A pressed, hard, granular cow's milk cheese from Italy with a delicately spicy taste, traditionally used as a grating cheese.

Pategrás (Patagras) The Cuban version of Gouda.

Pavé de Moyaux A large variety of Pont-l'Evêque.

Pecorino The name given to all Italian cheeses made from sheep's milk; in particular, those that are hard and cooked.

Pecorino Romano A straw-coloured, granular Italian cheese that may be eaten grated or straight from the block.

Pecorino Sardo *See* Fiore Sardo.

Pecorino Siciliano (Pecorino pepato) A variety of Pecorino made with grains of pepper.

Pélardon A tiny white goat's milk cheese from France, eaten fresh, when it has a full flavour.

Peneteleu (Penteleu) A Romanian version of Caciocavallo, similar to Kaskaval, made in the Penteleu Range of the Carpathian Mountains.

Pepato A Romano-type cheese seasoned with pepper.

Pera (Queso de Pera) A pasta filata cow's milk cheese made in Colombia and sold in tiny portions. Pera is similar to Provolone.

Petit-Suisse A very soft and creamy French cheese made from fresh milk with cream added.

Pfister A cow's milk cheese from Switzerland which looks a little like a small Emmental.

Picodon (Picardon) A tiny French goat's milk cheese from the Drôme region.

Pineapple An American cheese shaped like a pineapple. It matures in nets for several months, and is rubbed with oil or shellac to give it a hard, shiny exterior.

Pinzgauer bierkäse A spicy Austrian cheese intended for consumption with beer.

Plateau A washed-rind variety of Herve, which has all its flavour but none of its excessively strong odour.

Plattekees (Plattekaas) A type of fresh curd cheese from Austria.

Podhalanski A semihard cow's or sheep's milk cheese from Poland, with little holes and a firm rind. It is sold in slabs, sometimes in smoked varieties.

Pont-l'Evêque A square, golden-yellow cheese from France, with a soft texture and a rich and tangy flavour.

Port du Salut (Port Salut) A flat, cylindrical cheese originally from France, with a mild flavour similar to Gouda. Similar varieties are made all over the world, where they are called Trappist, Trappistenkäse, or Oka.

Potato A German cheese made from a combination of cow's, sheep's, or goat's milk, salt, mashed potatoes, and sometimes caraway seed.

Prato A Brazilian version of Gouda, similar to Patagras.

Prätost (Prestost) A homemade soft cheese from Norway, traditionally made by the pastor's wife with milk brought to her by parishioners.

Prattigau A cow's milk cheese from the Alps, often compared to Limburger.

Presukaca A pasta filata cheese equivalent to Kashkaval, made in Bosnia-Herzegovina by dipping the drained curds in hot water.

Provatura A soft member of the Caciocavallo family, made from buffalo's milk in Italy.

Provole An Italian pasta filata cheese made from buffalo's milk in a manner similar to Caciocavallo, and eaten when it is only a few days old.

Provolone The most famous variety of Caciocavallo. It is light in colour, mellow, smooth, and cuts without crumbling.

Pultost A lowfat Norwegian cheese made from sour cow's milk, occasionally with the addition of herbs, spices, or cream.

Quacheq A Yugoslavian sheep's milk cheese eaten either fresh or after it has ripened.

Quargel A naturally curdled Austrian soft cheese similar to Sauerkäse and Sauermilchkäse.

Quark A German sour-milk cheese made without rennet and eaten while very young.

Quartirolo A soft cow's milk Italian cheese.

Queijo de serra (Queijo da serra) A soft sheep's or goat's milk cheese from the mountains of southern Portugal; it comes in many varieties.

Queso Añejo See Añejo.

Queso blanco Literally, "white cheese." It is the principal Latin American cheese, soft and white, and made just about everywhere under various names, either fresh or semimatured.

Queso de bola The Mexican version of Edam.

Queso de crema A Latin American cheese similar to the French Petit-Suisse and Neufchâtel.

Queso de hoja A cow's milk, salt-cured cheese made in Puerto Rico.

Queso de la tierra See Queso del país.

Queso de prensa A hard cheese made in Puerto Rico from whole cow's milk.

Queso de puna A Puerto Rican cheese similar to Cottage cheese except that it is moulded into forms.

Queso del país (Queso de la tierra) Literally "cheese of the country" or "native cheese," a white, pressed, semisoft cheese made in Puerto Rico.

Queso fresco The generic term for fresh goat's cheese in Spanish-speaking countries.

Queyras See Champoléon.

Rabacal A Portuguese cheese made from sheep's or goat's milk or both; it is cylindrical, flat, and rather firm.

Raclette The collective name for a group of Swiss cheeses (Gomser is one). Raclette is from the French racler, "to scrape," and raclette cheeses are melted and scraped onto potatoes to make a dish also called raclette. Raclette cheeses must melt evenly and smoothly, and must be creamy but not too chewy when served.

Radener A hard skim (cow's) milk cheese from Germany.

Radolfzeller (Radolfzeller cream) A soft, creamy cow's milk cheese made in Lake Constance, which is bordered by Germany, Switzerland, and Austria.

Ragusano (Ragusana) A pasta filata cheese made from cow's milk in Sicily, used as a grating cheese when it has matured for more than six months.

Rasskäse A variety of Appenzeller with a much lower fat content and a pungent flavour.

Rayon A hard skim cow's milk grating cheese made in Switzerland and Italy.

Reblochon A French cow's milk cheese. Reblochon is mild, creamy, and fragrant, with a yellow washed rind.

Reggiano A hard grating cheese from Italy, similar to Parmesan.

Remoudou A Belgian cheese with a strong odour, similar to Herve and Limburger.

Requeijão A Brazilian cheese made from soured skim milk and rich cream.

Rheinwald See Schamser.

Richelieu The Canadian version of Bel paese.

Ricotta A soft Italian cheese made of the coagulated

matter from the whey of cow's or sheep's milk. Ricotta is now manufactured all over the world.

Ricotta Romana A regional version of Ricotta cheese made from sheep's milk.

Riddarost A rindless cheese from Sweden, with or without spices, that finishes its maturation process in its final foil packaging.

Ridder A semihard cheese from Norway, similar to Saint-Paulin.

Riesengebirge A mountain cheese made from goat's milk in the mountains of northern Bohemia.

Rinnen A sour-milk, spiced cow's milk cheese made in Poland.

Riola A soft cheese made in Italy from goat's or sheep's milk; it is similar to Mont d'Or, except that it is ripened for a longer period.

Robiola (Robbiole) A soft, rich cheese from Italy, similar to Crescenza.

Robiolino (Robbiolini) A soft, smooth cheese from Italy, very similar to Crescenza and Robiola but smaller and sold in bars or rolls.

Rollot A sharp, washed-rind cheese made in Picardy, France, and similar to Maroilles.

Romadur A soft, ripened cow's milk cheese from Germany, very similar to Limburger but milder.

Romanello A very hard cheese with a sharp flavour from Italy; its name means "little Romano."

Romano A very hard Italian cheese now made all over the world, including the United States and Australia.

Roquefort A soft, creamy, blue-veined sheep's milk cheese from France, with a strong smell and flavour.

Royal Brabant A small, Limburger-type cheese made in Belgium from cow's milk.

Royalp-Tilsit (Royalp) A Swiss version of the German Tilset, prepared with raw rather than pasteurized milk.

Rumi An Egyptian semihard cheese similar to Gouda.

Saanen A cow's milk cheese made in a manner similar to Emmental, but aged for at least three years until it is extremely hard.

Saarland Pfarr (Saaland Pfarr) A version of Prätost made by mixing whisky with the curds and then washing the cheese with whisky twice a week during maturation.

Saint Stephano A rare version of Bel paese made in Germany.

Saint-Marcellin A soft, sweet cheese from France, with blue mould cultivated on the surface but not in the interior of the cheese.

Saint-Nectare A supple, mild cow's milk cheese from France that is matured until its rind is spotted yellow to ochre-red.

Saint-Paulin A cheese similar to Port du Salut and Citeaux, made and consumed all over France and now in other countries throughout the world.

Sainte-Maure A log-shaped goat's milk cheese from France, pierced with a straw or stick to prevent breakage.

Salamana A soft, sheep's milk cheese from Greece, with a pronounced flavour, matured in a goatskin or bladder.

Saloio A small round cheese made near Lisbon in Portugal.

Samsø A mild, semisoft cheese with a hazelnut flavour, similar to the Swiss Emmental, with small, irregular holes.

Sapsago (Glarner Schabzieger, Schabziger, Glarnerkäse) A small, very hard, green skim-milk cheese from Switzerland that derives its colour from dried clover added to the curd.

Sardo *See* Fiore Sardo.

Sarrazin A Swiss version of blue-veined cheese.

Sartenais A goat's or sheep's milk cheese from Corsica, with a round shape and a strong flavour.

Sauerkäse A mellow, spicy, fragrant cheese from Austria, near the Swiss border.

Sauermilchkäse The generic name for a variety of small, soft cheeses with low fat content from Germany.

Sbrinz A hard cow's milk cheese from Switzerland, matured for a very long time, which gives it a sharp, full flavour. It is famous for being easy to digest.

Scanno A buttery cheese made from sheep's milk in Italy.

Scarmorze (Scamorze) An Italian pasta filata cheese sometimes formed in the shape of a pig.

Schabziger *See* Sapsago.

Schamser (Rheinwald) A wheel-shaped cheese made from skim (cow's) milk in Switzerland.

Schimmelkäse The name of a variety of blue-mould cheeses made in the Bavarian Alps.

Schloss A soft, ripened cheese similar to Romadur, made in Austria and Germany.

Schnittkäse A German smoked cheese similar in texture to Butterkäse.

Schützenkäse A Romadur-type cheese with an assertive flavour made in Austria.

Schwarzenberger A Limburger-type cheese made in Austria, Hungary, and Bohemia.

Selles-sur-Cher A savoury goat's cheese from France, covered with salt and finely powdered charcoal.

Serpa *See* Alentejo.

Serra *See* Queijo de serra.

Serra da Estrella A soft Portuguese cheese made in the Serra da Estrella mountain range from sheep's milk.

Sicille A round cheese with a hard rind, flavoured with paprika, from northern Africa.

Siraz A Serbian cow's milk cheese formed into largish pebble shapes which are dried in the sun.

Sirene The Bulgarian version of Feta cheese, made with cow's milk or sheep's milk.

Siriz Mjesine (Sir iz Mjesine) A skimmed sheep's milk cheese made in the Balkans and matured in goatskins.

Skyr A fresh cheese made from the whey of cow's milk in Iceland.

Slipcote (Slipcoat, Colwick) A soft, fresh cream cheese made from cow's milk in England.

Spalen A variety of Sbrinz named after the wooden containers in which the cheese used to be packed.

Spitzkäse A small spiced cheese made in Germany from skimmed cow's milk.

Stangenkäse A German cheese made from partly skimmed milk.

Steinbuscher A buttery, moist cheese made from cow's milk in Germany; it is often compared to Romadur.

Stepnoi (Stepnoj) A Russian version of Gouda.

Stilton A hard, blue-veined cow's milk cheese from England, with a crinkled brown rind and a flaky texture.

Surati A buffalo's milk cheese from India, famous for its nutritional and medicinal properties.

Sveciaost A Swedish cow's milk cheese similar to Gouda but with a more open texture.

Swiss cheese The American name for cheese of the Emmental variety.

Taffel (Taffelost) A Scandinavian table cheese made from cow's milk. Taffel has a dense texture and a spicy flavour.

Tafi A mountain cheese similar to Cantal, made from cow's milk in western Argentina.

Taleggio A soft, mild cow's milk cheese from Italy, with a thin reddish or pinkish rind.

Tamié (Tamie) A cheese produced at the French abbey of Tamié; it is similar to Reblochon.

Tanzenberger A Limburger-type cheese made in southern Austria.

Tel peynir A kneaded cheese made in Turkey from skimmed milk.

Telpanir An Armenian cheese with Turkish origins, made with the skimmed sour milk of cows or sheep and matured in wooden boxes for about a week.

Testouri A ball-shaped cheese made from beaten milk in North Africa.

Tête de moine *See* Bellay.

Texel A sheep's milk cheese made in Holland.

Tibet A very hard yak's milk cheese made in the Himalayas.

Tilsit (Tilsiter, Tilsitter) First made by Dutch immigrants who settled in the vicinity of Tilsit in East Prussia. Tilsit is known by various names around the world (Ragnit, Royalp-Tilsit, Soviet-ski), but is particularly popular in Germany. It is similar to Gouda and Edam, with pale yellow insides dotted with small irregular holes, and is sometimes flavoured with caraway.

Tomme au Marc A Tomme de Savoie that has been fermented in eau-de-vie made from grape pulp, known as Marc de Bourgogne.

Tomme d'Aligot (Aligot) A French mountain cheese, made from cow's milk and similar to Mozzarella. If not eaten fresh (within 48 hours) it is used as a base for Cantal.

Tomme de Savoie A traditional French cheese made from cow's milk, with a fresh and particular taste, sometimes bitter or sourish.

Tomme Vaudoise One of the few Swiss soft cheeses. Tomme Vaudoise has an almost liquid consistency enclosed by a faintly white rind. It has a mild taste and aroma.

Touareg A hard goat's milk cheese made in Africa by tribesmen; it is matured in the sun or by a fire.

Touloumisio A variety of Feta, matured in wooden barrels and skin bags.

Trapistaw A soft, washed-rind Trappist cheese made in Poland.

Trappist A pale yellow, mild, semihard cheese first made in 1885 in a monastery in Bosnia. It is now the generic term for any cheese made by monks of the Trappist order.

Trappistenkäse A version of Port du Salut made in Austria and Germany.

Travnik A soft, white, mild Bosnian cheese made from sheep's milk with goat's milk added.

Trecce A small pasta filata cheese from Italy.

Trouville A soft, ripened cheese very similar to Pont-l'Evêque, except that Trouville is made only from whole milk.

Tschil A rustic Armenian cow's or sheep's milk cheese.

Tulum A firm Turkish cheese, pressed and matured in a goat- or sheepskin bag (a *tulum*), with a strong, tangy taste.

Twarogowy A traditional Polish mountain cheese made from cow's or sheep's milk.

Twdr sir (Tvdr sir) A Yugoslavian sheep's milk cheese similar to Brick cheese.

Tworog (Tvorog) A Russian sour (cow's) milk cheese pressed into wooden forms.

Tybo A variety of the Danish Samsø, about half the size of Elbo.

Tylzscki (Tylzycki) The Polish version of Tilsit.

Urda (Urdâ) A soft Romanian cheese similar to Ricotta, flavoured with herbs. It is made from the whey that remains after making Brinza.

Uri A small, hard cow's milk cheese from Switzerland.

Vacherin à fondue A runny variety of Vacherin Fribourgeois, wrapped in a cloth and packed in chip boxes. As the name suggests, it is often used to make fondue.

Vacherin à la main A variety of Vacherin Fribourgeois, with a strong flavour.

Vacherin d'abondance A soft, brushed-rind cheese made from cow's milk in the Alps.

Vacherin Fribourgeois One of two types of Vacherin (the other is Vacherin Mont d'Or) made in the west of Switzerland. Fribourgeois is a soft cheese with a brownish-yellow rind.

Vacherin Mont d'Or The second type of Vacherin from the west of Switzerland. Mont d'Or is a soft, liquid cheese with a wrinkled, reddish rind and a mild, creamy flavour.

Västerbotten A larger and heavier version of Sve-ciaost, with a shorter maturation period and hence a milder taste.

Västgotaöst A Swedish cheese similar to Herrgårdsost but with irregular machine-made openings rather than round eyes.

Venaco A Corsican salted cheese with a powerful flavour, made from goat's or sheep's milk.

Vendôme A soft, ripened cow's milk cheese similar to Camembert.

Veneto A sharp cow's milk cheese from around Venice, similar to Asiago.

Vize (Vizé) A Greek grating cheese made from sheep's milk. It is similar to Romano.

Void A soft French cheese similar to Limburger, made from cow's milk.

Voljski (Volzky syr) A cow's milk cheese with an elastic texture from the Volga Basin. It is sold in slabs or blocks.

Vorarlberg A hard, moist, sour (cow's) milk cheese made in Austria; it has a strong flavour and taste.

Washed curd cheese A semisoft to slightly firm cheese that is made in the same way as Cheddar except that the milled curd is washed with water before it is salted, increasing the moistness of the cheese.

Weisslacker *See* Bierkäse.

Wensleydale A cow's milk cheese from Yorkshire, England, which comes in blue-veined and white varieties.

Werder A Prussian cheese similar to Tilsit but with more moisture and less sharpness.

Wilstermarsch (Wilster marschkäse) A Tilsit-like, sharp-tasting cheese made from cow's milk in Schleswig-Holstein, Germany.

Withania A cow's milk cheese made in Southeast Asia, named for the berries of the withania plant.

York *See* Cambridge.

Zakussotchny (Zakusocnyj) A soft cow's milk cheese from Russia.

Ziger (Zieger) The German name for whey cheese, known in the United States and Italy as Ricotta.

COFFEES

A list, by no means complete, of the names of quality coffees available from around the world. Often a coffee from a country is known merely by the name of the country, for instance, Kenya, but there are also names for varieties of coffee within a country, such as Brazilian Santos or Ethiopian Yirgacheffe.

AUSTRALIA

A mild, light, fruity, low-acid coffee bean.

BRAZIL

Santos beans are the most popular for their sweet, clear, neutral flavour. Varieties include: **Bourbon Santos**, bitter, made from the first few crops, which are grown from Mocha seed; **Red Santos**, sweet; **Flat Bean Santos**, made from the sixth year of crops; **New Crop Santos**, acidy. **Rio**, **Parana**, **Victoria**, and **Bahia** are other varieties of Brazilian coffee beans. They are mass produced, with a heavy, pungent, muddy taste.

BURUNDI

High-grade Burundi beans are rich and aromatic.

CHINA

Indigenous hill tribes from the mountain ranges of China produce arabica coffee for local consumption. Similar to Kenya, the coffee has a rich, mellow taste.

COLOMBIA

Supremo is one of the most-exported brands, sweet and aromatic. **Excelso** is the other most-exported. It is soft and slightly acid and not always consistent. **Medellin**, **Armenia**, **Manizales**, **Bogota**, and **Bucaramanga** are other famous names.

COSTA RICA

A high-quality coffee with a mild flavour and full body, and an acidity level that increases with elevation. **La Minita** has a full body, sweet aroma, and delicate aftertaste. **Tarrazu** has a robust flavour and a lively acidity. **Tres Rios**, **Santa Rosa**, **Montbello**, **Juan Vinas**, **Alajuela**, and **Heredia** are some other famous names.

CUBA

Cuban coffee beans make a pleasant coffee, like the Jamaican, but not as acidic because the mountains are not very high.

DOMINICAN REPUBLIC

Barahona has the best reputation; it resembles Jamaican High Mountain in its acidity. **Bani** and **Ocoa** are soft and mellow. **Cibao** and **Santo Domingo** are two other varieties.

ECUADOR

A medium-bodied coffee with occasional sharp acidity. **Chanchamayo** is one name.

EL SALVADOR

The best beans are labelled "strictly high grown," and are classic Central American coffees—pleasant, with a mild sweet taste and delicate fragrance.

ETHIOPIA

Harrar, graded as "Longberry" and "Shortberry," is the most famous. It is sometimes called **Ethiopian Moka**, and has winey, gamey, fruity, and spicy flavours. **Djimah** and **Lekempti** have earthy, wild gamey qualities. **Gimbi** is a "washed" coffee with a winey flavour. **Sidamo** is a washed coffee with fruity, vanilla tones. **Yirgacheffe** is also washed, and is fragrant and flowery. Other varieties include **Abyssinian** and **Jimma**.

GUATEMALA

The best grades are the high-grown "strictly hard bean." They are known for their rich spicy or smoky flavour. **Antigua** has a lively, complex flavour and spicy chocolatey overtones. **Heuheutanango** has a pronounced aroma and a distinctive winey taste. Other varieties are **Coban** and **Atilan**.

HAITI

The best grades are the "strictly high grown washed." They are sweet and mellow, resembling Jamaican **Blue Mountain**. **Haitian Bleu** is rich, acidic, sweet, and smooth.

HAWAII

Kona is grown on volcanic lava in the Kona district of Hawaii, between the twin volcanoes Mauna Loa and Mauna Kea. It is a rich coffee with a good aroma and a nutty, spicy taste. **San Juanillo Kauai** is a cheaper version of Kona.

INDIA

Mysore is the most famous variety, but other names are **Coorg**, **Bababudan**, **Shevaroys**, and **Billigris**. India also produces a kind of coffee with a process known as "monsooning," where unwashed beans are first exposed to dampness and then to the hot air of the monsoon winds. Monsooned **Malabar** is one of the best of this type, with a deep colour and a rich spicy flavour.

INDONESIA

Java coffees are spicy and full-bodied with a strong flavour. **Old Java** is a rare coffee aged for about three years, with a sweet mellow flavour. Other names are **Java Arabica**, **Old Government**, **Old Brown**, and **Rare Old Java**. Sumatra coffees are very strong and complex: **Mandheling** and **Ankola** are two fine varieties, with an almost syrupy richness and a unique musty flavour. Celebes **Toraja** is like Sumatra, but lighter and more acid. Celebes **Kalossie Sulawesi** is a rare coffee with nutty and dark chocolate flavours.

JAMAICA

Blue Mountain coffee is a legendary coffee with a very simple, sweet flavour and good aroma. The best varieties are **Wallensford Blue Mountain** and **Silverhill Estate Blue Mountain**. **High Mountain** has similar attributes, but less pronounced.

KENYA

A very good coffee with sharp acidity and excellent flavour and fragrance. **Kenya Peaberry** is a prized variety with an intense flavour. **Kenyan AA** is the largest bean, with **Kenyan A** and **Kenyan B** following behind. **Nairobi** is another variety.

MALAWI

Similar to Kenya, but lighter and less fine.

MEXICO

Mexican coffees have a fine acidity, delicate body, and mellow flavour. **Coatepec**, **Huatusco**, **Orizaba**, **Oaxaca**, and **Chiapas** are the best known; the **Margogype** from Mexico is the best of that variety of arabica coffee grown in Central America.

NICARAGUA

Jinotegas and **Matagalpas** are probably the best varieties of this mild-flavoured, medium-bodied coffee, but the quality is irregular.

PANAMA

Panama coffees have a good acidity, full body, and a mild pleasant flavour.

PAPUA NEW GUINEA

The high-grown milds resemble Kenya, but have less acidity and more sweetness. Varieties include **Sigri**, **Kiap**, and **Arona**.

PERU

Chanchamayos is full- to medium-bodied, delicate, flavourful, and gently acid.

TANZANIA

Similar to Kenya, with a rich winey flavour and aroma, but not as acid. The best is **Kibo Chagga**. Other names are **Kilimanjaro**, **Moshi**, and **Arusha**.

UGANDA

Bugisu is high-grown, with a full body and good acidity, like Kenya.

VENEZUELA

A very original coffee, different from the other American coffees, with a mild, sweet, and delicate flavour and aroma. **Meridas** is the best of the **Maracaibos**, which have a peculiar delicate flavour. **Caracas** has a distinctive, attractive flavour.

YEMEN

Yemeni coffee is called **Mocha**. It has a clear, distinctive, gamey flavour and a very heavy body. **Mocha Sanani** has a full body and spicy flavour. **Mocha Mattari** is aromatic, with a fruity, chocolatey flavour.

ZAIRE

Kivu and **Ituri** are coffees with a high acidity and pleasant flavour.

ZIMBABWE

A pleasantly acid coffee similar to Kenya but not as richly flavoured. **Smaldeel Estate** has dry fruit and cinnamon tones.

CONDIMENTS

PRESERVES

Butters Thick preserve from fruit pulp, sugar, spices
Conserves Two or more fruits made into jam with nuts and raisins
Jams Crushed fruit and sugar
Jellies Fruit juice and sugar
Marmalades Soft jelly with pieces of fruit or peel
Preserves Fruit that keeps its shape in syrup
Tutti-frutti Assorted fruits, sugar, brandy

PICKLES

Bread and butter pickle
Carrot pickle
Cauliflower pickle
Dill pickle
Ginger pickle
Green mango pickle
Lemon pickle
Okra pickle
Pickled beet
Pickled crab apple
Pickled onion
Sour pickle
Sweet pickle
Watermelon pickle
Zucchini pickle

RELISHES

Celery relish
Chowchow
Chutney
    Apple chutney
    Eggplant chutney
    Lime chutney
    Mango chutney
    Peach chutney
    Rhubarb chutney
    Sweet potato chutney
Corn relish
Cranberry orange relish
Green tomato relish
Horseradish sauce

Mostarda di Frutta (Mustard fruits)
Piccalilli
Sweet chilli sauce
Sweet pepper relish
Tomato relish
Zucchini relish

KETCHUPS

Apple
Cucumber
Grape
Mushroom
Oyster
Tomato
Walnut

MUSTARDS

Bavarian
Chinese
Dijon
English
Grainy
Hot
Japanese
Spicy brown
Sweet
Yellow

HOT SAUCES

Black bean
Chilli
Harissa
Nam prik
Piri-piri
Salsa
Sambal
Saus prik
Sherry pepper
Tabasco
Wasabi

ASIAN SAUCES

Fish (Nam pla)
Goma
Gomairi
Hoisin

Ketjap
Mirin
Miso
Mushroom
Oyster
Peanut
Plum
Ponzu
Satay
Shishimi
Shrimp paste
Soy
Sweet and sour
Tamari
Tentsuyu
Teriyaki
Tonkatsu

VINEGARS

Apple cider
Balsamic
Fruit
Herb
Malt
Rice
Wine

OILS

Almond
Canola
Coconut
Corn
Grapeseed
Hazelnut
Olive
Palm
Peanut
Sesame
Vegetable
Walnut

FRUITS

Apple
Apricot
Avocado
Banana
Bilberry
Blackberry
Blueberry
Boysenberry
Breadfruit
Cantaloupe
Cherimoya
Cherry
Citron
Clementine
Cloudberry
Coconut
Crab apple
Cranberry
Currant
Date
Fig
Gooseberry
Grape
Grapefruit
Guava
Honeydew
Huckleberry
Kiwi
Kumquat
Lemon
Lime
Lingonberry
Litchi
Loganberry
Loquat
Mango
Medlar
Melon
Nectarine
Orange
Papaya
Passionfruit
Pawpaw
Peach
Pear

Persimmon
Pineapple
Plum
Pomegranate
Prune
Quince
Raisin
Raspberry
Rhubarb
Rose hip
Rowanberry
Star fruit
Strawberry
Tamarind
Tangerine
Tomatillo
Tomato
Watermelon

GRAINS

Alfalfa
Amaranth
Arrowroot
Barley
Buckwheat (Kasha)
Bulgur
Corn (Maize)
Millet
Oats
Quinoa
Rice
Rye
Sago
Sorghum
Soy
Spelt
Teff
Wheat

LIQUORS, LIQUEURS, AND CHAMPAGNE BOTTLE SIZES

LIQUORS

Apple jack
Aquavit
Armagnac
Bourbon
Brandy
Cognac
Gin
Grappa
Kava
Mescal
Pisco
Pulque
Rum
Rye
Sake (Samshu)
Scotch
Tequila
Vodka
Whisky

LIQUEURS

Absinthe
Advocaat
Amaretto
Amontillado
Amoroso
Angelica
Anisette
Apricot brandy
Bailey's Irish Creme
Banana liqueur
Benedictine
Calvados
Cassis
Chartreuse

Cointreau
Creme de cacao
Creme de menthe
Curaçao
Cynar
Drambuie
Fernet Branca
Framboise
Frangelico
Galliano
Grand Marnier
Kirsch
Kummel
Kvass
Madeira
Malmsey
Mirabelle
Muscatel
Ouzo
Pastis
Peach liqueur
Pernod
Poire Williams
Port
Prunelle
Quetsch
Raspail
Retsina
Sambuca
Schnapps
Sherry
Shochu
Slivovitz
Strega
Triple sec
Vermouth

CHAMPAGNE BOTTLE SIZES

Split (Baby, Nip) quarter bottle
Bottle 0.75 litre
Magnum 2 bottles
Jeroboam (double magnum) 4 bottles
Rehoboam 6 bottles
Methuselah 8 bottles
Salmanazar 12 bottles
Balthazar 16 bottles
Nebuchadnezzar 20 bottles

NUTS

Almond
Brazil nut
Cashew
Chestnut
Hazelnut (Filbert)
Hickory
Peanut
Pecan
Pine nut
Pistachio
Walnut

SEEDS

Achiote (Annatto)
Anise
Caraway
Cardamom
Celery
Coriander
Cumin
Dill
Fennel
Flax
Poppy
Sesame (Benne)

SPICES

Ajowan *(Trachyspermum copticum)* a.k.a. ajuan, ajawain, omum. An Indian spice seed related to caraway and cumin. It looks like a large celery seed and tastes similar to thyme.

Allspice *(Pimenta dioica)* a.k.a. clove pepper, Jamaica pepper, myrtle pepper, pimenta, toute-épice. The dried berry is used whole or ground into a powder. The taste resembles a blend of nutmeg, cinnamon, and clove.

Amchur *(Mangifera indica)* a.k.a. amchoor. Unripe fruit of the mango tree, sliced and dried in the sun, and used powdered or in slices for the sweet-sour taste it adds to Indian cooking.

Anise *(Pimpinella anisum)* a.k.a. aniseed, sweet cumin. An annual plant, whose seeds are used whole or ground into a powder for use as a flavouring.

Anise-pepper *(Zanthoxylum piperitum)* A peppery, hot spice created by drying and grinding the berries of shrubs which grow in China. One of the ingredients of Chinese five-spice.

Annatto *(Bixa orellana)* a.k.a. achiote, annotto, arnatto, bija, bijol, lipstick tree, roucou. The seeds are ground and used as a seasoning in Latin American cooking.

Arrowroot *(Maranta arundinacea)* Ground arrowroot is used as a thickening agent.

Asafoetida *(Ferula assa-foetida* and *foetida)* a.k.a. asafetida, devil's dung, giant fennel, Persian gum, stinking gum. A very strong-smelling spice used ground in very small quantities.

Caraway seed *(Carum carvi)* The seeds of the caraway plant, a relative of parsley, are used dried or ground as a seasoning.

Cardamom *(Elettaria cardamomum)* The seeds of plants of the ginger family; they are very expensive and have a peppery, spicy taste.

Cassia *(Cinnamomum cassia)* a.k.a. Chinese cinnamon, false cinnamon. A close relative of cinnamon with a weaker aroma but similar pungency.

Cayenne pepper *(Capsicum frutescens)* Ground small red chilli peppers.

Celery seed *(Apium graveolens)* a.k.a. smallage. Tiny brown seeds which are aromatic and slightly bitter.

Chilli powder A blend of ground dried chillies and some combination of garlic, onion, cumin, oregano, allspice, salt, and other spices.

Chinese five-spice A Chinese spice mixture made of finely ground anise-pepper, star anise, cassia or cinnamon, cloves, and fennel seed.

Cinnamon *(Cinnamomum zeylanicum)* The bark of a small evergreen tree used ground or in whole pieces.

Clove *(Syzygium aromaticum)* The dried, unopened flower buds of the evergreen clove tree.

Coriander *(Coriandrum sativum)* The seeds have a hot, harsh flavour and can be used whole or ground.

Cubeb *(Piper cubeba)* The dried unripe berry of an Indonesian plant. Cubeb has a pungent, spicy flavour, similar to allspice but more peppery.

Cumin *(Cuminum cyminum)* The dried seed of a plant belonging to the parsley family, cumin is pungent, hot, and bitter. The seeds are used whole or ground.

Curry powder A blend of any number of different spices that can range from mild to very hot. Some of the spices generally used are black pepper, dried red chilli, cloves, cinnamon, cardamom, coriander, cumin, curry leaves, fenugreek, ginger, mace, mustard seed, poppy seed, and turmeric, which adds colour.

Dill seed *(Anethum graveolens)* The dried seeds of the dill plant, with a fresh, sweet aroma and a slightly bitter taste, similar to caraway seeds.

Fennel seed *(Foeniculum vulgare)* The seeds of the fennel plant—plumper, larger versions of anise seeds.

Fenugreek *(Trigonella foenum-graecum)* a.k.a. bird's foot, Greek hay, and methi. The seeds of Greek hay are dried, ground into a powder, and used as an ingredient in curries.

Galangal, Greater *(Alpinea glanga)* a.k.a. catarrh root, Laos, and lengkuas. A member of the ginger-root family, the spicy roots are grated and used as a seasoning.

Galangal, Lesser *(Alpinea officinarum)* a.k.a. Chinese ginger, East India root, galingal, kencur. A member of the ginger-root family, it is used in curries and stews, more as a vegetable than as a seasoning.

Ginger *(Zingiber officinale)* A root which may be used grated and fresh, or dried and powdered. It has a spicy, peppery flavour.

Grains of Paradise *(Elettaria granum-paradise)* a.k.a. Guinea grains. The seeds of a plant related to cardamom, they are hot and peppery.

Horseradish *(Armoracia rusticana)* A pungent root which is grated or scraped for use as a condiment.

Juniper *(Juniperus communis)* The juniper berry is used as a flavouring, usually crushed before use. It is most famously used to flavour gin, but is also used in food, and goes well with most other herbs—parsley, thyme, fennel, marjoram, bay.

Kokum *(Garcinia indica)* The dried skin of the fruit of the kokum tree, used like tamarind as a souring agent in Indian cooking.

Mace *(Myristica fragrans)* a.k.a. Banda mace, Penang mace. The threadlike tendrils (arils) on the surface of nutmeg, the fruit of an evergreen tree. Mace is sold dried and whole or dried and ground, and is used as a flavouring for cakes, soups, and stews.

Melegueta pepper *(Elettaria melegueta)* Tiny grains related to cardamom; they have a hot and peppery taste and smell very similar to cardamom.

Mustard, black *(Brassica nigra)* The seeds of a member of the cabbage family, black mustard is strong and pungent in flavour and closely related to brown mustard.

Mustard, brown *(Brassica juncea)* Bitter, hot, and aromatic, brown mustard seeds are more commonly grown than black.

Mustard, white *(Sinapis alba)* Large yellowish seeds, used extensively in the production of American prepared mustards.

Nasturtium seed *(Tropaeolum majus)* The seeds can be ground like pepper, and have a cresslike flavour.

Nigella *(Nigella sativa, and various species)* a.k.a. black caraway, black cumin, devil-in-the-bush, fennel flower, kalonji, nutmeg flower, Roman coriander, wild onion seed. Very small black seeds with an aromatic, peppery flavour.

Nutmeg *(Myristica fragrans)* The kernel of the apricot-like fruit of a variety of evergreen. It is dried and grated or ground and used in a variety of dishes.

Paprika *(Capsicum annuum)* Made from a sweet red pepper; varieties differ by country of origin: Spain, Portugal, and Hungary.

Pepper *(Piper nigrum)* Both black pepper and white pepper are made from the same berry—black pepper is the sun-dried green berry and white pepper is the ripe berry with the hull removed.

Pink peppercorn *(Schinus molle)* a.k.a. red peppercorn. The pink berries of a South American tree often used in combination with black and white pepper, but not a true pepper. Can be toxic in large quantities.

Poppy seed *(Papaver somniferum)* The ripened seeds of the opium poppy used whole or ground in cooking or baking.

Saffron *(Crocus sativus)* The aromatic, pungent dried stigmas of the crocus flower. This very expensive spice is a bright yellow colour and is used both to colour and season food.

Salt Ordinary table salt is sodium chloride. Other varieties include sea salt and rock salt, which can contain additional minerals.

Sassafras *(Sassafras variifolium)* a.k.a. filé gumbo, filé powder. Dried, powdered sassafras leaves and roots.

Sesame seed *(Sesamum indicum)* a.k.a. benne. The little seeds of the sesame plant have a nutlike flavour and come in a variety of colours: black, white, and tan.

Star anise *(Illicium verum)* a.k.a. Chinese anise, Indian anise. The star-shaped fruit of a small evergreen tree native to China. It is used whole, broken, ground, and in seed form, primarily in Chinese cooking.

Sumac *(Rhus coriaria)* a.k.a. elm-leaved sumac, Sicilian sumac, Tanner's sumac. The berries are dried and used whole or ground in cooking for their sour taste.

Tamarind *(Tamarindus indica)* a.k.a. Indian date. The fruit pod of the tamarind tree, used fresh or dried, whole or in block or concentrate form for its sour fruity flavour.

Turmeric *(Curcuma domestica)* a.k.a. Indian saffron, saffron of the Indies. The dried ground root of a member of the ginger family, turmeric is orange-yellow, with a gingery aroma and a somewhat bitter taste. It is sometimes used fresh.

Vanilla *(Vanilla planifolia)* The bean of a climbing orchid, used fresh or in extract form.

Zedoary *(Curcuma zedoaria)* Closely related to turmeric and used in the same way.

TEA

TYPES OF TEA

Black (fermented)
Green (unfermented)
Oolong (semifermented)
Pouchong (lightly fermented)

BLACK TEA CATEGORIES

Leaf grades
Orange pekoe (long, thin leaves)
Pekoe (small leaves)
Souchong (large, coarse leaves)
Flowery orange pekoe (tips or buds included)
Flowery pekoe (tips or buds included)
Bokea (stalks included)
Silver tip, white tea (unopened buds)

Broken grades (pieces of leaf)
Broken orange pekoe (used in most blends)
Broken pekoe (filler in blends)
Broken pekoe souchong (filler in blends)
Fannings (small, quick-brewing pieces)

GREEN TEA CATEGORIES

China
Gunpowder (tiny balls of aged leaves)
Young hyson (long, thinly rolled, aged leaves)
Imperial (loosely balled old leaves)
Hyson (old leaves)
Imperial twankey (old open leaves)
Hyson skin (poorer quality leaves)
Dust (remains)

India
Fine young hyson
Young hyson
Hyson number 1
Twankay
Sowmee
Fannings
Dust

Japanese leaf styles
Pan-fired (straight leaf)
Guri (curled leaf)
Basket-fired
Natural leaf

Japanese quality gradings
Extra choicest
Choicest
Choice
Finest
Fine
Good medium
Good common
Nibs
Fannings
Dust

OOLONG CATEGORIES

Choice
Finest to choice
Finest
Fine to finest
Fine up
Fine
On fine
Superior to fine
Superior up
Fully superior
Superior
On superior
Good to superior
Good up
Fully good
Good
On good
Standard

MAJOR TEAS OF THE WORLD

Ceylon (Sri Lanka)
Badulla
Dikoya
Dimbula
Galle
Haputale

Maturata
Maskeliya
Nuwara Eliya
Pussellawa
Ratnapura
Uva

India
Assam
Darjeeling
Dooars
Nilgiri

Indonesia
Java
Sumatra

Taiwan
Formosa
Lapsang
Special chun mee
Chun mee
Sow mee
Gunpowder
Formosa oolong
Formosa pouchong
Lapsang souchong
Tung ting

Japan
Gyokuro
Tencha
Sencha
Bancha
Spiderleg
I-chiban cha
Kuko-cha
Gen mai cha
Hoji-cha
Matcha uji

China
Keemun
Ningchow
Xi-chang
Yunnan
Hunan
Paklum

Panyong
Pakling
Ching wo
Yinfeng
Moyune
Tienkai
Hoochow
Pingsuey
Guangdong
Kwangsi
Anwhei
Ti kuan yin
Taiping houkui
Fenghuang dancong
Zengshan xiaozhong

Africa
Burundi
Cameroon
Congo
Kenya
Madagascar
Malawi
Mauritius
Mozambique
South Africa
Tanzania
Uganda
Zimbabwe

MAJOR TEA BLENDS

English breakfast
Irish breakfast
Russian
Earl Grey
Spice blends
Mint blends
Chinese restaurant

SCENTED TEAS

Jasmine
Rose
Orchid
Lychee

HERB TEAS (TISANES)

Alfalfa
Alpine strawberry
Angelica
Anise
Anise hyssop
Ash
Basil
Basswood flower
Bay
Bergamot
Black currant
Bog myrtle
Borage
Burnet
Calamint
Chamomile
Caraway
Catnip
Cinnamon
Clove
Clover
Comfrey
Cowslip
Dandelion
Epazote
Ephedra
Fennel
Fenugreek
Flax
Ginger
Ginseng
Goldenrod
Hawthorn
Hops
Horehound
Hyssop
Lemon balm
Lemon verbena
Liquorice
Linden
Marigold
Marjoram
Mint
Mullein
Nettle
Nutmeg
Passionflower

Pennyroyal
Purslane
Raspberry
Rose
Rosehip
Rosemary
Sage
Sarsaparilla
Sassafras
Savory
Skullcap
Strawberry
Sweet goldenrod (Blue Mountain tea)
Thyme
Vervain
Wild rosemary
Wintergreen
Yarrow
Yerba maté

VEGETABLES

Acorn squash
Adzuki bean
Agar-agar
Artichokes
Arugula (Roquette, Rocket)
Asparagus
Aubergine (Eggplant)
Bamboo shoot
Beet
Black bean
Blackeyed pea
Bok choy
Broad bean
Broccoli
Broccoli rabe
Brussels sprout
Cabbage
Cactus
Cardoon
Carob
Carrageen
Carrot
Cauliflower
Celeriac
Celery
Chard
Chayote
Chick pea (Garbanzo)
Chicory
Collard
Corn
Courgette (Zucchini)
Cucumber
Eggplant (Aubergine)
Endive
Escarole
Fennel
Garlic
Great northern bean
Green bean
Hubbard squash
Jerusalem artichoke
Kale
Kidney bean
Kohlrabi

Leek
Lettuce
Lima bean
Mangetouts (Snow pea)
Manioc (Cassava)
Mung bean
Mushroom
Navy bean
Okra
Olive
Onion
Parsnip
Pea
Pepper
Pinto bean
Potato
Pumpkin
Radicchio
Radish
Red bean
Red cabbage
Salsify
Savoy cabbage
Scallion
Shallot
Snow pea (Mangetouts)
Soybean
Spinach
Squash
String bean
Sweet potato
Taro
Truffle
Turnip
Water chestnut
Watercress
Yam
Yellow squash
Zucchini (Courgette)

WINES

FRENCH WINES

Major regions — Alsace, Bordeaux, Burgundy,
Champagne, Loire, Rhone Valley

White grapes
Aligoté
Bourboulenc
Chardonnay
Chenin blanc
Clairette blanc
Colombard
Gewürztraminer
Grenache blanc
Gros plant
Marsanne
Merlot blanc
Muscadelle
Muscadet
Muscat
Pinot blanc
Riesling
Sauvignon blanc
Semillon
Sylvaner
Tokay pinot gris
Viognier

Red grapes
Cabernet franc
Cabernet sauvignon
Cinsault
Gamay
Grenache
Merlot
Mourvedre
Muscardin
Petit verdot
Pinot meunier
Pinot noir
Syrah
Vaccarese

Alsace
Altenberg de Bergbieten
Altenberg de Bergheim
Brand
Eichberg
Geisberg
Gloeckelberg
Goldert
Hatschbourg
Hengst
Kanzlerberg
Kastelberg
Kessler
Kirchberg de Barr
Kirchberg de Ribeauville
Kitterle
Mambourg
Moenchberg
Muenchberg
Ollwiller
Osterberg
Rangen
Rosacker
Saering
Schlossberg
Sommerberg
Sonnenglanz
Spiegel
Steinert
Steinklotz
Wiebelsberg
Zinnkoepfle

Bordeaux
Barsac
Côtes de Blaye
Côtes de Bourg
Côtes de Castillon
Entre-Deux-Mers
Fronsac
Graves
Listrac
Loupiac
Ludon
Margaux
Médoc
Moulis
Pauillac

Pomerol
Sauternes
St.-Emilion
St.-Estephe
St.-Julien

Burgundy
Beaujolais
Chablis
Côte Chalonnaise
Côte de Beaune
Côte de Nuits
Côte d'Or
Hautes Côtes de Beaune
Hautes Côtes de Nuits
Maconnais

Champagne
Ambonnay
Ay
Beaumont-sur-Vesle
Bisseuil
Champillon
Chigny-les-Roses
Chouilly
Cumieres
Dizy
Grauves
Hautvillers
Louvois
Mailly
Montmirail
Montreuil
Oger
Pierry
Sillery
Tours-sur-Marne
Verzy
Vincelles

Loire
Anjou
Bonnezeaux
Bourgueil
Champigny
Chateaumeillant
Cheverny
Chinon

Côte Roannaise
Côteaux d'Ancenis
Côteaux de l'Aubance
Côteaux de Saumur
Côteaux du Giennois
Côteaux du Layon
Côteaux du Vendomois
Jasnieres
Menetou-Salon
Montlouis
Muscadet
Pouilly-Fumé
Pouilly-sur-Loire
Quarts de Chaume
Quincy
Reuilly
St.-Nicolas-de-Bourgueil
Sancerre
Saumur
Savennieres
Touraine
Vouvray

Rhône Valley
Beaumes de Venise
Chateauneuf-du-Pape
Condrieu
Cornas
Côte Rotie
Côtes du Rhone
Crozes-Hermitage
Gigondas
Hermitage
St.-Joseph
St.-Pèray
Tavel
Vacqueyras

GERMAN WINES

Major regions—Franken, Mosel-Saar-Ruwer, Nahe, Rheingau, Rheinhessen, Rheinpfalz

White grapes
Gewürztraminer
Kerner
Muller-Thurgau
Riesling

Rulander (Pinot gris)
Scheurebe
Sylvaner

Red grapes
Pinot noir
Spatburgunder

Franken
Wurzburg

Mosel-Saar-Ruwer
Bernkastel
Brauneberg
Eitelsbach
Erden
Graach
Grunhaus
Kasel
Lieser
Ockfen
Piesport
Serrig
Traben-Trarbach
Trittenheim
Waldrach
Wehlen
Wiltingen
Wintrich
Zeltingen

Nahe
Bingen
Kreuznach
Munster
Niederhausen
Schloss Bockelheim

Rheingau
Eltville
Erbach
Geisenheim
Hallgarten
Hattenheim
Hochheim
Johannisberg
Kiedrich
Kloster Eberbach

Ostrich
Rauenthal
Rudesheim
Winkel

Rheinhessen
Bodenheim
Guntersblum
Laubenheim
Nackenheim
Nierstein
Oppenheim

Rheinpfalz
Deidesheim
Durkheim
Edenkoben
Forst
Kallstadt
Ruppertsberg
Schweigen
Ungstein
Wachenheim

ITALIAN WINES

Major regions—Campania, Emilia-Romagna,
Lombardy, Piedmont, Tuscany, Veneto

White grapes
Albana
Aleatico
Cataratto
Drupecchio
Falanghina
Fiano
Freisa
Garganega
Greco
Grillo
Insolia
Malvasia
Moscato
Naseo
Oliveto
Pinot
Riesling
Saint Nicola

Silvaner
Terlaner
Termeno
Trebbiano
Verdicchio
Vernaccia
Zibibbo

Red grapes
Aglianico
Barbera
Brunello
Canaiolo
Cannonau
Cesanese
Corvino
Dolcetto
Giro
Grappello
Grignolino
Jaculillo
Lagreine
Lambrusco
Mangiaguerra
Marzemino
Merlot
Molinara
Monico
Nebbiolo
Negrara
Piede di Palumbo
Pinot noir
Prugnolo
Rossara
Rossese
Sangiovese
Schiava
Serpentario
Soriella
Teroldego

Campania
Capri
Falerno
Gragnano
Lacrima Christi
Ravello
Solopaca
Vesuvio

Emilia-Romagna
Albana di Romagna
Lambrusco di Sobara
Sangiovese di Romagna

Lombardy
Frecciarossa
Grumello
Inferno
Sassella

Piedmont
Arneis
Asti spumante
Barbaresco
Barbera
Barolo
Cortese di Gavi
Dolcetto
Erbaluce di Caluso
Freisa
Grignolino
Moscato d'Asti
Nebbiolo
Roero Arneis

Tuscany
Bianco di Pitigliano
Brunello di Montalcino
Carmignano
Chianti
Galestro
Montecarlo
Nobile di Montepulciano
Pomino
Santo Toscano
Vernaccia di San Gimignano

Veneto
Bardolino
Santa Maddalena
Silvaner
Soave
Terlaner
Valpantena
Valpolicella

Other
Aglianico del Vulture
Aleatico di Puglia
Amarone
Castelli Romani
Dolceacqua
Est, Est, Est
Frascati
Orvieto
Pinot bianco
Pinot grigio
Recioto
Ribolla Gialla
Verdicchio

SPANISH WINES

Major regions—Penedes, Rioja

White grapes
Albarino
Chardonnay
Macallo
Malvasia
Moscatel
Palomina
Parellada
Pedro Ximenez
Riesling
Sauvignon
Torrontes
Verdejo
Xarello

Red grapes
Cabernet sauvignon
Carinena
Fogoneu
Garnacha
Merlot
Monastrell
Tempranillo

Wines
Alicante
Almansa
Carinena
Condado de Huelva

Jerez
Malaga
Mancha
Mentrida
Navarra
Penedes
Ribeiro
Rioja
Tarragona
Toro
Valdeorras
Valdepenas
Valencia
Valle de Monterrey

AMERICAN WINES

Major regions—California, New York, Oregon, Washington

White grapes/wines
Catawba
Chardonnay
Chenin blanc
Colombard
Concord
Delaware
Fumé blanc
Gewürztraminer
Johannisberg riesling
Muscat
Pinot chardonnay
Pinot gris
Ravat
Riesling
Sauvignon blanc
Semillon
Seyval blanc
Trebbiano

Red grapes/wines
Alicante
Baco noir
Beaujolais
Cabernet sauvignon
Carignane
Chancellor
Gamay

Grenache
Lemberger
Mataro
Merlot
Mourvedre
Petit Sirah
Pinot noir
Zinfandel

AUSTRALIAN WINES

Major regions—Adelaide Hills, Barossa Valley, Bendigo, Central Victoria, Clare Valley, Coonwarra, Geelong, Glenrowan, Great Western, Hunter Valley, Lower Great Southern, Margaret River, McLaren Vale, Mudgee, Murrumbridgeel, Padthaway, Pyrenees, Riverland, Rutherglen, Swan Valley, Yarra Valley

White grapes/wines
Chardonnay
Gewurztraminer
Marsanne
Muscat
Riesling
Sauvignon blanc
Semillon

Red grapes/wines
Cabernet sauvignon
Pinot noir
Shiraz

SPORTS

FOOTBALL

PREMIER DIVISION
(and Nicknames)

Arsenal	Gunners
Aston Villa	Villains
Bradford City	Bantams
Charlton Athletic	Addicks
Chelsea	Blues
Coventry City	Sky Blues
Derby County	Rams
Everton	Toffees
Ipswich	Tractor boys
Leeds	Whites
Leicester City	Foxes
Liverpool	Reds
Manchester City	Citizens
Manchester United	Man U, Red Devils
Middlesborough	Boro
Newcastle United	Magpies
Southampton	The Saints
Sunderland	Rokerites
Tottenham Hotspur	Spurs
West Ham	Hammers

NATIONWIDE FIRST DIVISION

Birmingham City	The Blues
Blackburn Rovers	Rovers / Blue and Whites
Bolton Wanderers	The Trotters
Burnley	The Clarets
Crewe Alexander	The Railwaymen
Crystal Palace	The Eagles
Fulham	The Cottagers
Gillingham	The Gills
Grimsby Town	The Mariners
Huddersfield Town	The Terriers

Norwich City	The Canaries
Nottingham Forest	The Reds
Portsmouth	Pompey
Preston North End	The Lilywhites
Queen's Park Rangers	The Rs
Sheffield United	The Blades
Sheffield Wednesday	The Owls
Stockport County	The Hatters
Tranmere Rovers	Rovers
Watford	The Hornets
West Bromwich Albion	The Baggies, The Throstles
Wimbledon	The Dons/The Crazy Gang
Wolverhampton Wanderers	Wolves

SECOND DIVISION

Bournemouth	The Cherries
Brentford	The Bees
Bristol City	The Robins
Bristol Rovers	The Pirates
Bury	The Shakers
Cambridge United	The Us
Colchester United	The Us
Luton Town	The Hatters
Millwall	The Lions
Northampton Town	The Cobblers
Notts County	The Magpies
Oldham Athletic	The Latics
Oxford United	The Us
Peterborough United	Posh
Port Vale	The Valiants
Reading	The Royals
Rotherham United	The Merry Millers
Stoke City	The Potters
Swansea Town	The Swans
Swindon Town	The Robins
Walsall	The Saddlers
Wigan Athletic	Latics
Wrexham	The Robins
Wycombe Wanderers	The Chairboys

THIRD DIVISION

Barnet	The Bees
Blackpool	Seasiders
Brighton Hove Albion	Seagulls
Cardiff City	The Bluebirds
Carlisle United	The Cumbrians
Cheltenham Town	
Chesterfield	The Spireites
Darlington	The Quakers
Exeter City	The Grecians
Halifax Town	
Hartlepool United	The Pool
Hull City	The Tigers
Kidderminster	
Leyton Orient	The Os
Lincoln City	The Red Imps
Macclesfield Town	The Silkmen
Mansfield Town	The Stags
Plymouth Argyle	The Pilgrims
Rochdale	The Dale
Scunthorpe United	The Irons
Shrewsbury Town	The Town
Southend United	The Shrimpers
Torquay United	The Gulls
York City	The Minstermen

SCOTTISH PREMIER LEAGUE

Aberdeen
Celtic
Dundee
Dundee United
Dunfermline
Hearts
Hibernian
Kilmarnock
Motherwell
Rangers
St Johnstone
St Mirren

MAJOR INTERNATIONAL TEAMS

AC Milan
Ajax (Netherlands)
Anderlecht (Belgium)
AS Roma
Athletic Bilbao

Barcelona
Bayern Munich
Benfica (Portugal)
Feyenoord (Netherlands)
Hamburg SV
Inter Milan
Juventus
Lazio
Lyon
Panachlinaikos (Greece)
Paris St. Germain
PSV Eindhoven (Netherlands)
Real Madrid
Red Star Belgrade
Sparta Prague
Spartak Moscow
Sporting Lisbon
St. Etienne
Sturm Graz (Austria)
Valencia

CRICKET

COUNTY SIDES
(and name of the ground)

County	Ground
Derbyshire	Derby County Ground
Durham	Chester le Street
Essex	Chelmsford
Glamorgan	Sophia Gardens, Cardiff
Gloucestershire	Phoenix County Ground, Bristol
Hampshire	Southampton
Kent	Canterbury
Lancashire	Old Trafford, Manchester
Leicestershire	Grace Road, Leicester
Middlesex	Lords, St. John's Wood
Northamptonshire	Northampton County Ground
Nottinghamshire	Trent Bridge, Nottingham
Somerset	Taunton
Surrey	The Oval
Sussex	Hove
Warwickshire	Edgbaston, Birmingham
Worcestershire	New Road, Worcester
Yorkshire	Headingley, Leeds

TEST PLAYING NATIONS

Australia
Bangladesh
England
India
New Zealand
Pakistan
South Africa
Sri Lanka
West Indies
Zimbabwe

FORMULA ONE MOTOR RACING

GRAND PRIX AND CIRCUITS

Australian	Albert Park
Austrian	A1-Ring
Belgian	Francorchamps
Brazilian	Interlagos
Canadian	Gilles Villeneuve Circuit
European	Nurburgring
French	Magny Cours
German	Hockenheim
Hungarian	Hungarorin
Italian	Monza
Monaco	Monte Carlo
San Marino	Imola
Spanish	Circuit de Catalunya
UK	Silverstone

FORMULA ONE TEAMS

Arrows
BAR
Benetton
BMW Williams
Ferrari
Jaguar Racing
Jordan
McLaren
Minardi
Prost
Sauber

RUGBY

Rugby Union Teams

Bath
Bristol
Harlequins
Gloucester
Leicester
London Irish
Newcastle
Northampton
Rotherham
Saracens
Sale
Wasps

World Cup Sides

Argentina
Australia
Canada
England
Fiji
France
Ireland
Italy
Japan
Namibia
New Zealand
Romania
Scotland
South Africa
Spain
Tonga
Uruguay
US
Wales
Western Samoa

Rugby League Teams

Bradford Bulls
Castleford Tigers
Halifax Blue Sox
Huddersfield Giants
Hull FC
Leeds Rhinos
London B rocos
Salford Reds
St Helens
Wakefield Trinity Wildcats
Warrington Wolves
Wigan Warriors

HORSERACING

RACE COURSES

Aintree
Ascot
Ayr
Bangor
Bath
Beverley
Brighton
Carlisle
Cartmel
Catterick
Cheltenham
Chepstow
Chester
Doncaster
Epsom
Exeter
Fakenham
Folkestone
Fontwell
Goodwood
Hamilton
Haydock
Hereford
Hexham
Huntingdon
Kelso
Kempton
Leicester
Lingfield
Ludlow
Market Rasen
Musselburgh
Newton Abbot
Newbury
Newcastle
Newmarket
Nottingham
Perth
Plumpton
Pontefract
Redcar
Ripon
Salisbury
Sedgefield
Southwell
Taunton
Thirsk
Towcester
Uttoxeter
Warwick
Wetherby
Wincanton
Windsor
Wolverhampton
Worcester
Yarmouth
York

NAMES OF GRAND NATIONAL WINNERS
since 1970

1970	Gay Trip
1971	Specify
1972	Well to Do
1973	Red Rum
1974	Red Rum
1975	L'Escargot
1976	Rag Trade
1977	Red Rum
1978	Lucius
1979	Rubstic
1980	Ben Nevis
1981	Aldaniti
1982	Grittar
1983	Corbiere
1984	Hallo Dandy
1985	Last Suspect
1986	West Tip
1987	Maori Venture
1988	Rhyme 'N' Reason
1989	Little Polveir
1990	Mr Frisk
1991	Seagram
1992	Party Politics
1993	(Void race) Esha Ness
1994	Minnehoma
1995	Royal Athlete
1996	Rough Quest
1997	Lord Gyllene
1998	Earth Summit

1999   Bobby Jo
2000   Papillon
2001   Red Marauder

WINNERS OF THE EPSOM DERBY
since 1970

1970   Nijinsky
1971   Mill Reef
1972   Roberto
1973   Morston
1974   Snow Knight
1975   Grundy
1976   Empery
1977   The Minstrel
1978   Shirley Heights
1979   Troy
1980   Henbit
1981   Shergar
1982   Golden Fleece
1983   Teenoso
1984   Secreto
1985   Slip Anchor
1986   Shshrastani
1987   Reference Point
1988   Kahyasi
1989   Nashwan
1990   Quest for Fame
1991   Generous
1992   Dr Devious
1993   Commander in Chief
1994   Erhaab
1995   Lammtarra
1996   Shaamit
1997   Benny the Dip
1998   High Rise
1999   Oath
2000   Sinndar
2001   Galileo

MAJOR LEAGUE BASEBALL TEAMS

Six separate major leagues have been officially acknowledged by the Office of the Baseball Commissioner. This list includes only those teams that have been, or still are, members of the National or American leagues.

Anaheim Angels (formerly California Angels) *American League* (1997–present)
Atlanta Braves (formerly Milwaukee Braves) *National League* (1966–present)
Baltimore Orioles (formerly St. Louis Browns) *American League* (1954–present)
Boston Braves *National League* (1876–1952)
Boston Red Sox *American League* (1901–present)
Brooklyn Hartfords *National League* (1877)
Brooklyn Dodgers *National League* (1890–1957)
Buffalo Bisons *National League* (1879–85)
California Angels (formerly Los Angeles Angels) *American League* (1966–96)
Chicago Cubs *National League* (1876–present)
Chicago White Sox *American League* (1901–present)
Cincinnati Reds *National League* (1876–80; 1890–present)
Cleveland Forest Citys *National League* (1879–84)
Cleveland Spiders *National League* (1889–99)
Cleveland Indians *American League* (1901–present)
Colorado Rockies *National League* (1993–present)
Detroit Wolverines *National League* (1881–88)
Detroit Tigers *American League* (1901–present)
Florida Marlins *National League* (1993–present)
Hartford Dark Blues *National League* (1876)
Houston Astros (formerly Houston Colt .45s) *National League* (1965–present)
Houston Colt .45s *National League* (1962–64)
Indianapolis Blues *National League* (1878)
Indianapolis Hoosiers *National League* (1887–89); *Federal League* (1914)

Kansas City Cowboys *National League* (1886)
Kansas City Athletics (formerly Philadelphia Athletics) *American League* (1955–67)
Kansas City Royals *American League* (1969–present)
Los Angeles Dodgers (formerly Brooklyn Dodgers) *National League* (1958–present)
Los Angeles Angels *American League* (1961–65)
Louisville Grays *National League* (1876–77)
Louisville Colonels *National League* (1892–99)
Milwaukee Grays *National League* (1878)
Milwaukee Brewers *American League* (1901)
Milwaukee Brewers (formerly Seattle Pilots) *American League* (1970–present)
Milwaukee Braves (formerly Boston Braves) *National League* (1953–65)
Minnesota Twins (formerly 1901–60 Washington Senators) *American League* (1961–present)
Montreal Expos *National League* (1969–present)
New York Mutuals *National League* (1876)
New York Giants *National League* (1883–1957)
New York Yankees *American League* (1903–present)
New York Mets *National League* (1962–present)
Oakland Athletics (formerly Kansas City Athletics) *American League* (1968–present)
Philadelphia Athletics *National League* (1876); *American League* (1901–54)
Philadelphia Phillies *National League* (1883–present)
Pittsburgh Alleghenies *National League* (1887–91)
Pittsburgh Pirates (formerly Pittsburgh Alleghenies) *National League* (1892–present)
Providence Grays *National League* (1878–85)
St. Louis Browns (formerly 1901 Milwaukee Brewers) *American League* (1902–53)
St. Louis Browns/Perfectos *National League* (1892–98)
St. Louis Brown Stockings *National League* (1876–77)
St. Louis Maroons *National League* (1885–86)
St. Louis Cardinals (formerly St. Louis Browns/Perfectos) *National League* (1899–present)
San Diego Padres *National League* (1969–present)
San Francisco Giants (formerly New York Giants) *National League* (1958–present)

Seattle Pilots *American League* (1969)
Seattle Mariners *American League* (1977–present)
Syracuse Stars *National League* (1879)
Texas Rangers (formerly 1961–71 Washington Senators) *American League* (1972–present)
Toronto Blue Jays *American League* (1977–present)
Troy Trojans *National League* (1879–82)
Washington Senators *National League* (1886–89, 1892–99); *American League* (1901–60, 1961–71)
Worcester Brown Stockings *National League* (1880–82)

NATIONAL BASKETBALL ASSOCIATION (NBA) TEAMS

Anderson Packers (1949–50)
Atlanta Hawks (1968–present)
Baltimore Bullets (1947–55)
Baltimore Bullets (1963–73)
Boston Celtics (1946–present)
Buffalo Braves (1970–78)
Capital Bullets (1973–74)
Charlotte Hornets (1988–present)
Chicago Bulls (1966–present)
Chicago Packers (1961–62)
Chicago Stags (1946–50)
Chicago Zephyrs (1962–63)
Cincinnati Royals (1957–72)
Cleveland Cavaliers (1970–present)
Cleveland Rebels (1946–47)
Dallas Mavericks (1980–present)
Denver Nuggets (1949–50)
Denver Nuggets (1976–present)
Detroit Falcons (1946–47)
Detroit Pistons (1957–present)
Fort Wayne Pistons (1948–57)
Golden State Warriors (1971–present)
Houston Rockets (1971–present)
Indiana Pacers (1976–present)
Indianapolis Jets (1948–49)
Indianapolis Olympians (1949–53)
Kansas City Kings (1975–85)
Kansas City–Omaha Kings (1972–75)
Los Angeles Clippers (1984–present)
Los Angeles Lakers (1960–present)
Miami Heat (1988–present)
Milwaukee Bucks (1968–present)
Milwaukee Hawks (1951–55)
Minneapolis Lakers (1948–60)
Minnesota Timberwolves (1989–present)
New Jersey Nets (1977–present)
New Orleans Jazz (1974–80)
New York Knickerbockers (1946–present)
New York Nets (1976–77)

Orlando Magic (1989–present)
Philadelphia 76ers (1963–present)
Philadelphia Warriors (1946–62)
Phoenix Suns (1968–present)
Pittsburgh Ironmen (1946–47)
Portland Trail Blazers (1970–present)
Providence Steamrollers (1946–49)
Rochester Royals (1948–57)
Sacramento Kings (1985–present)
San Antonio Spurs (1976–present)
San Diego Clippers (1978–84)
San Diego Rockets (1967–71)
San Francisco Warriors (1962–71)
Seattle SuperSonics (1967–present)
Sheboygan Redskins (1949–50)
St. Louis Bombers (1946–50)
St. Louis Hawks (1955–68)
Syracuse Nationals (1949–63)
Toronto Huskies (1946–47)
Tri-Cities Blackhawks (1949–51)
Utah Jazz (1980–present)
Washington Bullets (1974–present)
Washington Capitols (1946–51)
Waterloo Hawks (1949–50)

NATIONAL FOOTBALL LEAGUE (NFL) TEAMS

The football league now known as the National Football League began in 1920 and was called the American Professional Football Association. In 1922, the name was changed to the National Football League. In 1926, the competing American Football League was formed, only to fold after a year of play. In 1946, the rival All-American Football Conference was created, merging with the NFL in 1950. In 1959, a new American Football League was formed, and in 1966 a merger agreement between the two leagues was announced: the AFL was absorbed into the NFL by 1970. In 1974, a new rival, the World Football League, was formed, folding in 1975; and the United States Football League began operations in 1983 and played its last season in 1986. Rival league team names are listed only when at least some of their teams have become NFL teams.

NFL Teams

Akron Pros (1920–25)
Akron Indians (1926)
Arizona Cardinals (formerly Phoenix Cardinals) (1994–present)
Atlanta Falcons (1966–present)
Baltimore Colts (formerly AAFC Baltimore Colts) (1950)
Baltimore Colts (1953–83)
Baltimore Ravens (1997–present)
Boston Braves (1932)
Boston Bulldogs (formerly Pottsville Maroons) (1929)
Boston Redskins (formerly Boston Braves) (1933–36)
Boston Patriots (formerly AFL Boston Patriots) (1970)
Boston Yanks (1944–48)
Brooklyn Lions (1926)

Brooklyn Dodgers (1930–43)
Brooklyn Tigers (formerly Brooklyn Dodgers) (1944)
Buffalo All-Americans (1920–23)
Buffalo Bills (formerly AFL Buffalo Bills) (1970–present)
Buffalo Bisons (1924–25)
Buffalo Bisons (1927)
Buffalo Bisons (1929)
Buffalo Rangers (1926)
Canton Bulldogs (1920–23)
Canton Bulldogs (1925–26)
Carolina Panthers (1995–present)
Chicago Bears (formerly Chicago Staleys) (1922–present)
Chicago Cardinals (1920–59)
Chicago Cardinals–Pittsburgh Steelers (the teams merged for one season) (1944)
Chicago Staleys (formerly Decatur Staleys) (1921)
Chicago Tigers (1920)
Cincinnati Bengals (formerly AFL Cincinnati Bengals) (1970–present)
Cincinnati Celts (1921)
Cincinnati Reds (1933–34)
Cleveland Browns (formerly AAFC Cleveland Browns) (1950–96)
Cleveland Bulldogs (1924–25)
Cleveland Bulldogs (1927)
Cleveland Indians (1923)
Cleveland Indians (1931)
Cleveland Rams (1937–42)
Cleveland Rams (1944–45)
Cleveland Tigers (1920–21)
Columbus Panhandles (1920–22)
Columbus Tigers (1923–26)
Dallas Texans (formerly New York Yanks) (1952)
Dallas Cowboys (1960–present)
Dayton Triangles (1920–29)
Decatur Staleys (1920)
Denver Broncos (formerly AFL Denver Broncos) (1970–present)
Detroit Heralds (1920)
Detroit Lions (formerly Portsmouth Spartans) (1934–present)
Detroit Panthers (1921)
Detroit Panthers (1926)
Detroit Tigers (1925)
Detroit Wolverines (1928)
Duluth Kelleys (1923–25)

Duluth Eskimos (formerly Duluth Kelleys)
(1926–27)
Evansville Crimson Giants (1921–22)
Frankford Yellow Jackets (1924–31)
Green Bay Packers (1921–present)
Hammond Pros (1920–26)
Hartford Blues (1926)
Houston Oilers (formerly AFL Houston Oilers)
(1970–96)
Indianapolis Colts (formerly Baltimore Colts)
(1984–present)
Jacksonville Jaguars (1995–present)
Kansas City Blues (1924–25)
Kansas City Chiefs (formerly AFL Kansas City
Chiefs) (1970–present)
Kansas City Cowboys (1926)
Kenosha Maroons (formerly Toledo Maroons)
(1924)
Louisville Brecks (1921–25)
Louisville Colonels (formerly Louisville Brecks)
(1926)
Los Angeles Buccaneers (1926)
Los Angeles Raiders (formerly Oakland Raiders)
(1982–94)
Los Angeles Rams (formerly Cleveland Rams)
(1946–94)
Miami Dolphins (formerly AFL Miami Dolphins)
(1970–present)
Milwaukee Badgers (1922–26)
Minneapolis Marines (1921–24)
Minneapolis Redjackets (1929–30)
Minnesota Vikings (1961–present)
Muncie Flyers (1920–21)
New England Patriots (formerly Boston Patriots)
(1971–present)
New Orleans Saints (1967–present)
New York Brickley's Giants (1921)
New York Bulldogs (formerly Boston Yanks)
(1949)
New York Giants (1925–present)
New York Jets (formerly AFL New York Jets)
(1970–present)
New York Yanks (formerly New York Bulldogs)
(1950–51)
New York Yankees (formerly AFC Brooklyn
Horsemen) (1927–28)
Newark Tornadoes (formerly Orange Tornadoes)
(1930)
Oakland Raiders (formerly AFL Oakland

Raiders) (1970–81)
Oakland Raiders (formerly Los Angeles Raiders)
(1995–present)
Oorang Indians (1922–23)
Orange Tornadoes (1929)
Philadelphia Eagles (1933–present)
Philadelphia Eagles–Pittsburgh Steelers (the
teams merged for one season) (1943)
Phoenix Cardinals (formerly St. Louis Cardinals)
(1988–present)
Pittsburgh Pirates (1933–40)
Pittsburgh Steelers (formerly Pittsburgh Pirates)
(1940–present)
Portsmouth Spartans (1930–33)
Pottsville Maroons (1925–28)
Providence Steam Roller (1925–31)
Racine Legion (1922–24)
Racine Tornadoes (formerly Racine Legion)
(1926)
Rochester Jeffersons (1920–25)
Rock Island Independents (1920–25)
San Diego Chargers (formerly AFL San Diego
Chargers) (1970–present)
San Francisco 49ers (formerly AAFC San
Francisco 49ers) (1950–present)
St. Louis All-Stars (1923)
St. Louis Gunners (1934)
St. Louis Cardinals (formerly Chicago Cardinals)
(1960–87)
St. Louis Rams (formerly Los Angeles Rams)
(1995–present)
Seattle Seahawks (1976)
Staten Island Stapletons (1929–32)
Tampa Bay Buccaneers (1976–present)
Tennessee Oilers (formerly Houston Oilers)
(1997–present)
Toledo Maroons (1922–23)
Tonawanda Kardex (1921)
Washington Redskins (formerly Boston Red-
skins) (1937–present)
Washington Senators (1921)

1960–69 AFL Teams

Boston Patriots (1960–69)
Buffalo Bills (1960–69)
Cincinnati Bengals (1968–69)
Dallas Texans (1960–62)
Denver Broncos (1960–69)

Houston Oilers (1960–69)
Kansas City Chiefs (1963–69)
Los Angeles Chargers (1960)
Miami Dolphins (1966–69)
New York Jets (formerly New York Titans)
(1963–69)
New York Titans (1960–62)
Oakland Raiders (1960–69)
San Diego Chargers (formerly Los Angeles
Chargers) (1961–69)

AAFC Teams

Baltimore Colts (1947–49)
Brooklyn Dodgers (1946–48)
Buffalo Bills (formerly Buffalo Bisons) (1947–49)
Buffalo Bisons (1946)
Chicago Hornets (1949)
Chicago Rockets (1946–48)
Cleveland Browns (1946–49)
Los Angeles Dons (1946–49)
Miami Seahawks (1946)
New York Yankees (1946–49)
San Francisco 49ers (1946–49)

1926 AFL Teams

Boston Bulldogs
Brooklyn Horsemen
Chicago Bulls
Cleveland Panthers
Los Angeles Wildcats
New York Yankees
Newark Bears
Philadelphia Quakers
Rock Island Independents

1997–98 NFL Teams
American Football Conference Teams

AFC East Division
Buffalo Bills
Indianapolis Colts
Miami Dolphins
New England Patriots
New York Jets

AFC Central Division
Baltimore Ravens
Cincinnati Bengals
Jacksonville Jaguars
Pittsburgh Steelers
Tennessee Oilers

AFC West Division
Denver Broncos
Kansas City Chiefs
Oakland Raiders
San Diego Chargers
Seattle Seahawks

Note: The Browns, currently not a team, will eventually be based in Cleveland, probably in the AFC Central Division.

National Football Conference Teams

NFC East Division
Dallas Cowboys
New York Giants
Philadelphia Eagles
Phoenix Cardinals
Washington Redskins

NFC Central Division
Chicago Bears
Detroit Lions
Green Bay Packers
Minnesota Vikings
Tampa Bay Buccaneers

NFC West Division
Atlanta Falcons
Carolina Panthers
New Orleans Saints
Saint Louis Rams
San Francisco 49ers

NATIONAL HOCKEY LEAGUE (NHL) TEAMS

Montreal Canadiens (1917–present)
Montreal Wanderers (1917–18)
Toronto Arenas (1917–19)
Ottawa Senators (1917–31) (1932–34)
St. Louis Eagles (1934–35)
Toronto St. Pats (1919–26)
Toronto Maple Leafs (1926–present)
Quebec Bulldogs (1919–20)
Hamilton Tigers (1920–25)
New York Americans (1925–41)
Brooklyn Americans (1941–42)
Boston Bruins (1924–present)
Montreal Maroons (1924–38)
Pittsburgh Pirates (1925–30)
Philadelphia Quakers (1930–31)
New York Rangers (1926–present)
Detroit Cougars (1926–30)
Detroit Falcons (1930–32)
Detroit Red Wings (1932–present)
Chicago Blackhawks (1926–present)
Los Angeles Kings (1967–present)
Minnesota North Stars (1967–93)
Philadelphia Flyers (1967–present)
Pittsburgh Penguins (1967–present)
St. Louis Blues (1967–present)
Oakland Seals (1967–70)
California Golden Seals (1970–76)
Cleveland Barons (1976–78)
Buffalo Sabers (1970–present)
Vancouver Canucks (1970–present)
New York Islanders (1972–present)
Atlanta Flames (1972–80)
Kansas City Scouts (1974–76)
Colorado Rockies (1976–82)
Washington Capitals (1974–present)
Edmonton Oilers (1979–present)
Hartford Whalers (1979–97)
Quebec Nordiques (1979–95)
Winnipeg Jets (1979–96)
Calgary Flames (1980–present)
New Jersey Devils (1982–present)

San Jose Sharks (1991–present)
Ottawa Senators (1992–present)
Tampa Bay Lightning (1992–present)
Anaheim Mighty Ducks (1993–present)
Dallas Stars (1993–present)
Florida Panthers (1993–present)
Colorado Avalanche (1995–present)
Phoenix Coyotes (1996–present)
Carolina Hurricanes (1997–present)

DIVISION NAMES (BEFORE 1994)

Adams
Norris
Patrick
Smythe

CONFERENCE NAMES (BEFORE 1994)

Campbell
Wales

BIBLIOGRAPHY

Anderson, Alan, ed. *The Complete Book of the Car.* Carlton Books Limited, 1997.

Bonnet, Corrine and Paolo Kelba. *Great Biblical Characters.* Gremese International, 1996.

Botting, Douglas and the editors of Time-Life Books. *The Pirate.* Time-Life Books, 1978.

Brownrigg, Ronald. *Who's Who in the New Testament.* Oxford University Press, 1993.

Brunner, Borgna. *1998 Information Please Almanac.* Information Please LLC, 1997.

Calvocoressi, Peter. *Who's Who in the Bible.* Penguin Reference, 1987.

Chevalier, Tracy, ed. *Twentieth-Century Children's Writers.* St. James Press, 1989.

Cochran, Thomas C. and Wayne Andrews, eds. *Concise Dictionary of American History.* Scribner, 1962.

Croteau, Maureen and Wayne Worcester. *The Essential Researcher.* Harper Perennial, 1993.

Crystal, David. *The Cambridge Factfinder,* 2nd ed. Cambridge University Press, 1997.

Drabble, Margaret. *The Oxford Companion to English Literature.* Oxford University Press, 1985.

Encyclopedia of Walt Disney Characters. Walt Disney Company, 1987.

Feder, Lillian. *Apollo Handbook of Classical Literature.* Crowell, 1964.

Fisher, Margery. *Who's Who in Children's Books.* Holt, Rinehart and Winston, 1975.

Freeman, William. *Dictionary of Fictional Characters.* Writer Books, 1963.

Gresswell, R. and Kay and Anthony Huxley, eds. *Standard Encyclopedia of the World's Rivers and Lakes,* 1965.

Guinness Book of Answers, 8th ed. 1991.

Hammer, Richard. *The Illustrated History of Organized Crime.* Courage Books, 1989.

Harris, William H. and Judith S. Levey, eds. *New Columbia Encyclopedia.* Columbia University Press, 1975.

Hogg, Ian V. *The Hutchinson Dictionary of Battles,* Helicon Publishing Ltd, 1995.

Horn, Maurice, ed. *The World Encyclopedia of Cartoons.* Chelsea House, 1980.

Jordan, Michael. *The Encyclopedia of Gods.* Facts on File Publications, 1993.

Kipfer, Barbara Ann. *The Order of Things.* Random House, 1997.

Ladd, John. *Guide to Football Grounds.* Ian Allen Limited, 1997.

Lenberg, Jeff. *Encyclopedia of Animated Cartoon Series.* Arlington House, 1989.

Lipschutz, Mark R. and R. Kent Rasmussen. *Dictionary of African Historical Biography.* University of California Press, 1989.

Magill, Frank N. *Encyclopedia of Literary Characters.* Harper, 1963.

Magill, Frank N. *Masterpieces of World Literature.* HarperCollins, 1989.

Mortimer, John, ed. *The Oxford Book of Villains.* Oxford University Press, 1992.

Parker, Peter and Frank Kermode. *A Reader's Guide to the Twentieth-Century Novel.* Oxford University Press, 1995.

Parrinder, Geoffrey, ed. *World Religions.* Facts on File Publications, 1983.

Plowright, Frank, ed. *Comic Guide.* Aurum Press, 1997.

Pringle, David. *Imaginary People,* 2nd ed. Scolar Press, 1996.

Rand McNally Cosmopolitan World Atlas 1996. Rand McNally, 1996.

Revell, Fleming H. *The Revel Bible Dictionary.* Fleming H. Revell, 1984.

Sadie, Stanley, ed. *The New Grove Dictionary of Music and Musicians.* Macmillan Publishing Ltd., 1980.

Salzman, Jack and Pamela Wilkinson. *Major Characters in American Fiction.* Henry Holt, 1994.

Sifakis, Carl. *The Mafia Encyclopedia.* Facts on File Publications, 1987.

Whitney, David C. and Robin Vaughn Whitney. *The American Presidents.* 7th ed. Prentice Hall, 1990.

World Almanac, 1998. K-III Reference Corp.

World Almanac. World Almanac Books. 1997.

Wright, John, ed. *The New York Times 1998 Almanac.* Penguin Reference, 1997.